The LIFE ON OTHER WORLDS SERIES is a selection of classic accounts of the afterlife and otherworldly life, told by those who are already there or who have been shown glimpses of what awaits us when our lives on earth are over. Descriptions vary, yet a thread of similarity runs through them all. May this collection serve as a travel guide as we embark on the greatest adventure of all—the journey into the mysterious realms beyond this world.

*

OTHER VOLUMES IN THE SERIES INCLUDE
Earths in the Universe (1758) Emanuel Swedenborg
The Realms Beyond (1878) Paschal Beverly Randolph
A Wanderer in the Spirit Lands (1896) Franchezzo
Intra Muros (1898) Rebecca Ruter Springer
The Angels' Diary (1903) Effie M. Shirey
Two Years in Heaven (1911) Rose the Sunlight
Spiritual Life on Mars (1920) Eros Urides
The Blue Island & Other Spiritualist Writings (1922) William T. Stead
The World Unseen (3 Vols.) (1954-59) Anthony Borgia

THE LIFE
BEYOND THE VEIL

SPIRIT MESSAGES RECEIVED AND WRITTEN DOWN BY THE

REV. G. VALE OWEN

VICAR OF ORFORD, LANCASHIRE

*

WITH AN APPRECIATION BY
LORD NORTHCLIFFE

AND AN INTRODUCTION BY
SIR ARTHUR CONAN DOYLE

EDITED BY
H. W. ENGHOLM

EDITOR'S NOTE (2012) BY
SASKIA PRAAMSMA

SQUARE CIRCLES PUBLISHING

THE LIFE BEYOND THE VEIL
A Compilation of Four Classic Books
Book I—The Lowlands of Heaven (1920)
Book II—The Highlands of Heaven (1920)
Book III—The Ministry of Heaven (1921)
Book IV—The Battalions of Heaven (1921)
By Rev. G. Vale Owen

Preface and Notes by H. W. Engholm
An Appreciation by Lord Northcliffe
Introduction by Sir Arthur Conan Doyle
Editor's Note (2012) by Saskia Praamsma

Cover: Syrp & Co.

SQUARE CIRCLES PUBLISHING
P. O. Box 9682 / Pahrump, NV 89060
www.SquareCirclesPublishing.com
ISBN: 978-0-9893962-8-8

www.LifeOnOtherWorlds.com

Contents

Editor's Note

THE four-volume classic, *The Life Beyond the Veil,* has been combined into one volume for inclusion in Square Circles Publishing's LIFE ON OTHER WORLDS SERIES, a collection of works about the afterlife which were communicated to psychics and spiritualists by those "on the other side."

To standardize the four books, I have numbered originally unnumbered chapters, shortened some of their names, and combined others. I have also removed several footnotes, inserting their content between brackets at appropriate points in the text, and standardized spelling and capitalization.

The original introductory material for each of the four volumes has been combined and rearranged into six sections: (1) H. W. Engholm's Prefaces to Books I-IV, (2) Identity of Those Who Communicated [created by me from information found at various points throughout the text], (3) H.W.E.'s General Notes, (4) Biographical Notes on G.V.O., (5) An Appreciation by Lord Northcliffe, and (6) Introduction by Sir Arthur Conan Doyle.

My editorial comments are followed by "—*Ed.*" to distinguish them from those of the original editor, H. W. Engholm [H.W.E.].

Not one word of the afterlife communications has been omitted or changed.

SASKIA PRAAMSMA
Square Circles Publishing
June 2012

H. W. Engholm's

Preface to Books I-IV

PREFACE TO BOOK I:
THE LOWLANDS OF HEAVEN

BOOK I contains the first of a series of communications from beyond the veil, received and written down by the Rev. G. Vale Owen, Vicar of Orford, Lancashire.

It should be clearly understood that these messages, while complete in themselves, deal chiefly with the "Sphere of Light" nearest to the earth in which the Vicar's mother, who is the principal communicator, states that she dwells, and that her impressions are chiefly individual to herself and are thus those of a newcomer and learner whose experiences are limited to a restricted area. Wider regions and greater heights and depths are explored, the interrelation of this and the afterlife is more fully explained, and both narrative and exposition of aims and principles are more vigorous, clear and comprehensive in succeeding messages, contained in other volumes of the series which follow this.

That said, however, the high importance and far-reaching significance of Volume I must be affirmed. It gives the most complete and the most detailed statement of conditions in the afterlife yet published. It must be read and studied in order to gain an understanding of the further messages.

The narrative brings one face to face with a Spiritual Universe of unimaginable immensity and grandeur, with sphere upon sphere of the realms of light which stretch away into infinity. We are told that those who have passed from our earth life inhabit the nearer spheres, amid surroundings not wholly dissimilar from those they have known in this world; that at death we shall enter the sphere for which our spiritual development fits us. There is to be no sudden change in our personality. We shall not be plunged into forgetfulness. A human being is not transformed into another being.

In the first sphere of light we find trees and flowers like those that grow in earthly gardens, but more beautiful, immune from decay and death, and endowed with qualities that make them more completely a part of our lives. Around us are birds and animals, still the friends of man, but nearer, more intelligent, and freed from the fears and the cruelties they suffer here.

We find houses and gardens, but of substance, color and atmosphere more responsive to our presence; water whose playing is music; wide-ranging harmonies of color. We find everything more radiant, more joyous, more exquisitely complex, and while our activities are multiplied, our life is more restful.

Differences in age disappear. There are no "old" in the Spheres of Light; there are only the graceful and strong.

Spirits from a higher sphere may descend to the lower, may even be sent on a mission to earth. But ere they can reach us they must first accustom themselves to the dimmer light and heavier "air" of the lower spheres. They must undergo a change ere they can penetrate the dense and murky atmosphere in which our world is enfolded.

That is why the spirit voices so often reach us in broken fragments which our dull intelligence can hardly piece together. That is why we can so rarely hear the words and feel the presence of those who are longing to reach and to comfort their friends.

So small a thing is the change which we call death, the narrative tells us, that many do not realize it. They have to be taught that they are in another world, the world of reunion. "She fell asleep," says one of the messages which describe the passing of such a spirit, "she fell asleep, and the cord of life was severed by our watching friends, and then softly they awoke her, and she looked up and smiled very sweetly into the face of one who leaned over her. . . . She began to wonder why these strange faces were around her in place of the friends and nurses she had last seen.

"She inquired where she was. When she was told, a look of wonder and yearning came over her face, and she asked to be allowed to see the friends she had left.

"This was granted her, and she looked on them through the veil, and shook her head sadly. *'If only they could know,'* she said, *'how free from pain I am now and comfortable! Can you not tell them?'*

"We tried to do so, but only one of them heard, I think, and he only imperfectly, and soon put it away as a fancy."

To many, indeed, these spirit messages will seem to shed new illumination upon passages in the Bible whose interpretation they have hitherto regarded as obscure. Others, whose faith may have wavered beneath the impact of modern criticism or under the trials of sorrow and bereavement, may well find in this new revelation the answer that will resolve their doubts and deepen into certainty their hope of ultimate reunion after death.

Here is a document which is placed before the reader as an authentic communication from the world beyond. No man can say what the limits of its influence will be, or how far-reaching an effect it may have upon the minds and lives of the men and women by whom it will be read.

But one thing is certain. A manuscript of such a character, coming from such a source, demands the most careful study—so tremendous are the claims made for these revelations, so rich in human interest is the actual narrative, so undoubted is Mr. Vale Owen's sincerity.

London

May 1920.

* * *

PREFACE TO BOOK II:
THE HIGHLANDS OF HEAVEN

BOOK II contains the second of a series of communications from beyond the veil received and written down by the Rev. G. Vale Owen, Vicar of Orford, Lancashire.

The messages in this volume are complete in themselves and all are given by one who calls himself Zabdiel and who in the opening line of the messages describes himself as the guide of Mr. Vale Owen.

Following on the communications which Mr. Vale Owen received from his mother, and which terminated on October 30, 1913, in rather an abrupt manner, Mr. Vale Owen again sat in the vestry of the Parish Church, Orford, on the evening of November 3 and received by automatic writing the words "Zabdiel your guide is here." From that date and until the evening of January 8, 1914, a series of communications amounting to some 60,000 words and occupying some thirty-seven sittings were given by this communicator.

These messages cover a wider range than those the Vicar received from his mother. The interrelation of this and the afterlife is more fully explained both in narrative and exposition; and in the last message of all the highest note of spiritual rapture is reached.

To criticize or attempt to elucidate these messages from Zabdiel is not my intention in this preface. The mass of information they contain, the new light they throw on the life beyond the veil, and the knowledge that is unfolded respecting spiritual causes which affect our life here must be left to the understanding of each individual who reads this volume.

That these communications come from a source outside the personality of Mr. Vale Owen will be very apparent to those who follow them closely. On the question of the origin of these scripts I am reminded of a letter which Mr. Vale Owen wrote to me regarding a portion of the messages published in *The Weekly Dispatch* in the latter part of February, 1920: "When I had read the last half-column I put it down with tears in my eyes. I tried it again later—same result. It comes from somebody who knows how to get into my soft places. It all bears out what I said to you: You are interpreting to me the script for the first time."

London
September 1920.

* * *

PREFACE TO BOOK III:
THE MINISTRY OF HEAVEN

ALTHOUGH during the year 1920 the whole of the messages contained in Volume III appeared in *The Weekly Dispatch,* their strict continuity was not observed for various editorial reasons. These 39 communications are now, however, set forth in consecutive order and in the manner in which they were received by the Rev. G. Vale Owen, commencing with the message from Kathleen [introduced in the following chapter—Ed.] on the evening of September 8, 1917. These messages were all recorded in the vestry of All Hallows, Orford, and Mr. Vale Owen invariably sat between the hours of 5:00 and 6:30 in the evening.

I have personally compared the proofs of this volume, word for word, with the original manuscripts. In no instance has a word been altered or a passage omitted. The original script was written down by the Vicar in pencil in the manner described by me in Volumes I and II of this series.

In the Note by Mr. Vale Owen (in the General Notes section for Volume III) he describes how in September, 1917, he was called to sit again, after a lapse of over three years and nine months, by messages spelled out by the planchette operated by his wife.

I have had the privilege of examining the records of these planchette messages. I found that week by week for practically the whole of a period of three years and more, the Vicar had kept in touch, by this means, with Kathleen and also many friends and members of his family who are beyond the veil.

It appears from a number of these records, that during the year 1917 the Vicar received several requests from Kathleen to sit again for messages. Then on September 7th, 1917, I found Mr. Vale Owen had recorded the following:

> "Kathleen wants an answer tonight."
> *"Well, will between 5 o'clock evensong and 6 o'clock do—
> in the vestry?"*
> "Yes, beautifully, thank you very much."

Then on the following evening, and about an hour after Mr. Vale Owen had recorded the first message in Volume III dated September 8, and which is signed "Kathleen," he was seated in the dining-room of the Vicarage watching his wife operating the planchette, when this message was spelled out:

> "Kathleen is here. George will tell you how we got on."
> *"How do you think we got on, Kathleen?"*
> "Very nicely for a start."

On carefully examining these planchette records, which fill many notebooks, I found several illuminating passages which throw much light on the communications Mr. Vale Owen received from time to time in the vestry.

The reality of communication with those beyond the veil stands out most vividly in these records. There is something about them that seems so perfectly natural. At the same time there is in these conversations so much relating to the sanctity of the home, that it is hardly to be expected these records will ever be made public.

To Mr. Vale Owen the authenticity of the messages is not only a vital matter but a fact that means everything to him. He, I know, realizes only too well the tremendous responsibility that falls upon him in permitting them to be given to the world. But to know the Vicar of Orford gives one a deep insight into the spiritual side of these matters. Without seeking any gain for himself he has regarded it a bounden duty to his faith to associate his name with these messages, and to know G.V.O. as I know him, is to realize that he has done this in all humility. It is in spiritual comradeship and with implicit faith in those who have thought fit to use him as their instrument that he has labored. No life could be more simple than the one which the Vicar and his family lead in the Vicarage at Orford, and to witness their struggle to make both ends meet on the stipend granted by the Church should be a sufficient answer to those who have been so ready to suggest that his unavoidable fame has brought affluence and ease.

When reading these scripts I have often been reminded of the 12th verse of the 16th chapter of the Gospel of St. John, wherein it is written: "I have yet many things to say unto you, but ye cannot bear them now." This was said by the Founder of Christianity nearly 2,000 years ago. Since then mankind has progressed in many directions. To any careful observer of the state of the world's progress today there are many indications of a spiritual awakening, a fuller realization and a loftier viewpoint of the deeper truths. There are possibly some amongst us now who are able at last to bear a little of the many things that have been promised to be revealed to us as the growth of our spiritual progress entitles us to understand them. It may be that this volume contains a little more of those "many things" designed to broaden our vision, strengthen our faith, and help us to realize more fully the wonderful things which God has in store for all those that love Him.

London
March 1921.

* * *

PREFACE TO BOOK IV:
THE BATTALIONS OF HEAVEN

THE messages recorded in Book IV were all received and written down by the Rev. G. Vale Owen in the vestry of All Hallows, Orford, Lancashire, after evensong. These thirty-four communications were first published in *The Weekly Dispatch*, and their termination on Sunday, September 26, 1920, brought to a conclusion an uninterrupted series which started in that journal on February 1, 1920.

. . . Volume IV contains the communications from one who gave the name of "Arnel," for such was the name disclosed to Mr. Vale Owen in the message dated February 5, 1918.

In the spring of 1921, and on an occasion when Mr. Vale Owen gave his first personal and public statement on the script, he was asked the question as to how he was sure that the messages were not from his own mind, but from some source beyond it. As this question may arise in the minds of many who read these scripts for the first time, I think it will be helpful to give the Vicar's answer as recorded at the time in the journal *Light*:

> He said it was a straight question, and deserved a straight answer. That was one of the things he *knew*. He was thinking of the great number of letters he had received, putting that question in various ways. It had been put to him many times, sometimes cynically, but now and then

in a very different spirit. He did not think that many of those who asked it realized one simple fact—that there was no one in the whole world whom the answer could affect so deeply as himself. He could assure his hearers that before consenting to make the messages public he had proved up to the hilt that they did not emanate from his own mind. He said to himself, I believe in a future life. My father, mother, and little child have passed into that life, and I am going there—it can only be a few years before I join them. Now, G.V.O., suppose you go over there and your mother says, "I am so glad to have you here. But with regard to those messages, they did not come from us." That would be hell to him, a hell that he could not face. The messages came from his mother and those on the Other Side. He made himself quite sure of it in more ways than one. He was certain, first of all, that they could not have come from his own subconscious mind, or if they did they must have been put there. He wrote them at the rate of twenty-four words a minute on an average. That was not a quick speed if one knew what one was writing about, but he made it a rule not to think of the sittings beforehand. The people who came through were quite unknown to him, except his mother. When he had written, say, on Monday, on Tuesday he put the question, "Is the writing correct?" More than once he had put the question, and had been stopped. Once his mother had communicated by the planchette (operated by his wife) in terrible trouble. He asked what was the matter, and she said, "I am in great distress. You have done nothing; but the writing, *that* is the matter. For the last fortnight it has not come from us. Do not tear it up. It has been given for some purpose. It is not bad, but *it is not from us.* Wait a fortnight." Later on she said, "The way is clear now."

In reply to a further question as to whether he saw any of the beautiful scenes described in the messages he replied that he did in a way, but not externally. When a city was described he could see it in his mind's eye. If he were an artist he could paint the scenes except for some of the details. He asked his mother, when she was communicating, how he could know that it was not his imagination. She said, "My dear boy, it *is* your imagination; what else can it be? We have trained you for many years, before you knew, so that we can use not only your hand but the whole of you, including your imagination, and by that imagination we have built up the images that you see."

Again being asked to describe his sensations when writing, Mr. Vale Owen said that was difficult for him to do. Many of his hearers who had read the script would know that they went right from regions of light to those of darkness. Angels could not always come right down to him, and he had to lift himself to them. That had at times been a great effort, especially when the messages were ethical and philosophical. He felt as if he was scarcely on earth. When the hells were described he felt that he had been through them, and he could now understand the look on Dante's face.

From the above we gain a little insight into the verity of these messages and the source of their origin, but much depends on the reader himself. There is no scientific proof possible to offer in matters such as is dealt with in the Vale Owen script. Their true value can only be gauged by spiritual standards and such appeal as they may make to an interior sense of reality. To those who have this vision, the glorious vista of the life to come, as described in these communications, will have a meaning too deep for words. In the ascending grandeur of these messages there is a revelation that will bring the reality of the Divine love and the glory of the Eternal Christ vividly into the hearts of all those who are ready and willing to receive it.

London

June 1921.

Identity of Those
Who Communicated

G. Vale Owen's mother

MRS. Owen, the Vicar's mother, who communicated the first messages the Vicar received during September and October, 1913, and from whom the major portion of the messages in Volume I came, died on June 8, 1909 [1904, according to Vol. IV Notes—*Ed.*], at the age of 63. She had not during her life shown any interest in the question of spirit communication. Her life was spent at Birmingham, where her husband, at first practicing as an architect and surveyor, was compelled by a breakdown in health to change his occupation to that of a chemist. She visited Orford little, and was never during her lifetime on earth in the vestry of the church where the messages were received.

* * *

Kathleen and Ruby

Kathleen was first heard of on July 28, 1917, when, as Mrs. Vale Owen, the Vicar's wife, was using the planchette, the following interchange took place, the questions asked in italic type:

> "Kathleen."
> *"Who is Kathleen?"*
> "A friend of Ruby's. Would you like to make my acquaintance?"
> *"Very much, if you are Ruby's friend."*
> "Ruby told me to come. She said she was sure you would welcome me for her sake."

Ruby was the daughter of the Rev. G. Vale Owen. She was born at Fairfield, Liverpool, on August 26, 1895, and died at the same address on November 21, 1896. According to messages received through the planchette by the Vicar's wife, when Ruby passed on to the other side she was taken to a home where was she was "mothered by Kathleen." Subsequently the child was brought, under the guardianship of Kathleen, to visit her parents when they were using the planchette. It was in this way Kathleen became acquainted with the Vale Owen family, and in consequence became an intermediary between Mr. Vale Owen and those who were communicating.

Kathleen, in answer to questions, said she had been a seamstress, living in Walton Breck Road, Anfield, Liverpool, and had passed over through consumption at the age of 23 [28, according to Vol. III Notes—*Ed.*], about three years before Ruby. This information, as well as other details connected with Kathleen, were given at different times between 1914 and 1920. In Vol. III, "The Ministry of Heaven," the importance of Kathleen respecting these messages is clearly defined (See Chapter 8, "The Importance of Kathleen").

* * *

Astriel

Intermingled with the messages from Mr. Vale Owen's mother, given in Volume I, came others from Astriel, who had been headmaster of a school at Warwick in mid-eighteenth century. His messages touch upon religious faith, philosophical and scientific matters. They have been separated from those of Mrs. Owen and placed in their proper order at the end of Volume I.

* * *

Presence Form

The meaning of the term "Presence Form," which appears in various places and for the first time in the message dated Monday, September 27, 1913, is explained in the following communication received by Mr. Vale Owen, in answer to his request that the term be defined:

> A "presence form" is the form in which a person becomes localized and visible in form at a distance from himself essentially. The form is not an empty sign or symbol, but is alive with the life of the person it so manifests, action and expression being responsive to the thought, will, action and spiritual state of its original. The personality is projected and becomes visible in any place where God (or those of His angels who are so authorized) wills the manifestation to take place.
>
> By this method the wishes, prayers, thoughts and the whole spiritual state of any one in the earth life, or in any of the regions of the spiritual world, may be manifested in any place or sphere at any moment when those to whom this high gift is entrusted shall will that it be so. A person is not always so manifested in the same presence form, which, from time to time, may be given a different aspect and take a different shape. Under whatever aspect he be manifested, however, that form is, for the time being, his real self projected.

* * *

Zabdiel

In the course of these communications Zabdiel has given no indication as to who he may have been during his earth life or of what period of our earth's history he lived here. To Mr. Vale Owen he always addressed himself as his friend and guardian, and his spiritual presence is very real to the Vicar of Orford.

The Experience of Mary A. and Zabdiel

I am privileged to be able to give for the first time in these notes the full story of an experience that befell a young woman who attended evening service at the parish church of Orford on Palm Sunday, 1917, and it seems to indicate very directly the presence of Zabdiel on this occasion. I myself have questioned at great length this young girl, Mary A., and her story coupled with the appeal expressed by Mr. Vale Owen to Zabdiel, the same evening, points very clearly to the fact that it was Zabdiel who was seen by the girl and thus came to the help of Mr. Vale Owen in response to his prayer. I give the story from notes made by Mr. Vale Owen himself at the time and I use his own words:

> After evensong on Palm Sunday, 1917, a girl of about eighteen or nineteen years of age came to me in the vestry. Without any preliminaries she asked, "Mr. Owen, is there such a thing as seeing angels?"
>
> I replied, "Certainly; why?"
>
> "Because I have seen one."
>
> "When?"
>
> "Tonight, in church."
>
> She then in answer to further questions explained that just as I had entered the pulpit she saw an angel near the "Shield," who passed over the heads of the congregation. As he passed, he turned and smiled—a very beautiful and sweet smile it was—and seemed to go towards me in the pulpit and there disappeared. This was the first experience of the kind she had had, and it gave her so great a shock that she had not recovered from it during the remainder of the service. Indeed, as she

spoke to me, she was visibly trembling. I told her that, had she not given way to fright, she would probably have seen him standing with me in the pulpit.

As to her reference to the "Shield," there are six shields on either side of the nave, attached to the corbels. Those on the south are illuminated with ecclesiastical insignia; those on the north with the arms of local families. The third from the chancel arch on the south side is just about half way down the nave, the pulpit stands outside the chancel on the north side.

The occurrence she related interested me on this particular evening for the following reason:

On account of extra work owing to the war, I had been feeling very unwell for some weeks past. Palm Sunday is a full day in most parishes, and that evening I was feeling very much spent. As the time for the sermon drew near I began to dread the ordeal and wondered what was going to happen. After saying my usual prayer before going into the pulpit, therefore, I made an appeal to my guide, Zabdiel. I told him I needed his help very really as I did not feel at all equal to the preaching of a sermon without notes, and was in acute pain. So I asked him to give me his help in a special degree that night. What the girl had told me assured me that my request had not been in vain, and it showed me who had brought me the help I already was aware I had received. For on entering the pulpit my pain had suddenly ceased and the preaching was no effort at all. Preoccupation might have explained it had the effect not been so marked and instantaneous. Before Mary A. had spoken to me I had decided that the effect was too great for such a cause, and had already thanked Zabdiel for acceding to my request.

Note by H. W. E.: When interviewing Mary A. in reference to the above experience I was very much impressed by the girl's obvious honesty. She is a typical Lancashire lass of the industrial classes, earning her living by working in a metal works. She told me that at the sight of the "angel," as she called the appearance, she was so thoroughly frightened that she bent her head down and clutched at her friend who was seated by her side, and did not dare to leave the pew until the service was over. From her manner in telling of her experience, it was obvious to me that she will never forget it.

A Message from Zabdiel

On Saturday evening, January 31, 1920, Mr. Vale Owen's wife received a message through the planchette, which instrument had been on various occasions operated by her and through which a considerable number of messages had been given from time to time that proved helpful and instructive to Mr. Vale Owen when he was receiving the different communications now published.

This occasion happened to be on the eve of the publication of the first of the series of the scripts in *The Weekly Dispatch.* The message was spelled out by the pointer of the planchette, running from letter to letter of the alphabet, written on the board over which the instrument was propelled. I give it here exactly as it was received; it reads as follows:

> "*Zabdiel.* My son, your script will be a blessing to the world. Zabdiel gives you his blessing. My son, we lately have done right well, giving you what we can, quietly working with you. When I gave those first writings to you we arranged long ahead what should be done when they came to be published. Long hours of work you gave to me. Do you think I should leave you to fight the great battle alone?"
>
> "*Any more from Zabdiel?*"
>
> "I have no more to say now except, God bless you all. God's blessing rest upon you in your endeavor to give to the world the truth."

Note by G.V.O.: When Zabdiel's messages terminated on January 3, 1914, I knew that phase of work had come to an end, and nothing had been said to me about any further communications. So I let the matter rest until September, 1917, when I was called to sit again by messages through the planchette operated by my wife. Also about September, 1917, I felt the same urge to write I had experienced in 1913, when the messages from my mother and Astriel first came through. . . .

* * *

Leader and his band

As stated in the course of the Vol. III messages dated November 16, 17, 22 and 23, these communications came from a band of people directed by one who was called the Leader. It transpired in a later script that the Leader's name was Arnel, which name he only used when communicating without collaborating with his band of helpers.

Kathleen was used by Leader and his band as their amanuensis when communicating their messages to Mr. Vale Owen in the vestry of All Hallows, Orford.

* * *

Arnel

The one who communicated the messages contained in Volume IV gave the name of Arnel. The Vicar first heard of Arnel when receiving messages from his mother in October, 1913. In answer to a question from Mr. Vale Owen as to why his mother (who was describing one of the Heavenly estates to which she had been sent on a mission) did not give the name of the ruler of the estate, she wrote the following through the Vicar's hand: "His name was Arnol, but these names sound so strange to earth ears, and people are always trying to find out their meaning, that we are rather shy of giving them." . . . It will be noted Mrs. Vale Owen spelled the name with an o.

Over four years later, on February 5, 1918, and when receiving the messages contained in Book IV, Mr. Vale Owen asked the communicator, whom he had up to then addressed by the general term "Leader" or "Leader of the Band of Communicators," to tell him his name. It was given as Arnel. The Vicar then asked Arnel if he was the one referred to as far back as October, 1913, and the answer was, "I am he of whom your mother told you . . . write it with one or other letter as you will; it shall suffice that you know me by that name hereafter."

Then again, in the message received on the evening of the fourth day of March, 1918, Arnel revealed a little of his earth life and the period of the world's history when he lived here. Again, at the end of the sitting in the vestry on March 8, Mr. Vale Owen questioned Kathleen (Arnel's spirit amanuensis), and from this and the previous communication we glean that Arnel was an Englishman who, in consequence of religious persecution, had to flee to Florence, and lived there in the English Colony during the early days of the Renaissance. He taught music and painting, and died, as he said, in mid-life, escaping thereby the further enmity of the Church and the State of those days. Through Mr. Vale Owen's hand the name Arnel was written at the conclusion of each communication from him and the sign of the cross affixed below it.

Regarding Arnel's spiritual status at the time he was communicating the messages in Vol. IV, it is recorded in the first message, dated February 5, that he was then a Temple dweller on the borders of Spheres Ten and Eleven, thus indicating that Arnel is a being of a high spiritual order.

Special note: Initials only are used throughout this volume when reference is made to any person outside Mr. Vale Owen's own family. The name Rose refers to Mr. Vale Owen's wife, and Rene is their daughter.

H.W.E.'s General Notes

How the Messages Came

IN the typewritten copies of the original manuscript, Mr. Vale Owen gave a description of how it came about that he acted as amanuensis for his mother and the spirit beings who in turn took her place at the sittings in the vestry, of the church at Orford:

> There is an opinion abroad that the clergy are very credulous beings. But our training in the exercise of the critical faculty places us among the most hard-to-convince when any new truth is in question. It took a quarter of a century to convince me—ten years that spirit communication was a fact, and fifteen that the fact was legitimate and good.
>
> From the moment I had taken this decision, the answer began to appear. First my wife developed the power of automatic writing. Then through her I received requests that I would sit quietly, pencil in hand, and take down any thoughts which seemed to come into my mind projected there by some external personality and not consequent on the exercise of my own mental-

ity. Reluctance lasted a long time, but at last I felt that friends were at hand who wished very earnestly to speak with me. They did not overrule or compel my will in any way—that would have settled the matter at once, so far as I was concerned—but their wishes were made ever more plain.

I felt at last that I ought to give them an opportunity, for I was impressed with the feeling that the influence was a good one, so, at last, very doubtfully I decided to sit in my cassock in the vestry after evensong.

The first four or five messages wandered aimlessly from one subject to another. But gradually the sentences began to take consecutive form, and at last I got some which were understandable. From that time, development kept pace with practice. When the whole series of messages was finished I reckoned up and found that the speed had been maintained at an average rate of twenty-four words a minute. On two occasions only had I any idea what subject was to be treated. That was when the message had obviously been left uncompleted. At other times I had fully expected a certain subject to be taken, but on taking up my pencil the stream of thought went off in an altogether different direction.

A Sample of the Actual Script

On the following page is a reproduction of a sheet from the actual script written down by the Rev. G. Vale Owen at the sitting of October 6, 1913. It will be noticed how the words and sentences have flowed from the pencil in a swift and steady stream. They are joined together as if the writer were striving to keep pace with the communication which was being impressed upon his mind.

This page of the manuscript is particularly interesting, for it shows a question written down by Mr. Vale Owen, and the answer to it immediately following in a steady flow of words.

REPRODUCTION (REDUCED) OF THE
ACTUAL SCRIPT

261

The text of the above MS. will be found on page 60, commencing "Our onward way . . ."

* * *

Sample of the script, which in this edition can be found starting on page 47.

Mr. Vale Owen always numbered a quantity of sheets of paper before he began to write. He placed these in a block before him on the table in the vestry. Then, using shaded candlelight to illuminate the sheet of paper and with his pencil in his hand, he would wait until he felt the influence to write. When once he started the influence was maintained without a stop until the message for the evening was concluded by the communicator.

How the Communicators Operated on the Other Side

It is particularly interesting to note the explanations given by his mother and others of their methods of impressing the mind of Mr. Vale Owen with the words they wished his hand to write. We select the following illustrative passages which, however, do not appear in the first volume of communications.

It transpired from a later script that when Mr. Vale Owen's mother was communicating, the girl Kathleen acted for her on the other side as an amanuensis, and controlled the actual writing down of the messages for all the communicators. In the case of Mr. Vale Owen's mother the difficulties of getting through antique words and expressions that were not modern did not, of course, arise in her case, but there seems no doubt from the character of many of her messages that she was not alone in giving them.

(Extract from a script)

Only in part are we able to make in anywise clear to you the method we are employing in this particular case. And that we will so far as we be able.

First, then, here we stand a group tonight of seven—sometimes more, at others less. We have already broadly settled what we will say to you, but leave the precise wording till we sight you and sense your disposition of mind.

Then, we take our stand a little distance away lest our influence, the emanations of our several minds, reach you in detail, and not as one stream but as many, and so confuse you. But from the little distance at which we stand they merge and mingle, and are focused into one, so that by the time our thoughts reach you there is unity and not multiplicity of diction.

When you sometimes hesitate, doubtful of a word or phrase, that is when our thoughts, mingling in one, are not quite perfected into the special word required. You pause; and, continuing their blending together, our thoughts at last assume unity, and then you get our idea and at once continue on your way. You have noticed this, doubtless?"

Yes, but I did not know the cause.

No. Well, now, to continue. We think our thoughts to you, and sometimes they are in such words as are too antique, as you say, for you to grasp them readily. This is remedied by filtering them through a more modern instrument, and it is of this we now would speak.

That instrument is your little friend Kathleen, who is good enough to come between you and us, and so render our thoughts available for you. This in more ways than one.

First, because she is nearer to you in status than we, who, having been longer here, have become somewhat removed from earth. She is of more recent transplanting, and not yet so far away that when she speaks you cannot hear.

For a like reason also she comes between. That is, by the words that form her present store. She can still think in her old tongue of earth, and it is more modern than our own—though we like it not so well, since it seems to us more composite and less precise.

But we must not find fault with what is still beautiful. We have, no doubt, still our prejudices and insularity; when we come down here we cannot but take on anew some of those traits we once had but gradually have cast aside.

The little lady Kathleen is nearer you than we in these respects, and the stream of our impelling we direct on you through her for that reason.

However, we stand a little apart from you, because the presence of us combined would overmatch you. You could not write down what we would give, and our purpose in coming is to give you such narrative of words as you and others may read with intelligence.

You glance at the dial of your timekeeper. You call it a watch. Why? That is one little instance of our preference for our older way of speaking. Timekeeper seems to us more explicit than the other word. The meaning of your glance is clear, whatever we call the thing on which it fall. So we bid you goodnight, good friend. . . .

We find sometimes, when we read what message we have given, that much which we tried to impress is not apparent there, and some lesser quantity of what we had not in mind appears.

This is but a natural consequence of the intervention of so thick a veil between the sphere from which we speak and that in which the recorder [i.e. Mr. Vale Owen) lives his life.

The atmosphere of the two spheres is so diverse in quality that, in passing from one to the other, there is always a diminution of speed, so sudden and so marked that a shock is given to the stream of our thoughts, and there is produced, just on the borderline, some inevitable confusion. This is one of the many difficulties we find.

Here is another. The human brain is a very wonderful instrument, but it is of material substance, and, even when the stream of our thoughts reaches and impinges upon it, yet, because of its density, the penetration is impeded and sometimes altogether brought to a stop. For the vibrations, as they leave us, are of high intensity, and the fineness of their quality is a hindrance to their effecting a correspondence in the human brain, which is gross by comparison.

Once again: there are many things here for which there are no words in any of the earth languages to express their meaning.

There are colors which your eyes do not see, but are present in your spectrum; there are more colors which are of higher sublimity than could be reproduced by that medium, which shows both the earth colors to you and registers those invisible to you, but present withal.

There are also notes and tones of sound of like nature, and too fine for registration by the atmosphere of earth.

There are forces also, not available with you, not able to be expressed to you. . . .

These and other matters are interpenetrating all our life and informing our environment. And when we come to speak of our life here, or of the causes we see in operation, of which you behold the effects alone, we are much perplexed and strive continually to find just how to say it so that it shall be both understood of you and also not too wide of the target as known to us.

So you will see that we have a task to do in speaking into your sphere from this of ours which is by no means easy. Still, it is worth the doing of it, and so we essay our best and try to rest content.

Mr. Vale Owen's Comments

In view of the above description, it is interesting to have the following remarks from Mr. Vale Owen, descriptive of his mental and physical condition during the time he was actually receiving the communications. In a letter to the editor of this volume, Mr. Vale Owen wrote:

> You point out to me the fact that, while in the script itself my communicators give not a little information as to the methods employed in the transmission of mes-

sages from their side to ours, yet, on my own part, I have never given you any definite description of the effect produced upon myself.

The effect of what, perhaps, we might term the more mechanical operations, as these impinge upon the organism of the human brain, the transmitters themselves describe in some detail. Vibrations, initiated by them and projected through the Veil, find their target in the mentality of the human instrument and are reproduced, on this side, in what is, in effect, a kind of inner clairvoyance and clairaudience. Viewed inversely, from the standpoint of the instrument himself, it assumes an aspect something like this: the scenes they describe seem to come along a kind of X-ray stream of vibrations and are received by means of the faculty of visualization. That is, he sees these scenes in his imagination as he, by a similar process, is able to visualize his garden or house, or other well-known place, when at a distance.

The words of the messages seem to travel on a celestial-mundane telephonic current. He can hear them interiorly in much the same manner as he is able to hum over a well-remembered tune, or to reproduce a speech he has heard with all its inflections and cadences, pathetic or uplifting—all this also interiorly, and without himself uttering a sound.

In addition, however, there is a deeper content in the operation. It is that effect upon the human instrument produced by the more or less intimate contact of spirit with spirit. This is actual "Spiritual Communion," and is recognized in the Creed of Christendom in the article "the Communion of Saints."

Here enters in an essentially spiritual element which, as our spirit communicators repeatedly tell us, it is not possible adequately to contain in any earthly form of words. It is uplifting to the boundaries, and on occasion, into the very domain, of ecstasy.

At times such as these earth and earth's affairs retreat into the background, and glimpses are had of what eternity and infinity mean, and of the Presence of God.

Then Christendom assumes an enlarged aspect and occupies a broader room. It is seen that the whole Church on earth is but a small portion of the Divine Kingdom, which includes within itself, not alone all races and all systems of religion here below, but also that realm of interstellar glories and powers in the mere contemplation of which the human heart grows faint and the reaches of human imagination fade into the boundless infinities pulsating with the heart-love of the One Ineffable Light.

It is almost needless to add that anyone who has ever experienced such contact as this has no room in his heart any more for any paltry sentiment of self-exaltation, or of spiritual pride. I know of no better teacher of humility than this realization of the smallness of the individual earth-dweller amid the myriads of those so much brighter ones who, with himself, form the one family of the Creator.

On the other hand, the sense of security, of comradeship, of oneness with them, and of the sweet intimacy of their love, is a sure warrant of, protection to us lesser ones to whom our angel friends bend down for our uplifting. Be a man prayerful, clean-living and of a humble mind, and no danger of devils can enter in between him and them.

Sincerely your friend,

G. Vale Owen.

P.S. For all this, yet so intimate and so perfect must be the sympathy of aim and affection existing between transmitter and receiver, that whenever any thought comes through which seems to be at variance with what is true, immediately a shock is felt and the instrument faces about, as it were, with a query in his mind, which

on the part of the communicator is as immediately observed and noted.

This sympathy is quite apart from the difference in
status, both in mental and spiritual capacity, between
the spirit-communicator and the human instrument,
and is not affected by it. As I have said above, they "bend
down" to us, and thus bridge over any such inequality.

Biographical Notes on G.V.O.

"What manner of man is he?"

THE Rev. G. Vale Owen is a typical clergyman of the Church of England, devoted to his parish and completely absorbed in his work.

Nothing was farther from his thoughts, a few years ago, than that he should be made a medium for "spirit" communications.

His career has been uneventful. Born in Birmingham in 1869, and educated at the Midland Institute and Queen's College, in that city, he was ordained by the Bishop of Liverpool to the curacy of Seaforth in 1893; then was curate successively of Fairfield, 1895, and of St. Matthew's, Scotland Road, 1897—both of Liverpool.

It was in 1900 that he went to Orford, Warrington, as curate-in-charge. Orford Church was built in 1908, when a new parish was formed and he became the first Vicar. His Vicarage was built so recently as 1915.

Though he feared that the quietude of his life in his parish would be disturbed, Mr. Vale Owen felt that the importance of the revelations which were sent through him did not permit him to follow his own wishes and withhold his name, and regarding himself as only an instrument for the transmission of the messages, he refused to accept any money payment for the publication of the scripts, great as had been the labor they had thrown upon him.

Though his personality was much discussed on the first appearance of the messages, that circumstance did not affect his absorption in the work of his parish. He felt that that parish was peculiarly his own, since his was the only church in the village, and he had become intimately bound up with every family in it during his twenty years' service.

Villagers speak of him as "G.V.O."—an abbreviation of his name which in itself is a sign of affection. One of them recounted an incident typical of the means by which he has won and retained their close friendship.

"Coming home late one night," he said, "I was startled to see a tall, dark figure dash past me at a run. It was our Vicar. I learnt afterwards that one of his young parishioners, who was ill, had become restless through pain, and had asked that Mr. Owen should come and talk to her and pray at her bedside. Her brother had at once cycled to the Vicarage, and Mr. Owen, who had retired for the night, had dressed at top speed and hurried to the house.

"He is always available at any hour, and such is his influence that invalids belonging to all denominations ask for him. Can you wonder why he is a welcome guest in every house?"

When Mr. Vale Owen went first to Orford his congregation worshipped in a large room of the village school. He told them they were "getting their religion too cheaply," and did not appreciate it enough. Then, obtaining donations from prosperous friends of the village, he called the parishioners together and

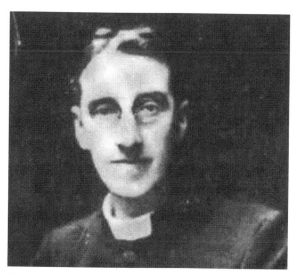

The Rev. G. Vale Owen

The Church of St. Margaret's & All Hallows, Orford, Warrington, Lancashire, of which the Rev. G. Vale Owen was the Vicar. [Reproduced from The Life Beyond the Veil, *Volume I,* The Lowlands of Heaven.—*Ed.]*

organized a system of weekly collections, to which every family subscribed according to its means. In this way he succeeded in getting a church built and an excellent organ installed.

When the War came, about two hundred Orford men served in the Forces. All of them regarded "G.V.O." as their chief "home pal" and wrote to him regularly of their adventures. All were "his lads," and he always wrote encouraging them to "play the game."

In appearance, the Rev. G. Vale Owen is tall, spare, and a little bent. One might at first judge him to be the shy recluse. But his deeply-lined face lights up readily with a smile and, most unassuming and approachable of men, he has a genius for friendship. There is no trace of the aloofness of the dreamer in his relations with anyone with whom he comes in contact. He is above all practical. The building of his new church at a time which many thought premature, is one of the standing evidences of that quality. To know him is to realize that he is a fitting instrument indeed to receive such communications as are set forth in these pages. His life has been one of strenuous endeavor to help his fellows to understand the reality of sacred things, to lighten their hearts and strengthen their courage; his first thought and his last have been for others. But G.V.O.'s point of view may perhaps best be shown by the following illustration. Amongst many thousands of letters received at the Vicarage at Orford during the early days of the publication of the script in *The Weekly Dispatch* was this:

> "Rev. Sir—Pray for the writer of this note who is in great trouble concerning a little child who is afflicted. I have read about you and I feel you must be very near to God, and if you were to say, 'Dear Father, help your child,' He would hear. Please do not fail to pray. The Lord understands. This is a cry for help from a mother's aching heart. God bless you."

Mr. Vale Owen's comment in speaking of this to a friend was:

". . . And yet *The Weekly Dispatch* says I am receiving no payment."

It was in this spirit that the Vicar of Orford gave permission for these communications to be placed before the world. He hoped that by so doing he would be instrumental in bringing light into many dark places, strengthening the faith of the people and doing, his humble duty to those fair angel friends, who, as he himself often remarked, "have been so gentle and patient with me during those precious hours I spent at their bidding in the vestry of the little Parish Church at Orford."

* * *

The Personality of Mr. Vale Owen

In the *London Evening News* of July 16, 1920, in the course of a review of the first volume of *The Life Beyond the Veil,* Sir William Barrett, F.R.S., referring to Mr. Vale Owen, wrote:

Here we have a beloved and honored clergyman, whose saintly and devoted life is known to all his parishioners, retiring to the vestry of his church and in the solemn silence of the place finds his hand guided by some unseen power, whilst evening after evening there is swiftly written down the record of a pilgrim's progress in the spiritual world. And this record is entirely independent of any conscious or voluntary guidance on his part. Only on two occasions had the Rev. Vale Owen any idea of what subject was to be treated, and often when he had anticipated one topic the writing disclosed a wholly different train of thought.

Reluctant at first to yield to this involuntary guidance, doubtful of its legitimacy and skeptical of the result, he was at last convinced that the messages were wise and helpful; that they did not originate from his own mind; but appeared to be impressed upon him by some extraneous spirit. Believing that these messages would afford hope and consolation to many stricken hearts, the author consented to their publication, but, as Lord Northcliffe[1] tells us, he refused to touch a penny of the large emolument he might have had. I wonder how many of the Rev. Vale Owen's critics and detractors—with a family to support, as I am informed is the case here—would have acted in this noble and utterly unselfish way!

. . . But although the fierce ray of publicity has penetrated the quietude of the peaceful Vicarage at Orford, Mr. Vale Owen is the last man on earth to whom this would make the slightest material difference. He has always been most emphatic, both in his letters and to all those with whom he has been brought in contact, in stating that it is the messages that are of paramount importance and not the man. It is, however, impossible altogether to accede to the wishes of Mr. Vale Owen in this respect. On Tuesday, June 15, 1920, the Vicar of Orford after considerable pressure was prevailed upon by the Hon. and Rev. James Adderley to preach at St. Paul's Church, Covent Garden, London. The scenes that took place in that famous old London Church were described in *The Daily Mail* the next morning as follows:

> There were all sorts and conditions of people—clergymen, Army officers, city men, girl typists, Covent Garden porters, women in working garb, women of leisure, widows in their weeds, laborers in corduroys. These and other types of humanity were all there. When he left the church Mr. Vale Owen was surrounded by men and women who grasped him by both hands. Men bared their heads and a number of women wept. When Mr. Vale Owen freed himself he stood on the steps and to

[1] Owner/publisher of *The Weekly Dispatch.—Ed.*

the hushed assemblage addressed a few simple words. As he descended the steps hundreds of people again rushed to greet him. It was with the greatest difficulty that his friends, clerical and lay, were able to escort him to the rectory across the road. Thousands of people have written to Mr. Vale Owen congratulating him on his writings. Many people in yesterday's congregation traveled specially from the north of England, Manchester and Leeds in particular, to hear his address.

The advent of Mr. Vale Owen to London on this occasion illustrated at once and in a remarkable manner the value of his personality. The Rev. James Adderley, standing beside the altar of St. Paul's, Covent Garden, before pronouncing the benediction, addressed the vast congregation saying:

> With regard to our preacher today, we are perfectly certain there is no fraud and no self-advertisement and no denial of Christianity. That is putting it only in a very negative way. I am not saying anything of the positive things we could say. If we had any doubt about it before we have none now, for if ever a man had an opportunity for self-advertisement and fraud our preacher has had it today standing in this church, packed from end to end, hundreds of people outside unable to get in; if he had been out for self-advertisement, was it psychologically possible that he could have preached such a sermon as he has today? Anybody knows he could not, and knowing that I asked Mr. Vale Owen to preach here because I thought it would do real good to people of all kinds, convinced believers and those who are skeptical, to have an opportunity of seeing a simple-minded humble Christian parson, who does believe in these experiments, and who has had the most extraordinary psychical experiences, of seeing what manner of man he is and of hearing what he has to say. If it has done nothing more, it may make people think a little more,

make them wonder whether there is not a new spiritual movement going on in the world and whether any religious person can afford to stand altogether outside or is not bound to come inside it, at least to learn something about it, to discuss it, to inquire into it; because if there is any meaning at all in religion, it means that these things are so real that those who believe in God and Jesus Christ cannot possibly neglect them.

* * *

Mr. Vale Owen's Worldwide Correspondence

As a natural consequence of the worldwide publicity and interest in these scripts during their publication in *The Weekly Dispatch* and other journals overseas, Mr. Vale Owen has received an enormous number of letters from every part of the globe. Of the great majority expressing gratitude, or making urgent enquiries, many were such as deeply to move him, and also to humble him by bringing realization of the immense volume of goodwill created. I cannot refrain quoting from a letter written to me by Mr. Vale Owen referring to a certain section of his correspondence, in view of the light it throws on a particular phase of his character. It was in answer to one in which I could not help speaking with indignation on the attitude of certain persons towards the scripts and even towards Mr. Vale Owen himself. Gently rebuking me, he wrote:

> Let us treat our anonymous post-carders and other revilers gently and with patience. They are following, not in a very high-minded way truly, the course they believe to be right and many would be prepared to make sacrifices for their cause—although some are not prepared to do this to the extent of backing up their opinions and convictions by coming out into the open with their names. But viewing the whole matter generally, I cannot but realize what a joy it will be some day, somewhere, to take them by the hand as brothers and sisters and to

tell them that we were not too bitter against them when their rather cruel words of misjudgment and attribution of false motives came from them, because we realized that they were but treading the road by which we ourselves had come. That is so in my own case, at least. I see my own former self reflected in their present attitude, and I hope it helps to keep me in humility and in love to them. Indeed, I owe them, for this reason, a debt not of resentment, but of gratitude. I refer not to their bitterness, but to their lack of enlightenment."

This letter is typical of the many that I have received from Mr. Vale Owen, and makes it unnecessary for me to insist on what I venture to call the Christ-like nature of G.V.O., as his parishioners, who are also his friends, his comrades and his followers, dearly love to call him. Of his practical energy and foresight in affairs of his parish, his buoyant cheerfulness and untiring labors, I have already spoken in my preface in Vol. I.

Manly though his attitude is towards this life and its trials and vicissitudes, and fascinating in every degree as is his personality, I must ask every reader of this volume to respect the wishes of Mr. Vale Owen as far as possible and center his attention upon the communications . . . and not on the one who was used as an instrument to give them to the world.

H. W. Engholm
London, *May 1920.*

* * *

The Life to Come a Living Reality

During the first week of the publication of the script in *The Weekly Dispatch*, the thoughts of thousands of people were turned towards Orford. This quite insignificant village had become famous in a day and was destined to be known throughout the world. No one realized more than Mr. Vale Owen during that momentous week that he had turned his back once and for all on the old order of things and that his outlook on life could never be quite the same again. Controversy about the scripts was already beginning to rage throughout the country, and the mailbags for the Vicarage were the largest that had ever been seen in that peaceful village of Lancashire. In the midst of this new condition of things I received a letter from the Vicar. A document written straight from the soul of a man who realizes the nature of the high task before him and its tremendous importance to the world. . . .

Extract from G.V.O.'s letter addressed to H. W. Engholm, February 11, 1920:

> It has taken me some years to think things out. I have done so and made up my mind. I have been down into the Valley of Decision and wrestled it all out. It was rather dark down there at times. But I have now come out of the Valley and I stand today upon the hilltop in the fierce light of day. I have given myself at last but wholly to the Great Cause, and any personal feelings count no more at all with me. So never hesitate to tell me what to do and I will do it gladly. When I went into our little church this morning it was quite dark. I knelt in my little corner, but there was so great a surging of spiritual forces all around that I had to get up and walk up and down the church for a time panting. At last I came to a stand in the chancel and this is what I realized. It was quite distinct and real.
>
> The whole spirit world near the earth was in motion. It was immense like the ocean beating against the rocks. High above stood Our Lord the Christ. He was stern and immovable, but He looked down our way and with Him there was a great host of fighting men all ready for the battle, and some were already engaged with the enemy. Between Him and me stood Zabdiel. He stood there straight and tall—taller and more majestic than I had ever realized him before. His hands

were straight down by his sides, clenched and determined as he poured down upon me a great stream of strength and determination which he in turn seemed to be drawing down from those above him. All this while the forces rushed and surged about him and me, but he was quite calm and like the Christ immovable. And as I stood there still, but still panting—for the power was really overwhelming—he gradually came down and stood on my right-hand side. But he towered above me as we stood together there comrades both.

G.V.O.

To Mr. Vale Owen, I know, the life to come is a living reality. He feels that he is now carrying out his humble duty to those fair angel friends, whose continual presence strengthens and sustains him night and day, and he will continue to do so until he is called to the presence of the Christ whom he daily strives to serve as a faithful and loving servant.

H.W.E.

An Appreciation

by Lord Northcliffe

I HAVE not had an opportunity of reading the whole of *The Life Beyond the Veil,* but among the passages I have perused are many of great beauty.

It seems to me that the personality of the Rev. G. Vale Owen is a matter of deep importance and to be considered in connexion with these very remarkable documents. During the brief interview that I had with him I felt that I was in the presence of a man of sincerity and conviction. He laid no claims to any particular psychic gift. He expressed a desire for as little publicity as possible, and declined any of the great emoluments that could easily have come to him as the result of the enormous interest felt by the public all over the world in these scripts.

NORTHCLIFFE[1]

---

[1] [Lord Northcliffe (Alfred Charles William Harnsworth) was a British newspaper magnate and owner/publisher of *The Weekly Dispatch.* His undated Appreciation was included in all four volumes of *The Life Beyond the Veil.—Ed.*]

Introduction by

Sir Arthur Conan Doyle

THE long battle is nearly won. The future may be checkered. It may hold many a setback and many a disappointment, but the end is sure.

It has always seemed certain to those who were in touch with truth, that if any inspired document of the new revelation could get really into the hands of the mass of the public, it would be sure by its innate beauty and reasonableness to sweep away every doubt and every prejudice.

Now worldwide publicity is given to the very one of all others which one would have selected, the purest, the highest, the most complete, the most exalted in its source. Verily the hand of the Lord is here!

The narrative is before you, and ready to speak for itself. Do not judge it merely by the opening, lofty as that may be, but mark the ever-ascending beauty of the narrative, rising steadily until it reaches a level of sustained grandeur.

Do not carp about minute details, but judge it by the general impression. Do not be unduly humorous because it is new and strange.

Remember that there is no narrative upon earth, not even the most sacred of all, which could not be turned to ridicule by the extraction of passages from their context and by over-accentuation of what is immaterial. The total effect upon your mind and soul is the only standard by which to judge the sweep and power of this revelation.

Why should God have sealed up the founts of inspiration two thousand years ago? What warrant have we anywhere for so unnatural a belief?

Is it not infinitely more reasonable that a living God should continue to show living force, and that fresh help and knowledge should be poured out from Him to meet the evolution and increased power of comprehension of a more receptive human nature, now purified by suffering?

All these marvels and wonders, these preternatural happenings during the last seventy years, so obvious and notorious that only shut eyes have failed to see them, are trivial in themselves, but are the signals which have called our material minds to attention, and have directed them towards those messages of which this particular script may be said to be the most complete example.

There are many others, varying in detail according to the sphere described or the opacity of the transmitter, for each tinges the light to greater or less extent as it passes through. Only with pure spirit will absolutely pure teaching be received, and yet this story of Heaven must, one would think, be as near to it as mortal conditions allow.

And is it subversive of old beliefs? A thousand times No. It broadens them, it defines them, it beautifies them, it fills in the empty voids which have bewildered us, but save to narrow pedants of the exact word who have lost touch with the spirit, it is infinitely reassuring and illuminating.

How many fleeting phrases of the old Scriptures now take visible shape and meaning?

Do we not begin to understand that "House with many mansions," and realize Paul's "House not made with hands," even as we catch some fleeting glance of that glory which the mind of man has not conceived neither has his tongue spoken?

It all ceases to be a far-off elusive vision and it becomes real, solid, assured, a bright light ahead as we sail the dark waters of Time, adding a deeper joy to our hours of gladness and wiping away the tear of sorrow by assuring us that if we are only true to God's law and our own higher instincts there are no words to express the happiness which awaits us.

Those who mistake words for things will say that Mr. Vale Owen got all this from his subconscious self. Can they then explain why so many others have had the same experience, if in a less exalted degree?

I have myself epitomized in two small volumes the general account of the other world, drawn from a great number of sources. It was done as independently of Mr. Vale Owen as his account was independent of mine. Neither had possible access to the other. And yet as I read this far grander and more detailed conception I do not find one single point of importance in which I have erred.

How, then, is this agreement possible if the general scheme is not resting upon inspired truth?

The world needs some stronger driving force. It has been running on old inspiration as a train runs when the engine is removed. New impulse is needed. If religion had been a real compelling thing, then it would show itself in the greatest affairs of all—the affairs of nations, and the late war would have been impossible. What church is there which came well out of that supreme test? Is it not manifest that the things of the spirit need to be restated and to be recoupled with the things of life?

A new era is beginning. Those who have worked for it may be excused if they feel some sense of reverent satisfaction as they see the truths for which they labored and testified gaining wider attention from the world. It is not an occasion for self-assertion, for every man and woman who has been honored by being allowed to work in such a cause is well aware that he or she is but an agent in the hands of unseen but very real, wise, and dominating forces. And yet one would not be human if one were not relieved when one sees fresh sources of strength, and realizes the all-precious ship is held more firmly than ever upon her course.

SIR ARTHUR CONAN DOYLE[1]

---

[1] [Sir Arthur Conan Doyle (1859-1930) was a Scottish author most noted for his Sherlock Holmes detective stories. After the deaths of his son, wife, and several other close relatives, he turned to Spiritualism for solace and became one of its most well-known advocates.—*Ed.*]

BOOK I

THE LOWLANDS
OF HEAVEN

Poem: Into the Light

The good God is, and God is good,
    And when to us 'tis dimly seen
'Tis but the mists that come between
    Like darkness round the Holy Rood,
Or Sinai Mount where they adored
    The Rising Glory of the Lord.

He giveth life, so life is good,
    As all is good that He has given.
Earth is the vestibule of Heaven;
    And so He feeds with angel's food
Those in His likeness He has made,
    That death may find us unafraid.

Death is no wraith, of visage pale,
    But waits attendant on our birth
Out of this darkened womb of earth,
    To lead us gently through the Veil,
To realms of radiance, broad and free,
    To Christ and immortality.

September, 1915.

* * *

Note: Subsequent to the reception of the portion of the script which is included in Vol. I, I received at three separate sittings the verses printed above. It was intimated to me, at that time, that the purpose for which this hymn was transmitted was that it should be regarded as a keynote to the messages received previously from my mother and her fellow workers.—G.V.O.

1

The Lowlands of Heaven

Tuesday, September 23, 1913.

Who is here?

MOTHER and other friends who have come to help. We are progressing very well, but are not able to give you all the words we would like to yet, as your mind is not so quiet and passive as we would wish.

Tell me something about your home and occupation.

Our occupation varies according to the needs of those to whom we minister. It is very various, but directed to the uplifting of those who are still in earth life. For instance, it is we who suggested to Rose [the Vicar's wife—*Ed.*] the creation of a band of people to come to her aid in case of her feeling any danger when she was in the room writing as we moved her hand, and that band is at present in charge of her case. Does she not feel their presence at times near her? She should do so, for they are ever near at call.

About our home. It is very bright and beautiful, and our companions from the higher spheres are continually coming to us to cheer us on our upward way.

(A thought here came into my mind. Could they see these be-ings from the higher realms, or was it with them as with us? I may say that here and there throughout these records the read-er will come upon passages which are quite obviously answers to my unspoken thoughts, usually beginning "Yes" or "No." This being understood, there will be no need for me to indicate them unless any particular instance seems to require it.)

Yes, we can see them when they wish that we should do so, but that depends on the state of our advancement and their own power of service to us.

Now will you please describe your home—scenery, etc.?

Earth made perfect. But of course what you call a fourth dimension does exist here, in a way, and that hinders us in de-scribing it adequately. We have hills and rivers and beautiful forests, and houses, too, and all the work of those who have come before us to make ready. We are at present at work, in our turn, building and ordering for those who must still for a little while continue their battle on earth, and when they come they will find all things ready and the feast prepared.

We will tell you of a scene which we witnessed not long ago. Yes, a scene in this land of ours. We were told that a cer-emony was about to take place in a certain wide plain not far from our home, at which we might be present. It was the cer-emony of initiation of one who had passed the gate of what we will call prejudice, that is, of prejudice against those who were not of his own particular way of learning, and who was about to go forth into a wider and fuller sphere of usefulness.

We went, as we were bidden, and found a great many peo-ple arriving from many quarters. Some came in . . . why do you hesitate? We are describing quite literally what we saw— chariots; call them otherwise, if you will. They were drawn by horses, and their drivers seemed to know just what to say to them, for they were not driven with reins like they are on earth, but seemed to go where the drivers willed. Some came on foot and some through space by aerial flight. No, not wings, which are not necessary.

When they had all gathered, a circle was made, and one stepped out, the one who was to be initiated, and he wore a robe of orange color, but bright, not like the color as you know it; none of our colors are; but we have to speak to you in our old tongue. The one who had had him in his care then took him by the hand and placed him on a green knoll near the middle of the clear space, and prayed. And then a very beautiful thing occurred.

The sky seemed to intensify in color—blue and gold mostly—and out of it descended a veil-like cloud, but which seemed to be made up of fine lacework, and the figures dominating were birds and flowers—not white, but all golden and radiant. This slowly expanded and settled on the two, and then they seemed to become part of it, and it of them, and, as it slowly faded away, it left both more beautiful than before—permanently beautiful, for both had been advanced into a higher sphere of light.

Then we began to sing, and, although I could see no instrument, yet instrumental music blended with our singing and became one with it. It was very beautiful, and served both as a reward to those who had earned it and a spur to those who had still to tread the path they two had trodden. The music, as I found out later by inquiry, proceeded from a temple grove outside the circle, but indeed it did not seem to come from any one point. That is a faculty of music here. It seems very often to be part of the atmosphere.

Nor was the jewel lacking. When the cloud cleared, or dissolved, we saw it on the brow of the initiate, gold and red, and his guide, who had one already, wore his on his shoulder—left shoulder—and we noticed it had increased in size and brightness. I do not know how this happens, but have an idea, not definite enough to tell you, however, and it is difficult to explain what we ourselves understand. When the ceremony was over we all separated to our own work again. It was longer than I have described and had a very heartening effect on the rest of us.

Over the hill on the farther side of the plain to that where we stood I noticed a light grow up and it seemed to us a beautiful form in human shape. I do not think it was an appearance of our Lord, but some great Angel Master who came to give power, and to do His will. No doubt some there could see more clearly than I, because we are able to see, and also to understand, in proportion to our stage of advancement.

Now, my boy, just think for a moment. Is this *from* your mind or *through* it, as you say? When you sat down to write, as you know, nothing was farther from your thoughts, for we had carefully refrained from impressing you, and yet you went off at once on the account as we influenced you. Is that not so?

Yes; I admit that frankly.

Quite right. And now we will leave—not you, for we are always with you in a way you do not understand—but we will leave this writing, with our prayer and blessing on you and yours. Goodnight and goodbye till tomorrow.

Wednesday, September 24, 1913.

Suppose we were to ask you to look forward a little space and try to imagine the effect of our communications as viewed in relation to the ultimate outcome of your present state of mind.[1]

---

[1] *Note By G.V.O.:* As my desire is that my readers should understand, so far as is possible, the conditions under which these messages were given, it may perhaps be well to append to the foregoing a note of explanation. I do this because it is apparent, from letters received, that many readers are perplexed at my perplexity. It would require a volume in itself to explain all the intricate factors which enter into such a process as this. I must therefore content myself with a very brief statement. I do not see nor hear my communicators with bodily organs of eye and ear. The method adopted

What then, think you, should have been the issue of events as we see them from our own sphere in the spirit world? It would be something like the effect of sunlight when it is projected into a sea-mist, which mist gradually vanishes away, and the scene it enveloped becomes clearer to the vision, and more beautiful than when dimly discerned through the enveloping mist.

So do we view your minds and, if the sun for awhile dazzles and perplexes rather than clarifies the sight, you know that the end is light, and the end of all that Light in whom there is no darkness at all. Yet light is not conducive to peace always, but, in its passage, often creates a series of vibrations which bring destruction to those species of living creatures which are not fashioned to survive in the light of the sun. Let them go, and, for yourself, go onward, and as you go your eyes will become used to the greater light, the greater beauty of the Love of God, the very intensity of which, blended as it is with infinite Wisdom, is perplexing to those who are not altogether of the light.

* * *

And now, dear son, listen while we tell you of one more scene which has gladdened us here in these regions of God's own light.

---

may perhaps be described as impressional. The impression, however, was so strong as to induce me to devote many hours a week, month after month, to the writing down of what came through to me in this way. As the messages proceeded my confidence in their authenticity gradually increased. This confidence was confirmed by communications sent to me through other people of psychic faculties of various kinds. Those quite independent lines of testimony all converged on the script and constituted so strong a case as to prove to me: (1) that the titles been given from people who hall passed into the larger realm of spirit; (2) that these people were the individuals they claimed to be; (3) that I had taken down their messages correctly. I came to the conclusion that to reject such proof would be to discount the value of all that the world accepts as evidence of fact. Then, and then only, did I feel myself justified in undertaking the responsibility of giving this script to the public.

We were wandering a short time ago in a beautiful wood-land place, and as we went we talked a little, but not more than a little because of the sense of music which seemed to absorb all else into its own holy silence. Then, standing in the pathway in front of us, whom should we see but an angel from a higher sphere. He stood and looked on us with a smile, but did not speak, and we became aware that he had a message for one of us especially. It was so, for, as we halted and stood in expecta-tion, he came forward and, lifting the cloak he wore—amber it was in color—he placed his arm and it round my shoulder and, laying his cheek on my hair—for he was much taller than I am—he said softly, "My child, I am sent to you from the Mas-ter Whom you have learned to trust, and the way before you is seen by Him but not by you. You will be given strength for whatever you have to do; and you have been chosen for a mis-sion which is new to you in your service here. You will be able, of course, to visit these your friends at will, but now you must leave them for a time and I will show you your new home and duties."

Then the others gathered round me and kissed me and held my hands in theirs. They were as glad as I—only that is not quite the word to use in my case, it is not peaceful enough. After awhile, when he had let us talk and wonder what his mes-sage meant, he came forward once more and this time took me by the hand and led me away.

We walked for a little time and then I felt my feet leave the ground and we went through the air. I was not afraid, for his strength was given to me. We passed over a high mountain range where many palaces were, and at last, after a fairly long journey, we descended in a city where I had not been before.

The light was not unkind, but my eyes were not used to such a degree of brightness. However, I soon made out that we were in a garden surrounding a large building, with steps up to it all along the front, at the top of which was a kind of terrace.

The building seemed all of one piece of material of different hues—pink and blue and red and yellow—which shone like gold, but softly. Up these we went, and at the great doorway, without any door to it, we met a very beautiful lady, stately but not proud. She was the Angel of the House of Sorrow. You wonder at the word used in this connection. What it means is this:

The sorrow is not of those who dwell there, but is the lot of those to whom they minister. The sorrowful ones are those on earth, and it is the business of the residents in this House to send to them vibrations which have the effect of neutralizing the vibrations of sorrowful hearts on earth. You must understand that here we have to get at the bottom of things, and learn the cause of things, and that is a very deep study, only learned in gradual stages bit by bit. I therefore speak of the causes of things when I use the word "vibrations," as one you will understand best.

She received me very kindly and took me within, where she showed me over part of the place. It was quite unlike anything on earth, so it is hard to describe. But I may say that the whole house seemed to vibrate with life, and to respond to our own will and vitality.

This, then, is my present and latest phase of service, and a very happy one it promises to be. But I have only just begun to understand the prayers which are brought to us there and registered, and the sighs of those in trouble we hear—or rather, they are also registered, and we see or feel them, as it were, and send out our own vibrations in answer. This in time becomes involuntary, but is a great effort at first, I find it so. But even the effort has a reflex blessing on those who work so.

There are many such places here, as I learn, all in touch with earth, which at present would seem impossible to me except that, as the effects are also registered back again to us, I know the amount of comfort and help we send. I only am on duty for a short space at one time, and then go out and see the sights of this city and its neighborhood. And very glorious, it all is, even more beautiful than my old sphere, which I also revisit to see my friends. So you can imagine the talks we have when we do meet. That is almost as great a joy as the work itself. Peace in Jesus our Lord is the atmosphere all around us. And this is the land where there is no darkness, and when those mists are of the past, dear, you will come here and I will show you all—until you are perhaps able to take me by the hand, as he did, and lead me to see the work in your own sphere. You think I am ambitious for you, dear lad. Well, so I am, and that is a mother's—shall I say weakness—or rather blessing?

Goodbye, dear. Your own heart at this moment is a witness that this is all real, for I can see it glowing happy and bright, and that is gladness also to me your mother, dear son. Goodnight, then, and God will keep you and yours in His peace.

Thursday, September 25, 1913.

What we want most to say to you tonight is to be understood as a very imperfect attempt to tell you what is the meaning of that passage of which you have often thought where our Lord tells St. Peter that he is an adversary to him. He, as you will remember, was on the way to the Holy City, and had been telling his Apostles that he would be killed there. Now, what he evidently wished to impress on them was the fact that, although to men his mission might seem to have ended in failure, yet to eyes which were enabled to see as He would theirs might see, His end was only the beginning of a much more powerful and glorious development of the life-giving mission which He had undertaken on behalf of the Father and for the uplifting of the world.

Peter, by his attitude, showed that he did not understand this. Which is all plain and easy enough, so far, to understand. But what is usually lost sight of is the fact that the Christ was pursuing one straight line of progress, and that His death was but an incident in the way of His onward path, and that sorrow, as the world understands it, is not the antithesis of joy, but may be a part of it, because, if rightly used, it becomes the fulcrum on which the lever may rest which may lift a weight off the heart of the one who understands that all is part of God's plan for our good. It is only by knowing the real "value" of sorrow that we understand how limited it is in effect, so far as making us unhappy goes. Now, He was about to inflict the heaviest sorrow He possibly could on the Apostles and, unless they understood this, they would be unable to use that sorrow to lift themselves above the turmoil of the world, and so, unable to do the work He had in hand for them to do. "Your sorrow shall be converted into joy," He told them, and so it came to pass, but not until they had learned the scientific value of sorrow—in a limited measure indeed, but in a measure nevertheless.

All this sounds very simple when it is written down thus, and no doubt it is simple, in a way, because all the fundamentals of God's economy are simple. But to us, and to me at the present time, it has an importance which may not be apparent to you. For the problem which is the chief study of the new House in which I spend so much of my time is this same subject, namely, the turning, or converting, of the vibrations of sorrow into the vibrations which produce joy in the human heart. It is a very beautiful study, but many perplexities enter into it because of the restrictions imposed on us by the sacredness of free will. We may not overrule the will of any, but have so to work through their wills as to produce the desired effect and yet leave them free all the time, and so, deserving, in a way and in a measure at least, of the blessing received. I get tired sometimes, but that will pass away as I become stronger in the work. What is your question? I think you wish to ask one.

No, thank you, I have no particular question in mind.

Wasn't there something you wished to ask about—something to do with the method by which we impress you?

I did think of asking you that this morning. But I had forgotten it. I suppose there is nothing much to explain, is there? I should call it mental impression.

Yes, that is correct, as far as it goes, but it does not go far. Mental impression is a phrase which covers up a great deal which is not understood. We impress you by means of these same vibrations, some of a different nature from others—all directed on your will. But I see you are not much interested in that matter at the present moment. We will return to it, if you wish, at another time. I want to speak of those things which are of present interest to you.

Then tell me something more about that home of yours and your new work.

Very well, then, I will try to do so as well as I can.

It is beautifully appointed within and without. Within are baths and a music room and apparatus to aid us in registering our work. It is a very large place. I called it a house, but it is really a series of houses, each house allotted to a certain class of work, and progressive as a series. We pass from one to another as we learn all we can from any particular house. But it is all so wonderful that people would neither understand nor believe; so I would rather tell you of the simpler things.

The grounds are very extensive, and all have a kind of relation to the buildings, a kind of responsiveness. For instance, the trees are true trees and grow much as trees do on earth, but they have a kind of responsiveness to the buildings, and different kinds of trees respond more to one house than to the others, and help the effect and the work for which that particular house was raised. So it is with the grouping of trees in the groves, and the bordering flower-beds of the paths, and the arrangement of the streams and falls which are found in different parts of the grounds. All these things have been thought out with marvelous wisdom, and the effect produced is very beautiful.

The same thing obtains on earth, but the vibrations there are so heavy, comparatively, both those sent out and those which respond, that the effect is almost unseen. Nevertheless, it is so. For instance, you know that some people can plant flowers and trees more successfully than others, and that flowers will last longer in some houses—that is families—than others; cut flowers, we mean. All that is the same thing in grosser state. Here these influences are more potent in action, and also the recipients more sensitive in perception. And that, by the way, is one of the things which help us to accurate diagnosis of cases which are registered here for us to deal with.

The atmosphere also is naturally affected by vegetation and by buildings, for, let me repeat, those houses have not been raised merely mechanically, but are the outcome—growth, if you will—of the action of the will of those high in rank in these realms, and so of very powerful creative wills.

The atmosphere also has an effect on our clothing, and enters into the influence of our own personalities in its effect on texture and color. So that while, if we were all of the same quality spiritually our clothing would be of the same tint and texture, by reason of the atmospheric influence, this is in fact modified by the degree in which our own characters differ one from another.

Also the tint of our robes changes according to the part of the grounds in which we happen to be. It is very interesting and instructive, and also very beautiful, to see them change as one turns down a sidewalk where different vegetation flourishes, or where the arrangement of the various species of plants is different.

The water also is very beautiful. You hear of water-nymphs and suchlike beings, in the earth life. Well, I may tell you that here, at any rate, these things are true. For the whole place is pervaded and interpenetrated with life, and that means with living creatures. I had some idea of this in the sphere from which I have lately come, but here, as I grow accustomed to the strangeness and newness of it, I see it all much more plainly and begin to wonder what it will be a few spheres onward. For the wonder of this place seems to be about as much as any place could hold.

But there, let it rest. He Who enables us in one part of His beautiful Kingdom will enable us in another. Which is a word for you, my dear son, and which I will leave with you now, and my blessing.[2]

Friday, September 26, 1913.

Our last installment was given in answer to a request by one of our band that we should try to impress you in a rather deeper kind of way than heretofore, but we were only able to begin, as it were, and not to complete our explanation. If you wish it therefore, we will continue the subject now.

Thank you; yes.

---

[2] *Note by G.V.O.:*—While writing the first part of this message I could not see the drift of the argument, which seemed to me to be rather thin and muddled. On reading it over, however, I am by no means sure of my estimate. Taking what is said of the vibrations of sorrow as merely a hint on fundamentals," and applying to it some such reasoning as that by which the wave theory is applied to the radiation of light and heat, the result would be something like this: In dealing with that combination of vibrations which cause sorrow, the method is not so much that of substitution as of readjustment. By directing on the sorrowful soul other classes of vibrations those of sorrow are, some of them, neutralized; and others are modified and converted into vibrations the effect of which is joy or peace. Viewed thus the above message does seem to hold some significance, and may perhaps throw light on the way in which troubles are actually dealt with in life. It certainly does seem to be part of the divine method, not that the outer aspect and circumstances of sorrow should be remedied (except in extremely rare cases), but that other elements should be infused which should have the effect of converting that sorrow into joy. This is merely a matter of everyday observation. To the unscientific mind this will probably seem to be drawing a very long bow. To others it may not seem so unreasonable to suggest that these "other vibrations "are really vibrations of other classes or "values." The passage referred to is John xvi. 20.

Then you must, for a moment, try to think with us as from our side the Veil. Things, you must understand, take on a very different aspect here from what they did as viewed from the earth plane, and an aspect, I fear, which to those still on earth will, in many cases at least, wear a semblance of unreality and romance. And the least things here are fraught with so much wonder to those who are newly come over that until they have divested themselves of the habit of thinking in three dimensional terms, they are unable to progress very far. And that, believe me, is a matter of no little difficulty.

Now, the term "vibrations" is one which will have to serve, but it is far from adequate as understood of things material. For such vibrations as those of which we speak are not merely mechanical in movement and quality, but have an essence of vitality in themselves, and it is by that vitality that we are able to appropriate and use them. That is the connecting link between our wills and the outward manifestation in vibrations, for that is really all that these are. They are just phenomena of the deeper life which envelops us and all things. By them, as raw material, we are able to accomplish things, and build up things which have a durability which the term itself would seem to belie.

For instance, it is by this method that the bridge over the chasm between the spheres of light and darkness is constructed, and that bridge is not all of one color. On the farther side it is shrouded in darkness and, as it gradually emerges into, or towards, the region of light, it assumes an ever brighter hue and, where it lands on the heights where begin the brighter lands, it is of pink hue and glistens in the light enveloping it like some rare kind of silver, or alabaster rather.

Yes, of course there is a bridge over the chasm. Otherwise how would those who have fought their way upward through the gloom get over? True—and I had forgotten it—there are some who do proceed through the awful realm of darkness, and climb up the regions on this side the chasm. But these are few, and they are those obstinate ones who reject the help and guidance of those guardians of the way who are stationed on the farther side to show those who are qualified the way across.

Also, you must know, those guardians are only visible to those poor people in proportion to the light that has been generated in their hearts; and so a certain amount of trust is needed if they would commit themselves to their keeping. This trust also is the outcome of a better mind by which they have become, in a measure, able to discern between light and darkness. Well, the complications of the human spirit are manifold and perplexing, and so let us get on to something easier of putting into words. I have called this a bridge, but I ought to have referred you to the passage, "The light of the body is thine eye." Read that in this connection, and you will see that it bears on the case, not only of those on earth but those here also.

I have called this a bridge, but, as a matter of fact, it has little likeness to a bridge on earth. For these regions are vast, and the bridge is more like a tract of country than anything else I can think of to call it to you. And remember I have only seen but a small part of these spheres, and so just tell you of that part which I know. Doubtless there are other chasms and bridges— probably numbers of them. Across the ridge, or bridge, then, those who seek the light make their journey, and that journey is but slow, and there are many rest-houses at which they stay, from time to time, on their progress across, and are handed on from one to another party of angel ministers, until the last stage lands them here on this side. Our work in the house, or colony, to which I now belong, is also directed to these progressive spirits, as well as to those on earth. But that is a different department from mine at present. I have not yet got that far in my study. For it is more difficult, because the influences around those in the darkness here are much more evil than the influences on earth, where good influences are ever mingling with the bad. It is only when careless and wicked people get over here that they realize the awful task before them; and that is why so many of them remain for ages in a condition of hopelessness and despair.

When they are safely over the bridge they are welcomed by those on the slopes where grass and trees grow, and they are just stupefied with delight, in spite of the gradualness of their preparation.

For they have not yet become used to love and its sweetness after their experience of the opposite down there.

I said this bridge landed on the heights; I speak comparatively. The landing place is highland as compared with those regions of darkness below. But, as a matter of fact, it is lowland, and the lowest land indeed, of the heavenly country.

You are thinking of the "great gulf," or chasm, "fixed," of the Parable. That is all quite in accord with what I have written. Also the reason why these who come over do so instead of attaining this side by aerial travel, or "flight," as you would perhaps call it, is because they are not able to make the journey so on account of their weakness spiritually. If they were to attempt it they would only fall into the dark valley, and then lose their way.

I have not been far into those dark regions, but I have been a little way; and the misery I saw was quite enough to suffice for some time to come. When I have progressed in my present work, and have for some time helped those poor souls from the vantage point of this house, I may be permitted, and probably shall be, to go farther among them. But that is not yet.

One thing more I may say—for it is time that you should cease. When they break away, and come to the other end of the bridge, I am told that the noises which are heard from behind them are horrible; and dull red flashes of fire are seen. How that is caused I am not able clearly to state, but we are told that both the yells and screeches and howls, and also the flashes, are made by those left behind who are enraged because of their powerlessness to recapture the fugitive, or to hold him as he is slipping away; for evil is ever powerless against good, be the good ever so small in amount. But I must not pursue this farther now, and what I am now saying is not what I have myself seen, but hearsay, that is, it is given to you at secondhand but it is true, nevertheless.

Goodnight, then, dear son, and may the All Father shed His light and peace on you and yours. . . . In His light shall you see light; and the shining of that light is of the peaceful ever-breaking dawn.

Saturday, September 27, 1913.

(I asked my friends to try to impress me more vividly.)

It is scarcely necessary that we should be careful to impress you more vividly than we have already done, for we have managed to get through the messages as we intended them, to help you to realize somewhat of our life, and conditions prevailing here. Only we would add that what should be clear to you is that when we come here we are not in our own proper element, but that what to you is a natural environment is to us as a mist, and through it we have to work as best we can.

Are you able to see me as I sit here writing?

We do see you, but with other eyes than yours. Our eyes are not accustomed to the effect of light as you have it on earth. Our light is of a different kind, a sort of interpenetrating element by which we are able to discern your inmost mind, and that is it to which we speak—to you yourself and not, of course, to your outward ears. So it is yourself we see, and not your material body, which is but an enveloping robe. When we touch you, therefore, you do not feel the touch physically but spiritually, and if you wish to apprehend our touch, you will have to keep this in mind and look deeper than the body and its mechanical brain.

You would wish to know something more of the way we work here and the conditions in which our life is spent. Not every one who comes over here is able to understand that one of the elementary truths which it is necessary to assimilate in order to progress is that God is no more visibly present here than He is in the earth life. They expect to see Him bodily, and are much disappointed when they are told that that is a quite mistaken idea of the way of His dealing with us. His life and beauty are quite apparent on earth to those who can look deeper than the externals of nature. And so it is here, with this modification: that life here is more tangible, and easier to lay hold of and use by those who study its nature, and it pulsates all around us, and we, being in a more sensitive state, are more able to feel it than when we were in the earth life. Still, having said this on the general conditions, it is true to add that, from time to time, manifestations of the Divine Presence are given us, when some particular purpose necessitates; and of one of these I will tell you now.

We were called to a tract of country where many people were to forgather, of different creeds and faiths and countries. When we arrived we found that a band of missionary spirits had returned from their period of duty in one of the regions bordering on the earth sphere, where they had been working among souls just come over who did not realize that they had crossed the borderline between earth and the spirit land. Many had been enlightened, and these had been brought to the place in order that they might join with us in a service of thanksgiving before going to their own proper homes. They were of various ages, for the old had not progressed yet in becoming youthful and vigorous again, and the young had not progressed to complete stature. They were all agape with happy expectation, and, as one company after another of their new companions in this life arrived, they scanned their faces, and the different colored robes, worn by the different orders and estates in wonder.

By and by we were all assembled, and then we heard a burst of music which seemed to invade us all and unify the whole great multitude into one great family. Then we saw a great cross of light appear. It seemed to lie on the slope of the great mountain which bordered the plain and, as we watched it, it began to break up into specks of bright light, and we gradually became aware that it was a large company of angels of a higher sphere who stood on the mountain in the form of a cross; and all about them was a golden glow, which we could feel at that distance as a warm breath of love.

Gradually they became more distinct to our vision as they emerged more perfectly into this, to them, lower environment, and then we saw, standing over the square where the arms of the cross joined the stem, a larger Being. We all seemed to know Him at once instinctively. It was a Manifestation of the Christ in what you have come to know as Presence Form.

He stood there silent and still for a long time, and then lifted His right hand on high, and we saw a column of light descend and rest upon it as He held it aloft. This column was a pathway, and on it we saw another company descending and, when they came to the uplifted hand, they paused and stood still with their hands folded on their breasts and heads bowed. Then slowly the hand moved out until it had swung round and down and the fingers pointed over the plain, and we saw the column stretch out towards us in mid-heaven until it bridged the space between the mountain and the plain, and the end of it rested over the multitude gathered there.

Along this column walked the company last become visible, and hovered above us. They spread out their hands then, and all slowly turned towards the mountain, and softly we heard their voices half speaking and half singing a hymn of devotion to Him Who stood there all so beautiful and so holy that at first we were awed into silence. But presently we also took up their words and sang, or chanted, with them; for that evidently was their purpose in coming to us. And as we sang there arose between us and the mountain a mist of bluish tint which had a very curious effect. It seemed to act like a telescopic lens, and brought the vision of Him nearer until we could see the expression on His face. It also acted similarly on the forms of those who stood just below Him. But we had no eyes for them, only for His gracious face and form. I cannot describe the expression. It was a blend of things which words can only tell in small part. There were blended love and pity and joy and majesty, and I felt that life was a very sacred thing when it held Him and us in one bond. I think others felt something like this too, but we did not speak to one another, all our attention being taken up with the sight of Him.

Then slowly the mist melted into the atmosphere, and we saw the cross on the mountain and Him standing as before, only seen more dimly; and the angels who had come over to us had gone, and hovered above Him. And then all gradually faded away. But the effect was a very definite sense of His Presence remaining and perpetual. Perhaps that was the object of the vision being given to the newcomers who, although they could not see so clearly as we could who had been here longer, yet would be able to see enough to encourage them and give them peace.

We lingered sometime longer, and then quietly went our ways, not speaking much, because we were so impressed with that we had witnessed. And also, in all these Manifestations there is always so much to think out after. It is so glorious that one is not able, while it is taking place, to take in all the meaning. That has to be thought out gradually; and we talk it over together, and each gives his impressions, and then we add them up, and find that a revelation has been given of something we did not understand before so well. In this instance what seemed to impress us most was the power He had of speaking to us in silence. He did not utter a word and yet we seemed to be hearing His voice speaking to us whenever He made a movement, and we understood quite well what the voice said, although it did not actually speak.

That is all I can tell you now, so, goodbye, dear son, and may you, as you will, see for yourself one day what our Lord has in store for them who love Him

Monday, September 29, 1913.

The idea of viewing things from the standpoint of a higher sphere than yours is one which should be given due weight when you read what we have already written. Otherwise you will often be mystified at the seeming incongruity in the association of ideas as we have given them. To us it is perfectly natural to link together the coming of our Lord in Presence Form and the other incident of the formation of that bridge which spans the great continent of the chasm. For what is there seen in the concrete—that is, of course, concrete to us here— is but a phenomenon of the same invisible power as that by which the Lord and His company of angel attendants bridged the gulf between the spheres in which we at present move and those from which these higher beings come.

You will understand that that Manifestation was to us very much what materialization is to you. It was the linking up of two estates in the Kingdom of the Father by bridging the space by higher vibrations than those which we are able to use in these lower spheres. How it is done we can only surmise, but, having passed through from your earth sphere into this, the connection between this and the next does not seem strange.

We would wish you could be further enlightened in regard to some of the wonders of our land, for then it would seem more natural to you, both during your sojourn on earth, and also when you come over here it would be less unfamiliar to your mind. The former in that you would see that earth is heaven in embryo, and heaven is but earth cleansed and made perfect and the latter for reasons quite obvious.

In order to help you in this matter, therefore, we will try to tell you of a system which we have here of separating and discerning between things that matter and those of lesser importance. Whenever we are perplexed about anything—and I speak just of our own immediate circle—we go up to the top of some building, or hill, or some high place where the surrounding country may be viewed from a distance. Then we state our difficulties, and when we have made the tale complete, we preserve silence for a time and endeavor to retreat into ourselves, as it were. After a time we begin to see and hear on a higher plane than ours, and those things which matter, we find, are those which are shown to us, by sight and hearing, as persisting on that higher plane, in those higher spheres. But the things which do not matter so greatly we do not see nor hear, and thus we are able to separate the one class from the other.

It seems all right, dear, but could you give me a specific instance by way of example?

I think we can. We had a case of doubt to deal with, and scarcely knew how to act for the best. It was that of a woman who had been over here for rather a long time, and who did not seem able to progress much. She was not a bad sort of person, but seemed to be uncertain of herself and everybody around her. Her chief difficulty was about angels—whether they were all of light and goodness, or whether there were some of angelic estate and yet who were of the darkness. For some time we could not quite see why this should trouble her, as everything here seemed to be of love and brightness. But we found at last she had some relatives who had come over before her, and whom she had not seen, and could not find where they were. When we got at her real trouble we talked it over among ourselves, and then we went to the top of a hill and stated our wish to help her and asked to be shown the best way. A rather remarkable thing happened, as unexpected as helpful.

As we knelt there the whole summit of the hill seemed to become transparent and, as we were kneeling with bowed heads, we saw right through it, and a part of the regions below was brought out with distinctness. The scene we saw—and we all saw it, so there could be no delusion—was a dry and barren plain in semi-darkness and, standing leaning against a rock, was a man of large stature. Before him, kneeling on the ground, with face in hands, was another smaller form. It was that of a man, and he seemed to be pleading with the other, who stood with a look of doubt upon his face. Then at last, with a sudden impulse, he stooped down and caught the prostrate form to his breast, and strode with him over the plain towards that horizon where a faint light glimmered.

He went a long journey with that burden and, when they came to a place where the light was stronger, he set him down and pointed out the way to him; and we saw the smaller form thank him again and again, and then turn and run towards the light. We followed him with our eyes, and then saw that the other had directed him to the bridge, of which I have told you already—only that end of it which is on the other side of the chasm. Still we could not understand why this vision had been shown to us, and we continued to follow the man until he had reached the large building which stands at the entrance of the bridge—not to guard it, but to watch for those who come and who require refreshment and help.

We saw that the man had been sighted from the watch-tower, for a flash of light signaled the fact to those below and to those on the next watchtower along the bridge.

And then the hill resumed its normal aspect again, and we saw no more.

We were more perplexed than ever now, and were descending the hill when our Chief Lady met us, and, in her company, one who seemed to be a high officer in some part of our sphere, but whom we had not met before. She said he had come to explain to us the instruction we had just received. The smaller man was the husband of the woman whom we were trying to help, and we must tell her to go to the bridge and she would be given a lodging there, where she could wait till her loved one arrived. The larger man whom we had seen was what the woman would call an angel of darkness, for he was one of the more powerful spirits in that dark land. But, as we had observed, he was capable of a good deed. Why then, we asked, was he still in the regions of darkness?

The officer smiled and said, "My dear friends, the Kingdom of God our Father is a very much more wonderful place than you seem to imagine. You never yet have met with a realm or sphere which was complete in itself, and independent and separate from all other spheres. Nor are there any such. That dark angel blends within his nature many spheres of knowledge and goodness and badness. He remains where he is first because of the badness remaining in him, and which unfits him for the regions of light. He remains also because, while he could progress if he would, yet he does not wish to do so at present, partly because of his obstinacy, and partly because he still hates the light, and thinks those who set out upon the awful uphill way fools because the pains and agonies are sharper then, by reason of the contrast which they see between the light and the darkness. So he remains; and there are multitudes such as he whom a kind of dull and numb despair prevents coming over. Also in his time of hatred and frenzy he is cruel. He had tortured and ill-treated this same man whom you saw with him from time to time, and that with the cruelty of a cowardly bully. But, as you saw, that wore itself out, and, when the man pleaded this last time, some soft chord in the heart of the other vibrated just a little, and, on the impulse, fearing a reversal of his intention, he liberated the victim who wished to make the journey, and pointed out to him the way, no doubt thinking in his heart that he was a fool and yet, perhaps, a wiser fool than he, after all."

This was new to us. We had not realized that there was any goodness in those dark regions before; but now we saw that it was but natural that there should be, or, if every one were totally bad, no one would ever desire to come to us here.

But what bearing has all this on the discerning between the things which matter and those of lesser importance?

All that is of good is of God; and light and darkness, as applied to His children, are not, and cannot be, absolute. They are to be understood relatively. There are, as we now know, many "angels of darkness" who are in the darkness because of some twist in their natures, some obstinate trait which prevents the good in them having its effect. And these one day may pass us on the road of the ages, and become greater in the Kingdom of the Heavens than we who now are more blessed than they.

Goodnight, dear son. Think over what we have written. It has been a very wholesome lesson to us, and one which it were well if many in your present life could learn.

2

Scenes That Are Brighter

Tuesday, September 30, 1913.

YOU would scarcely realize all that we feel when we come to earth in this way and commune with one still wending his way through the valley. We feel that we are of those who are more than ordinarily privileged, for, once we are able to convince people how much lies to their hand that they might use for the uplifting of the race, there seems to be no bounds to the possibilities of good and enlightenment. Still, we are but able to do a little, and must rest content until others will co-operate with us, as you have done, fearlessly, knowing that no evil can come to those who love the Father, and serve Him in His Son, our Savior Lord.

Now, in order to help those who still doubt us and our mission and message, let me say that we do not lightly leave our beautiful home to come down into the mists which surround the earth sphere. We have a mission and a work in hand which someone must do, and there is joy in the doing of it.

* * *

A little time since—to speak in earth phrase—we were sent into a region where the waters were collected into a large lake, or basin, and round the lake, at some distance from each other, were erected buildings in the form of large halls with towers. They were of varied architecture and design, and not all built of one material. Spacious gardens and woods surrounded them, some of them miles in extent, and full of beautiful fauna and flora, most of the species known on earth, but also some which would be strange to you now, although I think that at least a proportion of them lived once on earth. That is a detail. What I wish to explain to you is the purpose of these colonies.

They are for nothing else than the manufacture of music and musical instruments. Those who live there are engaged in the study of music and its combinations and effects, not only as to what you know as sound, but also in other connections. We visited several of the great houses and found bright and happy faces to welcome us and show us over the place; and also to explain what we were able to understand, and I frankly confess that was not much. Such as I personally did understand I will try to explain to you.

One house—or college, for they were more like colleges than manufactories, when I come to think of it—was devoted to the study of the best methods of conveying musical inspiration to those who had a talent for composition on earth; and another house gave attention rather to those who were clever at playing music, and others to singing, and still others made a special study of ecclesiastical music, and others concert music, and others operatic composition, and so on.

The results of their studies are tabulated, and there their duty ends. These results are studied again by another class, who consider the best method of communicating them to composers of music generally, and then another body do the actual work of transmission through the veil into the earth sphere. Here are pointed out to them the objects of their endeavors, namely, those who are likely to prove most ready of response to their inspiration. These have been carefully selected by others who are trained in selection of such. All is in perfect order; from the colleges round the lake to the church or concert hall or opera house on earth there is a chain of trained workers who are constantly active in giving to earth some little gift of heavenly music. And that is how all your best music comes to you. . . . Yes, you are quite correct. Much of your music is not from us; and much is sullied in its passage. But that is not the fault of the workers from those spheres, but lies at the door of those on your side of the Veil, and those on this side who are of the gloomy regions and to whom the character of the composer gives a foothold to tamper with that which comes from us here.

What were the towers for?

I was just going to explain that to you.

The lake is of vast extent, and the buildings at some little distance from it on all sides. But at certain times, previously arranged, the workers of some of these colleges, and now and again of all of them, send certain of their company to the tower-top, and, when all are assembled, then a concert, literally true to its name, is held. They all practice something they have previously agreed upon together. On one tower will be instrumentalists of one class, on another those of another class, and on the third vocalists; and on another, another class of vocalists; for there are many classes, not only four, as usually with you, but many toned voices. And other towers are devoted to other workers whose actual duties I could not understand. From what I could make out, some of these were expert in harmonizing the whole, or part, of the volume of sound combined from the different towers.

But I want to get on to the description of the thing itself—the concert or festival, or whatever you like to call it. We were taken to an island in the midst of the lake, and there, in a beautiful scene of trees and grass and flowers and terraces and arbors of trees and little nooks and seats of stone or wood, we heard the festival.

First there came a chord, long and sustained, growing louder and louder, until it seemed to invade the whole landscape and waterscape and every leaf of every tree. It was the key given to the musicians on the various towers. It died into silence and all seemed very still. Then, gradually, we heard the orchestra. It came from many towers, but we could not tell any single contribution apart. It was perfect harmony, and the balance of tone was exquisite.

Then the singers took up their part. It is of no use for me to try to describe this music of the heavenly spheres in earth language, but I may perhaps be able to give you some idea of the effect. Briefly, it made everything more lovely, not only beautiful, but lovely, too—for there is a difference in meaning of these two words as I use them here. All our faces took on a more lovely hue and expression, the trees became deeper in color, and the atmosphere gradually grew into a vapor of tints like a rainbow. But the vapor did not obscure anything; it seemed to bring everything nearer together rather. The water reflected the rainbow tints, and our clothing also became intensified in color. Moreover, the animals and birds about us also responded. One white bird I remember especially. Her beautiful milky feathers gradually grew brighter and, when I saw her last, before she flew into a grove, she shone like gold burnished and glowing, like transparent light or fire. Then, as the mists slowly faded away, we all became, and everything became, normal once again. But the effect remained, and if I could give it a name, I should say it was "peace."

* * *

That, then, is one little experience which I had in the Home of Music. What we heard will be discussed again and again by meetings of experts, a little altered here, and a little there, and then some use will be made of it; perhaps at some great service of thanksgiving here, or some reception of spirits come over from the earth life, or some other function. For music enters into so many phases of our life here, and, indeed, all seems music in these spheres of light—music and blended color and beauty, all breathing love among all, and to Him Who loves us as we are not able to love. But His love draws us onward, and, as we go, is all about us, and we must inbreathe it, as we do the beauty of His presence. This we cannot choose but do, for He is All in All here, and love is a delight which only you will understand when you stand where we have stood, and heard what we have heard, and seen the beauty of His presence, breathing and shimmering all around and above and beneath, as we learned some little more of His love.

Be strong and live the valiant life, for the end is worth the cost, as we ourselves have proved.

Goodnight, dear lad, and remember that sometimes in your sleep we are able to waft some faint echo of such music as this into your spiritual environment, and it is not without its effect on the aspect worn in your mind by your next day's life and work.

Wednesday, October 1, 1913.

What we said last evening relative to the Home of Music was but an outline sketch of all that we heard and saw; and we only went over part of the place. We are informed, however, that it is of much larger extent even than we thought at the time, and extends far away from the lake into the mountainous country outlying the plain in which the lake lies. In those mountains there are other colleges, all linked up with those we saw by means of a kind of wireless telephony, and a cooperative work is continually going on.

On our way back to our own home we turned aside to see another new thing. It was a plantation of very large trees in which was built another tower, not a single column, but a series of chambers and halls, with pinnacles and turrets and domes of manifold colors. These were all in the one building, which was very high and also spacious. We were shown within very courteously and kindly by one of the dwellers there, and the first thing that struck us was the curious aspect of the walls. What had from the outside appeared opaque, from the inside were translucent, and, as we went from hall to hall, and chamber to chamber, we noticed that the light which filled each was slightly different in tint from the one which led to it—not of different color, for the variance was not so marked as that, but just a slight degree deeper or lighter.

In most at least of the smaller compartments the light was of one definite and delicate hue, but every now and then, after passing through a more or less complete series of chambers, we came to a large hall, and in this hall were gathered all the component tints of the surrounding chambers. I am not quite sure whether I am exactly correct in saying that all the smaller laboratories only distilled one tint, but am telling you as nearly as I can remember. There was so much we saw that it is difficult to separate all into details; and it was my first visit, so I do not vouch for more than a true description of the general scheme.

One of these great halls was the Orange Hall, and in it were all the tints of that primary, from the faintest of light gold to the deepest of deep orange. Another was the Red Hall, where hues were ambient all about us, from the faintest rose-leaf pink to the deepest crimson of the rose or dahlia. Another, the Violet Hall, was radiant with hues ranging from the most delicate heliotrope, or amethyst, to the dark rich hue of the pansy. And now I must tell you that there were not only more but several more of these halls devoted to those tints which you do not know, but which you call the ultra-violet and the ultra-red, and most wonderful they are.

Now, these rays are not blended together in one hue, but each tint was distinct in its gradation, and yet all harmonized wonderfully and beautifully.

You are wondering to what purpose these buildings of crystal are put. They are for studying the effect of colors as applied to different departments of life, animal, vegetable and even mineral life, but the two former chiefly, together with clothing. For both the texture and the hue of our garments take their quality from the spiritual state and character of the wearer. Our environment is part of us, just as with you, and light is one component, and an important one, of our environment. Therefore it is very powerful in its application, under certain conditions, as we saw it in these halls.

I am told that the results of those studies are handed on to those who have charge of trees and other plant life on earth and other planets. But there are other results which are too rare in nature for such application to the grosser environment of earth and the other planets, so, of course, only a very small part of these studies is handed on in your direction.

I am sorry that I can tell you little more, partly because of these same limitations, and partly because it is rather scientific and out of my line. But this I may add, for I inquired while there. They do not gather the primary colors together in one hall in that colony. Why, I do not know. It may be, as some of my friends think, who understand these matters better than I do, that the force generated by such combination would collectively be too tremendous for that building and require a specially constructed one, and that, probably, away in some high mountain; as it is possible, they told me, that no vegetation would live within a long distance of such a place. And they add that they doubt whether people of the degree we met could safely control such forces as would be so generated. They think it would require those of much higher state and skill. But away in another and higher sphere there may be, and probably is, a place where this is done, and that place in touch with the one we saw. Judging from the way things are ordered here, that much is almost certain.

We left the colony, or university, as it might be called, and when we were at some distance away on the plain where we could see the central dome above the trees, our guide, who had come with us to speed us on our way, told us to stop and see a little parting surprise which the Chief had promised to afford us. We watched and saw nothing, and, after a while, looked at our guide questioningly, he smiled, and we looked again.

Presently one of our party said, "What color was that dome when we first paused here?" One said, "I believe it was red." But none could be sure. Anyway, it was then a golden tint, so we said we would watch it. Sure enough, presently it was green, and yet we had not seen it change, so gradually and evenly was the progress from one color to the other made. This went on for some time, and it was extremely beautiful.

Then the dome disappeared utterly. Our guide told us it was still there in the same place, but the disappearance was one of the feats they had managed to accomplish by combining certain elements of light from the various halls. Then above the dome and the trees—the dome still being invisible—there appeared an enormous rose of pink, which slowly deepened into crimson, and all among its petals there were beautiful forms of children playing, and men and women standing or walking and talking together, handsome, beautiful and happy; and fawns and antelopes and birds, running or flitting or lying among the petals, whose shapes swelled like hills and mounds and landscapes. Over these swells ran children with the animals, playing very happily and prettily. And then it all slowly faded away, and all was blank. We were shown several of these displays as we stood there.

Another was a column of light which shot up vertically from where we knew the dome was, and stood erect in the heavens. It was of the purest white light, and so steady that it looked almost solid. Then came a ray from one of the halls obliquely and gently struck against the side of the column.

Then came another from another hall, of a different color—red, blue, green, violet, orange; light, middle and dark, of all colors you know, and some which you do not know—and they all lodged against the white column about halfway up.

Then we saw the oblique lines of light taking shape, and they slowly became each a highway with buildings, houses, castles, palaces, groves of trees, temples and all manner of such, all along the broadways. And up these ways came crowds of people, some on foot, some on horseback, and others driving in chariots. All on one shaft of light were of one color, but manifold in hues. It was very lovely to see them. They approached the column and halted a little distance from it all round.

Then the top of the column opened out slowly, like a beautiful white lily, and the petals began to curl over, and lower, and ever lower, until they overspread the space between the people and the column. And then the base of the column began to do the same, until it formed a platform, circular in shape, between the different shafts of light, from the column to so far as the places on each causeway where the people halted.

Then they could move onward. But they mingled now, and their horses and conveyances, each retaining its own tint and color, but mingling with the rest. And we became aware that what we were looking at was a great multitude of lovely and happy people, gathered as if for a feast or festival, in an enormous pavilion of vari-tinted light. For their hues were now reflected against and into the roof and the floor, or pavement, and most wonderful was the radiance of it all. Slowly they formed into groups, and then we noticed that the center column was piped like a great organ, and we understood what to expect.

And it came very soon—a great burst of music, vocal and instrumental, a grand Gloria in excelsis to Him Who dwells in the light which is as darkness to His children, even as our darkness is as light when He sheds down on us a ray of His present power; for Omnipotent is the King Whose Light is life to all

His children, and Whose glory is reflected in the light such as we are able to endure. Something like that they sang, and then all that, too, faded away. I expected they would retrace their steps along the causeways, but these were withdrawn, and apparently it was unnecessary.

Your time is up, dear lad, so we must stop regretfully, with our usual love to you, my dear one, and those who love you and us, as we love them. God be with you, Who is Light, and in Whom no darkness can find a place to rest.

Thursday, October 2, 1913.

"Speak unto the children of Israel that they go forward." That is the message we would impress on you now. Do not lag behind in the way, for light is shed along it which will show you the path, and, if you hold fast to your faith in the All Father and His dear Son our Lord, you need have no fear of any beside.

We write this on account of certain lingering doubts still about you. You feel our presence, we know, but our messages have taken on such a complexion as to seem too fairy-like to be real. Know, then, that no fairy story ever written can equal the wonder of these Heavenly Realms, or the beauties of them. Moreover, much of the description you read in fairy books of scenery and buildings is not altogether unlike many things we have seen here in this beautiful land. Only a little yet have we been able to learn, but, from that little, we are convinced that nothing which can enter into the creative imagination of a man while in the earth life can equal the glories which await his wondering intellect when he puts off the earth body, with its limitations, and stands free in the light of the Heavenly Land.

Now, what we wish to try to tell you tonight is of a rather different order from our former messages, and has regard rather to the essential nature of things than to the phenomena of life as displayed for our instruction and joy.

If a man could take his stand here on some one of the high summits with which this landscape is crowned, he would behold some rather strange and unfamiliar sights. For instance, he would probably first observe that the air was clear, and that distance had a different aspect from that it wears on earth. It would not seem far away in the same sense, for, if he wished to leave the summit on which he stood and go to some point near the horizon, or even beyond, he would do so by means of his will, and it would depend on the quality of that will, and his own nature, whether he went fast or slow; and also how far he could penetrate into the regions which lie beyond the various mountain ranges and whose—I suppose we shall have to use the word—atmosphere is of rarer quality than that in which his present lot is cast.

It is on account of this that we do not always see those messengers who come to us from the higher spheres. They are seen by some better than by others, and are only truly and definitely visible when they so condition their bodies as to emerge into visibility. Now, if we go too far in their direction —that is, in the direction of their home—we feel an exhaustion which disables us to penetrate farther, although some are able to go farther than others.

Again, standing on that summit, the observer would notice that the firmament was not exactly opaque to the vision, but rather in the nature of light, but light of a quality which intensifies as the distance from the surface of the landscape increases. And some are able to look farther into that light than others, and to see there beings and scenes enacting which others less developed are not able to see.

Also, he would see all around him dwellings and buildings of various kinds, some of which I have described. But those buildings would not be merely houses and work-places and colleges to him. From each structure he would read not its character so much as the character of those who built it and those who inhabit it. Permanent they are, but not of the same dull permanency as those of earth. They can be developed and modified and adapted, in color, shape and material, according as the need should require. They would not have to be pulled down, and then the material used in rebuilding. The material would be dealt with as the building stood. Time has no effect on our buildings. They do not crumble or decay. Their durability depends simply on the wills of their masters, and, so long as these will, the building stands, and then is altered as they will.

Another thing he would notice would be flights of birds coming from out the distance and going, with perfect precision, to some particular spot. Now there are messenger birds trained on earth, but not as these are trained. In the first place, as they are never killed or ill-used, they have no fear of us. These birds are one of the means we use to send messages from one colony to another. They are not really necessary, as we have other quicker and more businesslike ways of communication. We use them more as pretty fancies, just as we use colors and ornaments for beauty's sake sometimes. These birds are always making flights, and are dear, loving creatures. They seem to know what their business is, and love to do it.

There is a tale here that once one of these birds, in his eagerness to outstrip his fellows, overshot the others and projected himself into the earth sphere. There he was seen by a clairvoyant man, who shot at him, and so astonished was the wanderer—not at the shooting, but at the sensation which he felt coming from the man's thoughts—that he realized that he was not in his right element somehow, and as soon as he realized that, he was back again here. What he had felt coming from the man's brain was the resolution and desire to kill, and, although he knew it was something uncanny, when he came to try to tell his other bird friends he was at a loss, because nothing of the kind is known here, and he could no more describe it than a bird from this realm could describe his life to one of the earth sphere. So the other birds said that, as he had a tale to tell which he could not, he was to return and find the man and ask him what word he should use.

He did so, and the man, who was a farmer, said "Pigeon-pie" would best describe his idea. The bird returned and, as they could not translate the term into their language, or make any meaning of it, they passed a resolution to the effect that whoever should wish to visit earth in future should place himself under guard until inquiries had been made as to whether he was in his own proper sphere or no.

And the moral of it all is this: Keep to your own appointed task which you will understand, and where you will be understood by those who are your fellow-servants in the work, and do not be too eager to shoot ahead before you are sure of your ground, or "atmosphere," or, thinking you are going forward, you may find yourself in a sphere which is below the one from which you started, and where the highest beings of that sphere are less progressed, in many ways, than the lowest of your own, and much less pleasant as company.

Well, that is a light story as a little interlude, and will serve to show you that we can laugh here, and be foolish wisely, and wise foolishly, on occasion, and that we are not grown-up much in some things since we left your earth and came over here. Goodbye, dear; keep up a merry heart.

Friday, October 3, 1913.

When you are in any doubt as to the reality of spirit communion think of the messages you have already received and you will find that in all we have written we have preserved a clear purpose throughout. It is that we may help you, and through you others also, to understand how natural all is here, if wonderful also. Sometimes, when we look back upon our earth life, we feel a wistful longing to make the way of those still there a little clearer and brighter than was our own in our forward glances into the future life. We did not understand, and so we went on in uncertainty as to what really awaited us.

Many, as we know, say that this is good, and yet, as we view things from our present vantage ground, we cannot agree that uncertainty is good when a definite goal is to be won. Certainty, on the other hand, gives decision and conduces to courageous action, and if we may be given to implant in just a few of earth's sojourners the certainty of life and brightness here for those who fight the good fight well, we shall be amply repaid for our journeys hither from our own bright home in light.

* * *

Now let us see if we can impress you to write a few words of the conditions which we found when we arrived here—the conditions, that is, of those who pass over here when they first arrive. They are not all of an equal degree of spiritual development, of course, and therefore require different treatment. Many, as you know, do not realize for some time the fact that they are what they would call dead, because they find themselves alive and with a body, and their previous vague notions of the after-death state are not, by any means, lightly thrown away.

The first thing to do, then, with such as those is to help them to realize the fact that they are no more in the earth life, and, to do this, we employ many methods.

One is to ask them whether they remember some friend or relative, and, when they reply that they do so but that he is dead, we try to enable them to see this particular spirit, who, appearing alive, should convince the doubter that he is really passed over. This is not always the case, for the ingrained fallacies are obstinate, and so we try another method.

We take him to some scene on earth with which he is familiar, and show him those whom he has left behind, and the difference in his state and theirs.

If this should fail, then we bring to his recollection the last experiences he underwent before passing, and gradually lead up to the time when he fell asleep, and then try to connect up that moment with his awakening here.

All these endeavors often fail—more often than you would imagine—for character is built up year by year, and the ideas which go to help in this building become very firmly imbedded in his character. Also we have to be very careful not to overtax him, or it would delay his enlightenment. Sometimes, however, in the case of those who are more enlightened, they realize immediately that they are passed into the spirit land, and then our work is easy.

We once were sent to a large town where we were to meet with other helpers at a hospital to receive the spirit of a woman who was coming over. These others had been watching by her during her illness, and were to hand her over to us to bring away. We found a number of friends round the bed in the ward, and they all wore long dismal faces, as if some dire disaster was about to happen to their sick friend. It seemed so strange, for she was a good woman, and was about to be ushered into the light out of a life of toil and sorrow and, lately, of much bodily suffering.

She fell asleep, and the cord of life was severed by our watching friends, and then, softly, they awoke her, and she looked up and smiled very sweetly at the kind face of one who leaned over her. She lay there perfectly happy and content until she began to wonder why these strange faces were around her in place of the nurses and friends she had last seen. She inquired where she was, and, when she was told, a look of wonder and of yearning came over her face, and she asked to be allowed to see the friends she had left.

This was granted her, and she looked on them through the Veil and shook her head sadly. "If only they could know," she said, "how free from pain I am now, and comfortable. Can you not tell them?" We tried to do so, but only one of them heard, I think, and he only imperfectly, and soon put it away as a fancy.

We took her from that scene, and, after she had somewhat gained strength, to a children's school, where her little boy was, and, when she saw him, her joy was too great for words. He had passed over some few years before, and had been placed in this school where he had lived ever since. Then the child became instructor to his mother, and this sight was a pretty one to see. He led her about the school and the grounds and showed her the different places, and his schoolmates, and, all the while, his face beamed with delight; and so did the mother's.

We left her awhile, and then, when we returned, we found those two sitting in an arbor, and she was telling him about those she had left behind, and he was telling her of those who had come on before, and whom he had met, and of his life in the school, and it was as much as we could do to tear her away, with a promise that she should return soon and often to her boy.

That is one of the better cases, and there are many such, but others are otherwise.

* * *

Now, while we waited for the mother who was talking with her son, we wandered over the grounds and looked at the various appliances for teaching children. One especially engaged my attention. It was a large globe of glass, about six or seven feet in diameter. It stood at the crossing of two paths, and reflected them. But as you looked into the globe you could see not only the flowers and trees and plants which grew there, but also the different orders from which they had been derived in time past. It was very much like a lesson in progressive botany, such as might be given on earth and deduced from the fossil plants of geology. But here we saw the same plants alive and growing, and all the species of them from the original parent down to the present representative of the same family.

We learned that the task set for the children was: to consider this progression up to this particular plant or tree or flower actually growing in that garden and reflected in the globe, and then to try to construct in their minds the further and future development of that same species. This is excellent training for their mental faculties, but the results are usually amusing. It is the same study which full-grown students are also at work upon in other departments here, and is put by them to a practical end. One of them thought it would be a useful method to help the children to use their own minds, and so constructed the ball for their especial use. When they have thought out their conclusion, they have to make a model of the plant as it will appear after another period of evolution, and fearful and wonderful some of those models are, and as impossible as they are strange.

Well, I must not keep you longer, so we will continue when you are able to write again. God bless you and yours. Goodnight.

Monday, October 6, 1913.

Well, dear, you have had a very happy Harvest Thanksgiving, and we were with you although you did not see us, and were too busy to think about us very much. We love to come and join with our fellow-worshippers still incarnate, and also to give what we are able to help in their worship. It may surprise you to know that here in these Realms of Light, we too, from time to time, hold such services as yours, and join in thanking our Father for harvest plenty. We do this by way of supplementing the thanksgiving of our brethren on earth, and also for our own uplifting. We have here no such harvests as yours, but still we have services of thanksgiving for other blessings which are to us what harvest is to you.

For instance, we thank Him for the beauty all around us and all the glories of light and love which sustain us in vigor for our work and progress, and have services of thanksgiving for such blessings as these. At such times we usually are given some Manifestation from the Higher Spheres, one of which I will tell you about now.

We were holding our Eucharist in a valley, where two lofty hills stood some little distance apart, one on each side, but at one end of the vale. We had offered up our praises and worship, and stood with heads bowed down awaiting, in that silent peace, which always fills us at such times, for the word of Benediction from him who had been the chief minister. He stood a little way up the hillside, but he did not speak, and we wondered why.

After a while we all slowly raised our heads, as if by one consent and impelled thereto by some inner voice, and we saw that the hill on which he stood was covered with a golden light which seemed to rest upon it like a veil. This slowly drew together and concentrated around the form of the Priest, who stood as if oblivious of anything about him. Then he seemed to come to himself again, and, stepping out of the cloud, he advanced towards us and told us that we were to wait awhile until we were able to see into the higher sphere from which certain angels of that sphere had descended and were present. So we waited, well content; for we have learned that when such an injunction is given it will presently be justified.

The cloud then lifted and spread out over the valley, farther and farther, until it covered the whole sky above us, and then it gradually descended and enveloped us, and we were in a sea of light far brighter than the light of our own sphere, but yet not dazzling to our eyes, but soft and mellow. By and by we were able to see by means of it, and then we saw the vision prepared for us.

The two high hills at the end of the valley glowed with fire, and each was the side, or arm, of a Throne, and about that Throne all colors of the rainbow played, much like that scene of which you read in the Book of Isaiah and of the Revelation. But we did not see the One Who sat on the Throne, at least not in bodily form. What we did see was a Manifestation of Him as to His Fatherhood. On the terrace, which was instead of the seat of the Throne, we saw a great company of Angels, and they were all bending in worship and love over a cradle. In the cradle we saw a child who smiled at them, and at length raised his hands towards the open space above him, where a light seemed to stream down from above.

Then into his arms there descended a golden globe, and he stood up and held it on his left hand. It seemed alive with the light of life and sparkled and glowed and became brighter and brighter until we scarcely noticed anything else but that ball itself and the child who held it, and whose body seemed to be irradiated through and through by its living light. Then he took it in his two hands and opened it in two halves, and held it aloft, turning the open circles towards us. One was filled with a pink radiance, and the other with blue. In the latter we saw the heavenly realms set in concentric circles, and each circle full of glorious and beautiful beings of those realms. But the outer circles were not so bright as the inner ones, and yet we could see the inhabitants more plainly because they were more nearly of our own estate than those others. As the innermost circles were neared, the light became too intense to see clearly what they held. But the very outermost circle we recognized as that of our own order.

The other bowl of pink light was different. There were no circles apparent in it. But yet, in perfect order, we beheld all the different species of animal and vegetable life as they are on the planets, including Earth. But we saw them not as they are with you, but in perfection, from man to the lowest form of sea-animal, and from the largest tree and most luscious fruit to the tiniest weed which grows. When we had viewed these awhile the child gently brought the two halves together, the glorious Heavens and the perfect Material Creation, and, when he had joined them, we could see no mark of the joining, nor tell which was one half and which the other.

But as we looked on the reunited ball, we saw that it was enlarging, and, at last, it slowly floated up from the hand of the child and rose into the space above him, and stood there poised, a beautiful ball of light. Then there gradually emerged into view, standing on the great sphere, the figure of the Christ, Who in His left arm held a cross, the base of which rested on the globe and the top was some little space above His shoulder. In His right hand He held the child, on whose forehead we now noticed a single circle of gold worn as a fillet on his head, and over his heart a jewel like a great ruby. Then the globe began slowly to ascend into the heaven above, and the higher it went the smaller it grew to our sight, until it melted into the distance over the space between the two hills.

Then we were in our normal state again, and all sat down to wonder at what we had seen, and the meaning of it. But although some seemed to have some glimmerings as to the meaning of it, nobody was very illuminative. Then we thought of our minister, who had first received the baptism of the cloud, and, as it seemed to us, in a more intense degree than the rest of us. We found him sitting there by himself on a rock, with a quiet smile on his face, as if he knew we should come to him at last, and was waiting till we remembered him. He bade us sit down again, and, still sitting on the rock where he could be seen by all, he told us of the Vision.

It had been explained to him as to its more obvious meanings, and these he was able to hand on to us, leaving us to think it over and work out the higher and inner teaching for ourselves, each according to his own phase of mind. This is what is usually done, I find, when teaching is given to us by such means as this.

The pink hemisphere represented the Creation which was inferior to our Sphere, and the blue one our own and that superior to us. But these were not two Creations, but one; and there was no break between these two hemispheres or any of their sub-departments. The child was the embodiment of the beginning, progress and end, which has no ending—our onward way. The ruby stood for sacrifice, and the crown for achievement, and the ascension of the globe and the Christ and the child led our aspirations into those realms which are at present beyond our attainment.

But of course, there is much more than this mere outline in it, and we are, as I said, left to work it out for ourselves. This, according to our custom, we shall do, and, at future gatherings, give our conclusions from time to time, and discuss them.

Thank you. May I now ask you a question which I have been requested to put to you?

No need to put it into words. We can see it in your mind, and knew it before you wrote.[1] The dove which Miss E. saw above the altar of your church was a Manifestation, in presence form, such as that I have just related. It was for your invisible congregation, and symbolized, in a way they would readily understand, the gentleness of the presences about the altar, that they were there indeed in love, and ready to help those who were willing to receive their help, and, in token of their gentleness, a dove was seen hovering near them and unafraid; a state of mind which those who are not progressed are not always able to maintain in the presence of those from the higher realms whose bright holiness sometimes, in the minds of those who are not able to judge proportionately, by reason of their still lingering imperfections, eclipses their other virtues and make the poor doubting ones afraid.

Wednesday, October 8, 1913.

Because of certain matters which are of importance to those who would understand our meaning in its inner sense,

---

[1] A member of the congregation of All Hallows, Orford, had told me a few days previously that she had seen clairvoyantly a dove hovering over the altar during the celebration of the Holy Communion.—G.V.O.

we have decided to endeavor tonight to give you some instruction which will be of help and guidance when dealing with those things which lie beneath the surface of things, and which are usually not taken into account by the ordinary mind.

One of these is the aspect which thoughts wear when projected from your sphere into ours. Thoughts which are good appear with a luminance which is absent from those of a less holy kind. This luminance appears to issue from the form of the thinker, and, by means of its manifold rays of divided colors, we are able to come at some knowledge as to his spiritual state, not alone as to whether his state is of the light or of the darkness, and of what degree in light, but also of the points in which he excels or comes short in any direction. It is by this that we are able to allot to him the guardians who will best be able to help him in the fostering of that which is good in him, and in the cleansing away of that which is not good or desirable. By means of a kind of prismatic system we divide up his character, and so reach our conclusions, which are based on the result.

In this life such a method is unnecessary, for it is a matter concerning the spiritual body, and here, of course, that body is patent to all, and, being a perfect index of the spirit, shows forth his characteristics. Only I may say that the colors of which I have spoken are here communicated, in a degree, to our clothing, and those which are dominant over the others serve to classify us into our various spheres and grades. But thoughts, which are the effect of spirit action, are seen in the effect they, in their turn, produce on the environment of the thinker, and not only are seen, but felt, or sensed, by us in a more accurate and intense way than with you.

Following on this line of reasoning, you will naturally see that when we think anything very intensely our wills are able to produce an outward manifestation which is really objective to those who behold it. Thus are many beautiful effects produced.

Can you give me a particular instance, by way of illustration?

Yes; it will help you to see what we mean.

A company of my friends and myself, who were being instructed in this knowledge, met together in order to see how far we had progressed, and resolved on an experiment to that end. We selected a glade in the midst of a beautiful wood, and, as a test, we resolved all to will one particular thing, and see if we were successful. What we selected was the producing of a phenomenon in the open space which should be so solid and permanent as to allow of us examining it afterwards. And that was to be a statue of an animal something like an elephant, but rather different; an animal which we have here, but which has ceased to inhabit your earth.

We all sat round the open space and concentrated our wills on the object to be produced. Very quickly it appeared and stood there before us. We were much surprised at the quickness of the result. But, from our point of view, there were two defects. It was much too large; for we had failed to regulate the combination of our wills in due proportion. And it was much more like a live animal than a statue, for many had thought in their minds of the live animal itself, and also of its coloring, and so the result was a mixture between stone and flesh. Also many points were disproportionate—the head too large and the body too small, and so on, showing that more power had been concentrated on some parts than on others. It is thus we learn our imperfections, and how to remedy them, in all our studies. We experiment, and then examine the result, and try again. We did so now.

Taking our minds off the statue so produced, and talking together, it gradually faded away. And then we were fresh and ready for our next trial. We decided not to select the same model as before, or our minds would probably run into more or less the same grooves. So we, this time, chose a tree with fruit on it—something like an orange tree, but not quite the same.

We were more successful this time. The chief points of failure were that some of the fruit was ripe and some unripe. And the leaves were not correct in color, nor the branches rightly proportioned. And so we tried one thing after another, and found ourselves a little more successful each time. You can imagine somewhat of the joy of such schooling as this, and the laughter and happy humor which result from our mistakes. Those among you who think that in this life we never make jokes, and never even laugh, will have to revise their ideas some day or they will find us strange company—or perhaps we shall find them so. But they soon learn what the love of this land is, where we can be perfectly natural and unrestrained, and indeed are compelled to be so if we wish to be accepted into respectable company, as you would phrase it. I fear the obverse is rather true on earth, is it not? Ah well, live and learn, and those who live in this life—and not merely exist, or worse— learn very quickly. And the more we learn, the more we marvel at the forces at our command.

Astriel,[2] who came yesterday—is he here now?

Not tonight. But he will, no doubt, come again, as you wish it.

Thank you. But I hope you will come and write, too.

Oh yes, we will do so, for it is practice both for you and for us also, for, in thus impressing you, we are learning to use our wills and powers in a similar way to that I have been describing. Do you not see the image of the things we are telling you in your mind.

---

[2] Astriel's messages were given on various dates which, however, were not consecutive. Why they were given in this way is not apparent. The effect, however, was to cut into the communications given by Mr. Vale Owen's mother in such a way as rather to break the continuity of her messages as well as to destroy the sequence of those of Astriel himself, I have deemed it advisable, therefore, to collect them into a separate chapter. [See Chapter 6, "Astriel's Messages."]

Yes, very vividly sometimes; but I had not thought of it in that way.

Ah well, my boy, you see now, do you not, that we had an object in writing what we have above? All the time you were thinking it was rather thin (and perhaps it was—we do not say to the contrary), and you were wondering whither it all was tending, and, in your mind, you were just a very wee bit disgusted. Now, were you not, dear? Well, we were smiling all the time; and now you understand that you were interpreting our thoughts, more or less, as we sent them forth, and the object we had was to explain to you how those scenes appeared before you so vivid and so real, as you described them.

Goodbye, dear lad, and God bless you and your dear ones now and always.

3

From Darkness Into Light

Friday, October 10, 1918

WERE we to impress you to write on matters which to us are of everyday concern, you would perhaps be able to compare them with your own daily life, and you would see then that we and you are both at school, and that the school is a very large one, with many classes, and many instructors, but with one scheme running throughout the course of instruction, and that scheme a unity of progress from the simple to the complex, and that complexity does not mean perplexity, for, as we learn more of the wisdom of the Divine Author of all, we see how beautifully composite is the realm in which He exerts His Loving Will to the end we may, by our very joy of knowledge, give homage to the Glory of Him Who holds all things in the hollow of His Hand.

And so, dear lad, we will once again take up our theme, and tell you of our doings here in these bright realms, and of how the Father's love encompasses us all around as a radiant cloud in which all things appear to us more plainly, as we progress in humility and in love.

One of those things which matter here is that due proportion be meted out between wisdom and love. These are not contrary the one from the other, but are two great phases of one great principle. For love is to wisdom as the tree is to the leaves, and if love actuate and wisdom breathe, then the fruit is healthy and sound. By way of illustrating this we will give you a concrete instance of how we are taught to consider duly both love and wisdom in our dealings with ourselves and others to whom we are permitted to minister.

We were given a task to perform a short time ago in which a party of us, to the number of five, were to go to a colony in a rather distant part of this land, and inquire of them by what means could best be given help to those on earth who were in doubt and perplexity as to God's Love. For we were often hampered by our lack of experience in dealing with such cases, and these cases, as you know, are many.

The Principal of the College was a man who in earth-life had been a statesman of no little ability, but his fame was not so great, and it was only when he came over here that he found play for his powers, and understood that the earth is not the only field in which earth's training may be put to use and effect in the Kingdom of God.

We stated to him the object of our mission, and he was very courteous and kind, for all his high office. I suppose you would call him a great angel, and indeed, if he could come to earth and assume visibility, his brightness would be somewhat awe-inspiring. He is very beautiful, both of form and countenance; radiant and beaming and glowing would perhaps describe him best. He listened and encouraged us, now and then, with a quiet word, to state our difficulties, and we forgot that he was so high in estate, and talked without fear or restraint. And then he said, "Well, my dear pupils—for so you are good enough to become for a little time—what you have told me is very interesting, and also very general in the work in which you are now engaged. Now, if I were to solve your perplexities you would go back to your work with light hearts, but you would probably find that the solution, when it came to work out, would not be without many flaws in the working, for just those points which are most necessary to remember are those little things which can best be learned by experience; and experience is the only thing which can show you how great these little things are. Come, therefore, with me, and I will teach you what is necessary for you to learn in a better way."

So he went with him, and he led us into the grounds which surrounded his house, and there we found there were gardeners at work tending the flowers and fruit trees, and doing the general work of a garden. He took us some distance along the walks, winding here and there, and through plantations of trees and shrubs, where birds were singing and small pretty furry animals played here and there. At length we came to a stream and by it stood a stone arbor, which reminded me of a miniature temple of Egypt, and he led us within. Then we sat on a seat under a network of flowering plants of different colors, and he sat on another bench at right angle to us.

Drawn on the floor, in indented lines, was a plan, and he pointed to it and said, "Now, this is a plan of my house and these grounds through which I have led you. Here is marked this little place in which we sit. We have come, as you will see, a considerable distance from the gate where I met you, and you were all talking so much of the pretty things you saw as you came that not one of you gave heed to the direction in which you came. It will be good practice, therefore, and not altogether lacking in pleasure, for you to find your way back again to me, and, when you arrive, I shall perhaps be able to give you some help by way of instruction on the difficulties you have stated to me."

With that he left us, and we all looked at one another, and then burst out laughing at ourselves for being so foolish as not to guess his object in leading us to this place by so circuitous a route.

We then examined the plan again and again, but it was all lines and triangles and squares and circles, and we could make little of it at first.

Gradually, however, we began to understand. It was a map of the estate, and the arbor was in the center, or nearly so, but the entrance was not shown, and, as there were four paths leading up to it, we did not know which to take to get back again. We, however, reasoned that it did not matter much for all seemed to lead to the outer circle, because there were so many paths between us and that, which crossed and re-crossed each other. I must not tell you of all our endeavors to solve the problem, as it would take much too long.

At last I had a thought which I considered, and then, thinking it might perhaps help, told the others. They said it was the very thing they had been waiting for, and would very likely prove the key to the riddle. It was nothing more wonderful than just to go out and take whatever path led in the most direct line onwards from any we were forced to leave. That is awkward—what I mean is this: to go by those paths which would lead us in the straightest line from the arbor in any direction whatever. Then, when we had reached the boundary, which we saw by the plan was a perfect circle, we could skirt that and must inevitably reach the gate sooner or later.

So we set off, and a long and very pleasant journey it was, and not without adventure, for the place was extensive, with hills and valleys and woods and streams, and all so beautiful that we had to keep our object very firmly before our minds or we should have forgotten to choose the correct path when we came to two ways.

We reached the outermost boundary, however, although we did not, I think, take quite the best and most direct route. This boundary, I may say in passing, was composed of a wide stretch of grassland, and we saw, by the shape of its border, that it was circular, although we could not see much of it. So we turned to the left and then, as we went on, the bend of the circular estate seemed endless. Still we followed it and eventually came to the gate where first we had met our instructor.

He greeted us encouragingly, and we went up on to a terrace before the house, and then told him all our adventures—much more than I have narrated to you—and he listened as before, and then said, "Well, you have not done so badly, for you have gained your object, you have returned to the gate. And now let me tell you the lesson you have learned.

"First of all, the thing is to make sure of the direction you wish to go; and then the next thing is to take, not the path which seems shortest, but the one which seems surest to lead you right in the end. That path will not always be the quickest, and may lead you to the borderland where infinity shades off from the realm you know. Still, beyond the border line you are the better able to see both the extent and also the limitation of the estate you are negotiating, and it is only a matter of steadfastness and patience, and the goal you desire is quite sure to be won.

"Also, from just beyond the boundary between the local and the infinite, you are able to see that, although it contains within itself paths winding and many, and valleys and groves from which you cannot see very far away, yet that, viewed as a whole, it is perfectly symmetrical—a true circle in fact, which, for all the seeming maze and medley within, yet, as a circle, contains within itself a perfect geometrical entity, simple in itself, considered as a unit from the larger, wider point of view; perplexing when passing through its paths inside the boundary line.

"Also, you noted that, as you followed that curve on its outer side, you were able only to see a little portion of it at one time. Still, knowing that, from its shape, it would lead to the place you sought, you were content to follow on in faith based on reasoned conclusions, and, true enough, here you are and prove by your presence that your reasoning was, at least in the main, sound.

"Now, I could pursue this subject considerably further, but I will hand you over now to some of my friends who are with me here and help me in the work, and they will show you more of our home and its surroundings, and, if you wish, will be glad to accompany you farther afield, for there is much of interest to show you. Also you will be able to talk over with them the lessons I have been happy enough to be able to give you, and among you you will, no doubt, have something more to tell and to ask me when we meet a little later."

So he bade us goodbye, and a band of happy people came from the house and led us within. But, as the time is up for you to go to other duties, we must cease now, with our love and assurance to you of our delight in coming thus to commune with you, if only for this little while. God bless you, dear lad, and all our loved ones. Mother and friends.

Saturday, October 11, 1913.

We were able to give you only a very brief account last evening of our visit to the home of our instructor on account of the shortness of time. We will now continue, and relate some of our experiences in that region. It is a region where there are many such institutions, and they are mostly devoted to the study of the best way of helping those on earth who are in doubt and perplexity as to the problems which stretch out into the realms beyond. You will be able, by meditation, to amplify our own instruction if you view the place and our experience there in the light of a parable. So we pass on to other scenes, and will describe them as well as we can.

Our guides led us to a place outside the boundary of the estate of which we have already spoken, and we found that the grassland was very extensive. It is one of those plains of Heaven where Manifestations from the higher Heavens are sometimes given. The call goes forth and vast multitudes assemble, and then some of the glories of the higher spheres are manifested, as well as is possible in these lower realms.

We passed over this tract until we at length began to ascend, and presently found ourselves on a tableland, where there were several buildings scattered about, some larger than others. In the center was a large structure, and this we entered and found ourselves in a large and spacious hall, the only compartment in the place. It was circular in shape, and round the walls were carvings of a curious kind. We examined them and found that they were representations of the heavenly bodies; and one was the earth. But they were not fixed, but turned on pivots, half in and half out of the wall. There were also models of animals and trees and human beings, but they were all movable, and mostly stood on pedestals in niches or alcoves. We inquired the meaning and were told that this was a purely scientific institution.

We were taken up to a balcony on one side of the circular space. It projected somewhat, and so we could see the whole at once. Then we were told that a small demonstration would be made for our benefit in order that we might get some idea of the use to which these things were put.

We sat there waiting, and at length a blue mist began to fill the central space. Then a ray of light swept round the hall and rested on the globe which represented the earth. As it hovered about it the sphere appeared to absorb the ray and became luminous, and after a time, the ray being withdrawn, we saw the earth globe was shining as from within. Then another ray was sent on to it of a deeper and different kind, and the globe slowly left the pedestal, or pivot, or whatever it rested on, and began to float out from the wall.

As it approached the center of the space it entered the blue mist and immediately on contact began to enlarge until it became a great sphere glowing with its own light and floating in the blue space. It was exceedingly beautiful. Slowly, very slowly, it revolved on its axis, evidently in the same way the earth does, and we were able to see the oceans and continents. These were flat patterns, like those on the terrestrial globes used on earth. But as it revolved they began to assume a different aspect.

The mountains and hills began to stand out, and the waters to sway and ripple; and presently we saw minute models of the cities, and even details of the buildings. And still more detailed grew the model of earth, till we could see the people themselves, first the crowds and at last the individuals. This will be hard for you to understand, that on a globe of some, perhaps, eighty to a hundred feet in diameter we were able to see individual men and animals. But that is part of the science of this institution— the enabling of these details being seen individually.

Still more distinct grew these wonderful scenes, and, as the globe revolved, we saw men hurrying about the cities and working in the fields. We saw the wide spaces of prairie and desert and forest and the animals roaming in them. And as the globe slowly circled we saw the oceans and seas, some placid and others tossing and roaring, and here and there a ship. And all the life of earth passed before our eyes.

We looked at this a long time, and our friend who belonged to this settlement spoke to us from below where we sat. He told us that what we were looking at was the earth as it was at that moment. If we wished he would now show us the retro-progress of the ages from the present time to the beginning of man as an intelligent being. We replied that we would indeed be glad to see more of this wonderful and beautiful phenomenon, and he left us to go, I suppose, to the apparatus by which these things were controlled.

I may here pause to explain a matter which I see is in your mind. The place was not dark, it was light everywhere. But the globe itself shone with such extra intensity that, without any unpleasant sensation whatever, it obscured everything which was outside the blue cloud, which cloud seemed to be the circumference of the radiating beams shed by the globe.

Soon, then, the scenes began to change on the revolving sphere, and we were taken back through the thousands of years of the life of the earth and the generations of men and animals and plant life which had been from the present to the ages when men were just emerging from the forest to settle in colonies on the plains.

Now, I must explain here that history was not followed as historians follow it. These phenomena were not of nations and centuries, but of eons and species. The geologic periods passed before us, and it was intensely interesting to watch what men called the iron age and the stone age, the ice age, the floods, and so on. And those of us who understood enough to follow it noticed that these ages were rather arbitrarily named. For the ice age, for example, might correctly describe the state of things in one or two regions of the earth, but there was by no means ice everywhere, as we saw as the sphere revolved. Also we noticed that very frequently one continent was in one age and another continent in another age at the same time. The exhibition ended, however, when the earth was well progressed, and, as I have said, the advent of man was already an accomplished fact.

When we had satisfied our eyes for awhile looking on the beauty of this many-colored and ever-changing jewel, and had realized that this was indeed no other than the old earth we thought we knew so well, and found we knew so little, the globe gradually became smaller and floated back to the niche in the wall, and then the light faded out from it and it looked like an alabaster carving, just as we had seen it at first set there as an ornament.

We were so interested in what we had seen that we questioned our kind guide, and he told us many things about this hall. The earth sphere which had just been used could be made to serve other purposes than the one we had seen. But that had been selected because its picturesqueness was suited to us who were not scientifically trained. Among other uses was that of illustrating the relation of the heavenly bodies one to another, and their evolution into their present state. In this, of course, the globe we had just seen played its appropriate part.

The animals about the walls were also used for a like purpose. One would be vivified by these powerful rays and brought forth into the center of the hall. When so treated it could walk of itself like a live animal, which it was temporarily, and in a certain restricted way. When it had ascended a platform in the center space, then it was treated with the enlarging rays—as I may call them, not knowing their scientific name—and then with others which rendered it transparent, and all the internal organism of the animal became plainly visible to the students assembled. Those who were of that settlement said that it was a very beautiful sight to see the whole economy of the system of animal or man at work so displayed.

Then it was possible to bring over the living model a change, so that it began to evolve backward—or should I say "involve"?—towards its simpler and primal state as a mammal, and so on. The whole structural history of the animal was shown in that life-like process. And often when the first period of its separate existence as a separate creature was reached, the process was reversed, and it passed through the different stages of development, this time in their correct order and direction, until it became again as it is today. Also it was possible for any student to take charge and continue the development according to his own idea, and this not of the animals alone, but of the heavenly bodies, and also of nations and peoples, which are dealt with in another hall, however, specially adapted to that study.

It was a student from one of these establishments, in this same region, who erected the globe in the children's garden, of which I told you. But that is, of course, a much simpler affair, or so it appeared to us after visiting this colony of beauties and wonders.

That will have to suffice for this time, although there is a lot more we saw while there. But I must not start off again, or I shall be keeping you too long.

You have a question. Yes, I was present on Monday at your Study Circle.[1] I knew she saw me, but could not make her hear me.

Goodnight, dear.

Monday, October 13, 1913.

One more experience we had in that colony which you would like to hear about. It was one which was new to me and very interesting. We were being shown over the different establishments which formed a complete group, when we came to a kind of open-air pavilion. It was principally composed of a huge circular dome resting on tall pillars, and the interior space so enclosed was open to the air. In the center of the platform to which we ascended by a flight of steps which were all round the building, was a kind of square altar some four feet high and three feet square. On this stood a bronze tablet, something like a sundial, marked with lines and symbols and different geometrical figures.

---

[1] The reference to the Study Circle needs a note of explanation. It was on the previous Monday. I sat in the Sanctuary between the rails, and the members were facing each other in the choir stalls. Miss E. sat on my right at the Sanctuary end of the stall. She afterwards told me that, when I was summing up the debate, she saw my mother step forth from the altar and come forward behind me with outstretched arms and a look of intense yearning and love on her face. She was exceedingly bright and beautiful, and her body looked as substantial as that of any of the others present. Miss E. thought she was going to clasp me in her arms, and it was so vivid that she forgot, for the moment, that the form was not of flesh and blood, and, therefore, could not be seen by the others. She was on the point of crying out when she suddenly recollected herself but had to look away in order to suppress her exclamation. It was about this I wished to ask the question.—G.V.O.

Above it in the center of the dome was an opening which led, as we were told, into a chamber where the instruments used here were controlled.

We were told to stand round the dial (as I will call it) and our guide left us, and, going without, ascended to the roof of the dome, and so entered the chamber above us. We did not know what was going to happen, and so stood gazing at the disc.

Presently the place took on a different aspect, the air seemed to be changing in color and intensity. And when we looked about us we saw that the landscape had disappeared, and between the pillars there stretched what appeared to be gossamer threads in the form of curtains. They were of various tints all interwoven, and, as we looked round, these seemed to separate into their own colors and then to take on more definite forms. This continued until we found ourselves standing in a glade with the circular belt of trees gently waving in the breeze.

Then birds began to sing, and we saw their bright plumage, as they flew from one tree to another. Gradually we saw the distance deepen between the trees and could see far into a beautiful forest. The dome also was gone and the sky was above us, except where the trees stretched aloft like a canopy.

We turned again to the altar and the disc. These were still in place, but the figures and signs on the latter were now shining with a light which seemed to come from within the altar.

Now we heard the voice of our guide from above telling us to watch and try to read the tablet. We could make little of it at first, but at length one of our party more clever than the rest said that the signs were really representations of the various elements which went to make up the vegetable and animal bodies of the spiritual realms. It is difficult to explain the way in which the connection between the two was apparent to us. But when once pointed out it became quite clear that this was so.

Now our guide joined us once more and explained the use of the building. It seems that before the students are able to progress much in the science of creation as studied in this region, they have to get a thorough knowledge of the fundamental elements with which they have to deal. This is, of course, quite natural. This building is one of the first where they come to study, and the table, or dial, is a kind of register of these elements on which the student above in the chamber where the controlling instruments are can see the combination of elements he has brought about, and also the proportion of each element entering into the combination.

Our guide was somewhat advanced in the science, and had contrived the forest scene by means of this same skill. As the learners progress they are able gradually to achieve the result they wish without the scientific apparatus which at first is necessary. One instrument after another is left out until at length they are able to depend solely on their will.

We asked our guide to what practical purpose the knowledge was put when acquired. He replied that the first use was the training of the mind and will of the student. That training was very excellent and very strenuous. When the student had become proficient he moved on to another college in this region where another branch of the science was learned, and then had to pass through many more stages of training. The actual use of his knowledge did not fall to his lot until he had passed through many spheres of progress. In the higher of these he was allowed to accompany some great Master, or Archangel, or Power (I do not know the exact and correct title) on one of his missions of service in the Infinite Creation of the One Father, and there witness the sublime process at work. It was thought that this might be the creation of some new cosmos or system, either material or spiritual. But that is so high above this state in which we are at present that we have only a general idea of the duties of those High Beings, and it is a matter of a few ages of progress from here to there, if our ways lie in the direction of that particular system of Heavens. And the chances are that, for us five women who visited the place I have been describing, our onward path will lead us somewhere else.

But we love to know all about the different spheres of service, even if we be destined never to be chosen for them. We cannot all be creators of cosmoi, I suppose, and there are other things as necessary, great and glorious, no doubt, in those far reaches beyond us nearer to the Throne and Dwelling of Him Who is all in all to all.

As we returned across the wide grasslands we were met by a party of these same students who had been to another college to study a different branch of science. They were not all men; some were women. I inquired if their studies were all on the same lines as that of their brothers, and they replied in the affirmative, but added that while the men students mostly looked after the purely creative part, they were permitted to add to and round off the work with their genius of motherhood, and that the two aspects blending enhanced the beauty of the finished work—finished, that is, so far as it was possible as conditioned by the limitations of their 'present spheres. For here were not so much spheres of perfect accomplishment as of progress towards those higher spheres.

By the time we had returned to the first colony where we had met our instructor of the circular estate—

Why do you not give me his name?

His name was Arnol[2] but these names sound so strange to earth ears, and people are always trying to find out their meaning, that we are rather shy of giving them. The meanings are

[2] Arnol here referred to, for the first time, eventually communicated through the Rev. G. V. Owen a series of messages of a very high order, which are published in Volumes III and IV of *The Life Beyond the Veil*—H.W.E.

mostly incomprehensible to you, so we will just say the name in future, as you wish it, and leave it there.

Well, it saves a lot of roundabout wording, doesn't it?

Yes, and yet if you understood the conditions under which we give you these narratives you would probably say that the longer was the more sure route. Remember our experience and teaching on Arnol's estate.

What makes it so difficult for you to give names? I have heard of this difficulty more than once.

There is also a difficulty in explaining the difficulty—from your point of view so apparently simple a matter. Let us put it in this way. You know that with the old Egyptians the name of a god or goddess was much more than a name as understood by the hardy materialistic Anglo-Saxon from whose race came the question: "What's in a name?" Well, from our point of view, and that also of the ancient wisdom of Egypt, based on data obtained from this side the Veil, there is a great deal in a name. Even in the mere repetition of some names there is actual power, and sometimes peril. That we know now as we did not when on earth. And so we here acquire a reverence for the entity "the Name," which to you would probably seem foolish. Nevertheless, it is partly for this reason that names do not come through to you so plentifully as many rather feeble investigators would wish.

Also the mere utterance and transmission of some of these names is, when we are in this earth region, a matter of more difficulty than you would perhaps deem. It is a subject, however, which is hard to explain to you, and only one which you will be able to understand when you have become more familiar with the fourth dimension which obtains here—which term, also, we use for want of a better. We will just refer you to two or three instances and there leave the matter.

One is the giving to Moses of the Name of the great Officer of the Supreme Who visited him. Moses asked for that Name, and got it—and neither he nor any one else to this day has been able to say what it means.

Then the lesser Angel who came to Jacob. Jacob asked for his name, and it was refused him. The Angels who came to Abraham and to others in the Old Testament very seldom gave their names. Likewise in the New Testament, most of the Angels who come to minister to earth's denizens are simply so called; and where the name is given, as in the case of Gabriel, it is little understood as to its inner significance. Of the new name which no man—that is, man on earth—knoweth.

What is your name, mother—I mean your new name? Is it permissible for you to give it?

Permissible, yes, but not wise, dear. You know I would give it if it were so. But this for the present I must withhold even from you, knowing that you will understand my love even if my motive is not very clear.

Yes, dear, you know what is best.

Some day you, too, will know, and then you will see what glory awaits those whose names are written in the Book of the Life of the Lamb, a phrase also which is worth thinking over, for in it is a glorious and living truth which those who use that Name so lightly surely apprehend little or not at all.

God bless you, dear, and Rose and the children. Ruby once more bids me in her pretty way, to say she is coming to see you soon, and hopes you will be able to take down her commands—that is the word she used, bless her, who is graceful humility itself, and loved by all who know her. God bless you, dear. Goodbye.

Wednesday, October 15, 1913.

How would you begin to explain to one who had little idea of a spirit world about him the truth of survival beyond the grave and the reality of this life and all its love and beauty? First you would probably endeavor to bring home to him the fact of his present actual existence as an immortal being. And then, when he had really grasped the significance of that, as it affects his future, he would perhaps be open to a few words of description as to that life which he will find himself possessed of, and in touch with, when he puts aside the Veil and emerges into the greater light of the Beyond.

So we feel that if men could but understand that the life they now live is life indeed, and not merely an ephemeral existence, they would then be more inclined to count worthy of consideration the words of those who have proved for themselves both the reality of this persistence of life and individuality, and also the blessedness of the lot awaiting those who on earth are able to strive and to prevail.

Now, it is no small matter that men should so live their lives on earth that when they step over the threshold into the larger, freer sphere they should take up and continue their service in the Kingdom without a more or less protracted hiatus in their progress. We have seen the effect of the career of so many, as it is viewed in extension into this land, that we feel we cannot too much emphasize the importance of preparation and self-training while opportunity offers. For so many do put off the serious consideration of this, with the idea of starting afresh here, and when they come over they find that they had very little realized what that starting afresh really implied.

Who is this writing?

Still your mother and her friends. Astriel is not here tonight, but will be with us on another occasion. We will let you know when it is he and his party communicating.

Well, to proceed then. We have already told you of the Bridge and the Chasm—

Yes. But what of your further experience in Arnol's domain, and of your return to your own proper sphere? Have you nothing more to tell me of that episode?

No more than that we learned much, made many friends, saw a great deal more than we here set down, and shall visit the place again soon. Now let us get on to what we wished to say, and which will perhaps be as useful as if we were to continue our description of the Colony in that other region.

The Chasm and the Bridge bring back your mind to what we told you of them. We wish to relate an episode which we witnessed at the place where the Bridge—as I will continue to name it—emerges on to the uplands of life and light.

We were sent thither to receive a woman who was expected to arrive, having fought her way through those dreadful, dark regions which lie below the Bridge. She had not come over the great causeway, but through the horrors of the darkness and gloom in the region below. With us went a strong Angel from a sphere above us, who was specially commissioned for the task. This was one of the Sister Angels who organize our homes where the rescued are taken.

Can you give me her name?

Bearn—no, we cannot get it through. Leave it, and we may be able to do so as we proceed.

When we arrived there we found that a light was glimmering some way down the rocky way which went down into the valley, and knew that some angel was there on the watch. Presently it grew more dim, and we noticed that it was moving away from us into the distance below. Then after a time we saw a flash far out over the valley, and this was immediately answered by a stream of light from one of the towers on the Bridge. It was not unlike what you know as a searchlight, and indeed answered a purpose somewhat similar. It shot out downward into the gloom and remained steady. Then Bea—our Angel Sister—told us to abide where we were for a time, and she went quickly through the air to the tower top.

Then we lost her in the light, but one of my companions said she thought she saw her speeding along the ray of light which slanted downwards towards the depths. I did not; but afterwards we found that she had seen correctly.

I ought to pause here to explain that that light was not so much to enable the spirits to see (which they could do of their own power), but to give strength for the work and protection against the hurtful influences which held sway in the region below. It was for that reason that the first angel had sent out his signal, and it was understood by the constant watchers on the Bridge and answered in the way I have told. The ray of light is, in some way I do not understand yet, impregnated with power of life and strength—the best description I am able to give—and it was sent to help him whose strength was in want of succor.

By and by we saw the two return. He was a strong Angel, but looked fatigued, and we learned later that he had encountered a band of very malignant spirits who did their best to get the woman back again amongst them. That is why he needed help. He walked on one side and she walked on the other side of the poor torn and tortured soul who was more than half in a swoon. They went very slowly for her sake now, walking in the ray of light towards the tower on the Bridge. We had never seen anything like this before, except once, and that I have recounted to you. I mean the Pavilion of light and the assembling of the people of many colored dresses. But this was, in a way, much more solemn; for here was anguish in the midst of joy, and there joy alone. They reached the Bridge, and the rescued one was taken into one of the houses and tended, and there remained until she had sufficiently recovered to be banded over to our care.

Now, there are several points in this narrative which held new knowledge for us, and some which confirmed what had been mere surmises up to the time of that experience. Some of these I will name.

It is a mistake to think that Angels, even of such estate as those two who went and rescued that poor woman, are unable to suffer. They do suffer, and that frequently. And it is possible for the malicious ones to hurt them when they venture into their regions. Theoretically I cannot see why the evil ones should not now and then prevail so as to get them into their power. So well, however, are the powers of light and good organized, and so watchful, that I have not heard that this catastrophe has ever been known actually to happen. But their fight is a real fight, and fatiguing also. That is the second point. Even these high Angels can become fatigued. But neither their suffering nor their fatigue do they mind. It may sound a paradox, but it is nevertheless true, that it is a joy to them to suffer so when some poor struggling soul is to be helped.

Also that light-ray—or perhaps I should say "ray of power and vitality"— was so strong that, had they not protected the woman by surrounding her with a certain negative influence, it would have harmed her, because it would have been too great a shock to one so unprepared as she.

Another point is this. That ray was seen far out in the region of gloom, and we heard a murmur coming, as it seemed, from hundreds of miles away, down across the valley. It was a strange experience, for the sound was that of many voices, and some were of rage and hate, and others of despair, and others cries for help and mercy. And these and other different cries seemed to be gathered each in its own particular locality, and to come from different directions. We could understand but little, but afterwards, while we waited for the rescued one, we asked Beanix—(I am afraid I cannot do better than that, so it will have to stand. We will call her Beanix, but it does not look quite correct when written down)—we asked her about those cries and where they came from. She said she did not know, but that there was provision for their registration, both collectively and individually, for their analysis, and that they should be scientifically treated in this science of love, and that then help would be sent out according to the merit of those who cried, and also in such form as would best be of service. Each cry was an evidence either of good or bad in some human soul in that region, and would receive its appropriate answer.

When the woman was handed over to us we first let her rest and surrounded her with a quiet restful influence, and then, when she was strong enough, led her away to a home where she is being cared for and tended.

We did not ask her any questions, but let her ask the few she was able to put to us. But I found that the poor thing had been in that dark land for more than twenty years past. Her life history on earth I have partly learned, but not enough to make a connected narrative. And it is not well to remind them too vividly at first of the earth they have left so long ago. They usually have to work back from the present through their experience in the spirit life, in order to understand it and the relation of the whole—cause and effect, sowing and reaping—all explained.

That must serve for this time. Goodbye, dear, and God's blessing and our prayers shall be with and for you. May He keep you in His peace.

Amen.

4

City and Realm of Castrel

Friday, October 17, 1913.

BY the time we had reached the Home where we were charged to leave our poor sister, now so blessed, we were aware of another mission allotted to us. We were bidden to go to another district farther to the East. . . . You again hesitate, but that is the word we want. By the East we mean the direction from which the Brighter Light is seen over the mountains which border the plain where the Vision of the Christ and the Cross had been given to us. We often speak of that direction as the East because it reminds us of the Sunrise.

We set off, the five of us, all women, and kept before us the description we had received of the place we were to seek. We were to look for a great city among the mountains, with a golden dome in the midst of it, and the City itself surrounded by a colonnade on a terrace which ran round the City on all sides. We walked over the plain, and then went through the air, which requires more exertion, but is more speedy, and, in a case like ours, more convenient in enabling us to get a view of the country.

We sighted the City and descended before the principal gateway, by which we entered the main thoroughfare. It ran straight through the City and emerged through another gateway on the other side. On each side of this broad street there were large houses, or palaces, in spacious grounds, the residences of the principal officials of that district of which the City itself was the Capital.

As we came towards the City we had seen people working in the fields, and also many buildings, evidently not residences, but erected for some other useful purpose. And now that we were within the City walls we saw the perfection of both buildings and horticulture. For each building had a typical garden to match it both in color and design. We passed on, waiting for some sign as to our destination and mission, for on such occasions as this a message is always sent on ahead, so that the visitors are expected.

When we had gone some way we entered a large square, where beautiful trees grew on lawns of the greenest of green grass, and fountains played a harmony together; that is to say, there were perhaps a dozen fountains, and each had a tone of its own, and each was composed of many smaller jets of water, each being a note. These are manipulated, on occasion, so that a fairly complicated piece of music can be played, with an effect such as that produced by an organ with many stops. At such times there are large numbers of people assembled in the square, or park, as I might call it, both of the citizens and also those who dwell outside among the hills and pastures. But when we came to it the fountains were playing a simple series of chords, in perfect harmony, and with most pleasing effect.

Here we lingered for awhile, for it is exceedingly restful and beautiful. We sat and lay upon the grass, and presently there came towards us a man who, by the smile on his face as he approached, we knew was the one who had been expecting us. We arose and stood before him in silence, for we did not feel inclined to begin the conversation, as we saw he was an angel of some degree considerably above us.

Please describe him, and give me his name if possible.

All in good time, dear. We learn to eliminate impatience here as a thing which confuses without adding impetus to the matter in hand.

He was tall—much taller than the average man on earth. I should say he would be some seven and a half feet high in earth measurement. I am considerably taller than I was when with you, and he was much taller than I am. He wore a cream-colored tunic, almost to his knees, bare arms and legs, and no sandals.—You see I am answering what you are questioning in your mind.—No, he had nothing on his head, but a beautiful veil of soft brown hair, parted in the middle and curling round his face and neck. One broad fillet of gold he wore, and in the center and at the sides were set three large blue stones. He wore a belt of silver and some pink metal mingled, and his limbs shone with a soft glow. And these points, together with others, told us of his high degree.

There was also a calm benevolence and power in his firm but kindly countenance which gave both peace and trustfulness to us, as we stood before him, but also induced a reverence which we were glad to pay to one of such real worth as he.

He spoke at last, quietly, modulating his voice, as we instinctively knew, to our case. We could, nevertheless, detect the reverberating power in the tone of it. He said, "My name is Cast—," I am sorry. These names seem to be one of my weaknesses. They always perplex me when I try to reproduce them down here. But never mind his name for the moment. "I am C.," he said. "You have already heard of me from your own Superior, and now we meet in person. Now, my sisters five, come with me, and I will tell you why you have been sent to this city and to me." So we followed him, and on the way he chatted pleasantly, and we were quite at ease in his presence.

He led us down an avenue at right angles to the square, and then we emerged into another square; but we saw at once that this was a private square, and that the great palace, which lay away across the parklands before and around it, was the residence of some great Lord. We were guided through the park until we approached the great building, which stood, like some Greek temple, on a plateau which had a flight of steps on all sides of it.

The building was immense, and stretched before us, to right and left, and had high arches and entrances and porticoes, and surmounting it was a great dome. It was the landmark we had seen when approaching the city, only we found that it was not all gold, but gold and blue. We inquired who lived here, and he answered, "Oh, this is my home; that is, it is my city home but I have also other houses out there in the country parts where I go from time to time to visit my friends whose duties lie in those districts. Come within and you shall be given the welcome which is your due, who have come so far to see us."

He spoke quite simply. I have come to know that here simplicity is one of the marks of great power. One might have thought that the proper way to usher one into the presence of a great noble would be to send servants to lead us to the Palace, and then that he should receive us in state. But they look at things differently here. No purpose would have been served in this case by such ceremony, and so it was dispensed with. In cases where ceremony is helpful or desirable it is observed and sometimes with much grandeur. When it has no use it is not observed.

And that is how we came to the House of Castrel—now you have his name as well as I am able to give it; of whom more another evening. You have to go now, so goodnight, dear, and all blessing to you and yours from these glowing and beautiful realms. Dear lad, goodnight.

Saturday, October 18, 1913.

So he led us within, and we found that the interior of the house was lofty and very magnificent. The entrance-hall in which we stood was circular in shape, and open right up to the great dome above, which did not stand over the center of the building, but receded a little from the portico over this entrance. The rotunda was richly embellished with stones of many colors, and hangings of silk-like texture, mostly of deep crimson. Doorways led off down long passages in front and on either side of us. Doves flitted about the dome itself, and evidently had means of ingress and egress. The material of which the arching roof of this dome was built was a kind of semi-opaque stone, and permitted the light to filter through in a softened glow. When we had looked about us for a time we found that we were alone, for Castrel had left us.

By and by, from down a passage on our right, we heard laughter and happy voices, and there presently emerged a party of women, with a few children among them. They numbered about twenty in all, and came to us, and took our hands in welcome, and kissed us on the cheek, and smiled on us, so that we were happier, if possible, than before. Then they drew away, and stood at a little distance, except one who had remained in the rear. She came forward and led us to a recess in the wall, where she bade us be seated.

Then, standing before us, she addressed each of us by name in greeting, and said, "You will wonder why you have come here, and what this City and place is to which you have been sent. This house in which you now are is the Palace of Castrel, as, no doubt, you already know. He is ruler of this wide district, where many occupations are followed, and many studies are pursued. I hear you have already been to the Colony of Music, and farther on to other settlements, where different branches of science are carried on. Now, we are in touch with all of these, and are constantly receiving their reports as to progress in this or that branch. These are considered and dealt with by Castrel and his officers, from the harmony point of view, as I will call it. Co-ordination, however, would express what I mean.

"For instance, a report will arrive from the College of Music, and another from that of Light, and another from the settlement where the Creative faculty is studied, and from other branches of service. These are all very carefully examined and analyzed and tabulated, and, where necessity requires, the results are tested here, in one or other of the laboratories attached to this City. You will have seen some of these as you approached. They are scattered over the country to a great distance. They are not quite so complete in detail as those you have visited elsewhere, but, when any new apparatus is required, a mission is dispatched to inquire as to the construction, and these return and erect it in the spot most fitting in relation to the other establishments in this district; or perhaps it is added to the other apparatus already in existence in one or other of the buildings.

"You will understand, therefore, that an Overlord such as he who controls so varied a combination of knowledge must be well advanced in wisdom, and also is kept very busy at his work. It is this work you have been sent to see, and, while you remain with us, you will have ample opportunity of visiting some of the outlying stations. You will not, of course, understand all, or perhaps very much, of the scientific side of the work, but enough will be shown you to help you in your future work. Now come, and I will show you over this house, if you would care to see it."

We replied that we would, and thanked her for her kindness. So we went all over the principal parts of that magnificent dwelling. That is the only word I can find for it. Everywhere was color blended with color, bold but harmonious, and in such a way that, instead of being glaring, it had sometimes an exhilarating and sometimes a soothing and restful effect. Jewels and precious metals and beautiful ornaments, vases and pedestals and pillars—some standing alone as an ornament, each by itself, some in groups—hangings of glittering material which, as we passed through some doorway, swung into place again with a musical murmur, fountains with fish, courtyards open to the sky, in which grass and most beautiful trees and flowering shrubs grew, of such colors as are not known on earth.

Then we ascended to the roof, and here again was a roof garden, but one of large extent, with grass and arbors and shrubs and fountains once again. It was mostly from this garden that messages and messengers were sighted; and also there were appliances by which correspondence could be carried on with distant regions by a kind of what you would perhaps call wireless telegraphy, but it was really different from that, inasmuch as the messages arrive in visible form mostly, and not in words.

In this mansion we stayed for a considerable period, and visited both the City and also the district around, a district which in earth measure would be reckoned in thousands of miles across, but all in constant touch with the city and its communicating stations, and with this central Palace itself. Time would fail to tell you all, so I will just give you a few details and leave you to imagine the rest, which, however, I know you will fail to do.

The first thing which puzzled me was the presence of children, for I had thought that all children were reared in special Homes by themselves. The lady who had received us was the Mother of the place, and those who had attended her were some of her helpers. I asked one of these about these children who looked so happy and beautiful, and so perfectly at ease in this grand place. She explained that these were still-born children, who had never breathed the atmosphere of earth. For this reason they were of different character from others who had been born alive, even from those who had only lived a few minutes. They also required different treatment, and were able much sooner to imbibe the knowledge of these spheres. So they were sent to some such home as this, and were trained until they had progressed in mind and stature to such a degree that they were able to begin their new course of knowledge. Then, strong in heavenly purity and wisdom, they were taken in hand by those teachers who were in touch with the earth itself, and were taught what they had not been able to learn before.

This was interesting to me, and presently I began to see that one reason I had been sent here was to learn this very thing, in order that there might be awakened in me by that knowledge the desire to know my own who had so passed into this land, and of whom I had not hoped to be called Mother. 0, the great and sweetest yearning which came to me when I realized this! I will not dwell upon it, but confess that for a time tears of unutterable joy dimmed my eyes at this one more blessing added to my already abundant store. I sat down on the grass beneath a tree, and hid my face in my hands, and bowed my head upon my knees, and there I remained helpless, from the too exquisite rapture, which filled and vibrated through my being till I shook all over. My kind friend did not speak to me, but sat down by my side, and put her arms around my shoulders, and let me sob out my joy.

Then, when I had somewhat recovered, she said very gently, "Dear, I also am a mother, the mother of one such as you will find here all your own. So I know what is in your heart at this moment, for I have experienced your present joy also."

Then I raised my eyes to her face, and she saw the question I could not ask her, and, taking my hand, she raised me, and, with her arm round my shoulder still, she led me towards a grove, where we heard children playing, their happy shouts and laughter coming through the trees—for I was very faint from all that great joy that filled me, and how should I sustain the greater joy to come?

Dear, that was not very long ago, and it is still so fresh to me that I find it hard to write for you clearly as I could wish. But you must forgive me if I seem to be too profuse, or too disjointed in my words. I had not known this truth, and when it was revealed to me so suddenly, and all the—to me—tremendous significance of it—well, I must leave you to try to understand. Suffice to say, I found in that glade what I did not know I possessed, and such a gift as this is more readily bestowed in this land than one is able with due self-control to receive.

I must add, before I cease, what I ought to have said before, but was carried on in spite of myself by the recollection of that sweet hour. It is this: When young children come over here they are first schooled in this life, and then have to learn what experience they have lacked on earth. The more training they have acquired in the earth life, the sooner they are sent to complete it. Those who are stillborn have had no earth training at all. Nevertheless, they are children of the earth and, as such, they must return and acquire it. Not until it is safe for them to do so, however, and then under proper guardianship until they are competent to go alone. Their return to the neighborhood of the earth sphere is consequently longer delayed, and one who has lived a long and busy life on earth has less to learn of earth life when he comes over here, and so can pass on to other and higher studies.

Of course, these are only the broad governing principles, and, in application to individuals, account has to be taken of personal characteristics, and the rule modified and adapted as the particular case requires or merits.

But all is well for all who live and love, and those who love best live the loveliest life. That sounds rather too alliterative, but let it stand, for it is true. God bless you, dear. Goodnight.

Monday, October 20, 1913.

We were walking down the principal street of that beautiful city on a tour of inspection. We wanted to understand why it was laid out in so many squares, and what was the use of some of the buildings we had noticed on both sides of that broad way. When we had arrived at the farther gateway, we saw that the city stood very high above the surrounding plains. Our guide explained that the reason for this was that those on the towers might see as far as possible, and also might be seen by those in the distant settlements of this district. This was the Capital City of the region, and all business going on found its focus here.

On our way back we visited several of the buildings, and were everywhere kindly received. We found few children, other than those in Castrel's Home. Here and there, however, there were groups in the squares, where the fountains played and were surrounded by basins into which their waters fell. These were all connected with one broad stream which issued forth from one side of the City, and fell into the plain below, a brilliant waterfall of many tints and of sparkling brightness. It took its way across the plain, a fairly broad stream flowing gently over the sands, and we saw, here and there, some children bathing in it, and throwing it over their beautiful bodies in great enjoyment. I did not think much of this until my guide remarked that these children were encouraged to bathe in the waters, as they were electrically charged, and gave strength to them, for many came here very weak and required such nourishment.

I expressed my surprise at this, and she replied, "But what would you have? You know that, although not of material flesh and blood, yet our bodies here are solid and real as those we have laid aside. And you know that these bodies of our present state correspond to the spirit within much more accurately than those others used to do. Now these little spirits are, most of them, only beginning to develop and need bodily nourishment to help them on the way. Why not?"

Why not, indeed! Surely I was slow to learn all that that phrase I have already given you implied, "Earth made perfect." I fear many of you when you come over here will be much shocked to see how very natural all things are, even if more beautiful than on the earth. So many expect to find a vague shadowy world over here, totally diverse from earth in every possible way. And yet, come to think of it, and with common sense, what good would such a world be to us? It would not mean a gradual progress for us, but a vast leap, and that is not the way of God.

Things here when first we arrive are certainly different from those of the old life, but not so different as to make us feel dumbfounded by their strangeness. Indeed, those who come over after living an unprogressive life on earth, find themselves in spheres of so gross a character as to be, to them, indistinguishable from earth itself. That is one of the reasons why they are not able to realize that they have changed their state. As you progress through the lower spheres into the higher, this grossness gradually gives place to more rare conditions, and the higher you go the more sublimated is the environment. But few, if any, pass into those spheres where no trace of earth is seen, or no likeness to the earth life. I doubt if, as a rule, any do. But of this I must not speak dogmatically, for I have not myself reached, or even visited, a sphere where there is absolutely no likeness to God's beautiful earth. For it is beautiful, and we have to learn its beauties and wonders here, as part of our training. And, learning so, we find that earth is but one further manifestation outward from our own spheres, and in tune with us and our present environment in many very intimate ways. Were it not thus we could not be communing with you at this moment.

Also—and I merely say this as it appears to me who am not very wise in these things—I do not see how people passing over from the earth life into this could possibly get here were there a great gap between us, a gigantic void. How could they cross it? But that is simply my own thought, and there may be nothing in it at all. Only of this I am fairly certain: if people would but keep in mind the Oneness of God and His Kingdom, and the gradual progression which, in His wisdom, He has ordained for us, then they would much better understand what death is and what is beyond. It would probably be utterly absurd to many to be told that here we have real solid houses and streets and mountains and trees and animals and birds; and that animals are not here for ornament alone, but also for use; and that horses and oxen and other animals are put to use. But they enjoy their work in a way which makes one glad to watch them. I noticed a horse and rider coming along the street once, and I wondered which was enjoying the canter the more of the two. But I fear this will not be accepted by many, so I will get on to another theme.

One of the buildings in the broad street was a library where records were kept of reports from the outlying stations. Another was a laboratory where some of the reports could be tested by actual experiment. Another was a lecture hall where professors gave their results to those of their own and other branches of science. Another had a somewhat curious history.

It stood well back from the street and was built of wood. It looked like polished mahogany, with streaks of gold in the grain. It was erected long ago as a Council Chamber for the Chief of that time, long before Castrel took over the work. Here he used to assemble the students in order that they might each give an exhibition of their knowledge in practical form.

A young man arose on one occasion, and, going to the center of the auditorium, stood there and stretched out his hands, and remained facing the President. As he stood there his form seemed to change and become more radiant and translucent, until at last he was surrounded by a large halo of light, and there were seen about him many Angels from the higher spheres. His smile had some enigma in it. which the Prince was trying to read, but could not. Just as he (the Prince or Chief) was about to speak, there came through the open door a little boy-child, and looked round in surprise at all the great crowd.

He paused at the edge of the circle and looked on the multitude of faces of those who sat there in tiers, one above the other, round the circle, and seemed abashed. He was just turning to run away again when he caught sight of the one who stood in the center, now glowing with light and glory. Immediately the little lad forgot everybody else, and, running as fast as his little legs would carry him, he went straight to the center of the circle with outstretched hands and a look of great joy in his face.

The one who stood there then lowered his arms, and, stooping down, took up the little one and laid him on his shoulder, and then, approaching the Prince, he gently laid the little fellow in his lap and began to walk back towards the place where he had stood. But as he went his form grew dim, and, before he had reached the spot he had left, he had become quite invisible, and the whole space was empty. But the little boy lay in the Prince's lap, and looked up into his face—a very beautiful face it was—and smiled.

Then the Prince arose, and, holding the child on his left arm, he reverently laid his right hand on his head, and said, "My brothers, it is written, 'A little child shall lead them,' and these words come to my mind but now. What we have seen is a Manifestation of our Lord the Christ, and this little one is of those who are of the Kingdom, as He said. What message did He give you, child, as you lay in His arms, and He brought you to mine?"

Then for the first time the boy spoke and said, with a child's accent, and still very shy of the large audience, "If you please, Prince, I must be good and do as you instruct me, and then He will show me, from time to time, new things for your City and Realm. But I don't know what it means."

Nor did the Prince, nor the students at first. But he dispersed them and took the little one home to his own house, and thought the matter out. He came to the conclusion it was Eli and Samuel over again, without the more unpleasant details. As a matter of fact, as it turned out, he had read the matter correctly. The child was allowed to play about the laboratories and scientific schools, and watch and listen. He never was in the way, and did not bother them with questions. But now and again, when some extra-difficult piece of work was on hand, he would make some remark, and when he did so, it was always the key to the solution. Also—and this was considered, as time went on, to be the principal object He had in giving that Manifestation—the students learned simplicity; that is, that the simpler the solution they could find to any problem in particular, the better it fitted into the general scheme with other solutions.

There were many other lessons also which they learned from the Vision itself; for instance, the fact that His Presence was among them always, and that at any time He might become visible, for, when He came that time, He walked out from among the assembly of students. Also, the outstretched arms taught them of self-sacrifice even in those happy realms where glories shone about them, even as it had shone about His form as He stood there. But the child: he grew as His Divine Sponsor had grown, in wisdom and stature, and when the Prince of that time was taken into a higher spheres he succeeded him in his high office.

Well, all this is long ago, and still the old hall stands today. It is always kept carefully tended and made beautiful without and within with flowers. But it is not used now for lectures and discussions, but for service of worship. One of the artists of the City made a painting of the scene, and that was placed there behind the Altar, like many on earth. And from time to time worship is offered to the Great Father of all, in the sanctifying Presence of His Anointed Son, and, on some of the greater occasions, the Prince who was there when that Vision was given will descend from the higher spheres with the little boy, now a great Angel-Lord, and others who have held the office since their time; and those who assemble there know that some great blessing and Manifestation will be given. But only those who are fitted by their developed state are present at such times, for the Manifestation would not be visible to those who have not reached a certain stage in progress.

God's spheres are wonderful in their beauty of light and glory; but most wonderful thing of all seems the Presence of His Spirit through all these infinities and eternities, and His tender love to all, both wise and simple; and to you and me, dear, in that He has so ordained the co-operation of the different estates within His Realm that we can talk together thus, you and I, dear, through the thin Veil which hangs between.

Tuesday, October 21, 1918.

Of that city I could tell you much more than I have done. But I have other matters to deal with, and will, therefore, give you just one more item of our life there and then pass on to other things.

We were lodging in a cottage within the Palace grounds where the children often came to see us, and my own little one among them. They seemed to be glad to come and see their little friend's mother and her fellow visitors, and were never tired of hearing about the other places we had visited, and especially the children's homes and schools. They would weave garlands of flowers and bring them to us as gifts, with the hope at the back of their minds that we would in return join them in one of their games. This we often did, and you will easily imagine how I enjoyed those romps with these dear little children in that quiet and peaceful place.

We were once playing with them at a game they had invented among themselves, a kind of Jolly Hooper game such as you used to play, and we had won nearly all the others on to our side, when the few who were left facing us suddenly stopped in their song and stood still, looking beyond us. We all turned round, and there, standing in the entrance of a long avenue of trees at the edge of the glade, was no other than Castrel.

He stood there smiling at us, and, although his aspect was so kingly, yet there was so much gentleness and humility blended with his strength and wisdom, that he was very lovely to look upon, and to be near. He came slowly forward and the children ran to him, and he patted one and another on the head as he came. Then he spoke to us. "You see," he said, "I knew where I might find you, and so I needed no guide. And now I am obliged to cut your play short, my sister-visitors, for there is a ceremony on hand at which you ought to be present. So you little ones must continue your games alone while these big children come with me."

Then they ran to us and kissed us happily, and made us promise to come and continue our games as soon as we were at liberty.

So we followed the Prince Castrel along the avenue of trees which formed a leafy tunnel meeting overhead. We walked to the end and emerged into the open country, and here our guide paused and said, "Now I want you to look yonder and tell me what you see!"

We, one and all five of us, told him we saw a large undulating plain, with many buildings here and there, and, beyond, what appeared to be a long range of high mountains.

"Nothing else?" he asked.

We replied that we could see nothing else of importance, and he continued, "No, I suppose that is about the limit of your vision at present. But my sight, you see, is more developed than yours, and I can see beyond those mountains yonder. Now listen, and I will tell you what I see. Beyond that range I see other mountains higher still, and beyond them still more lofty peaks. On some of these are buildings, others are bare. I have been in that region also, and I know that among those mountains, which from this point are viewed foreshortened, are plains and tracts of country as wide as this of which this City is the chief.

"I am now looking at the shoulder of a mountain, not on the horizon, as I see it, but far beyond your own range of vision, and I see a large and glorious City, much more extensive and much richer and more magnificent than this. The principal gateway fronts in this direction, and before it is a large flat space. Through this gateway are emerging horses and chariots with drivers, and other horses with riders. They have now assembled and are about to start. Now their leader emerges from the crowd and comes to the front. He gives an order and the crowd of citizens raise their hands and wave a God-speed to them. Now their Prince moves forward to the edge of the cliff on which the City is erected. He leaves the edge and proceeds by aerial flight. His chariot leads the way and the others follow. And they come," he added with a smile, "in this direction. Now we will go to another place, and you shall witness their arrival."

None of us asked the reason of their visit. It was not that we were afraid to do so. I think we could have asked him anything. But we somehow felt that all that it was meet that we should know then had been told us, and so we were content to wait. But he said, "You are curious to know the reason of their coming. That you will shortly be permitted to see." So we went with him to the wall of the City, and stood there looking over the plain towards the hills. We could see no more than we had said.

"Tell me," he said, "which of you first sights them."

We looked long and eagerly, but could not see anything. At last I thought I saw a star begin to twinkle over the mountains far away in the depths of space. Just at that moment one of my companions exclaimed, "I think, my lord, that star was not there when first we came here."

"Yes," he replied, "it was there, but not visible to you. So you are the first to see it?"

I did not like to say I had seen it also. I should have said that before. But he continued, "I think there is some one else who sees that star. Is that not so?" and he turned to me with a quiet smile. I am afraid I reddened and mumbled something awkwardly. "Well," he said, "watch it. You others will also be able to see it presently. At this moment it is several spheres away, and I did not expect any of you to be able to see quite into that region." Then, turning to us two, he bowed courteously, and said, "Ladies, I congratulate you on your good progress. You are rapidly advancing towards a higher grade, and, if you continue, your sphere of service will soon be enlarged, believe me." We were both made very happy by this speech.

But now the star had considerably brightened, and ever, as we looked, it seemed to enlarge and expand, and this continued a long space of time. Then I noticed that it was no longer a round disc, but was gradually assuming another shape, and, at last, I was able to see what the shape was. It was a harp of light, somewhat in the shape of a lyre, and seemed to be like a jewel set with many diamonds. But as it came nearer and nearer, we were able to see that it was made up of horses and chariots and men, and that in that order they were speeding through space towards us.

Presently we heard shouts of welcome from the people on other parts of the City walls and knew that they had sighted them also.

"Now you see the nature of their business in this City."

"Music," I suggested.

"Yes," he answered, "it has to do with music. That is the main object of this visit, anyway."

As they drew nearer we saw that the company numbered some hundreds. It was a beautiful sight to see. There they came along the path of the heavens, horses and chariots of fire—you know the old familiar phrase; believe me, it is little understood—with riders of light radiating their glory far around them, as they sped along their heavenly way. 0, these citizens of those higher realms are all too beautiful for us to describe to you. The lowest in rank of these was just about of Castrel's degree. But his own glory was constrained and hidden, in order that he might be both Prince of this City and also a citizen. Yet, as his companions and peers drew near, we noticed that he also began to change. His face and form glowed with an ever-increasing radiance until, at length, he shone as bright as the least bright of those who came along the sky. I could understand, when I thought of it afterwards, why it was necessary for him to condition himself to the lower sphere in which he served. For, as he stood before us now, even though he had not attained the full intensity of his native brightness, yet none of us dared approach him, but drew a little distance away, and left him to stand alone. We were not afraid, but unaccustomed—that is as well as I can put it.

The members of the flashing jeweled harp at last were speeding over our own country, and when they had come half the way between us and the first range of hills, they slowed down and gradually reformed. This time the band took the shape of a . . . [that word we could not give above was "planet"—the second formation, we mean—not "planet," but "planetary system." I do not know whether it was the solar system, of which the earth is a unit, or other—some other system I rather think; but I do not know]. Then sweeping down they landed on the space before the principal gate of the City.

Castrel had left us for some time now, and, as they landed, we saw him issue on foot from the City gate, attended by his principal men. He was robed in light—that is nearly all I could see. But the diadem he wore shone more brilliantly than I had ever seen it; and so did the girdle he wore. He approached the leader and knelt before him. This Angel was much brighter even than Castrel. He descended from his chariot and, hastening to our own Prince, lifted him up and embraced him. The action was full of grace and also of love, and, for the few seconds they were together, there was complete silence on the walls. But when the embrace was done, and the words of blessing—in a language we do not understand—were spoken, Castrel bowed his head before the other and then, standing up, looked to the City walls and raised his hand, and there was a burst of music and voices as the citizens broke into a glorious anthem. I have told you of the singing in another region. This was much more sublime, for this was a plane in advance of that. Then they too, followed by the other visitors, entered the City amidst the shouts of the populace and the pealing of bells and strains of instrumental music and the singing of the thousands upon the walls.

So they passed along the street to the Palace, and, as he turned into the avenue which led off the main street, the Angel Prince, our visitor, halted, and, standing in his chariot, turned round, and, lifting his hand, blessed the people in their own tongue, and then went on down the avenue and was, with his glittering attendants, lost to view.

Dear, I have tried my very best to give you even a faint description of that incident. I have failed miserably. It was much more glorious than I have been able to describe. I have spent my time also on the description of this arrival scene because that I could understand better than the mission on which they had come. That is far too deep for me, and concerned the teachers of the City and the great men of that land. All I could get to know was that it was chiefly concerned with the studies of the most advanced in that Colony of the connection of music with the creative faculty. I cannot understand more than that. But perhaps others will be able to say more about it than I can.

That is all, dear, tonight. Are you waiting for our blessing? God bless you, dear lad. Lift up your eyes and keep your ideals bright, and believe that the most glorious of glories you can imagine are to the real and actual glories of this life of ours, just as candlelight to that of a sun.

Wednesday, October 22, 1913.

If all the world were one great diamond or pearl reflecting or radiating the light of the sun and distant stars, how bright would be its vicinity. Yet in a measure it does this, but only to a very limited degree because of the lack of luster on its surface. And as the reflecting capacity of the earth is to that more perfect mirror which a pearl would furnish, so is the earth life to ours here in these realms of light and beauty, the Summerland of God.

As we gaze out over the wide plains and valleys of the Heavenly Land, we are scarce able to remember the effect of the atmosphere of earth as it had relation to our vision of terrestrial things. But we do remember certain qualities which here are absent. Distance is not obscured, for instance. It fades away. Trees and plants do not appear for a season, and then die. They bloom perpetually, and then, when plucked, they are fresh for a long time, but they do not droop and wither. They, too, fade, or melt, away into the atmosphere. This same atmosphere is not always white. In the neighborhood of the City of the Prince Castrel there is a sense of golden sunshine all around. It is not a mist, and does not obscure, but bathes all things in its golden radiance without invading the various colors themselves. In other places it is of a faint pink or blue. And every region has its own peculiar tint, or sense, of color, according to the nature of the people and their employment and bent of mind.

The tint of the atmosphere seems to be governed by this principle; but also it is reflex in its action on the people themselves. Especially is this the case with visitors from other regions. The more highly developed, on coming into a new tract of country, are able to tell by this alone the general character and occupations of the people there. The influence, however, very quickly extends to themselves. It does not change them in character, of course, but it does affect their sensations, and is almost instantaneously seen in the changing hue of their robes.

Thus, as one visits a strange district, one very speedily begins to feel, within and without, that sense of brotherhood and sisterhood which is one of the most delightful of blessings I have found. Everywhere you go you find brothers and sisters. Try to think of it and see what it would mean if it were thus on earth. Then the Angels' greeting of Peace and Goodwill indeed would be realized and earth would be the ante-chamber of the Heavenly Home.

We returned from that City asking ourselves what difference our visit had made in us, and what we had learned. For my own part, it was not difficult to see that the very fact of my own little girl being there was enough. She is a gift I had not expected. But as we returned leisurely across the plain, we found that each had received some special blessing for herself alone.

As we had approached the City by the air, we preferred now to go afoot across the plain until we reached the mountains. And as we went we talked of what we had seen. Now, I could fill many pages with that talk, and I assure you it would not be uninteresting. But time and space are to you, and to publishers, of more account than they are to us, so I will hasten on to what I have to tell.

We reached our own sphere just as our Mother Angel had also returned from a journey to the Bridge of which I have already told you. She brought with her this time one you know.

Name, please.

Mrs. S. She had been through a rather trying experience. When first she came over she was taken to a place where she might have progressed rapidly. Hers was a perplexing case, so many mixed traits that it was very difficult to place her exactly. So she was given the chance and helped in every way. But, you must know, freewill and personality are very important things here, and are never overruled when help is being offered. She soon grew restless, and it was seen that she would have to be given her way. So she was warned and advised and then taken to the parting of the ways to choose her own road, as she wished to do. A guardian was appointed to keep constant watch in order that if help were sought any time it would be near at hand.

Well, she did not seem to know where to go or what to do, to find what she wanted—peace. So she wandered on and spent a considerable period in the neighborhood of the Bridge. It was only when she had learned for herself that her own willful course led again and again into places where the darkness always increased, and people, sights and sounds were of a nature not to radiate happiness, but sometimes terror, that at last she wandered along the borderland, and, by and by, turned a little towards the light and was gradually helped back again to the Home she had left. She is now progressing, slowly, to be sure; but still with an ever softening heart, and more humility and trust, and she will do well in time. That is why I have seen so little of her, and been of so little use. But I may be able to help a little now and again as time goes on. Perhaps that is why she has been brought to the place where I am destined to spend a more or less protracted period of service. I did not know her in the earth life except through you, and your friendship with her children may be the link which will enable her to receive any little help I am able to give.

You see, everything is considered here, even the things which seem so casual and transitory in the earth life. They are all registered and viewed in their relation to one another, all the seemingly casual talks or chance meetings, a book read, a hand shaken in the street for the first time and never again, a few friends meeting, in the same way, at a mutual friend's house and never meeting again—everything and every item is registered, considered, coordinated and used when, and if, occasion offers. And so may it be in this case.

Be, therefore, not remiss to weigh well all you do and every word you say; not in anxiety, but rather by cultivating a habit of will to do good; always and everywhere to radiate kindness of heart, for in the Kingdom these are not of small account, but go to make robes bright and bodies radiant.

And so, dear, goodnight once again—a wish not without its significance to you, if otherwise to us, for here all is good to them who goodness love, and night is absent always where the True Light shines for ever, and all is Peace.

5

Angelic Ministry

Thursday, October 23, 1913.

PERCHANCE if we were to tell you of our progress in these heavenly spheres we should weary you, for much detail has to be negotiated, and nothing passed over as being too small. But it may be helpful if we supplement what we wrote in this vein last evening by giving you now an instance by way of illustration of this point.

We received a message a short time ago of the arrival of a sister at the Bridge, who had come over from the further side where lie the regions of gloom, and I and another were sent to conduct her to this Home. We went quickly and found our charge awaiting us. She was quite alone, for her attendants had left her thus in order that she might profit by a quiet period of meditation and reflection before beginning her further advance.

She was seated on a slope of grass under a tree whose branches spread like a canopy over her. Her eyes were closed, and we stood before her waiting. When she opened them she looked at us for some time in an inquiring manner. As she did not speak, I at last addressed her "Sister." At that word she looked at us hesitatingly, and then her eyes began to fill with tears, and she put her face in her hands, bowed her head upon her knees, and wept bitterly.

So I went to her and laid my hand upon her head and said, "You are our sister now, dear, and as we do not weep, so neither must you."

"How do you know who or what I am?" she replied, as she raised her face and tried to force back her tears, while there was just a touch of defiance in her voice.

"We do not know who you are," I answered.

"What you were we do know. We know that you were always a child of our Father, and so, always our sister. Now you are our sister in a fuller sense. What else you are lies with you. You are either one whose face is set toward the Sunshine of His Presence, or one who, fearing the task before you in that direction, will turn back again across the Bridge."

She was silent for a while, and then said, "I dare not. It is all too horrible over there."

"But," I urged, "you must choose; for you cannot remain where you are. And you will come the upward way, will you not?—and we will lend you a sister's hand and give you a sister's love to help you on the way."

"Oh, I wonder how much you know of what lies yonder," she said, and there was agony in her voice. "There they called me sister, too; they called me sister in mockery, while they heaped upon me infamy and torture and—oh, I must not think of it or it will drive me mad again. But I don't know how I shall proceed; I am so stained and vile and weak."

But I saw that this would never do, so I cut her short. I told her that, for the present, she must try to forget these experiences, until we had helped her, and then it would be time enough to begin her task in earnest. I knew that task was going to be a heavy and bitter one; but there is only one way onward, nothing can be glossed over; everything must be viewed and understood for exactly what it is—every act and word up to the present time—God's justice acknowledged, and God's Love through all—and that is the only onward and upward way. But that must rest a while until she was capable of enduring it. And so we comforted her and gradually led her away.

Now, as we went she began to look around and ask about the things she saw, and what kind of country lay ahead, and what the home was like to which she was being led, and so on. We told her all she could understand. We told her of our Angel Mother who had charge of the place, and of our fellow workers there. In the midst of our conversation she stopped suddenly and said she felt she could go no further. "Why?" we inquired, "are you tired?" and she answered, "No; afraid."

We saw something of what was in her mind, but could not quite understand it as a whole. There was something we could not lay hold of. So we led her on to talk of herself, and at last we unearthed the difficulty.

It seems that when the guardian at the other end of the Bridge had heard her cry for help far away in the gloom, he at once directed a ray of his light in the direction, and sent a messenger to help her. This spirit found her fainting by the side of a dark murky stream whose waters were foul and hot, and bore her to the Bridge Gatehouse. Here she was tended and revived and brought forward across the Bridge to the place where we found her.

Now it chanced that when this spirit worker had found her she had felt a presence but could not see any one near. She therefore called aloud, "May you be cursed if you touch me!" thinking that perhaps it was one of her old tormentors and companions in wickedness. Then she remembered no more until she recovered her senses again in the Gatehouse. As we walked and talked of the workers of these realms the memory of that incident suddenly came back to her mind. She had cursed one of God's ministers, and she was afraid of the light because the words were evil. Truly, she did not know whom she had cursed; but a curse is a curse against whomsoever directed, and it lay upon her heart.

My companions and I consulted together briefly and came to the conclusion that we must return. The other sins of this poor soul might be dealt with presently. This, however, was against one of our fellow-workers of the realms of light and love, and we saw that she would find no rest among us, and our services would little avail her until that wrong had been righted. So back to the Bridge we went, and right across it to the Gatehouse at the further end.

There we found the spirit helper who had brought her to that place, and she asked and obtained forgiveness. Indeed, he was awaiting us; for he was stronger and more progressed than we, and so was greater in wisdom, and he knew that she would compel herself to return. So as we drew near he came from the gateway where he had been standing watching us coming along the road, and, when she saw his kind face and forgiving smile, she knew at once it was he whom she sought and, falling on her knees, obtained his blessing.

* * *

I fear this is not a very exciting message tonight. I have given it to show you how even the seemingly slight things have to be reckoned with here. As a matter of fact, I believe that some higher intelligence than our own was controlling us all the time; for that little incident proved a very important episode in the progress of that poor sinful woman. It was a long journey back to, and across, the Bridge, and she was very weak and weary. But when she saw the face of the one against whom she had sinned, and heard his words of love and forgiveness, it showed her, for the first time, that whatever she should have to endure in future it would be sweet in the end, and each task done would earn its own blessing. And that is no mean support

to such as she who had so much to face of repentance and ago-
nizing shame of remembrance of the Great Love of God which
she had flouted and denied.

What is she doing now?

That was not very long ago, and she has been progressing
but slowly. There is so much to keep her back. But she does
progress, nevertheless. She is in our Home, but has not yet
been given any special work to do for others. She will be so
employed eventually, but not for a long time to come.

Sin may be negative in its essential parts, but it is negation
of the Love and Fatherhood of God, and that is a far more terrible thing than mere offence against a commandment. It is the
contamination of the very nature and spring of our inner spirit
life, of the Sanctuary of the Spirit of God. And the cleansing of
a polluted Sanctuary is more than the washing of an ordinary
dwelling. The very intensity of the Light of the Presence in this
spiritual state shows up every speck and mote, and happy are
those who keep that Sanctuary clean and bright, for such shall
know how sweet it is to live and to love in Him.

Monday, October 27, 1913.

Once again we take up our tale of the Heavenly Life, and
hope to be able to tell you a little more of the love and blessedness which we experience in these bright realms. Our Home is
situated on the slope of a thickly-wooded hill in a clearing, and
our patients—for they are really such—are tended by us here
in peace and quiet after their distressing experiences in one or
other part of those lands where the light is dim, and darkness
seems to enter into their very souls. They come here more or
less exhausted and weak, and are only allowed to go onward
when they have become strong enough for the way.

You would perhaps like to know somewhat of our methods here. Chiefly these may be summed up in one word: Love.
For that is the guiding principle in all our work. Some are so

overjoyed with the realization of the fact that we do not seek to judge and punish, but only to help them, that they are, from that very cause ill at ease from its unfamiliarity.

One of our poor sisters met our Mother Angel a little while ago in the garden, and was turning down a side path in order to avoid meeting her, not of fear but of reverence. But our bright Angel went to her and spoke kindly to her, and when she found she could talk quite freely she asked a question. "Where is the Judge," she inquired, "and when is the Judgment to take place? I am trembling all the while with the thought of it, for I know my punishment will be a very dreadful one; and I would know the worst, and get it over."

To this the Mother replied, "My child, your judgment will take place whenever you desire; and from your own words I can tell you that it has already begun. For you own that your past life is worthy of punishment, and that is the first step in your judgment. As to the Judge, well, she is here; for you yourself are judge, and will mete out to yourself your punishment. You will do this of your own free will by reviewing all the life you have lived and, as you bravely own up one sin after another, so you will progress. Much of your punishment you have already inflicted upon yourself in those dark regions from which you have lately come. That punishment, indeed, was dreadful. But that is past and over, and what you have now to endure will be dreadful no longer. All dread should now be past. Painful, deeply painful, I fear it will be. But all through you will feel that He is leading you, and this more and more as you go on in the right way."

"But," persisted the inquirer, "I am perplexed because I do not see the Throne of the Great Judge Who will reward some and punish others."

"You will, indeed, some day see that Throne, but not yet. The judgment you are thinking of is very different from what you imagine. But you should have no fear and, as you progress, you will learn more, and understand more, of God's great love."

That is what perplexes many who come over here. They expect to find all set ready for their dismissal from the Presence into torture, and cannot understand things as they are.

Others who have cultivated a good opinion of their deserts are much disappointed when they are given a lowly place, sometimes a very lowly one, and not ushered immediately into the Presence of the Enthroned Christ to be hailed with His "Well done." Oh, believe me, dear son, there are many surprises awaiting those who come over here, some of a very joyful kind, and others the reverse.

I have, only lately, seen a very learned writer, who had published several books, talking to a lad who, in the earth life, was a stoker in a gasworks, and being instructed by him. He was glad to learn, too, for he had partly learned humility; and the curious thing was that he did not so much mind sitting at the feet of this young spirit as going to his old friends here and owning up his mistakes, and his vanity of intellect in his past life. This, however, he will have to do sooner or later, and the young lad is preparing him for the task. It is also whimsical to us to see him still clinging to his old pride, when we know all about him, and his past and present status, which latter is rather low, and all the time he is trying to think he is hiding his thoughts from us. With such their instructors have to exercise much patience, which is also very good training for them.

And now let us see if we can explain a difficulty which is perplexing many investigators into psychic matters. We mean the difficulty they have in understanding why we do not give them information which they desire about one thing or another which they have in their minds.

You must try to realize that when we come down here we are not in our proper element, but are hampered with limitations which are now strange to us. For instance, we have to work according to the laws which are in vogue in the earth realm, or we could not make you understand what we wish to do or say. Then we often find that when any one has his mind fixed on some particular person whom he wishes to hear or see, or some special matter about which he wishes to inquire, we are limited by the straitened means at our disposal. Other reservoirs of power in that inquirer are closed, and those only are open to us which he himself has willed should be open. And these are frequently not enough for us to work with.

Then again, the activity of his will meets the activity of ours midway, as it were, and there is a clash, and the result is either confusion or nil. It is nearly always better to allow us to work in our own way, trustfully, and afterwards to examine critically what we manage to get through. If information on any particular point is desired, let that point be in your mind at times as you go about your daily occupation. We shall see it and take account of it, and, if it is possible and useful and lawful, we shall find opportunity and means, sooner or later, to answer it. If you ask a question while we are with you manifesting in one way or other, do not demand, but just put your thoughts before us, and then leave it to us to do what we can. Do not insist. You may be sure that, as our desire is to help, we shall do all we can.

* * *

And now to a case in point. You have been wanting to know about Ruby and others. You have not insisted, and, therefore, we have been able to use conditions freely and are able to give you some information.

Ruby is happy as ever, and getting quite expert in the work she has in hand. I saw her only lately and she says she will be able to come to speak to you or Rose very soon. Now you are wondering why she cannot come tonight. She has other duties, and also we have to fulfill ours according to plan. One thing she said was this: "Tell dear daddy that his words to the people are brought here, and some of the things he tells them are discussed among us because they happen to be of those things we have not learned of the earth life."

This seems well nigh impossible. Have I got this right?

There you go, you see. Now what do you think these dear angel children are, that you speak so? Do you not understand that the studies of those who came over here very young are mostly of the life and conditions of their new homeland, and that only little by little are they allowed to complete their knowledge of the earth and its life which, nevertheless, has to be learned quite thoroughly as they proceed onward? So it is that every means is used, with discretion, to teach them. And what better or more likely way could you name than by enabling the father to be instructor of his own child? I am not going to say any more about that. It is enough. Think it over in a commonsense way and you will perhaps come to a more enlightened frame of mind.

Well, but if what you say is true, one will be almost afraid to instruct one's people at all. And don't be cross.

Dear lad, no, I am not cross. But in you, at least, I have been grateful to find a certain enlightenment as to the conditions of this life and their naturalness, and up crops one of those silly ideas of the nebulous order right in the midst of your mind.

You are quite right, however, to think that you should be careful how you give instruction. But this applies not only to you but to every one; and to all thoughts and words and deeds of every one. They are all known here. One crumb of comfort you can take, however. You maybe sure that when anything unworthy or base is thought or spoken, that is never allowed to find its way into such a sphere as that in which Ruby is. So make your mind easy there, my dear, and do not fear to speak out your mind; for silence is sometimes less welcome here than erroneous teaching, when that teaching is sincere.

And now, goodnight, and best love to you all. God bless you, dear lad, and keep you brave and true.

Tuesday, October 28, 1913.

Whatever we have been able to give you in these messages has been transmitted to you by means of impressing your mind with our thoughts and words. In doing this we take, and make use of, as much as we find there, so that we may the more easily get our own thoughts through. Frequently, however, we have been obliged, of necessity, to call your spirit away from the earth surroundings and give you a vision of the places we are describing, and you have written down what you have seen.

No, we did not actually take you out of your body, because you have been really conscious all the time. What we did was to engage and absorb your attention that we might infuse power into your interior sight—the sight of your spiritual body—and at those moments you were scarcely conscious of your surroundings. You forgot them and became oblivious of them, and then we were able to impart to you, in a measure, the power of distant vision; and to this we added the incidents as we had witnessed them ourselves.

For instance, when we described the coming of the Harp of Light to the City of Castrel we showed you the city as it is, but we reconstructed the incidents of the crowds on the walls, and the meeting outside the gates, and all the parts of the ceremony which we wished you to write down. That is what was done. *How* it was done you will understand some day when you come over here.

* * *

We are now going to try to show you another scene. And here we may say that we use the word "try" because, although with a good subject we do not often fail, yet we are not omnipotent, and there are many things which may intervene to hinder our endeavor and modify our success.

Well then, give us your attention a while and we will tell you of a ceremony which we witnessed when a company of people came to visit our colony to learn about our work. You must understand that we go to each other's homes, and learn of one another in this way, and get to know what we can of the various aspects of work going on in different parts.

We were standing near the top of the hill behind this Home watching their coming. At last we saw them high in the air and far away over the wide-spreading plain. The sky behind them was streaked with horizontal layers of crimson, gold and green; and by that we knew from what region they came, and the nature of their work. They were students in a distant settlement whose principal branch of knowledge was proper use of ceremonial and ritual, and its effects on those who use it.

We watched them coming along the heavenly way, and then a party of our own people, who were waiting on the plain, rose into the air and proceeded to meet the visitors. It was very interesting to see them meet in the air. High up in the heavens they approached each other, and when they were some little distance away our party sounded a welcome on what looked and sounded like post-horns, and then others produced other instruments and, while they played, others sang a welcome.

They had halted now and we saw that behind them was a chariot and two horses. It was very much like the chariots of old times. There is no reason why we should not use carriages of modern build; but shelter is unnecessary, and the old open vehicles have persisted to the present day. When the visitors came near they halted, and there the two parties faced each other, standing in the air. Try to imagine it. It seems strange to you, but one day you will see that it is quite natural to our present state, and, if progressed enough, we are able not only to stand but to kneel, lie or walk in the midst of space, very much as if it were on solid earth.

Then the leader of our band and the Chief of the visitors approached each other between the two ranks. They took each other by both hands, and kissed each other on the forehead and cheeks. And then our leader took his visitor's left hand in his own right and led him towards the chariot, our party dividing to give them passage, and bowing respectfully as they passed. When the two Chiefs had entered the chariot, their followers ran together with outstretched hands and gladly saluted one another as the others had done. And then all turned their faces towards us and came on at a leisurely walking pace until they descended at the foot of the hill.

I cannot make you see the effect of an approach by air. I have tried to do so more than once, but that is outside your imagination. So I can only tell you that it is most beautiful to watch. The movement of these high spirits, such as Castrel and Arnol and others of their rank, when walking on the ground, is not only most graceful, it is fascinating in its beauty of poise and movement. But in the air it is much more so. The soft, graceful, gliding motion, full of quiet and gentle dignity and of strength and power, is princely and angelic. So these two now came to us.

They descended, and then walked by a winding path to the Chief's house. He rules here with our Mother Angel, and I do not think there is much difference in their status or rank. For, except by direct questioning, which we hesitate to use, it is not easy to tell which of two people so nearly, if not quite, equal is the one who by a little degree excels. For so great is the love and harmony between such, that command and obedience seem to blend into one gracious and smiling endeavor of service, and we are at a loss sometimes to distinguish between the estate of two so highly developed as these.

The Chief's residence would very forcibly remind you of a mediaeval castle, set on a rock half-way up a mountain-side and surrounded by waving trees and foliage of many tints—

green, red, brown and gold—and multitudes of flowers and green patches of grass.

They passed under the gateway, and so within, and we saw them no more. But we noticed that the presence of that radiant company within illuminated the windows of the castle as if suddenly some thousands of electric lamps had been set going. And the colored lights we saw were most beautiful, for they did not melt into one tint but mingled together, each preserving its own hue, and streaming through the apertures like so many streams of rainbow radiance.

I have often mentioned gateways, but you will have observed that I have not spoken of gates. Now, so far, I have not seen a gate to any of the many gateways I have seen here. You read in the Book of the Revelation of the Holy City and its gates, but I have thought of it, being reminded of it by these gates to what are, evidently, similar cities to that which St. John saw in Presence Form, and I doubt whether that city had gates to the gateways. And that may be what he means when he says that the gates shall not be shut by day and—remembering that in the cities as he knew them on earth, the gates were not shut by day except in times of war, but were shut by night continually—he adds, by way of explanation, that there is no night here in this land. These are only my thoughts, and may not be correct, but you can look up the passage and refresh your memory and decide for yourself.

I was not present at the festival within the Castle, so will not describe it, as I only heard of it at second hand, and prefer to tell you of things I myself have witnessed, which I can do more vividly. It was a most glorious affair, however, as one can well credit when so many high spirits brought their glory together.

Ah well, dear lad, you will see it all some day soon, when you and your dear ones will all be here in God's good land on which His love and blessing descend like dew upon sweet meadowlands, with the fragrance all around. And is it strange if we who learn continually how much more blessed it is to give than to receive, should seek to waft some of this sweetness on our breath through the Veil that those on your side may breathe it too and taste how sweet and gracious the Lord is, and how blessed are they who rest on Him? Whose blessing we invoke on you and yours, now and ever. Amen.

Thursday, October 30, 1913.

Place your hand against your head and you will notice that we are then able the more readily to speak to you so that you will be able to understand.

Like this?

Yes. It helps you and us, both.

How?

Because there is a stream of magnetism proceeding from us to you, and by doing as we have suggested it is not so quickly dissipated.

I don't understand a word of all this.

Maybe not. There are many things you have yet to learn, dear, and what we are saying now is one of those things, little in itself but still of account. It is often these small things which help to success.

Now, while we are not overanxious to explain the methods we employ in the transmission of these messages, because we can only make you understand imperfectly, still we may say this: the power we use is best described as magnetism, and by means of this the vibrations of our minds are directed on your own. Your hand being so placed serves as a kind of magnet and reservoir in one, and helps us. But we will not continue this, but get on to something we can better make clear to you.

In our life in the Summerland we endeavor to help both those who come over to us and also their friends still on earth.

Indeed, the two phases of service are inseparable, for those who pass over here are often much distressed, and so unable to progress until they know that those they have left behind are being helped from this side. So we often make excursions to the earth plane for this reason.

Last week we received a woman who had left a husband and three small children, and she begged to be allowed to go and see how they were managing at home. She was so anxious that at last we took her, and arrived at evening time just as they were all sitting down to supper. The man had just come in from work and he was going to have his meal before putting them to bed. They were two girls, aged about seven and five, and a little boy of two. They all sat round the table in the kitchen, a fairly comfortable room, and the father told the eldest girl to say grace. This is what she said, "God provide for us all, and mother, for Christ's sake. Amen."

The woman went round to the little one, and laid her hand on her hair and spoke to her, but could not make her hear. She was troubled at this, but we bade her wait and watch. By and by the girl spoke, after a long silence, during which she and her father had been thinking of the one who had passed away, and she said, "Dad, do you think mammy knows about us now, and Auntie Lizzie?"

"I don't know," he replied, "but I think she does, because I have felt very miserable the last few days, as if she was worrying about something; and it might be Auntie Lizzie."

"Well," said the child, "then don't let us go. Mrs— will look after baby, and I can help when I come home from school, and we shan't have to go then."

"Don't you want to go?" he said.

"I don't," answered the child. "Baby and Sissie would go, but I don't want to."

Well, I'll think about it," he said. "So don't worry. I dare say we shall manage all right."

"And mother will help, and the angels," persisted the little girl, "because she can speak to them now, and they will help if she asks them."

Now, the father said nothing more; but we could see his mind, and read in it the thought that if this little child had such faith, he ought to have as much at least, and by and by he made up his mind to try the thing and see how it would work out. For the parting with his children was not to his mind, and he was very glad to find an excuse to keep them.

I cannot say that the mother obtained much comfort from her visit. But on our way back we told her that the faith of that child, if it was reinforced by that of the father, would form a powerful medium of help, or we were much mistaken.

On our return we reported all to our Mother Angel, and immediately measures were taken to ensure that the family should not be broken up, and the mother was bidden to strive to progress in order that she should be able to help also. Then a change came over her. She set to work in real earnest, and will soon be allowed to join parties on their journeys earthward now and then, and to add her little mite to their stronger service.

But now we must leave that case for a time and tell you of another. A man came to our colony a short time ago who also had lately passed over. He was wandering about seeking somewhere to his mind, and thought this settlement looked something like what he wanted. You must not think he was alone. There accompanied him, but at a distance, a watcher who was ready to help when required. The man was one of those curious mixtures we sometimes get. There was considerable goodness and light in him, but that could not be used for furthering his development on account of its being checked and held in ward by other traits which he could not be brought to rearrange.

He was met on a path some distance away from the hill where our Home is by one of the workers in another Home, and the latter stopped and questioned him, for he noticed a strange and perplexed look in his face. When he stopped he received a signal from the guardian, who was some distance away, and was informed of the problem, and so, all instantaneously, was equipped to deal with it. He spoke kindly, and the following conversation ensued:

A. You seem to be not very familiar with this region. Can I help you in any way?

B. *I don't think so, although it is kind of you to offer to do so.*

A. Your difficulty is one which we might deal with here, but not so thoroughly as we would like to do.

B. *I am afraid you don't know what that difficulty is.*

A. Well, partly, I think. You are perplexed because you have not met any of your friends here, and wonder why.

B. *That is so, certainly.*

A. But they have met you.

B. *I have not seen them; and I have been wondering where I could find them. It seems so strange. I always thought that our friends were the first to meet us when we pass over, and I cannot understand it at all.*

A. But they did meet you.

B. *I didn't see any one I knew.*

A. That is quite correct. They met you and you did not know them—would not know them.

B. *I don't understand.*

A. What I mean is this. When you came over here you were immediately taken charge of by your friends. But your heart, good in some respects and even enlightened, was hard and blindly obstinate in others. And this is the reason you did not recognize their presence.

The other looked long and doubtfully at his companion, and at last stammered out a question.

B. *What is wrong with me, then? Everybody I meet is kind and happy, and yet I don't seem to be able to join any party, or to find my own proper place. What is wrong with me?*

A. The first thing you must learn is that your opinions may not be correct. I'll tell you one which is at fault, to begin with. This world is not, as you are trying to imagine it, a place where people are all that is good or all that is evil. They are much as they are on earth. Another thing is this: your wife, who came over here some years ago, is in a higher sphere than the one in which you will be placed when you have at length got the correct perspective of things. She was not mentally your equal in the earth life, and is not so now. But you are on a lower plane than she is, on general lines and all things considered. That is the second thing you have to accept, and accept ex animo. You do not accept it, as I can see by your face. You will have to do so before you can advance. When you have done so, then you will probably be enabled to communicate with her. At present that is not possible.

The man's eyes became dimmed with tears, but he smiled rather sweetly and sadly as he quoted, "Sir, I perceive that you are a prophet."

A. Quite right; and that brings me to the third thing you will have to accept; and that is this. There is one watching over you always, always at hand to help you. He is a prophet, or rather a seer, like me; and it was he who put that saying into your mind to repeat to me.

Now the stranger's face became grave and thoughtful. He was trying to get the right and true view of things. He, asked, "Is it vanity, then, that is my fault?"

A. Yes; but vanity of a rather difficult kind. In many things you are sweet and humble, and not without love, which is the greatest power of all. But there is a certain hardness in your mind rather than in your heart, which must be softened. You have got into a mental rut, and must get out of it and look farther afield, or you will go about like a blind man who can see—a contradiction and a paradox. There are some things you see clearly enough, and to others you are totally oblivious. Learn that to change your opinions in the face of evidence is not weakness or backsliding, but is the sign of an honest mind. I tell you this, further; had your heart been as hard as your mind you would not be wandering here in the fields of God's sunshine, but in darker regions yonder beyond those hills—far beyond them. Now I have explained, as well as I am able, your rather perplexing case, friend. The rest is for another to do.

B. *Who?*

A. The one I have already told you of; the one who has you in charge.

B. *Where is he?*

A. One minute, and he will be here.

The message was sent, and the guardian stood beside his charge, who, however, was unable to see him.

A. Well, he is here. Tell him what you want.

B. looked full of doubt and anxiety, and then said, "Tell me, my friend, if he is here why I cannot see him."

A. Because in that phase of your mind's activity you are blind. That is the first thing you have to realize. Do you believe me when I say you are, in some directions, blind.

B. *I can see very well, and the things I see are fairly plain, and the country quite natural and beautiful. I am not blind in that respect. But I am beginning to think there may be other things just as real which I cannot see, but shall see someday perhaps, but—*

A. Now, stop there, and leave the "but" alone. And now look, as I take your guide by the hand.

He then took the watching guide's right hand in his own, telling B. to look intently, and tell him if he saw anything. He could not be certain, however. He thought he saw some kind of transparent form which might or might not be real, but was by no means sure.

A. Then take his hand in yours. Take it from me.

The man held out his hand and took that of his guide from the hand of A., and burst into tears.

Had he not progressed so far as to make that action, he would not have seen his guide, nor have been able to feel his touch. The fact that he put out his hand at the command of A. showed that he had progressed during their conversation, and he immediately received his reward. The other held his hand in a firm grasp for some time, and all the while B. saw him and felt him more and more clearly. Then A. left them together. Soon B. would be able to hear, as well as see, his guardian, and no doubt he will go on now from strength to strength.

This will show you what difficult cases we sometimes have to deal with. Light and gross darkness, humility and hard, obstinate pride all mixed up together, and hard to separate or to treat successfully. But such problems are interesting, and, when mastered, give great joy to the workers.

Ruby[1] sends her love and this message to her parents, "Believe me, my darlings, the doing of a good and kind action, and the thinking and speaking of kind words by those we love on earth are immediately telegraphed here, and we use them to adorn our rooms, as Rene [the Vicar's daughter—*Ed.*] adorns her rooms with your flowers. God bless you, dear lad. Goodnight.

* * *

Note: With this message the communication from Mr. Vale Owen's mother ceased and the messages were continued by a spirit entity named Zabdiel. These are given in a further volume of *The Life Beyond the Veil* entitled "The Highlands of Heaven."—H.W.E.

---

[1] This message from Ruby seems to have reference to boxes of flowers we had been sending to our daughter [Rene], who was away at school.—G.V.O.

6

Astriel's Messages

Tuesday, October, 7, 1913.

BY the aid of others, who are with us now for the first time, we are going to try to give you a little instruction in the verities of the Faith as they appear to us on this side the Veil.

In regard to those truths which men have embodied in the Creeds we have little to say, for so much has been said already that, until much has been unsaid once again, men are ill-prepared to receive what we should have to say. We, therefore, prefer, for the present time, to leave you to look out for yourselves such truths as you find there, merely observing, as in passing, that all the articles are true if rightly interpreted.

We would pass on, therefore, to speak of things of which men do not consider so much at the present time. These will engage their attention the more when they have finished their wrangling over aspects of the truth which, after all, are aspects merely, and not the fundamental truth itself. If they would endeavor to view things in a right proportion, then many of those matters which absorb so much of their time would stand to them as among the lesser things which matter little, and they would then be the better able to devote their attention to the deeper truths which are established here as well as with you on earth.

One thing it may be well to notice is the efficacy of prayer and meditation. You have already received some instruction on this subject, and we would add to it.

Prayer is not merely the asking for something you wish to attain. It is much more than that, and, because it is so, it should receive more careful consideration than it has yet received. What you have to do in order to make prayer a power is to cast aside the temporal and fix your mind and spirit on the eternal. When you do that you find that many items you would have included in your prayer drop out from the very incongruity of their presence, and the greater and wider issues become to you the focus of your creative powers. For prayer is really creative, as the exercise of the will, as seen in our Lord's miracles, such as the feeding of the five thousand. And when prayer is offered with this conviction, then the object is created, and the prayer is answered—that is, the objective answers to the subjective in such a way that an actual creation has taken place.

This does not happen when the prayer is wrongly directed. Then the projection of the will glances off at a tangent, and the effect is only proportionate to the scattered rays by which the objective is touched. Also, when the prayer is mixed with motives unworthy it is proportionately weakened, and also meets with opposing or regulating wills on this side, as the case may require; and so the effect is not attained as desired.

Now, all this may sound rather vague, but it is by no means vague to us. For you must know that there are appointed guardians of prayer here whose duty it is to analyze and sift prayers offered by those on earth, and separate them into divisions and departments, and pass them on to be examined by others, and dealt with according to their merit and power.

In order that this may be done perfectly, it is necessary that we study the vibrations of prayer as your scientists study the vibrations of sound and light. As they are able to analyze and separate and classify the rays of light, so are we able to deal with your prayers. And as there are light rays with which they are confessedly unable to deal, so many prayers present to us those deeper tones which are beyond the range of our study and knowledge. These we pass on to those of higher grade, to be dealt with in their greater wisdom. And do not think that these latter are always found among the prayers of the wise. They are frequently found in the prayers of children, whose petitions and sighs are as carefully considered here as those of nations.

"Thy prayers and thine alms are come up for a memorial before God." You will remember these words spoken by the Angel to Cornelius. They are often passed over without being understood as the literal description of those prayers and alms as they appeared to that Angel, and were passed on, probably by himself and his fellow workers, into the higher realms. It is as if he had said, "Your prayers and alms came before my own committee, and were duly considered on their merits. We passed them as worthy, and have received notification from those Officers above us that they are of exceptional merit, and require a special treatment. Therefore I have been commissioned to come to you." We are trying to put the case as emphatically as we can in your language of official business in order to help you to understand as much as you may be able of the conditions here obtaining.

If you will examine other instances of prayer in the Bible in the light of the above, you may get some glimpses of the reality as seen by us here in our own land. And what applies to prayer also may be applied to the exercise of the will in directions not so legitimate. Hate and impurity and greed and other sins of the spirit and mind take on here a solidity which is not seen or realized in your sphere; and these also are dealt with according to their merits. And, alas, those who say that Angels cannot grieve, know little of our love for our brethren still battling on earth. Could they see us dealing with some of these misusings of the Father's great gift they would probably love us more and exalt us less.

Now we will leave you to consider this matter further for yourself, if you think it worthwhile, and, as we see you are willing to continue somewhat, will touch on another matter which may be both of interest and of help to you.

* * *

On the top of your church tower there is a weather-vane in the form of a cock. You will call to mind that you yourself decided the form that this should take. Is not that so?

I had entirely forgotten it until you called it to mind. You are quite correct, however. The architect asked me about it, and I hesitated between a fish and a cock, and eventually decided on the latter. I am wondering, however, whatever you have to say of it.

No doubt. You see, these things are trifles to you; but there are few things which are trifles to us. Now, the fact that the likeness of a cock stands above your tower is the direct consequence of certain activities which took place in your mind five years ago. That is a case of creation. Many would smile at this, but we do not mind that, for we, too, are able to smile, and some of our smiles would perplex you, I assure you.

The meaning you had in your mind when your apparently not very important decision was made was that all might be reminded that St. Peter denied his Lord. I suppose you meant it as a caution against the repetition of such offence today. But you did not realize that that apparently trivial decision was registered here and dealt with quite seriously.

I must tell you that the building of a new church is an event which is the cause of much activity here. There are officers to be appointed to attend the services and guard the building, and a whole host of ministering spirits to be allotted to the different departments of duty in connection with a new place of worship. Your clairvoyant friends have seen some of these already, but only a very few comparatively. Every detail is considered, not only in respect of the character of the minister and congregation and choir and so on; and the best among us, that is, the most suitable, chosen to help you according to the traits we observe; not only these things but the structure and all structural details are considered minutely, especially where symbolism enters in, for that has an importance not realized among you as it is with us. So it came about that the weather vane was also considered, and I have chosen that because of its seeming triviality in order to show you that nothing is missed.

It was decided that, as the cock had been chosen in preference to other symbols, we would answer that choice, according to our custom, by giving to the church some appropriate offering in response. And that offering was the church bell, for which a choir-boy collected the money. You had no bell when first your church was consecrated. The bird stood aloft, but could not utter his warning as his original had done to St. Peter. And so we gave him voice, and your bell today gives tongue—as it did tonight at evensong. And we are glad to see that he who chose the one makes the other speak day by day, for that is surely fitting.

Do you think we have our fancies here? Well, perhaps that is so; and yet you were thankful for that bell, were you not, good friend?

We were indeed. And I thank you for your kind message. Might I know who you are, if you please?

We are spiritual ministers from a sphere where your own friends and mother have visited from time to time, and she told us of you and said how much she would like us to know you more nearly and, if possible, to give you some message. She and her friends come to us for instruction. Speaking for my own degree, some members of which are here with me, I would say that we have been glad to come and to know you. But we knew you and your church before your mother told us.

Thank you, sir, for your kindness. Would it be permissible for me to ask your own name?

Permission certainly, but I fear you would not know it, nor understand it.

Nevertheless, sir, tell me, if you will.

Astriel, who leaves you with his blessing.+[1]

Thursday, October 9, 1913

We have come again at the request of your mother, and are glad to have this one more opportunity of speaking to you from this side. Never imagine that we are troubled to come to the earth sphere, for although it does mean an experience of less brightness in environment than is our usual lot, yet the privilege counterbalances that and more.

Perhaps if we endeavor to enlighten you on the chemistry of the heavenly bodies it may be both interesting and helpful to you. We do not mean the physical aspect of the science, as understood by modern astronomical scientists, but the deeper study of their constitution.

Every star, as you know, is itself a center of a system which comprises in itself not only the planets in revolution round the star, but also the particles of matter which suffuse that system, but are too sublimated to be cognized by any system of chemistry which is possible to those who dwell in physical bodies, and in their research are compelled to use both material instruments and material brains. These particles are

---

[1] Astriel always concluded his communications with the sign of the cross.— H.W.E.

between the purely material and spiritual, and indeed may be used both in the physical and the spiritual economies. For the two are merely two of many phases of one progressive economy, and act and react each on the other, like a sun and his planet.

Gravitation is applicable to these particles also on both sides, and it is by means of this force—as we will call it, as being a name you know, and also a very little understand—that we cohere these particles together and are able, from time to time, so to clothe our spiritual bodies as to become visible to the photographic plate, and sometimes to the human eye. But we do more than this, and over a wider range. Were it not for these particles all space would be dark; that is, no light would be able to be transmitted from planet or sun or star to the earth; for it is because of the reflection and refraction of these that the rays are visible. Not that they are transmitted, for their transmission and passage depend on other elements of which we will now say no more than this: It is not the rays of light, nor is it the so-called light-waves which are visible to the human eye, but their action on these minute particles which, on the impact of these rays, become visible as waves.

Your scientists have much to learn yet on this subject, and it is not our business to impart much which men can learn by the powers they possess. If we did so then the benefit derived from your earth schooling would be materially lessened, and that is why we are careful to give you just so much as will help you onward without neutralizing the good effect of individual and collective endeavor. Bear this in mind, and it will then perhaps be seen to have a bearing on whatever we deem it advisable to explain to you in such messages as these.

The stars, then, send forth their light. But in order to send it forth they first must possess it themselves. And as they are not self-constituted personalities, in order that they may have it they must be given it. Who does this, and how is it done?

Now, of course, it is easy to answer "God, for He is the Source of everything." That is true enough, but, as you know, He employs His ministers, and these are without number, and each unit with an allotted task.

The stars receive their power of transmitting light from the presence of myriads of spiritual beings about them, all ordered and regulated in their spheres, and all working in conjunction. These have the stars in their charge, and it is from them that the energy proceeds which enables the star to do its appointed work.

What we want you to understand is that there is no such thing as blind or unconscious force in all God's Kingdom of Creation. Not a ray of light, not an impulse of heat, not an electrical wave proceeds from your sun, or any other star, but is the effect of a cause, and that cause is a conscious cause; it is the Will of some conscious being energizing in a certain and positive direction. These beings are of many grades and many species. They are not all of the same order, nor all of the same form. But their work is controlled by those above them, and these are controlled by powers of higher grade and sublimity still.

And so these great balls of matter, whether gaseous or liquid or solid, whether star or comet or planet, are all held together, and their forces energized and given effect not by the operation of some mechanical law, but by conscious live beings at the back of, and working through, those laws. We use the word "conscious" in preference of "intelligent," because the latter term would not accurately describe all the ministers of the Creator. As you understand the word, indeed, it would describe only a very limited number. And it may surprise you to know that those to whom you would apply the term are those which stand between the lower and the higher. For while the lower workers are not really beings of intelligence, the higher are more sublime than that term would imply.

Between the two there are spheres of beings who would bear describing as intelligent beings. Mark well that I am not speaking now in the terms we should use here, and which you will use when you come over here and have studied the conditions somewhat. I am using earth language, and endeavoring to put the matter from your point of view.

Now you will, from what we have already written, be able to see how intimate is the relationship between spirit and matter, and when the other evening we spoke of your own church building and the allotting of guardians and workers, among other things, for the care of the material edifice, we were only telling you of the same principle at work on a minute scale. Nevertheless it is the same principle exactly. The scheme which provides for the upkeep of all those millions of suns and of their planets took note also of the rearrangement of certain congeries of atoms—some in the form of stone, others wood or brick—which resulted in that new entity which you call a church. These are held together, each atom in its place, by the outflowing power of will. They are not placed there and left solitary. Were this done the building would soon crumble away and fall to pieces.

And now, in the light of what we have written, think of what people call "the difference of feeling" on entering a church, or a theatre, or a dwelling house, or any building. Each has its own suitable emanations, and these are in consequence of this same principle at work which we have tried to describe. It is spirit speaking to spirit—the spirits of the discarnate workers speaking, through the medium of the material particles and their arrangement and purpose, to the spirits of those who enter that place.

You grow tired, and we find it hard to impress you, so, with our blessing, we will leave you now, and, if you will, we shall come again. God be with you and your dear ones and your people, in all things and all days.

ASTRIEL+

Thursday, October 16, 1913.

Should we perchance say aught that may seem strange and unreal of this our life in the spiritual spheres you will keep in mind that here are powers and conditions which on earth are hidden from the outer knowledge of men. These powers are not altogether absent from your environment, but they are mostly deeper than the physical brain can bear to penetrate. They may be sensed or felt to a degree by the more spiritually developed—no more than this. For those who spiritually rise above the general level do touch the borders of those spheres which at present are supernormal to the average man. And no amount of mental capacity or knowledge can achieve this exaltation of spirit, for these things are spiritually discerned, and only thus.

We who are present with you this evening have come at the invitation of your mother once again to speak to you of our work and life as it is presented to us, and as we are privileged to know it. This so far as we are able. For the rest, we have told you of our limitations in transmission of such knowledge which, for this reason, must of necessity be incomplete.

Are you Astriel?

Astriel and other friends.

First, my brother, we give you greeting of love and peace in our common Savior and Lord. He is here to us what He is there to you. But we understand now much which was not clear to us when we walked amidst the shadows on the earth. And this we would say with all solemnity: let those who today amongst you are searching into the meaning of His Divinity, and the relation of that to His Humanity, do so fearlessly and reverently. For such are guided more than they know from these realms. And be it always in the mind of those who are sincere that they can do no irreverence to Him Who Himself is Truth in inquiring what the Truth is as He revealed it.

Nevertheless, friend, we tell you, with this same fearlessness, and with great reverence also, that what goes by the name of Orthodoxy among Christians in the Church on earth is not a fair and true presentation, in many ways, of the Truth as we have come to know it here. Also we see among you too much unreadiness to go forward, and lack of courage and faith in the providence of God Who will, if men will follow, lead them more and more into the light, the radiant, glowing light, as it envelops those who are brave, to show them the right and holy way towards His Throne. Let such remember that that Throne shall be shared only by the brave who are strong to overcome, and these are they who are valiant to do and dare, and pay the price at the hands of those their fellows who are less courageous and less enlightened.

Now we continue our instruction, and you will accept it so far as you can. What you do not feel able to receive leave, and perhaps, as you proceed on your way, you will find it fall into place little by little until you understand it all.

We were telling you formerly about the heavenly bodies and their correlation to each other. Now we will tell you somewhat of their creation and of the aspect they wear to us as viewed on their spiritual side. For you will understand that every star and planet, and every thing material, has its spiritual counterpart. You do understand this, we know, and are going to build what we now have to say on that knowledge.

The heavenly bodies are the expression in matter of ideas originating among those high in the Heavenly Spheres of Creative Power. They are all and each the effect of thoughts and impulses proceeding from those spheres. When a world is in process of creation those High Beings are constantly energizing, and projecting into the forming matter their spiritual influence and, so to speak, character. Thus, although the planets of your system are all conformable to one great scheme of unity, they are diverse in their individual characteristics. These characteristics answer to the characters of the Great Lords in Whose charge they severally are. Astronomers are correct when they say that certain of the elements which go to form the earth are found in, say, Mars and Jupiter, and in the Sun itself. But they would err if they should say that they are found in the same proportion, or in similar combination. Every planet differs in these things from its fellow, but all conform to the one broader scheme which governs them as a system. What is here said of the units which go to make up the Solar system may be applied to the wider range of things. Considering the Solar realm as a unit, it is not identical, either in composition of elements or in planetary constitution, with other systems. Each differs from its fellow also.

Now, we have explained the reason of this. It issues in the individual mind of the Chief Lord of the particular system. Under him are other great Lords who work in unison with his one governing idea. But these also have freedom in those things which are under their charge, and so on downward to the minute things of creation—the flowers and trees and animals and the formation of the face of the planet. It is on account of this latitude in creation and control that you have such diversity in detail; and because of the limit of restriction to the exercise of that free individuality that you have the unity which you find interpenetrating every department and sub-department of creation.

Under these supervisors there are also myriads of lesser ministers of different grades downward until some of the lowest orders may scarcely be termed persons, for they merge into the lower species of life which you might term sensory, as distinguishing them from those who, like ourselves, are possessed not only of intelligence, but also of that independence in judgment which we know as freewill.

Are you speaking of fairies, pixies, and elementals generally, of which some writers tell us?

Yes, these are real things, and mostly benevolent; but they are far below the human sphere, and therefore are less known than the higher grades of ministry, such as the spirits of men, and those who have attained to angelic degree.

Now, a little more about the earth itself. Geologists tell how some of the rocks are alluvial and others igneous in formation, and so on. But if you will carefully examine some of these you will find that they give off a certain vapor, or one might almost say magnetic influence. That is the effect of the original inspiration into them by those who formed them originally. And these characteristics are worthy of deeper study than they have hitherto received. The chemical composition has been, more or less, ascertained. But the more subtle influences proceeding from the ever-vibrating particles has been neglected. Yet when it is remembered that no piece of rock or stone is still, but that all its particles are in movement orderly and constant, it is only one step onward then to realize that, in order that this movement be maintained, there must be present some great force and, at the back of that force, a personality of which it is the expression.

This is true, and the baleful influence which some gems do exercise on those whose sentiments towards them are not governed aright, is an evidence of this. On the other hand, you have heard of lucky-stones, which is a phrase which shows some rather vague notion of the underlying truth. Eliminate all idea of chance from these matters, and substitute an orderly system of cause and effect, and remember the consequence of ignorance in traversing all natural law, and you will see that there may be something in what we have been trying to explain.

For the sake of emphasis we have limited our consideration to the mineral creation, but the same truth may be adapted to the vegetable and animal kingdoms also. Of this we will not speak tonight. What we have said has been said with the object of showing that there is a field for those who have a scientific turn of mind, and who are not afraid to go farther afield than scientists have hitherto allowed themselves to go.

The whole may be summed up in a few words, if which be accepted then the conclusion we have intimated must, of necessity, be accepted too. The whole material creation is nothing in itself and by itself. It is but the expression, on a lower plane, of personalities on higher planes, the effect of which their wills are the causes. As a man leaves the imprint of his character on his work day by day, so these great Creative Lords and their ministers have left the impress of their personality on these material phenomena.

Nothing is still, all moves continuously. This movement is controlled and orderly, and that is a warrant of the constant energizing of personality. As the lower grades of service are dependent on those higher Lords for their existence and continuance, so are these latter to those of grade more sublime, as these are to the One Supreme Energy, the Self-Existent One, Whose Will is our life, and Whose Wisdom is more wonderful than we can express in words or in thoughts. To Whom be reverence done from all who are in Him, and from us who, in the Christ our Lord and Savior, dwell in Him, and He is us. Amen.+

Friday, October 24, 1913.

We have come tonight with our friends, your mother and her companions, at their invitation once again, in order to speak to you some message of friendly help and counsel. And in thinking over what would most interest you, we concluded that if we were to say something to you of those powers which watch over the world, we might, perchance, be able to lead you, and those who are willing to follow with you, a little onward towards the great body of knowledge which awaits your searching when you have laid aside those trammels of the earth life, and stand free to progress into the greater glories of the realm of spirit.

Who writes this, please?

We are they who came before, friend; Astriel, as you know me, and my fellow-workers of the Tenth Sphere of progress. Shall we proceed, then?

If you please; and I thank you for your courtesy in coming down here into this dim realm, as it must seem to you.

You say "coming down here," and that fairly well expresses the condition of things from your point of view. Yet not altogether, nor perfectly. For if the planet on which you live your present life is dependent in space, then "up" and "down" are terms which must be very restricted in their meaning. You already have noted this in your writing or, rather, you were impressed to note it.

When we said "the powers which watch over the world," we did not, of course, mean to localize these powers on one side of this planet, but to imply the all-enveloping watch which the heavenly powers keep about the sphere which is called Earth. These powers are resident in zones of which the Earth itself is the center, and they lie in concentric circles around it. The inferior zones are those near the planet's surface, and progress in power and glory as the distance is increased. But yet, space must be enlarged in meaning when applied to these spheres; for distance has not the same obstructive sense to us as it has to you.

For instance, when I am in the tenth of these zones, my cognizance is limited, more or less, by that Tenth zone as to its outer or superior boundary. I may, on occasion and by permission, visit the Eleventh zone, or even go higher; but residence in those higher zones is not permitted me. On the other hand, the zones inferior to the Tenth are not impossible to me; for the zone in which I dwell, being a sphere, includes within itself, even geometrically considered, all the nine inferior spheres. So that we may, for the sake of clarity of understanding, put it thus: The Earth is the center about which many spheres are, and is enclosed in all those spheres. And the residents in the earth life are potentially in touch with all those spheres, and actually so in ratio to their altitude spiritually considered—spiritually, because these spheres are spiritual and not material.

Even the material Sphere of Earth is only so phenomenally, for it is a manifestation in matter of all these zones of spiritual power which envelop it; and of others, too, of other degree which interpenetrate it. Leave these latter aside, for the present at least, and consider the matter as we have limned it.

You will now have some idea of what aspiration and prayer and worship mean. They are the means of communion with the Creator and His High and Holy Ones Who (to put it in a way which you will understand) dwell in the highest, or outermost, of these spheres, and include within Himself and These all the zones within that highest Zone or Sphere.

And so the Earth is enveloped by, and included in and affected by the spiritual powers, of varying degree and kind, entrusted by the Creator-God to all these ministers of all these spheres which are around it.

But as you progress outward you come into a more complicated state of affairs. For not the Earth only but every planet in this Solar system has its like complement of spiritual zones or spheres. So, as you go farther and farther from the Earth, you come to a realm where the spheres of Earth and the nearest planet interweave with each other. As every planet is served with like attendance, so the complication is multiplied, and you will begin to see that the study of these spheres is not so simple as some good people among you evidently think it to be, who demand from us information as to the meaning of this thing.

Draw a diagram of the Solar system, with the Sun at its center, and the planets roughly in their respective places around him. Then begin with Earth and encircle him with, say, a hundred circles. Do the same with Jupiter, Mars, Venus and the others, and treat the Sun in like manner; and you will have a faint idea of our work and its absorbing interest, but profound depths of meaning, who include in our studies that of the Spheres of God.

Nor have we yet reached the limit of our problem. For what applies to the Solar system must be applied also to that of every other star and its planets. Then each system having been separately considered, each and all must be studied in their correlation to the others. Think of it a while and you will acknowledge, I think, that there will be no lack of employment for your mental energies when you come over here.

Now, we are sometimes asked how many spheres there be. Well, having explained what we have above, I do not apprehend that we shall be asked that question by you. Did you ask it, we, who are only of the Tenth of these zones, would perforce have to answer, We do not know, and much doubt whether our answer to you would differ were you to put that question a million million of eons hence, and we having progressed all the while.

And now, friend and fellow spirit, we wish to ask you to consider one other aspect of this matter. We have said that these spheres are spheres of spiritual power. Now, two worlds affect each the other by means of that which your scientists name gravitation. Also, two spheres of spiritual power, coming into contact, cannot fail to act and counteract each on the other. Referring to your mental diagram of the Solar system you will see that Earth is, of necessity, acted on by a large number of spheres, and that the greater number of these are they which are those of the Sun and other planets.

Yes, friend, there is, after all, something in the astrological idea, and perhaps your scientists do well to give it a wide berth, for it may not be much understood by, and would probably be fraught with danger to, such as they who do not understand that spiritual power is spiritual power. It is real and tremendous, and every sphere of all these is reinforced or modified by the others. The study of these things should be approached with the utmost reverence and prayer, for these are realms where Angels of high estate go softly, and we of lesser estate look on and wonder after the Sublimity of that Being Who unifies all this in Himself, and Who has no Name that can be transmitted to us who only can reach out after Him a little way and then our arm is shortened; who only can see a little way and then the light beyond is darkness by reason of its intensity.

But we testify to you, friend, and those who will think reverently of things they cannot understand, that if wonder gives us pause time and again as we proceed, yet never do we lose that sense of a Presence Whose breathing is of Love, and Whose leading is as gentle as a mother's leading of her little child. So we, as you do, take His hand and do not fear; and the music of the Spheres is around us as we go on from glory to the glory beyond. Come this way ever, our brother in Him. Never faint nor weary of the road, for the mists are thinning as you proceed, and the light strengthens into the further light which issues onward into the unknown, but never feared, so we tread gently and humbly, as little children do, amid the glories of the planets and the heavens of suns and spheres, and of the Love of God.

Friend and brother, we say goodnight to you, and thank you for enabling us in this our service. May it be of some help, however little or much, to few or many seeking after the truth. Goodnight once more, and be assured of our help in blessing.+

Saturday, October 25, 1918.

We will, if it is to your mind, continue our message of yesterday in regard to those spheres of power which affect the earth.

Still concerning the Solar system, we say that, on considering what we have already said, you will see that we have not yet mentioned all the complications which enter into the study of these spheres. For not alone do the concentric circles of zones about all the planets and the sun commingle with all the rest, but also the relative combination is continually changing with the changing positions of these bodies and their consequent proximity to, or distance from, one another. So that it is quite literally correct to say that during no two seconds of time is the influence from them impinging on the surface of the earth the same.

Nor is any combination of their influences identical in its effect or intensity all over the earth at the same time, but differs in different localities. There must further be taken into our calculations the stream of radiation coming to this Solar system from the systems of the other stars. All these things have to be reckoned in, for bear still in mind that we are speaking of zones and spheres of spiritual beings whose powers are energizing continuously, and whose wakefulness never fails.

This, then, is a rough outline of the conditions which obtain among the planetary systems whose outer manifestation is visible to the eye and telescope of the astronomer. But what is thus observed is but a very little mite when compared with the whole. It is but as a small shower of spray which besprinkles the voyager, as he stands in the prow of the vessel, and scatters itself in globules of mist around him. He sees the miniature globes of water where they float reflecting the light around them, and says they are innumerable. But if this be so, then what of the ocean itself from whence they came, and of which they are, and to which they will return?

As that small cloud of spray-mist is to the ocean, so is the star-bemisted heaven, as seen from the surface of the earth, to the whole. And as the depths of the ocean are to the eye of him who gazes over the vessel's side, so are the depths of space and all that it holds to the human intelligence.

Now let us think a little further afield. Space itself is but a term used to describe the indescribable. It is, therefore, without definite meaning. One of your poets began a poem on space and gave it up in despair. Wisely, for had he intended to do adequate justice to the theme he would have been compelled to continue that poem for ever.

For what is space, and where are the boundaries of it set? Is it illimitable? If so it has no center. Where, then, is God His Dwelling Place? He is said to be at the Center of all Creation. But what is Creation? A creation which has relation to space, or a creation which is invisible?

Now it is useless, for all practical purposes, to speculate on things we do not understand. It is well to feel after these things sometimes in order that we may discover our own limitations. This done, let us now speak of such things as we, in a measure, are able to understand.

All these zones of which we have spoken are inhabited by beings according to their degree, who progress from one sphere to a higher as they accumulate knowledge within themselves. You will see from what we already have written that, as we advance from the lowest to the higher spheres, there comes a region of spheres which are interplanetary, inasmuch as they embrace within their circumference more planets than one. Still advancing, we come to a state where the spheres are of such a diameter that they are interstellar; that is, they embrace within their circumference not only more planets than one, but more stars, or suns, than one. All these are filled with beings, according to their degree of sublimity, of holiness and of power, whose influence extends to all, both spiritual and material, within the sphere to which they have attained. We have but advanced, you see, from planet to star, and from star to stars in their grouping. Beyond are spheres more awful still and more tremendous. But of these we in this Tenth Sphere know but little indeed, and nothing certain.

But you will be able faintly to realize, by a large effort of your imaginative powers, the meaning we had in mind when we wrote last evening of Him Whose Name is to us unknown and unknowable. So, when you worship the Creator, you have, I suppose, no very definite idea of the Order of Creator you intend. It is easy to say you mean the Creator of all. But what do you mean by all?

Now, know this—for this much, at least, we have progressed to know—that you do right to worship the Creator and Father of all, whatever you mean if you mean anything definite by that very inclusive word. Still, your worship passes first into the lower spheres, and through them to the higher, and some worship goes farther and into higher spheres than other worship does, according to its worth and inherent power. And some goes very far indeed. Far above us is the Christ Sphere of glorious intensity of light and awful beauty. Your worship, then, proceeds, to the Father through Him, that is, through the One Who came to earth and manifested the Christ to men.

Now, for all that all we have said is true, yet it is truth expressed quite inadequately by reason of the limitations both of us who are speaking to you, and of your own earth state. For you will understand that when we speak of, proceeding through these spheres, we are really using phrasing of a local character, as of a journey from one locality through another to a third. And I fear, friend, that I can do little more at this present time than remind you that these states of which we have been thinking are rather better expressed as spheres than as zones. For, I would repeat, the higher include within themselves all the lower, and he who moves in any of them is present in all those inferior to his own. For which reason it is not without some degree of truth that we speak of Him Who is all, and in all, and throughout all; and of the Omnipresence of God.

Now, we feel that we have labored this theme overlong and should cease further endeavor to put into the little wineglass of earth knowledge and wisdom to understand the vintage of these wide vineyards of the heavens. One thing is enough to know for you and us: The Husbandman and the Vinedresser, both, are sure in their power and in their wisdom to deal with us. Toward them is our journey set, and ours is to do the thing we find to hand, to do it thoroughly and well, and finish it quite, and then to reach out for the task set next in order. When that is finished well, then another will be awaiting us. We shall never find that we have reached the end, I think. For as one progresses one comes to feel the possibility more and more of a truth beneath those words "for evermore," "world without end." But we doubt if you do yet, friend, and we say this with courtesy.

And now we bless you, and leave you in the hope we may come again, for it is well, and there is sweetness in it, to bend to whisper into willing ears of some of the minor glories of our Heavenly Realms. Be sure, friend—and tell others who will hear it—that this life which awaits you is not a mere bodiless dream in a twilight region somewhere beyond the boundary of the real and actual. No; it is strenuous and intense, this life of ours. It is filled with service and endeavors crowned, one after another, with success; of patient pressing onward, and of indomitable wills attuned each to other in comrade service for the Lord of Love, Whose Life we sense and inspire, but Whom we do not see, and Whose Home is too sublime for us to know.

Onward we press, and often take the hand of one a little behind us, and with the other seize the skirt of one a little on before. And so we go, my brother; yes, and so do you, and others working with you. And if we are a little way on before, well, there are many who lag behind. Take their hand in your own, and gently, remembering your own comparative frailty, and if the task be too heavy for you, do not loose that hand you hold, but reach the other out—and here is mine and that of many another with us. You shall not fail, so you keep your own vision and your life both bright and pure. Nay, rather shall that Vision grow more glorious, for is it not written, friend, that such as are pure in heart shall see GOD?

Friday, October 31, 1913.

They who say that we come to earth in order to help are correct. But they who hope that we shall help to such a degree that their own endeavors will be unnecessary are in error. It is not permitted to us so to enable you as to lessen the value of earth's schooling. And although this seems so reasonable as to be almost of the nature of a truism, yet many there are who look to us to do what only they themselves can do; and that in no ordinary measure, but almost, as it were, miraculously.

Who is writing, please?

We are with your mother—Astriel and friends.

Thank you. I thought the wording was not quite like that of my mother and her companions.

No, I suppose it is not. Partly, of course, because we are of different character, different sphere, and also different sex, which is not without its peculiar characteristics here as with you. And partly, also, because we are of a different earth period from your mother and her friends.

Do you mean you lived on earth some considerable time ago?

Yes, friend, in England, when George the first was king, and some of us earlier still.

About yourself, Astriel—who, I suppose, are the leader of your band—can you kindly tell me anything?

Certainly. But you do not realize that it is more confusing to give these earth details than it might seem to you. I will say what I can, however. I lived in Warwick, and was a teacher in a school there headmaster. I cannot give the exact year when I passed over here with any certainty unless I look it up, and it does not really signify.

Now shall we say what was in our minds? We are permitted to help, but with discretion. When people suppose that we ought to help them in scientific investigation, for instance, they surely forget that God has given them minds of their own to use in His service. And to that end they are left to tread their own natural way, and when they have done what they are able, we, now and again, point the way onward and help them to further knowledge.

Can you give me an instance in point?

I remember that once I was impressing a man who was investigating the laws of psychology in the matter of visions and dreams. He wanted to find out what was the cause of certain dreams being prophetic—the connection between the dream itself and the incident which it foreshadowed. He applied to me, and I told him that he must continue his investigations and use his own mind, and, if it were well, he would be given to understand.

That night I met him when he fell asleep and conducted him to one of our observatories where we experiment with the object of portraying, in visible form, the events hovering about the present moment; that is, events which have happened shortly before, and those which will happen shortly in the future. We were not able to go far back or far ahead at that particular establishment. That is done by those in the higher spheres.

We set the instruments in order and cast upon a screen a picture of the neighborhood in which he lived, and told him to watch intently. One particular item was the entry into the town of some great personage with a large retinue. When the display was over he thanked us and we conducted him back to his earth body again.

He awoke in the morning with a feeling that he had been in the company of certain men who had been experimenting in some branch of science, but could not recall what it had been about. But as he was going about his work that morning the face of the man he had seen in the procession came to his mind vividly, and he then remembered several scraps of his dream experience.

On opening a newspaper a few days afterwards he saw an intimation that a visit was projected to the town and district of this same personage. Then he began to reason things out for himself.

He did not remember the observatory, nor the screen pictures we had shown him, as such. But he did remember the face and the retinue. So he reasoned in this way: when our bodies sleep we ourselves, at least sometimes, go into the sphere of four dimensions. That fourth dimension is such as enables those who dwell there to see into the future. But coming back to this realm of three dimensions, we are not able to carry over with us all we have experienced when we ourselves have been in the realm of four. Yet we do manage to hold such items as are natural to this lower realm, such as the face of an earth dweller and a retinue in procession.

The connection, then, between such a dream as foreseen and the events themselves is the relation of a state of four dimensions to a state of three. And the former, being of greater capacity than the latter, covers at any moment a wider range of view, as to time and sequence of events, than the latter can do.

Now, by such use of his own mental faculties he had arrived at as great an advance in knowledge as I could have given him direct; and by so doing he had also advanced in mental training and power. For although his conclusion was not such as would pass muster here without rectification in several points, yet it was roundly and broadly correct, and serviceable for all practical purposes intellectually. I could not have infused into him more than he had found out for himself.

This, then, is the method of our work, and, when people find fault with us and impatiently demand that this method should be altered to suit their ideas of what is the proper way, well, we have to leave them to themselves, and, when their minds are more humble and receptive, we return and continue.

And now, friend, let us tell you the immediate bearing of this on your own case. You sometimes wonder why we do not make these messages more vivid, as you put it, so that you may have no doubt or difficulty in believing that they come from us to you. Well now, think of it all in the light of the above, and you will see that, from time to time, you are given just so much as will help you to help yourself. Your training, remember, is still proceeding; you have not yet arrived, nor will you while you are in the earth life. But if you go on trustfully and faithfully you will find that things will grow more plain. Accept what is not self-contradictory. Do not look out too much for proof or disproof; but rather for consistency in these messages. We do not give you too much, but we give you all that will help you. Be critical, certainly, but not unbalanced. There is much more truth than falsehood round about you and your life. Look out more for the truth and you will find it. Beware of the false, but not superstitiously afraid. When you take your way along a mountain-path your mind is alert in two directions—for the right and safe foothold, and against the unsafe places. Yet you give more attention to the positive than the negative; and rightly so, or you would go slow on your journey. So tread that you do not slip; but go forward also fearlessly, for it is those who fear who lose their balance, and come most often to disaster.

God be with you, friend. His Presence is glorious here, and shines through the mists which envelop the earth, and that radiance may be seen by all—except the blind, and these cannot see.

* * *

Note: The reader will probably feel that the ending of this present series is somewhat abrupt. I felt so, too, and when at the next sitting Zabdiel[2] took up the tale I stated as much. On which the following conversation ensued:

What of the messages I have received from my mother and her friends? Are they to cease? They are incomplete—there is no proper conclusion to them.

Yes; they will stand very well as they have been given to you. Remember, they were not meant to be in the form of a complete history, or a novel. Scrappy they are, but not unhelpful to those who read with a right mind.

I confess I am rather disappointed at the ending. It is so abrupt. Lately something was said about publication. Is it your wish that they should go forth as they are?

That we leave to your own discretion. Personally I do not see why they should not. I may tell you, however, that this writing you have been doing lately, as all former writing you have received from us, is preparatory to a further advance—which I now propose to you.

That was all the satisfaction I obtained, so there seemed to be no alternative but to regard this installment as a preliminary to further messages—G.V.O.

---

[2] As stated in General Notes, these messages were continued further. The second part was given by Zabdiel (of the same Sphere as Astriel), and is about as long as this first portion. It is published in Book II of *The Life Beyond the Veil,* and is entitled The Highlands of Heaven.—H.W.E.

BOOK II

THE HIGHLANDS
OF HEAVEN

Poem: Angelic Love

I

Open your world to me,
Fair angel friends,
Your world of peace and beauty and delight,
Of people robed in radiance and bedight,
On brow and breast and shoulder, with the gem
Of Order and Degree of Ministry
  In those broad acres of Eternity
Or here below, as is allotted them.
  Open your world to me:
Yet not too broad make the Shekinah beam
  To fall upon my poor dull vision yet,
  Lest I lose heart by contrast; lest I fret
To leave my duty now, before the theme
Of this my present course be here complete—
But just enough to keep and guide my feet
  Till this life blends
  Into the Life Supreme,
  Fair angel friends.

II

  Open your hearts to me,
  Fair angel friends;
Open to me your large, untiring love,
And let me see how placidly you move
Amid the wonders of the Universe,
  Where wish is act accomplished; where each breast
  Heaves glowing and responsive to the quest
Of kindred spirit seeking to converse.
  Open your loves to me—

Yet you will know, your clearer eyes will see
How much 'tis well to give and to withhold—
Lest I to claim for earth be over bold
The licence of your larger liberty;
But just a gleam vouchsafe, nor seek to hide
How blest are loves where love is purified;
How our love tends
Toward the love to be,
Fair angel friends.

* * *

Note: Subsequent to the reception of the portion of the script which is included in this volume, I received the verses printed above. It was intimated to me, at that time, that the purpose for which this hymn was transmitted was that it should be regarded as the keynote to this series of messages.—G.V.O.

1

Introductory

Monday, November 3, 1913.

ZABDIEL, your guide, is here and would speak with you.

I shall be glad if he will be good enough to do so.

I am able now for the first time, friend, to join in these messages which your mother and her friends are giving through you to your fellows. Now the time has come when I may continue to develop, with your help, the instructions given you, if it be your wish so to continue.

I am much indebted to you, sir. Please tell me what is your wish now.

That you sit and write down my messages, here and at this time, as you have done for the past few weeks for your mother and her friends.

Will my mother, then, cease and give place to you?

Yes, that is her wish. From time to time, however, you shall hear of her, and from her and others of your circle of friends.

And what is the nature of your projected course of instruction?

That of the development of evil and good, and of God's present and future purpose with the Church of the Christ and, throughout, of mankind generally. It is for you, my friend and charge, to say whether you will proceed, or cease here and go no further. I warn you that, although I shall observe the rule here held advisable of leading onward rather than revealing by cataclysm, yet much that I shall have to say will be of a nature disturbing to you for a time until you have assimilated it and have come to understand the logical sequence of the teaching I shall have to impart.

What of those messages I have received from my mother and her friends? Are they to cease? They are incomplete—there is no proper conclusion to them.

Yes, they will stand very well as they have been given to you. Remember, they were not meant to be in the form of a complete history or a novel. Scrappy they may be, but not unhelpful to those who read with a right mind.

I confess I am rather disappointed at the ending, it is so abrupt. Lately something was said about publication. Is it your wish that they should go forth as they are?

That we leave to your own discretion. Personally I do not see why they should not. I may tell you, however, that this writing you have been doing lately, as all former writing you have received from us, is preparatory to a further advance which I now propose to you.

When do you wish to begin?

Now; and you may proceed as you are able from day to day, as you already have done. I know your work and your engagements and shall order my own accordingly, so far as my work with you is concerned.

Yes, I will do my best. But I confess, quite candidly, I fear the task. What I mean is, I do not feel developed enough, for, from

*what you say, sir, there is some pretty stiff mental work afoot in
what you propose.*

My grace shall be sufficient in the strength of our Lord the
Christ, as heretofore.

*Well, then, will you begin by telling me something more than I
know about yourself?*

It is not on myself that I would fix your mind, friend, but
on the messages proceeding through me to you, and through
you to our fellow Christians fighting their way through the
mists of controversy and doubt and misdirected zeal. I want
to help them and you, my charge; and to such as have shall be
given, and these shall hand it on to others. It is for you still to
choose.

*I have already chosen. I said so. If you are good enough, Zab-
diel, to use a poor instrument like me, that is your business,
not mine. I will do my best. I can only promise so much as that.
Now, what of yourself?*

My mission is of more importance than my own personality which will best be delineated through the thoughts I am
able to give you. The world is suspicious of one who claims
more than they can understand. They believe when they read,
"I am Gabriel who stand in the Presence," because that was said
long ago. But if I should say to you, "I am Zabdiel who come to
you from High Places with a message from those who are accounted in the Heavenly Realms as Holy Ones and Princes of
Love and Light"—well, you know, my friend and charge, what
shape their lips would take. And so I pray you let me speak, and
judge me and us by what message I am charged with whether it
be true and high or no—and it will suffice for you and for me.
One day, dear friend, you shall look on me as I am, and know
me better in that day, and be glad.

*Very well, sir, I leave it to you. You know my limitations. I am
neither clairvoyant nor clairaudient nor a psychic in any real*

way, I take it. But what has already been written, I admit, has convinced me that it is external to myself. I think I am convinced that far. So, if you will, I will. I cannot say more, and I know I am not offering you much.

It is enough, and what you lack I must endeavor to supply of my own strength. Now, I will say no more at this time, for I know you have to go; you have work to do. God be with you, my charge, in the Lord Christ. Amen.+

Tuesday, November 4, 1913.

May grace and peace be yours, friend, and quietness of mind.

In order that what I have to say be not misunderstood, I would begin by telling you that in these realms we do not dwell so much on those things which are not of immediate importance but search out such matters as most concern our present onward way, master them, and so proceed from step to step on firm and sure ground. Truly, the things of infinity are not altogether absent from our minds—the nature and presence of the Absolute and Ultimate One, and those conditions which are about Him, these are not altogether thrust aside. Yet we are content to let them rest not understood, knowing, as we judge from our own experience in these lower realms, that those beyond us must hold for us blessing even greater than our present state. And so we go onward in perfect trust and confidence, happy to advance, and yet not impatient of the future towards which we surely move. So when I tell you of evil and good I shall deal more of those things which we are able to make plain to you, and these will be but as one dewdrop is to a rainbow, and less than this indeed.

There are those who say there is no evil. These are in error. If evil is the negative of positive good, it is real as the good is real. For it were as rational to say there were no such condition as night, but that this is but the negative aspect of light and day, as to say that evil is not and yet good is. For both are conditions of attitude which individual beings assume toward the One Who Is, and, as each attitude is a qualifying medium of an appropriate effect, so a condition of rebellion is the secondary cause of trouble and disaster to the rebel.

Divine Love.

The very intensity of the Love of God becomes terrible when it meets with an opposing obstacle. The swifter the torrent the greater the surf about the opposing rocks. The greater the heat of a fire the more complete the dissolution of the fuel which is cast into it, and on which it feeds. And although to some such words may seem horrible in the saying of them, yet it is the very intensity of the Love which energizes and flows through the creation of the Father which, meeting opposing and disharmonious obstruction, causes the greater pain.

Even in the earth life you may test and prove this true. For the most bitter of all remorse and repentance is that which follows on the realization of the love borne to us by the one we have wronged.

This is the fire of hell, and none else. And if this do not make hell a reality, then what thing could? We who have seen know that only on repentance and the realization that all God's actions are acts of love do the pangs of hell descend upon the sinner, and not until then in their full intensity.

Human Blindness.

But if this be so, if evil be real, then also are evil beings real. Blindness is inability to see. But not only is there such a condition as blindness; there are also people who are blind. Blindness is also a negative condition, or less. It is the condition of one who has four senses instead of five. But real it is, nevertheless. Yet it is only when one who is born blind is told of the sense of sight that he begins to feel his lack of it, and the more he understands the lack of it the more his lack is felt. So it is with sin. It is usual here to call those who are in the darkness the "undeveloped." This is not a negative term, which would be "retrogressed." So of both I say not "loss" but "lack." The one born blind has not lost a faculty but lacks it.

The sinner also rather lacks than loses his faculty to apprehend the good. His is rather the condition of the blind from birth than the blind from misadventure.

And herein is the explanation of the words of St. John that they who have been brought into the knowledge of the truth cannot sin—not as theoretically considered, but as practically considered. For it is difficult to see how they who have enjoyed the light and all the beauty it reveals should put out their eyes and so, become blind.

Those, therefore, who sin do go from lack of knowledge, and inability to appreciate the good and beautiful, and as the blind come to disaster unless they be warded by those who can see—guides either incarnate or discarnate—so with those who are spiritually blind.

Yet you may say that people do go back and fall from grace. Those who do so are such as those who are partly blind or of imperfect sight—color-blind as to one or more colors. These have never seen perfectly, and their lack is only unknown to them until opportunity offers, and then their imperfection is manifest. For a color-blind person is one whose sight is, in little or more measure, undeveloped. It is only by using his vision that he maintains what vision he has, and if he neglects to do this then he retrogresses. So with the sinner.

But it may perplex you to be told that many who live apparently good and upright lives on earth are found here among the undeveloped. Yet so it is. They have gone through life with many of their higher spiritual faculties undeveloped, and when they step into the world where all is spiritual, their lack is seen, and only gradually do they come to understand what they have lacked unknowing so long, just as many color-blind people live their lives and pass hence and never know their imperfect state of vision; which also is hidden from their fellows.

Suppose you give me a case by way of illustration.

One who teaches the truth in part only must learn here to teach it whole. Quite a large number of people accept the fact of inspiration, but deny that it is an ordinary and perpetual means of God's grace for men. When they come over here they, in turn, become inspirers, if so qualified, and then learn by how much they were indebted in their earthly course to those who used this method with them unknown. They must first develop this lacking knowledge and then they may progress, and not till then.

Now, evil is the antithesis of good, but both may be present, as you know, in one person. It is only by freewill that that person is held responsible for both good and evil in his heart. Of this freewill, and the nature and use of it, I must further speak at another time.

God be with you, friend, and keep you in His Grace. Amen.

Saturday, November 8, 1913.

Evil and Good.

If you will give me your mind now for a little while I will endeavor to continue my words in reference to the problem of evil and its relation to that which is good. These are indeed relative terms and neither of them absolute as considered from the point of view of a man on earth. For it is not possible that one in whom both have a part be able to define either perfectly, but only, or chiefly, as the effect of each is seen in its working.

Also let it be remembered that what seems to be good or evil to one man does not of necessity so appear in the eyes of another. Especially is this true of those of different creed and habit of thought and manner of life in community. What, therefore, is possible in the matter of distinction between these two is that the broad and fundamental principles which underlie each should be grasped clearly, and the minor shades of these qualities be entrusted to the future when they will be gradually made more plain.

Now, evil is rebellion against those laws of God which are manifest in His working. It is the endeavor of a wise man that he should walk in the same direction as that towards which these laws flow. He who from willfulness or ignorance opposes this current finds at once that an obstacle is presented to him, and if he persists in his opposition, then disaster will ensue.

For the Life of the Supreme, which operates and energizes through creation, is a force to oppose which is destruction. And if a man were powerful enough in himself to bring such opposition to stand in the way of that tremendous force as would check, even for a moment, its flow, annihilation would be his lot when the pent-up energy once again burst forth upon him. But no man is able thus, and to this degree, to oppose God; and it is therefore that our weakness itself is our surety against annihilation such as this.

For a longer or shorter period sometimes, and often indeed for some thousands of years, as you reckon time on earth, a man may maintain his obduracy. But no man is created who is able to continue so everlastingly. And that is a merciful limit which our Father Creator has placed around and in us lest He lose us, or any one of His children, away from Him, and without return for ever.

Let us therefore, having looked on this phase of aberration from man's natural walking with God, now look the other way in the direction in which all things are tending. For truly, evil is but a transitory phase and, whether it pass away from His economy in whole or no, from every individual most surely it will pass away when its opposing force is spent, and he be left free to follow on in the glorious train of those who brighten as they go from glory to further and greater glory.

For this reason also will the Kingdom of the Christ one day be altogether purged of evil, because individuals make up that Church and, when the last has been ingathered, then will it be complete in its radiating glory to minister perhaps, and as many here believe, to other worlds in need of such help and succor as your world is today.

Evolution.

As we stand on the earth plane, where I stand now, and look through the Veil of difference of condition which is between us and you in the earth life, we often see many people at one time, and sometimes but few. These people differ in brightness according to the degree of holiness in each; that is, according to the degree in which each individual in himself is able to reflect the divine light of spirit which streams past and through us to you. Some appear very dim, and these, when they come over here, will go to regions dim or less dim according to their own dimness.

So that every one will both appear to others and others will appear to him, as natural to the particular environment and atmosphere in which their lot is cast. This is "their own place." Let me illustrate this in order to make it more plain to you. If an electric spark be projected into thick darkness, the contrast is too great to appear congruous. We should say that that spark was out of its proper element, and created a disturbance amid the darkness which brought, just for a minute, things to a standstill. Men groping their way along the dark country lane stand still and rub their eyes until they can see to pursue their way once more. The night animals also for a moment are startled and cease to move.

But if that flash be projected into the atmosphere in the daylight of noon, the disturbance is less, and if it could be projected into the sun it would there lose contrast and blend with his brightness.

So those whose radiance is great go into those spheres whose brightness agrees with their own; and every one into the sphere which agrees with his—be it less or more. But those whose bodies—spiritual bodies I mean—are of gross texture, and do not radiate much light, but are dim, go into those dim spheres where only they may be so much at ease that they may work out their own salvation. They are not at ease indeed in any sense of the word; but only they would be less at ease in a brighter sphere than in those dim regions until they have grown in brightness themselves.

All who pass over here from the earth have some of the darkness which envelops it like a thick pall of mist. But many of these have already in their wills endeavored to rise through that mist into the clearer realms: and these do quickly here what they fain would have done below.

And now we are looking upward, and there indeed lies the Royal Road, the King's Highway to His Holy City and the Dwelling Place of His present Majesty. Along that way we follow step by step; and every step we go we see that far away the light increases ever, and our comrades and ourselves grow in brightness, as in beauty, the further we go. And it is a matter of no small joy that we are permitted, for periods differing according to the needs of you on earth, to come back on our steps and help you on the road we know to be so radiant and so full of the Beauty of His Presence.

And this, my friend and ward, we will endeavor, if you still keep of the mind you are at this present time. I think you will so persevere. But know you that many do set out and then, distrusting the brightness because it dazzles their unaccustomed eyes, turn back to paths more dim where their sight is less distrained. And so we look upon them as they go, and sigh, and turn to seek another, if perchance he should prove strong to bear more of our brightness than the one for whose return hither in our ways we must await, till the due time shall come to us and him.

God keep your feet that they do not slip, and your eyes that they be not dimmed, and, although in words of earth you will not be able to write down what you may know, yet so much of it will we endeavor that you write that others may be led so to ask that they may have, so to seek that they shall find, and (if they be very courageous—these two cities being taken) so to dare as to knock, and so to knock that that Gate be opened and the brightness and glory within revealed.+

Monday, November 10, 1913.

As I stand on the plane of earth, above and beyond lie the spheres, into some of which I have penetrated, and of the Tenth of which I am a member. These spheres are not so much what would correspond to localities on earth, but rather estates of life and power, according to the development of the individual. You have already received some instruction as to the multiplicity of these spheres of power, and I do not purpose to pursue my own on those lines. I would rather lift your mind into the realms of light and activity by another channel, and this I now proceed to do.

All that is good is potent to accomplish things in two directions. By the power within, a good man, be he incarnate or discarnate, can and does both lift up that which is below him, and also draw down that which is above; not alone as by prayer, but also, of his own right, by power.

Now, this is by reason of his attunement to the Divine Will; for by so much as he is able to correspond with his Divine environment, by so much is he able to work through that environment; that is, to energize and to accomplish things. The things he may so accomplish are manifold even to one who has risen only into a small number of spheres, and these things, when projected through the Veil into your earth life, are accounted wonderful.

For instance, there are here such as have charge of the elements which condition the earth and those things which grow upon the earth. Let us take one example which will serve to illustrate the others: Those who have charge of vegetation.

These are under one Mighty Prince; and are divided and subdivided into departments, all in perfect order. Under these again are others of lower estate who carry out their work under direction, and in conformity to certain unalterable laws laid down in the higher spheres. These are what you know as elemental spirits, and are multiple in number and in form.

The laws of which I speak are very complex the further we proceed from the sphere of their origin; but if we could trace them upstream and arrive at their origin we should find, I think, that they were few and simple, and at last, in the source and spring of their origin, unity. Of this I, who have been only a little way, can but reason on what I have observed in my upward progress; and this would lead me to hazard that the one law, or principle, from which all the lesser laws and principles are radiated might best be described by the word Love. For, understood as we understand things, Love and Unity are not much diverse, if not actually identical. We have discovered this much at least, that everything which divides in all the regions and estates on this our own level, and in those spheres below us down to the earth sphere, is in one way or another an abnegation of Love in its most intense and truest meaning.

Unity in Diversity.

But this is a most difficult problem to discuss with you here and now; for it would be very difficult to explain to you how all the diversity you see around you is due, as it seems to us, to this same disintegrating action, and yet is all so wonderfully wise and so beautiful. Still, if you substitute for the word negation the idea of Unity less one part, and then Unity less two parts, and so on, you may perchance get some glimmer of what philosophy is held among us on this subject of Unity radiating into diversity of operativeness.

Although the activity of these lower orders is all regulated by law, yet a great amount of freedom is found within its bounds. And this is to us a matter of much charm because, as you will agree, there is much beauty in diversity, and in the ingenuity displayed by those who energize among plant life.

Some of these laws which govern the elementals and those above them I am unable to understand yet. Some I do understand but am unable to transmit to you. But a few I may tell you, and you will, in your own proper time, learn more as you progress in these heavenly mansions.

It would seem, then, that one rule they must observe in their work is that, having planned out any scheme of development for a family of plants, that scheme must be pursued, in its main elements and essentials, to its natural consummation. All their armies of subordinates are kept within the limits of that unalterable law of evolution. If an oak family is planned, then an oak family that must remain. It may evolve into subdivisions, but these must be subdivisions of the oak. It must not be allowed to branch off into the fern family, or seaweed. These also will be developed along their own line.

Another law is that no department of spiritual workers shall be able to negative the operations of another. They may not, and often do not, work in conformity; but their operations must be along lines of modification, rather than absolute negation, which would mean destruction.

Thus we find that if the seed of two plants of the same family be mixed the result will be a mule plant, or a blend, or a modification. But the seed of one family being mixed with that of another family is without effect. And in neither case is effect annihilation.

A parasite may entwine itself around a tree. But then ensues a fight. In the end the tree is usually worsted and pays the penalty of defeat. But it is not suddenly laid low. The fight proceeds, and indeed sometimes the tree wins. But it is recognized here that those who invented and carried out the parasitic idea have in the main won the battle of forces.

Thus the war goes on, and when you view it from this side you will see how very interesting it all is.

And now I must tell you something which I have hinted already, and which you may find difficult of acceptance. All these main principles, even when diverse in action, are planned in spheres higher than my own by high and powerful Princes who hold their commission secure under others higher still, who hold theirs from others above them.

I use the word "diverse" in preference to "antagonistic," for among those High Ones antagonism does not find a place, but diversity of quality in wisdom does, and is the cause of the wonderful diversity in nature as it works out in its procession from those higher heavens outward through the lower spheres into that of matter which is visible to you on earth. Where antagonism enters is in those spheres where the radiating wisdom has become more attenuated by reason of its journey outward in every direction through spheres of innumerable myriads of free-willed beings, and diluted and refracted in its passage.

And yet, when you consider the stars of different size and complement, and the waters of the sea, naturally still but by the motion of the earth and the gravitation of bodies at a distance allowed to have no rest; and then the more rarefied atmosphere which, also responding to the pulls and pushes of the forces which impinge upon the earth, whips into motion the heavier liquid; and all the diversity of form and color of grass and plant and tree and flower and insect life, and life more evolved, the birds and animals, and of the continuous movement among them all; and the way in which they are permitted one to prey upon another, and yet not to annihilate wholly, but every species must run its race before it pass away—all this and more;

then will you not, my ward and friend, confess that God is indeed most wonderful in the manner of His working, and that the wonder justifies most fully the measures He has permitted His higher servants to adopt and use, and the manner also of their using?

In His Holy Name I bless you, friend—and that is peace.+

2

Men and Angels

Wednesday, November 12, 1913.

IF it were possible, friend, that we should be so united as to be enabled to look out on things from one point of view and vantage, these matters in hand would be so much the easier to explain. But you look hence from one side of the Veil which hangs between things and the region of their causation, and I from the other side, so that our outlook is normally in opposition; and when I would make things appear simple to you I must perforce turn me about and look the other way, and, so far as I am able, with your eyes rather than my own.

This doing so far as in me lies, therefore, I call you to gaze with me into the upward reaches of creation, inversely to their natural course and flow from the High Ones outward towards the spheres where what is material begins to assume and claim a place.

As we go we find that what things we have known as belonging to our environment in the lower spheres begin to assume other aspects: they are transformed to the vision, and transubstantiated to the sense of inward perception, and yet are related to those things which obtain in the sphere of matter, or those next above as the sun is related to the twilight of earth.

Degrees of Light in the Spheres.

Taking first this same matter of light. Light is known on earth by reason of its contrast with darkness, which is merely a state of absence of light, and intrinsically of no content or value. So that when we speak of darkness we mean a lack of certain vibrations which enable the retina of the eye to register the presence of external things.

Now in the regions of spiritual darkness on this side of the Veil a like condition of affairs also obtains. For those who are in darkness are those whose sense of sight lacks the vibrations from without which enable others to have knowledge of those things which to them are external but present withal. Their state is a state of inability to receive these vibrations. When their spiritual faculties do undergo change then they are able to see more or less clearly.

But also these vibrations which convey the knowledge of things to their sense of sight are, in those regions, of a more gross quality than in the regions of spiritual health. So that even to those good spirits who penetrate into those regions, and whose sense of sight is more perfect, yet the darkness is quite apparent, and the light by which they see is dim. So that, as you will understand, there is response between the spirit and the spirit's environment, and that response is so accurate and perpetual and sustained as to constitute a permanent state of life.

As we go higher in the spheres this responsive action between the spirits and their environment is also maintained and that which we may call the external light becomes more and more perfect and intense the higher we go. So it is that those who dwell in, as we will say, the Fourth Sphere may not penetrate into the fifth, to remain there, until they have become so developed as to sustain with ease the degree of intensity of light there obtaining. Having attained to that Fifth Sphere they soon become used to its light. And if they return to the Fourth, as they do from time to time, that Fourth Sphere seems dimmer to them, while still they are able to see with comparative ease. But if they should descend straight to the Second or First Sphere, they would only with difficulty be able to use those denser vibrations of light and, in order to do so, are obliged to train themselves to see in that same sphere which once was but their normal abode.

When we come down to your earth sphere we see by reason of the spiritual light which men have in themselves. And those who are of higher spiritual grade than others we see so much the more clearly.

Were it not for faculties we possess other than that of sight, we should, as I suppose, have difficulty in finding our way about, and to those to whom we wish to come. But we have these other faculties, and by their use are able to do our work in ministering to you.

You will now be able to understand that there is a quite literal truth in the words, "Who dwells in light which no man can approach." For few in the earth life are able to rise many spheres beyond; and the light which streams from above is blinding even to those who are much progressed.

Now think what of beauty this evermore perfect light implies. You have colors on earth which to mortal eyes are entrancing. Just over the border on this side are colors which are much more beautiful and more varied. What then must be the beauty in this one thing alone as we advance into the greater light! Even what I myself have seen, who have only come this little way, is more than I can even hint at in this language in which I am trying to speak to you now, and which today is as a foreign tongue to me, who am also limited to the use of what store of words you yourself possess.

But those who love beauty will find a never-failing supply to their great joy and, as light and holiness go hand in hand, so, as they progress in the one, will they in the larger enjoyment of the other. This is the Beauty of Holiness, and it is past all imagination of mortal men. But it is worthy of meditation, and if you will keep it in mind then what things are beautiful on earth will speak to you more really of the greater beauties of the Heavenly Realms where the joy of life is all one can desire. Which one day shall be yours, good friend, if you keep in the right and onward way.+

Saturday, November 15, 1913.

Geometrical Astronomy.

And now, my friend and ward, I would that I might enable you to see one other matter from this standpoint where I stand, and that is the real relation of spirit power and energy to the phenomena of development among the heavenly bodies as men of science have observed them and tabulated them and, reckoning up their joint message, have made their deductions, and from these have, with some penetration and wisdom, formulated the laws according to which these things come about.

The term "heavenly bodies" has a dual significance and will be interpreted according to the measure and quality of the individual mind. To some these orbs are creatures of the heavens material, and to others they are none else but manifestations and results of the energizing of spirit life. The mode of operation of this spirit life, also, is not understood by all alike; and by some the term is used most vaguely. To say that God made all things is to say a big thing in few words. But the significance of the truth herein embodied is somewhat tremendous; and for all but those who are able to rise into clearer light than that which hovers about the dim places of the earth plane, it would be nearer the truth to say that herein is a truth not so much embodied as entombed. Out of the simplest wisdom are made the greatest things; and out of the most elementary of geometrical figures arise the most wonderful combinations of perpetual movement. For it is only the purest and simplest things that are competent to be used most freely and without entanglement. And this state of affairs alone gives warrant of perpetuity, whether on earth or in the vast reaches of space through which go these worlds and systems, eternally because perfectly ordered in their course.

Now, it is not too much to say that the appointed paths of all these bodies of the heavenly systems are shaped of two principles: that of the right line, and that of the curve. It is even more true and exact to say that their orbits may be said to be shaped out of one form only, and that the right line itself. All go onward impelled in a right and straight course and yet not one that is known to us but travels in a curve. Astronomers will explain why this is, but I will note one instance by way of example here.

The earth, we will suppose, is set forth on its journey. It travels in a straight line from one point. That is its potential movement. But directly it leaves that point it begins to fall towards the sun, and we find after a while that it is moving in an ellipse. There is no straight line here, but a series of curves worked together in one figure, which is the orbit of the earth.

And yet the pull of the sun was not in the fashion of a curve, but in a right line, direct. It was the combination of these two straight lines of energy—the impetus of the earth and the gravitation of the sun—which, being perpetually exerted, bent the orbit of the earth from a straight into an elliptical shape, and one in which many elements of curve entered to build it up complete. I leave out other influences which modify this one again in order to concentrate your mind on this one great principle. I put it in formula, thus: Two straight lines of energy operating on one another produce a closed curve.

Both, you will note, are quite orderly in their working; and both are beautiful and of wonderful power. For, that any body of matter move at all should seem wonderful and is so in truth. Yet each modifying the other, and the greater dominating the lesser without depriving it of its essential power and freedom of movement, these by their joint action—exerted and directed apparently in opposition—produce a figure of greater beauty than the two straight lines, which are as the parents to the child.

Now, you would not, I take it, say because these forces are seen to be exerted against one another that this is a bad scheme and plan whose origin is of evil. For you see these two bodies still continuing their journey through space year after year, and century after century, and you come to think it rather a matter for awe and reverence than for contumely. It displays a wisdom which is beautiful in its working and mighty in operation; and you praise God Whose mind conceived all this, for He must be very wise and very great indeed. And you do well.

The Orbit of Human Life.

Yet when other His works you contemplate, but understand them not so well as this, sometimes you men are too ready to doubt Him and His ways of working. You see a like opposition of forces in human life, and you say His plan is here imperfect. You think He might have made a better way; and many doubt His wisdom and His love because, seeing but a minute section of the curve of the great orbit of existence, they cannot but conclude that all is falling, falling to destruction; or at least that a straight and right line would be the better course, and not these combinations which curve the impetus of human life from its direct onward way of evolution—without disaster and without pain.

My dear friend and ward, these things might be otherwise than as they are, but they would not be near so lovely in their completed orbit then as they will be in the path on which He Who made all and sees the end of things sent them forth. These forces which in opposition produce straining and travail and pain are as those which make the orbit of the earth what it is;

and He Who sees the perfect form has seen it well to work thus, and in patience looks on towards the consummation of this His perfect scheme.

We here do see not all nor much of the road ahead; yet more than you we see, and so much as enables us to content ourselves and press onward, helping others on the road, content and trusting that all will be well ahead however far we go. For now we do not seek with much labor to reckon on the course we are traveling wrapped round with earth mist which hinders us to see, but we view the way from the clear sunlight atmosphere of these heavenly realms; and I tell you the orbit of human life, as it works out towards completion, is beautiful too—so beautiful and so lovely withal that we are full often brought to arrest in wondering awe at His Majesty of Love and blended Wisdom, to Whom we bow in lowly adoration not to be expressed in any words of mine, but only in the yearning of my heart.

Amen, and my blessing upon you, friend. Look up and be fearless for, believe me, all is fair ahead and all is well.+

Monday, November 17, 1913.

"What thou seest write in a book." These words were spoken by an Angel to John in Patmos, and he carried out the command as he was able. He wrote his account and handed it to his brethren; and from that time till now men have striven to wrest from that account its meaning. They have tried one method and another, and confess themselves perplexed. Yet their perplexity is of their own making, friend, for had they read as little children read they would have been able to turn the door with the right key, and to enter into the Kingdom to see what beauties there await such as are able to take a simple man's simple words simply, and believe.

But men have loved perplexity ever, and seek in it to find profundity and depth of wisdom. And they fail, for, looking on the surface of the glass, they are dazzled and blinded at the reflected light, which they should have looked through and beyond at the glories there revealed.

So do men add perplexity to perplexity and call it knowledge. But knowledge is in no wise perplexing, but the lack of it is. So when I seek to explain aught to you, and through you to others, do you not look so much on the surface of things, at the precise method by which this comes to pass; and do not start in doubt at words and phrases familiar to you as your own, for these are my material by which I build up my house; and only such as I find stored in your mind can I use.

Moreover, all these years past you have been watched and prepared, partly to this very end, that we should use you thus, and that where we lack, for, further contact with your material sphere, there you yourself should come to our aid. We can show you things—you must write them down. Thus what thou seest write in a book, and send it forth to be dealt with by men, each according to the measure of his own capacity, and each as his faculties are quickened to the perception of spiritual things. Let that suffice, then. Come with us and we will tell you what we are able.

You say "we." Are there others besides?
Angel Visitants to Earth.

We work all together, friend. Some are here present with me bodily, others still in their several spheres are able to send forth their help from those realms without their leaving them. Also there is a certain help which only may be given thus. For you will know that, as the diver at the bottom of the sea must be tended with air by those above continually for his support, so it is likewise helpful that we be ministered to the while we also minister. By this we are enabled the more clearly to speak to your mind of the higher verities while we stand on this dim and grosser lower plane as on the bed of the ocean where our natural air is scanty and our light looms far above. Think of it and us in this wise and you will be able to understand a part of our task.

Some there are who ask why angels do not come in plenty nowadays as in the olden times. Here are many errors in few words, and two pre-eminent. For first, angels of high estate did never come in plenty to the earth plane, but one here and another there amid the ages; and those were accounted worthy of a forward place in the annals of great events. Angels do not in this wise come to earth and visibly appear, except it be on some very rare and special commission. This were an extension of our difficult task: first must the diver get to the dark and very deep waters, and then must he so condition himself that he become visible to those nearly blind creatures whose habitat is on the ocean floor.

No; we work for men, and are present with them, but in other ways than this, according to rule and varying method as each task requires. And that is the second error made; for we are present and do come to earth continually. But in that word "come" more lies hidden than I may reveal. For even those on this side, in the spheres between us and you, do not understand yet our powers and the ways of their using, but only in part as they learn in the course of their progress. And so let it rest thus. And now I will explain to you another matter of interest.

The Wrestling of Jacob.

The audience which Jacob had of the Angel at Jabbok when he wrestled with him and prevailed: What, think you, was that wrestling; and what the reason of the withholding of the Angel's name?

I think that the wrestling was a bodily wrestling; and that Jacob was allowed to prevail in order to show him that his wrestling with his own nature during his residence in Padan Aram had not been in vain—that he had prevailed. I think the Angel withheld his name because it was not lawful to give it to a man still in the flesh.

Well, the first answer is better than the second, which, my charge, is not saying a very great deal. For, see you, if he did not give it because it was not lawful to give, why was it not lawful?

Now, the wrestling was real and actual, but not form to form as men do usually wrestle. The Angel might not be touched of mortal hands with impunity. He had manifested in visible form, and that form was even tangible, but not rudely to be treated. For the power of that Angel was such that the mere touching of the thigh of Jacob produced dislocation. What, then, had Jacob taken that form within his arms? But the Angel was held there by the will of Jacob: not because Jacob's was the stronger will, but because of the Angel's condescension and courtesy. While Jacob wished he stayed, but courteously asked to be permitted to go. Do you wonder at this great indulgence? Think of the Christ of God and His humiliation among men and you will wonder no longer. Courtesy is one of the outward manifestations of love, and may not be disregarded in that long course of training which makes us what we are and do become.

So was the Angel held because he gave that much. But Jacob is not so winning. In him his newly realized strength of will and character overbears his finer sentiments, for the time, and demands a blessing. This he obtains, but not the Angel's name.

The Power of a Name.

It were not quite accurate to say it was not lawful that it should be given. Sometimes the names are given. But in this case not; and for this reason: There is much power in the use of a name. Know this, and remember it; for much disaster continually ensues by reason of the misuse of holy names, disaster wondered at and often felt to be unmerited. Jacob for his own sake was denied that name. He had shown his willingness to demand a blessing, but must not be given to be enabled to demand too much. He had come into contact very nearly with great power, and must be restrained in the drawing on that power, or the fight he had still to fight would not be then his own.

Now, I see in your mind a question as to the possibility of demanding unwisely from us and thus obtaining. Things are so ordered that not alone is this possible but continually is it done. Strange as it may seem to you, help is often demanded from these spheres in such a way that it must be given, and yet it were, time and again, better that the asker's own resources should have been employed, and he thereby have risen to greater strength than by this the other way. If a name be called with vehemence by those on earth the owner of that name cannot but be notified of it. He attends and acts as possible and best.

I cannot but think that Jacob made a better advance in his contest with Esau, and with his sons and with the famine, and with the many trials he had to meet, by bringing to bear on them his own strength of personality than had he been able continually to call to his aid his Angel-guide to do what he could do himself. This help would be often refused and he, unable to understand, would probably have been hindered in his faith and perplexed. Sometimes the help would have been given, and in so patent a way as to require little aspiration to understand, and so, little advancement.

But I will not pursue this to greater length. My object in citing Jacob's case was to show you that you are not farther from us, nor we from you, because you do not see us nor hear our voices. We speak and you hear, but more deeply in yourself than with the outward ear. You do see, but the vision is more inward than that of the outward faculty of sight. And so do you be content; for we are so, and will continue to use you, so you continue in quietness of spirit and in prayer to the Highest through His Son, Whose ministers we are and in Whose name we come.+

Tuesday, November 18, 1913.

When all things visible were created one thing was left not quite complete because the last and greatest of all, and that was man. He was left to develop and, being given to possess great power, he was shown the onward way that he should tread, and left to tread it. But not alone. For all the hierarchy of the heavenly realms were his beholders to see how he would do with those gifts which had been given him.

I do not speak at this time of evolution expressly, as understood by scientists, nor of fall and uprising again, as taught by those who profess theological knowledge, but rather of the broader aspect, as we contemplate man's aspirations and what has come of them. And looking forward, also, it is permitted us to weigh his future, and to see a little way ahead into those long reaches and realms of wide expanse which lie before us all.

Courage in Thinking.

Nor in doing this am I able to constrain myself within the limits of doctrinal theology as understood by you. For it is indeed constrained and straitened so greatly that one who has lived so long in wider room would fear to stretch himself lest he foul his elbows against the confining walls of that narrow channel; and hesitates to go at any pace ahead, fain as he is to travel, lest worse than this be his lot.

No, my friend, shocking and startling as it be to those whose orthodoxy is as the breath of their body to them, more saddening is it to us to see them so much afraid to use what freedom of will and reason they have lest they go astray, mistaking rigid obedience to code and table for loyalty to Him Whose Truth is free.

Think you for a moment. What manner of Master-Friend is He to them who tremble so at His displeasure? Is it that He is, waiting and watching, with sinister smile, to catch them in His net who dare to think and think in error sincerely? Or is this He Who said, "Because you are lukewarm, and neither cold nor hot, I will reject you"? Move and live and use what powers are given prayerfully and reverently and then, if you do chance to err, it will not be of obduracy and willfulness but of good intent. Shoot with strong arm and feet well and firmly set, and if you miss the mark by once or by twice, your feet shall still be firm and the word "Well done!" for you shot amiss, yet in His good service, and as you were able to do, so you did. Be not afraid. It is not those who strike and shoot and sometimes miss the mark whom He rejects, but the craven who fear to fight for Him at all. This I say boldly for I know it is true, having seen the outcome of both manner of lives when those who have lived them issue forth among us here, and seek their proper place and the gate by which they may pass onward this way.

And now, my ward and fellow-servant in the Army of the Lord, listen well awhile, for I have that to say which may be not very familiar to your way of thinking, and I would that you record it aright.

The Divinity of the Christ.

Many there are among you who do not find it in them to accept the Christ as God. Now, there is much light talk of this matter on both sides of the Veil. For not with you on earth alone but also here we have to seek in order to know, and miracles of revelation are not thrust upon us nor is our own freedom of reasoning constrained by any higher power than our own. Guided we are, as you are, too, but not forced to believe this or that in any of the many ways in which this might be done. So there are here, also, many who say that Christ is not God, and so saying think they have made an end of the matter.

It is not my present purpose to prove to you the contrary and positive truth, nor even to state that truth affirmatively.

It is rather that I would endeavor to show you and them what manner of question this is, and how it is not conducive to an understanding of it, by even the little we may, to speak in terms without first defining them.

First, then, what is meant by God? Do they mean a localized personality when they think of the Father—a person such as a man is? If so it is obvious that the Christ is not He, or this would create a double person, or two personalities in one in such a way that distinction of each would be impossible. It is not that way the Oneness of which He spoke is to be sought. Two equal persons united is an unthinkable condition, and one which reason rejects at once.

Or is it meant that He is the Father in manifestation as Man? So, then, are you and so am I His servants. For the Father is in all of us.

Or is it that in Him was the fullness of the Father, undivided? So in you and in me also dwells the Father, for Him it is not possible to divide.

Yet if it be said that the Whole of the Father dwells in Him but not in us, I say that is an opinion and no more, and also an illogical one; for if the Father as a Whole dwells in the Christ, then either the Christ is the Father without distinction, and none else, or the Whole Father dwelling in the Christ must cease to dwell in Himself of necessity. This also is not reason.

So it is first necessary that we understand that the Father is the Name we give to the highest aspect of God we are able to think of. And even this we do not understand, for it is frankly confessed that He is beyond our understanding.

I cannot define Him to you, for I have not seen Him Who to all less than Himself is not visible entirely. What I have seen is a Manifestation of Him in Presence Form, and that is the highest I have attained hereto.

Then the Christ in His Unity with the Father must be also above us as to our understanding, as He is above us in Himself.

He tells us so much as we are able to think of, but not to understand very much. He manifested the Father, and such qualities of the Holy Supreme as were capable of manifestation in the body to us. Little more we know, but grow in knowledge as we grow in humility and reverential love.

As He is One with the Father, so we are One with Him. And we dwell in the Father by our dwelling in Him Who is the blending of what we call the Human and the Divine. The Father is greater than He, as He Himself once said. By how much greater He did not say, and we could not have understood had He told us.

It may be said by those who read this that I have cut away the scaffolding and left no building within. My purpose, friend, I stated at the first. It was not now to rear a building, but rather to point out that the first thing to build is a sure foundation; and that any structure raised on one not sure must, now or later, fall, and much labor be in vain. And this indeed have men been doing more than they realize; and that is why so much is mist when it might be plain to view. Not all, of course, but enough to make the road much brighter than it is.

I speak not so much to instruct, in this present message, but rather to give men pause. For ratiocination may be fascinating to certain minds, but is not meat for the soldier. It flatters with its perfect logic and well-balanced argument, but is not durable to withstand the wear and tear of the wide elements of the spheres. It is not always so wise to affirm, as to say, "I do not know this yet." Pride often blinds one to the beauty of a humble mind; and it is not true that he who answers a deep problem offhand is a fountain of wisdom; for assurance is sometimes nearly akin to arrogance, and arrogance is no wise true or lovely.

You and I, my friend and ward, are One in Him Whose Life is our assurance of Life continued. In Him we meet and bless each other, as I bless you now, and thank you for your kindly thoughts towards me.+

Wednesday, November 19, 1913.

Love and its Opposite.

And so, dear friend and ward, my words to you are such as many will not receive; yet know this, that many shall come from east and west and sit down at the Feast of the Christ who without knowing Him as to His Natural Divinity, yet love Him for His human kindness and love; for that, at least, they all can understand. And none can comprehend the other His aspect in the fullness of its meaning. And so let us think of other things, and first the relation men incarnate should foster towards Him if they would progress in the way He showed them.

Foremost must they love. That is the first commandment of all, and the greatest. And hard have men found it to keep. They all agree that to love one another is good; and when they come to translate the sentiment into action, how sadly do they fail. And yet, without love no thing in all the universe would stand, but fall into decay and dissolution. It is the love of God which energizes through all that is; and we can see that love, if we look for it, everywhere. The best way to understand many things is to contrast them with their opposites. The opposite of love is dissolution; because that comes of refraining from the exertion to love. Hatred is also of the opposite, and yet not the essence of it; because hatred of one person is often a mistaken method of expressing love to another.

And what is said of persons is also true of doctrines and aims. Many express their devotion to one cause by their hatred of another. It is foolish and faulty, but not altogether of evil. When a man hates another man, however, he is likely to cease to love more and more until it becomes an effort to love any-thing at all.

This is one of those things which make for difficulty in this life of the spheres. For not until a man has learned to love all without hating any is he able to progress in this land where love means light, and those who do not love move in dim places where they lose their way, and often become so dull in mind and heart that their perception of the truth is as vague as that of outward things.

There are, on the other part, mansions here which sparkle with light in every stone, and send forth radiance over the country round to a great distance by reason of the high purity in love of those who dwell in them.

Will you describe such a residence as this, and those who live in it? It would help more than this general description, I think.

It is not easy, as you will know one day. And if I accede to your request, you will understand the result will not be true to fact, inasmuch as it will be inadequate. Nevertheless, I will do as you desire. What residence particularly would you wish me to describe?

Tell me of your own, please.

In the Tenth Sphere are conditions which do not obtain in those of lower degree, least of all in your own sphere of earth.

Now we "see through a glass darkly."

If it were possible that I should take you now into that sphere you would not see anything at all, because your condition is not yet fitted to it. What you would see would be a mist of light, more or less intense according to what region of that sphere you were in. In the lower spheres you would see more, but not all, and what you were able to see you would not understand in every part.

Suppose you take a fish out of the water and put him in a globe and take him through a town, how much, think you, would he firstly see, and secondly understand? I think he would see some few inches beyond the circumference of his habitat—the water, which is his natural environment. Put your face where he can see you, and then your hand instead. What would he know of these things?

So would you be in these spheres; and only by training would you be able to energize and use your faculties therein with ease and profit. Now further, how would you, in the language of the fishes, describe to them the Abbey of Westminster, or even your own village church? If that fish were to make known to you how unreasonable you were when you told him you were hindered by his own limitations; or if he told you that he did not believe there was such a place as the church or Abbey, which you named but could not describe to him, how would you convince him that the unreason was of his own, and not of your, making?

Zabdiel's Heavenly Home.

Still, since you wish it, I will tell you what I can of my own house and home; and you will probably think I might have done better when I finish, and best of all had I refrained altogether.

The country in which we built our house touches many spheres, and among them those whose natures radiate many colors according to their virtues, and which coincide most nearly with those of the people with whom I dwell. These colors are mostly other than those you know, but all those you know are here, and in almost infinite combination and hue. According to the occupation in which we are mentally engaged at any time the blend of colors varies, and the atmosphere takes on that tint.

Then the house also vibrates and responds to the thoughts and aspirations, whether of prayer sent onwards, or help willed backward through the spheres behind us, in, which direction lies the earth plane.

Music also proceeds from us, not necessarily by mouth, but more often directly from the heart; and this is taken up also in response by the buildings around us, which are part of our energizing; and also the trees and flowers, and all plant life is affected and responds. Thus color and music are not merely inanimate here, but fraught with our life, and vibrate to our will.

The house is four-square, and yet the walls are not four alone, nor at angles each to the others. They, too, are blended, and the outer and inner atmosphere mingles through them. These walls are not for our protection, but for other uses, and one is to concentrate our vibrations, to focus them in their transmission to distant regions where our help is needed and desired. Thus we reach the earth also and sense your doings there, and send you words of instruction, or help in other forms, in answer to the prayers which come to us for us to deal with.

Here also descend those of higher spheres and, by means of these houses and other influences prepared, become tangible to us that we may commune with them on matters which perplex us.

From this house also we send such strength to those who from time to time are commissioned to us from the lower spheres as enables them, for the period of their sojourn among us, to endure the conditions of this sphere with no great discomfort; and also to converse with and to see and hear us, which otherwise they might not do.

As to the aspect of this house from without, I will give you the description of one of those of a lower sphere which is nearer your own. He told me that when he came in sight of it he was reminded of the words, "a city which is set on a hill whose light cannot be hid." He was a long distance away, but paused and descended to the ground to rest (for he came so far by aerial travel). He shaded his eyes, and gradually was able to look again at the mansion on the hill, far away, in its brightness.

He said he saw the great towers; but they shone so brightly with their blue light that he could not tell where they actually ended, because the light shot up into the heavens above and seemed to continue them there indefinitely. Then the domes—some were red and some gold, and the light from these was likewise too dazzling to see where they ended, or what was their size. The gates and walls likewise shone silver and blue and red and violet, and blazed with dazzling light which bathed the hill below, and the foliage of the trees around, and he wondered how he would enter and not be consumed.

But we saw him, and sent messengers to deal with that his difficulty; and when at last he turned to bless us and depart, his mission being ended, he said to us, "A thought strikes upon me at this time of parting. My fellow workers will ask me what manner of place is that to which I have been; and how shall I tell them of this glory when once again I am altogether of my own sphere, and resume its more straitened powers?"

And we replied, "Son, you will never quite be as you were, hereafter. For in you will remain somewhat of this sphere's light and perception. But what you in your heart are able to remember will be of larger measure than you can give to them. For they would not understand if you could tell them; and to tell them you would perforce have to use the language which is current here. Therefore tell them to bend their wills to further development, and one day they shall come and see for themselves what you have seen but are unable to relate."

And so he went away in great joy uplifted. This be your own also, friend, and the words we gave him now I give to you.+

3

The Earthly
and the Heavenly

Friday, November 21, 1913.

NOT every one who runs reads aright, for they who run are sometimes of too impatient a mind in regard to those things which are not of apparent importance, and only the apparent is of importance to such as these. And so it comes to pass that much that is written very plainly is no word to them, and its message of significance is left unheeded.

This is so in the various signs which are written in what men term nature; that is, the surface phenomena of spirit power energizing in and through matter. Thus it is also in the movement of peoples and nations, as they work out their destiny according to their own proper and peculiar characters.

And thus it is, in perhaps a less degree, in the discoveries of science, as popularly understood. Let us for a short while consider this last and see if there is any message to those who would search more deeply than most, who have time to run only and not to read.

Recurring Science.

Science, as history, repeats itself, but never in exact duplicate. Broad principles govern, from time to time, the search for knowledge, and are succeeded by others in their turn which, having served, then also fall behind into a secondary place in order that other principles may receive the more concentrated and undivided attention of the race. But from time to time, as the ages go by, these principles return again—not in the same order of sequence—to receive the attention of a new race. And so the march of human progress goes on.

Items of discovery also are lost and found anew, often in other than their original guise, and with some strange features added, and other old features lacking.

In order to make what is here set down more plain, I will come to details by way of example.

There was a time when science did not mean what it means to men today: when there was a soul in science, and the outer manifestation in matter was of secondary interest. Thus it was with alchemy, astrology, and even engineering. It was known in those days that the world was ruled from many spheres, and ministered to by countless hosts of servants, acting freely of their own will but within certain strait limits laid down by those of greater power and higher authority. And men in those days studied to find out the different grades and degrees of those spiritual workers, and the manner of their service in the different departments of nature and of human life, and the amount of power exercised by each several class.

And they found out a considerable number of facts, and classified them. But inasmuch as these facts, laws and regulations and conditions were not of the earth sphere but of the spiritual, they were fain to express them in a language apart from that of common use.

When another generation grew up whose energies were directed in other ways, these, not considering well what manner of knowledge was contained in the lore of their ancestors, said the language was allegorical, or symbolic; and thus doing they also made the facts themselves assume a shadowy form, until at last there was little of reality left.

Tales of Faerie and Magic.

Thus it happened with regard to the study of the spiritual powers of varying degree and race, and this issued in the fairy tales of Europe and the magic stories of the East. These are really the surviving lineal and legitimate descendants of the science of the past, added to, subtracted from, and distorted in many ways. And yet if you study to read these tales in the light of what I have said, you will see that, when you have separated the essentials from the more modern embroidering, there are to be found there embedded, like the cities of Egypt under the sands of the ages, solid facts of science or knowledge as spiritually considered.

Would you, please, give a specific instance, by way of illustration?

There is the story of Jack and the Beanstalk. In the first place, look at the name. Jack is colloquial for John, and the original John was he who wrote the Book of the Revelation. The Beanstalk is an adaptation of Jacob's Ladder, by which the upper, or spiritual, spheres were reached. Those spheres once attained are found to be real countries and regions, with natural scenery, houses and treasures. But these are sometimes held by guardians not altogether in amity with the human race who, nevertheless, by boldness and skill of mind are able to wrest those treasures away and return to earth with them. And also they are able, by natural quickness of character, to prevent those guardians from regaining possession of these treasures of wisdom and depriving the human race of the right won by the conquest of the bolder sort.

Now, this is picturesque, and is made to assume a quaint and even ludicrous guise by reason of its being handed down from age to age by those who did not understand its deeper import. Had they done so most certainly they had not nicknamed the original as Jack. But, as his customary attire of dress will show you, this came about in an age when things holy and spiritual were had in light esteem by reason of the inability of men to realize the actual presence of spiritual beings among them. So, also, they garbed a demon, and gave him spiked ears and a tail, and for a similar reason—that his actuality to them was mythical. The personality they made of him was mythical indeed.

The story I have named is one of many. Punch and Judy might represent the transactions in which the two who stood out most reprobate were Pilate and Iscariot. And from the manner in which these solemn, and indeed awful, incidents are related, the levity of the age in such matters is apparent.

Well, so it is, and has been ever. But now, today, the spiritual is returning among men to claim a place, if not adequate to its importance, at least of greater consideration than of these last centuries.

The Passing of Materialism.

Thus, in other guise outwardly, but inwardly more akin, the broad principle which governed the Egyptian astrologers, and the wisdom which Moses learned and used to such effect, is returning today to lift men up a little higher and to put a meaning into that dead materialism of the past which, handling things produced of the energizing of life—shells, bones and fossil stones—denied the Author of Life His place in life's grand arena. It spoke of the orderly working of natural law—and denied the One Source of all order and all working. It spoke of beauty—and forgot that beauty is not unless the spirit of man perceives it, and that spirit is because He Who is Spirit is for ever.

We are watching, and we are guiding as we may and opportunity is given us. If men respond to our prompting there is an age to come more full of light and the beauty of love and life than that just passing away. And I think they will respond, for the new is better than the old, and from behind us we feel the pressing of those of higher wisdom and power as we look earthward. And so we do what we are impressed is their intention and desire.

We are not given to be able to see very far ahead. That is a special study, and it is not of the duties of the band of workers to which I am attached. But we are glad to find our endeavors in many hearts meet with ready response, and we hope for greater opportunity, as years go by, to show men how near we are to them, and how great they are potentially if they but be humble in spirit, and quiet, and strive after holiness and purity in thought and desire, looking to Him, the Example of man at his greatest, and seeking to reproduce in themselves that beauty of holiness they may read, even as they run; for a glance at that One His Life should entrance one who has in himself to see what beauty is. For Him we love, and to Him we do reverence, Whose peace be to you in all things, all your days, dear friend. Amen.+

Monday, November 24, 1913.

The Interrelation of the Spheres.

Moreover, friend, it is a good thing and a helpful to bear in mind our presence at all times; for we are near, and that in ways both many and various. When we are personally near at hand we are able to impress you with helpful thoughts and intuitions, and so to order events that your work may be facilitated and your way more clear than otherwise it would appear to you.

When in person we are in our own spheres, we still have means whereby we are informed not alone of what has happened in and around you, but also what is about to happen, if the composition of circumstances pursue its normal course.

Thus preserving contact with you, we maintain and ensure our guardianship that it be continuous and unceasing, and our watchfulness that it shall in nowise fail on your behalf. For here, and through the spheres between us and you, are contrivances by which intelligence is sent on from one sphere to those beyond and, when necessity require it, we enjoin others to carry out some mission to you, or, if the occasion so requires, we come to earth ourselves, as I have done at this time.

But further still, and in addition to this, we are able each to come into contact with his own charge direct in certain ways, and to influence events from our own place. Thus you will understand that the whole economy of the Creator, through its manifold spheres of light, is unified in action and correlated. So that no part is but is influenced by all those other parts, and what you do on earth not only is registered in the heavens, but has effect on our minds and thoughts, and so on our lives.

Be, therefore, of very careful mind and will; for your doings in thought and your doings in word and your doings in act are all of great import, not alone to those you see and touch around you, but also to those around you unseen and untouched by you, but who see and touch you constantly and often. Not these alone, but those who go about their business in their own spheres are so affected. It is so in my own, I know, and how much higher I do not hazard to say. But, were you to ask me I would reply that your doings are multiplied by transmission through the spheres of light by seventy times seven; and that no end is found to their journey within the ken of man or angel. For I little doubt, if that at all, they find out at last the very Heart of God.

Be ye, therefore, perfect, because your Father Who is in the Heaven of the Heavens is perfect; and no imperfect thing can find acceptance and approval to enter where He is in His awful Beauty.

And what, then, of those spheres where they who do not love good and beauty dwell? Well, we are also in touch with those, and the help sent there is as readily sent as to the earth sphere; for those realms of darkness are but further removed, and not disconnected, from us. Those who are there are learning their lesson as are you in your earth sphere, but theirs is more dim than yours—no more than this. For still are they sons and daughters of the One All Father, and so our brothers and sisters too. And these we help when they cry, as we help you at your petition. It has been given you already to know somewhat of the conditions of life there obtaining. But what your mother wrote I may here supplement a little.

Purified by Suffering.

Light and darkness are states of the spirit, as you know. When those dwelling in the darkness cry for light, that means that they are become out of touch with their environment. So we send them what help is needed; and that is usually direction by which they find their way—not into regions of light, where they would be in torture, and utterly blinded, but—into a region less dark, and tinctured by just so much of light as they may bear until they outgrow that state and cry in their longing for more.

When a spirit leaves a dark region for one less dark he experiences an immediate sense of relief and comfort by comparison with his former state. For now his environment is in harmony with his own inner state of development. But as he continues to develop in aspiration after good, he gradually becomes out of harmony with his surroundings, and then, in ratio to his progress, so his discomfort increases until it becomes not less than agony. Then in his helplessness, and approaching near to despair, having come to that pass when his own endeavors can go no further, he cries for help to those who are able to give it in God's Name, and they enable him one stage

onward nearer to the region where dimness, rather than darkness, reigns. And so he at last comes to the place where light is
seen to be light; and his onward way is henceforth not through
pain and anguish, but from joy to greater joy, and hence to
glory and glory greater still.

But oh, the long, long ages some do take until they come
into that light, ages of anguish and bitterness; and know all the
time that they may not come to their friends who wait them
until their own unfitness is done away; and that those great
regions of darkness and lovelessness must first be trod.

But do not mistake my words of their meaning. This is no
vengeance of an angry God, my ward and friend. God is our
Father, and He is Love. All this sorrow is of necessity, and is ordered by those laws which govern the sowing, and the reaping
of that which is sown. Even here, in my own place, where many
things both wonderful and lovely we have learned, yet not yet
have we attained to plumb and sound this mystery to its lowest
depth. We do understand, as we were unable when in the earth
life, that it is of love that these things are ordained. I say we are
able to understand where formerly we were able but to say we
trusted and believed. Yet little more of this awful mystery do
we know; and are content to wait until it is made more plain to
us. For we know enough to be able to believe that all is wise and
good; as those in those dark hells will know one day. And this
is our comfort that they will and must be drawn onward and
upward into this great and beautiful universe of light, and that
then they will confess, not only that what is is just, but that it is
of love and wisdom too, and be content.

Such have I known, and do know, and am of their number
in the service of the Father. And it seems to me their praise
and blessing of Him is nowise lacking in love in comparison of
ours who have not journeyed through those awful depths. Nay,
friend, for I will confess to you this one thing else: that sometimes, as we have paid our united worship together prostrate

before the Light of the Throne of the Heavens, I have felt that there is something in their worship lacking in mine; and have almost half-wished that I might have that in me too.

Yet this would not be right; and doubtless the Father takes, in His Love, what is in us to give Him. Nevertheless, it is very sweet, that saying of the Master, and rings true here where love is seen in the beauty of its nakedness: Because she is forgiven much, therefore she loves the more.

God keep you in His Love, my friend and ward, and naught else matters so you do respond to His sweet caress, and rest in Him. Amen.+

Tuesday, November 25, 1913.

If it were but a little of faith a man should have in him he would be able to understand what I have written by your mind and hand. But not to many is it given to see into the truth of things, and to know them as true indeed. So has it been down the ages, friend, and so will it be yet for ages many. So far it is given to see, but yet we look forward and onward still, and ahead we think we see a world of men moving and doing in a greater light than that which is about them today; and in that day they will see and understand how near are we to them, not in books alone, but in the daily lives they lead. Meanwhile we do our part, ever watchful, ever hopeful and, if our joy is sometimes mingled with a sadness we cannot altogether put away while men and we do not go hand in hand, as is our wish, still, again, we know that we are coming nearer together; and all is well.

And now to our present task, my ward; for while it is day I would that we work together; for when the night descends then you will find another day, but not as now; and other op-portunities of service, but not such as these. So let us do what we can while we have command of these present conditions, and we shall do better work when wider spheres are opened to us—both to you and me.

Science, as you know it, is not coterminous with what you know, for we look deeper into those fundamentals which are of spiritual origin; and worldly science is but now beginning to admit this truth into her councils. Thus we are already drawing nearer each to other; or rather it would be more true to say that those among you who are searching into the meaning of the phenomena of your sphere are coming nearer to us as we draw them upward to higher and deeper searching.

For this we are thankful, and it emboldens us to continue in the same path; and this we do in sure faith that men will continue to follow where we lead, so we be careful to lead them wisely and well.

The Origin of Species.

I now would tell you somewhat of the inner meaning of what men call the origin of species in animal life. But now, and at once, I would say the term is all too large; for the origin of the different creations in animal life is not found in the realm of matter, but has its genesis in these realms. We have learned here that, when the Universe of systems was moving towards its present form and constitution, those who had charge to watch and work took their counsels from those of higher degree, and on those counsels shaped their own wisdom.

At that time it was seen that in the heavenly spheres there were many diversities both of the forms of life as bodily manifest, and of mind in its working. And it was resolved that the universe was meant to reflect the personalities and types of those who were commissioned to carry out the work of its development. To this conclusion they were divinely guided, for when their plan was completed it was given them by revelation to know that the Divine approval was upon it in general kind; but that it was not of absolute perfection. Nevertheless, it received the imprimatur of the All Father Who vouchsafed them freedom to work out His will according to their own capacities and powers.

Thus arose the different orders and species of animal and vegetable and mineral life, and also of human type and racial character. And these things being initiated, again the Divine Mind pronounced His general approval or, as our Bible has it, He found it to be "very good."

But high as were those who were chief in this matter of creation, yet they were less than the Only Omnipotent and, as the work of ordering the universe was very great, and wide in extent, the imperfections of their work became magnified as they worked out; so that, to a single mind, and one of low degree, as is that of a man, those imperfections loomed vast and great. For it is not competent to one who is so small and undeveloped to be able to see both good and evil equally, but the evil is the easier seen to him, and the good too high and wonderful for him to grasp its meaning and power.

Man's Place in the Universe.

But if men would keep in mind one thing, they would find the existence of this imperfection, mingled with so much more that is wonderful and wise, the easier to understand. That one thing is this: that the Universe was not created for him alone, any more than the sea was created alone for the use of the sea-animals that dwell therein, or the air for the birds. Man invades both sea and air and calls them of his kingdom to conquer and to use. And he is right. They do not belong to the fish and the birds. The dominion is to the greater being, and that being is man. He is lord by permission, and rules the earth in which, and over which, his Maker has placed him.

But there are greater than he and, as he rules the lesser and uses them for the development of his faculties and personality, so these rule him and use him likewise.

And this is just and wise, for these Angels and Archangels and Princes and Powers of God are His servants also, and their development and training is necessary as that of men. But by how much these are greater than he, respectively, so must the means and material of their training be of higher nature and sublimity than those which are given him to use. According to the innate power of any being, man or angel, so is his environment proportioned and constituted.

Let men remember this and keep it in mind, and then they will the better appreciate the dower of free will given to them, a gift which no one of all the heavenly hierarchy may take from him. And they would not if they might; for in so doing their material would be deteriorated in quality, and the less capable of enabling them in their own advancement.

Now, I fear that some who read what I have written will say that hereby man becomes merely the tool of those of higher grade, to do with him what they will for their own advantage. Not so; and for the reason I have just stated—that he is, and ever must remain, a free-willed being.

But more, the one great power which animates those who serve the Father here is Love. These are no mere despots of oppression. Power and oppression are correlatives of earth creation. Here power means an issuing forth of love, and the greater the power the greater the love which is sent forth.

And this, moreover. Let those whose fight with evil is fierce and dire remember and realize well the privilege and high destiny which is theirs to attain. For in this is a warrant and sure token that man has been permitted into the Council and work of those of very high degree, to join with them in this great task of working out salvation for the whole universe on the lines laid down so long ago.

And this task is one which a man with courage will grapple with full eagerly, for it is he who will understand so much as this: that what angels and Princes of high estate are doing he is doing with them in his own sphere and degree and, knowing this, he will rejoice and be strong.

Seeing also that his work is one with our own, and ours is his, and with only one object set before us both, which is the betterment of all life and all things, he will know that our strength is at his call, so he call wisely and with due humility and simple trust. For so we delight to help men, who are our comrades in this fight, and our fellow workers in the one great field of the Universe of God.

We see more than you do of the awful travail of those who err from this service, and yet we do not despair, because we see also the more clearly the meaning and purpose of it all. And thus seeing, we know that men will one day rejoice as we do when they too shall, each in his own time, ascend to the higher spheres of service and, from this point of vantage, continue his development. In that day he too will use for his training the material we are using, and of which he is a part and portion, when others have taken his place, and he the place of those who now are lifting him upward.

"To him that overcometh," said the Christ, "will I give to sit with Me in My Throne, even as I overcame, and am set down with My Father in His Throne." To the strong is the Kingdom, my dear charge and ward, and to the one who has shall be given.

* * *

This much now, and I must cease for this time. But the matter is much greater than I have been able to tell in this short message. If God permit I will tell you more anon.

And now, do well and you shall fare well; and if you be strong, then out of your strength shall sweetness come. For so it is in these realms that they are most sweet and lovely whose strength is greatest. This remember, and it shall solve many problems which perplex men much. God's light be with and around you always, and you shall not stumble then.+

4

Earth the Vestibule of Heaven

Wednesday, November 26, 1913.

MANY things there are of which I might speak to you, matters of organization, and of the exercise of power as its influence and effect are seen by us as it passes on its way through our spheres to that of earth. Some of these things you would not be able to understand, and others, perhaps, but few among you would believe if they understood them. So I confine myself to the simpler principles and the mode of their working; and one of these is the modus operandi of the connection obtaining between us and you in the matter of inspiration.

Inspiration

Now, this is a word very expressive if understood aright; and very misleading if not so understood. For, that we inbreathe into the hearts of men knowledge of the truth of God is true. But it is only a very little of the truth. For more than this we do give to them and, with other things, strength to progress and to work God's will, love to work that will from high motive, and wisdom (which is knowledge blended with love) to work God's will aright. And if a man be said to be inspired, this is not a singular case, nor one exceptional. For all who try to live well, and few do not in some degree, are by us inspired, and so helped.

But the act of inbreathing is not a very close way of describing the method of our work. It would the better apply as used subjectively of the one so-called inspired. He breathes in our waves of vibrating energy as we direct those waves to him. So a man breathes in and fills his lungs of the fresh breeze on the hillside, and is refreshed. Even so he breathes in the refreshing streams of power we waft towards him.

But we would not limit the meaning of the word to those alone who in elegant words tell out to the world some new truth of God, or some old truth refurbished and made as new. The mother tending her child in sickness, the driver of the engine along the railway, the navigator guiding the ship, all, and others, do their work of their peculiar powers self-contained, but, as occasion and circumstances require, modified and supplemented by our own. This is so even when the receiver of our help is unaware of our presence; and this more often than not. We give gladly while we are able; and we are able so long as no barrier is opposed to us by him we would help.

This barrier may be raised in many ways. If he be of obstinate mind, then we may not impose on him our counsel; for he is free to will and to do. And sometimes when we see great need of our help being given, the barrier of sin is interposed and we cannot get through it. Then those who counsel wrongly do their work, and grievous is the plight of those to whom they minister.

Each man, and every woman too, chooses his own companions wittingly or unwittingly. If he flout the idea that we are present in the earth sphere, or that any influence may proceed from what to him is the unseen and unknown, that matters not so he be of good intent and right motive. He opposes to us no barrier of absolute negation. We help him gladly, for he is honest, and will some day in his honesty own his error—some day soon. Only this, that he is not then so sensitive to catch our meaning; and he will often mistake us, not knowing what we would impress upon his mind.

If the water-wheel be well oiled on its axle, then the water turns it easily; but if it be rusty, then the force must be increased in volume, and the wear, both of the wheel and its axle, is greater, and it moves more heavily. Also, the sailors may be accurate in obeying the instructions of the captain, even if he were totally strange to them. But if he be known to them well, then they are the better able in the storm, of a dark night, to catch his meaning in the orders he gives, for they know his mind and need little words and few to tell them of his wishes. So they who know us more naturally and more intimately than others are in better fettle to receive our words.

Inspiration, therefore, is of wide meaning and extent in practice. The prophets of old time—and those of today—received our instruction according to the quickening of their faculties. Some were able to hear our words, some to see us—both as to their spiritual bodies—others were impressed mentally. These and other ways we employ, and all to one end, namely: to impart through them to their fellowman instruction as to the way they should go, and in what way they should order their lives to please God, as we are able to understand His will from this higher plane. Our counsel is not of perfection, nor infallible. But it never leads astray those who seek worthily and with much prayer, and with great love. These are God's own, and they are a great joy to us their fellow servants. Nor need we go far afield to find them, for there is more good in the world than evil, and, as in each good and evil is proportioned, so are we able to help, and so is our ability limited.

So do every one these two things—see that your light is kept burning as they who wait for their Lord, for it is His will we do in this matter, and it is His strength we bring. Prayers are allotted us to answer, and His answer is sent by us His servants. So be watchful and wakeful for our coming, who are of those who came to Him in the wilderness, and in Gethsemane (albeit I think they would be of much higher degree than I).

And the other to bear in your mind is this: See you keep your motive high and noble, and seek not selfishly, but for others' welfare. We minister best to the progress of those who seek our help for the benefit of their brethren rather than their own. In giving we ourselves receive, and so do you. But the larger part of motive must be to give, as He said, and that way the greater blessing lies, and that for all.

Remember His word, "I have power to lay down my life—but I lay it down for my sheep." This He did in very truth, and with no dissembling of motive. Nevertheless, in laying down that life He took life up again more glorious, and that only because His gift was empty of self, and full of love. So do you, and you will find your sweetness in the giving and receiving, both. It is a task most difficult of perfect fulfillment, but it is the right and good way, and must needs be trod. And He has shown us how.

The vessels of the flower empty themselves of their scent to the enjoyment of man, but only to be filled again with more and, so doing, come to more perfect maturity day by day. The word of kindness is returned, and two people made happy by the initial act of one. Kind words later beget kind deeds. And so is love multiplied, and with love, joy and peace. And they who love to give, and give for love's own sake are shooting golden darts which fall into the streets of the Heavenly City, and are gathered up and carefully stored away till they who sent them come and receive their treasures once again with increase.+

Thursday, November 27, 1913.

Like attracts Like.

Following on what I have given you, I may add that very few there are who realize in any great degree the magnitude of the forces which are ambient around men as they go about their business day by day. These forces are real, nevertheless, and close at hand. Nay, they mingle with your own endeavors, whether you will or no. And these powers are not all good, but some are malicious, and some are betweenwise, and neither definitely good or bad.

When I say "powers" and "forces," it is of necessary consequence that personalities be present with them to use them. For know this, not as of formal assent, but consenting thereto *ex animo*, that you are not alone, and cannot be or act alone, but must act and will and contrive in partnership, and your partners you do elect, whether you do so willingly or no.

So it behoves that all be curious in their selection, and this may be assured by prayer and a right life. Think of God with reverence and awe, and of your fellow-men with reverence and love; and do all things as knowing we watch you and mark down your inner mind with exact precision, and that, as you are and become now, so you will be when you are awakened here; and what things now to you are material and positive and seem very real will then be of another sphere, and your eyes will open on other scenes, and earth be spoken of as that other sphere, and the life of earth as a journey made and finished, and the money and furniture, and the trees in your garden, and all you now seem to own as your peculiar property will not be any more at hand.

Then you will be shown what place and treasures and friends you have earned in the school of endeavor just ended and left behind for ever. And you will be either full of sorrow and regret, or compassed with joy unspeakable and light and beauty and love, all at your service, and those your friends who have come on before, now eager to show you some of the scenes and beauties of their present home.

Now what, think you, will that man do whose life on earth has been a close compartment, with no window for outlook into these spiritual realms? He will do as I have seen many do. He will do according as his heart is fashioned. Most such are unready to own their error, for such are usually positive that the opinions built up during a lifetime, and which have served them so well, cannot be so grievously in error. These have much to pass through before the light will serve their atrophied spiritual sight.

But those who have schooled themselves to sit loose to what are counted for riches and pleasures on earth shall find their laps not large enough for the treasures brought by loving hands, nor their eyes so quick as they may catch all the many smiles of welcome and delight at the surprise they show that, after all, the real reality is just begun, and the new is much better than the old.

And now, my ward and friend, let me show you a scene which will point what I have written.

The Squire and his Wife.

On a hillside green and golden, and with the perfume of many flowers hovering about like music, kissed by color, there is an old gabled house with many turrets and windows like those which first in England were filled with glass. Trees and lawns and, down in the hollow, a large lake where birds of many colors, and very beautiful, sport themselves. This is not a scene of your sphere, but one on this side of the Veil. It were of little profit that I argue to show the reasonableness of such things being here. It is so, and that men should doubt that all that is good and beautiful on earth is here with beauty enhanced, and loveliness made more lovely is, on our part, a matter of wonder quite as great.

On one of the towers there stands a woman. She is clad in the color of her order, and that color is not one you know on earth; so I cannot give it a name. But I would describe it as golden-purple; and that will, I fear, convey little to you. She looks out towards the horizon far away across the lake, where low-lying hills are touched by the light beyond. She is fair to look upon. Her figure is more perfect and beautiful than that of any woman on earth, and her face more lovely, Her eyes shine out a radiance of lovely violet hue, and on her brow a silver star shines and sparkles as it answers to her thoughts within. This is the jewel of her order. And if beauty were wanted to make her beauty more complete, it is there in just a tinge of wistfulness, which but adds to the peace and joy of her countenance. This is the Lady of the house where live a large number of maidens who are in her charge to do her will and go forth on what mission she desires from time to time. For the House is very spacious.

Now, if you study her face you will see at once that she is there expectant; and presently a light springs up and flashes from her eyes those beautiful, violet rays; and from her lips a message goes; and you know that by reason of the flash of light of blue and pink and crimson which darts from beneath her lips and seems to take wing far too quickly for you to follow it across the lake.

Then a boat is seen coming quickly from the right between the trees which grow on its borders, and the oars flash and sparkle, and the spray around the gilded prow is like small spheres of golden glass mingled with emeralds and rubies as it falls behind. The boat comes to the landing-place, and a brilliantly robed throng leap on to the marble steps which lead them up to the green lawn above. One is not so quick, however. His face is suffused with joy, but he seems also full of wonder, and his eyes are not quite used to the quality of the light which bathes all things in a soft shimmering radiance.

Then from the great entrance, and down towards the party, comes the Lady of the House, and pauses a short distance from the party. The newcomer looks on her as she stands there, and utter perplexity is in his gaze, rapt and intent. Then, at last, she addresses him, and in homely words this shining saint of God welcomes her husband, "Well, James, now you have come to me—at last, dear, at last."

But he hesitates. The voice is hers, but different. Moreover, she died an old woman with gray hair, and an invalid, And now she stands before him a lovely woman, not young nor old, but of perfect grace and beauty of eternal youth.

"And I have watched you, dear, and been so near you all the time. And that is past and over now, and your loneliness is gone forever, dear. For now we are together once again, and this is God's Summerland where you and I will never grow old again, and where our boys and Nellie will come when they have finished what is theirs to do in the earth life."

Thus she talked, that he might get his bearings; and this he did at last, and suddenly. He burst into tears of joy, for it came to him that this indeed was his wife and sweetheart; and love overcame his awe. He came forward with his left hand over his eyes, just glancing up now and then, and when he was near she came quickly and took him into her arms and kissed him, and then throwing one arm about his neck, she took his hand in hers and led him up the steps, with slow and gentle dignity, into the house she had prepared for him.

Yes, that house was the heavenly counterpart of their home in Dorset, where they had lived all their married life until she passed hence, and where he had remained to mourn her absence.

This, my ward, I have set down by way of pointing, with homely incident, the fact that the treasures of heaven are not mere words of sentiment, but solid and real and, if you will not press the word, material. Houses and friends and pastures and all things dear and beautiful you have on earth are here. Only here they are of more sublime beauty, even as the people of these realms are of a beauty not of earth.

Those two had lived a good life as country squire and wife, both simple and God-fearing, and kindly to the poor and the rich alike. These have their reward here; and that reward is often unexpected in its nature as it was to him.

This meeting I myself witnessed, for I was one of those who brought him on his way to the House, being then of that sphere where this took place.

What sphere was it, please?

The Sixth. And now, friend, I will close, and would I might show you now some of these beauties which are in store for the simple-hearted who do what they can of love, and seek the righteousness of God to please Him rather than the high places among men. These shall shine as the stars and as the sun, and all around them shall take on more loveliness by reason of their presence near. It is written so, and it is true.+

Friday, November 28, 1913.

We will now try to think of that passage where the Christ of God and Savior of man speaks to His own as being chosen out of the world. Not alone chosen of the world, but taken out of it. If, then, out of the world, in what abode do they dwell?

First it is necessary to understand in what sense our Savior speaks of the world. The world in this case is the realm where matter is of dominant importance to the mind, and those who count it so are dwelling, as to their spiritual state and spiritual bodies, in another sphere than those who hold the inverse idea, namely, that matter is but the mode of manifestation adopted and used by spiritual beings, and subservient to those who use it, as a workman uses clay or iron.

Our Spiritual Status.

Those who are held to be in the world, therefore, are spiritually in the sphere which is near the earth; and these are sometimes called earthbound spirits. It matters not whether they be clothed with material bodies, or have shed them and stand discarnate; these are bound and chained to the world, and cannot rise into the spheres of light, but have their conversation among those who move in the dim regions about the planet's surface. These, then, are holden of the earth, and are actually within the circumference of the earth sphere.

But He had lifted His chosen out of this sphere into the spheres of light and, although still incarnate, yet as to their spiritual bodies, they were in those higher spheres. And this explains their manner of life and conduct subsequently. It was from these spheres that they drew all that indomitable courage and great joy and fearlessness which enabled them to count the world as being not of their necessity, but merely as the field where they must fight their battle, and then go home to their friends awaiting. What is true of them is true today.

It is from the spheres of gloom that fear and uncertainty come to so many, for these are the lot of those who dwell therein discarnate, and not quickened so that they may be able to realize their spiritual environment; nevertheless they move and energize in it, and receive in themselves those qualities for which they have fitted themselves by their manner of thinking and of life.

So it is scientifically exact to say that a man may be in the world as to his material body, but not of the world as to his spiritual body.

When these two sorts of men come over here they go each to his own proper sphere and, for lack of clarity of reasoning and judgment, many are very much surprised to find themselves allotted to a place of which they had heard with their outer ears, but had not further inquired as to its reality.

Now, in order to make this more clear, which is of the very elements of knowledge to us on this side, I will tell you of an incident of my own knowledge and experience.

The man who thought he knew.

I was once sent to receive a man who required some careful dealing with, for he was one who had many rather decided opinions as to these realms, and whose mind had been filled with ideas of what was right and proper as to the life continued here. I met him as his spirit attendants brought him from the earth region, and led him to the grove of trees where I awaited him. He walked between them and seemed dazed somewhat, as if he sought what he could not find.

I motioned the two to set him to stand alone before me, and they retired some little distance behind him. He could not see me plainly at first; but I concentrated my will upon him, and at last he looked at me searchingly.

Then I said to him, "Sir, you seek what you cannot find, and I may help you. First tell me, how long have you been in this country of ours?"

"That," he answered, "I find difficult to say. I had certainly arranged to go abroad, and thought it was into Africa I was going. But I do not find this place in any way what I expected."

"No, for this is not Africa; and from that country you are a long distance away."

"What is the name of this country, then? And what tribe of people are these? They are white, and very handsome, but I never came on any quite like them, even in my reading."

"Well, there you are not quite exact for a scientist such as you are. You have read of these people without realizing that they were anything more than puppets without life and natural qualities. These are those you have read of as saints and angels. And such am I."

"But," he began, and then paused. He did not believe me, and feared to offend, not knowing what consequences should ensue; for he was in a strange country, among strange folk, and without escort.

"Now," I told him, "you have the biggest task before you you have ever encountered. In all your journeys you have come to no barrier so high and thick as this. For I will be quite plain to you and tell you the truth. You will not believe it. But, believe me, until you do believe it and understand, you will not have peace of mind, nor will you be able to make any progress. What you have before you to do is to take the opinions of a lifetime, turn them upside down and inside out, and own yourself no longer a scholar and great scientist, but the veriest babe in knowledge; and that nearly all you thought worthy of any consideration at all as to this country was either unworthy a thinking being, or absolutely wrong. These are hard words; they are such of necessity. But look well on me, and tell me, if you can read me, whether I be honest and friendly or no.

He looked on me long and very seriously, and said at last, "Though I am altogether at sea as to what you mean, and your words seem to me like those of some misguided enthusiast, yet your face is honest enough, and I think you wish me well. Now, what is it you want me to believe?"

"You have heard of death?"

"Faced it many a time!"

"As you are now facing me. And yet you know neither one nor the other. What kind of knowledge call you that which looks on a thing without knowing what it is?"

"If you will be plain, and tell me something I can understand, I may be able to get the hang of things a little better."

"So. Then first of all you are what you would call dead." At this he laughed outright and said, "Who are you, and what are you trying to do with me? If you are bent on trying to make a fool of me, say so and be done with it, and let me get on my way. Is there any village near at hand where I can get food and shelter while I think over my future course?"

"You do not require food, for you are not hungry. Nor do you require shelter, for you are not bodily tired. Nor do you observe any sign of night at all."

At this he paused once again, and then replied, "You are quite right; I am not hungry. It is strange, but it is quite true; I am not hungry. And this day, certainly, has been the longest on record. I don't understand it all."

And he fell into a reverie again. Then I said, "You are what you would call dead, and this is the spirit land. You have left the earth, and this is the life beyond, which you must now live, and come to understand. Until you grasp this initial truth, further help I cannot give you. I leave you to think it over; and when you wish for me, if you so should wish, I will come to you. These two gentlemen who led you here are spirits attendant. You may question them and they will answer. Only, this remember: You shall not be suffered to ridicule what they say, and laugh at them, as you did but now at my words. Only if you be humble and courteous will I allow you their company. You have in you much that is of worth; and you have also, as many more I have met, much vanity and foolishness of mind. This I will not suffer you to flaunt in the faces of my friends. So be wise in time and remember. For you are now on the borderland between the spheres of light and those of shade, and it lies in you to be led into the one, or to go, of your own free will, into the other. May God help you, and that He will if you will."

Then I motioned to the two attendant spirits, and they came and sat down by him; and I left them sitting there together.

What happened? Did he go up or down?

He did not call for me again, and I did not go to him for a long time. He was very inquisitive, and the two, his companions, helped him in every possible way. But he gradually found the light and atmosphere of the place uncomfortable, and was forced to withdraw to a region more dim. Here he made a strenuous effort, and the good at length prevailed in him. But it was a fierce and protracted fight, and one of much galling and bitter humiliation. Still, he was a brave soul and won. Then they were called by those to whom he had been committed by them, and led him once again to the brighter country.

There I went to meet him, in that same spot in the grove of trees. He was a much more thoughtful man, and gentler, and less ready to scoff. So I looked on him silently, and he looked on me and knew me, and then bent his head in shame and contrition. He was very sorry that he had laughed at my words.

Then he came forward slowly and knelt before me, and I saw his shoulders shake with sobbing as he bid his face in his hands.

So I blessed him, with my hand upon his head, and spoke words of comfort and left him.

It is often thus.+

Monday, December 1, 1913.

The Penalty of Spiritual Blindness.

Not to many is it given to see the light amid the darkness, nor to know the darkness for what it is. But that is a state of their own making; for to every one who would know the truth there is sent out from these spheres such help and enablement as is needed according to his nature and capacity.

This has ever been, and thus it is today. For God is One, not alone as to His Nature, but also as to His manifestation in the outer spheres of His Kingdom.

When He sent forth this present universe of matter He endowed His servants with qualities which made them competent to carry out His purpose, giving them liberty within certain bounds, as I have formerly explained. And one of the laws which governed them was that, among all minor and temporal variations and seeming diversity in the operation of the powers which were put into their hands, unity should be the guiding principle of all, and to that end all should tend eventually.

This principle of unity and consistency has ever been before those high Princes and Dominions, and has never been departed from. Neither is it unregarded today. This men forget, and themselves disregard who marvel that we should interest ourselves in you, our brethren less developed, insomuch as to touch you, and to speak to you and guide you personally and by personal contact of our presence.

Also, it is on our part a marvel that men should be found who hesitate on the way, and fear that to speak to us is a wrong, and displeasing to Him Who Himself came into the world for this same reason; that He might show how both spiritual and material were but two phases of one great Kingdom, and the unity of both together.

Throughout His teaching this is the one great motive, and for this it was that His enemies put Him to death. Had His Kingdom been of this world alone He had not discounted their temporal aspirations, nor their manner of life as to its ease and grandeur. But He showed that the Kingdom was of those higher realms, and that the Church on Earth was but the vestibule to the Presence Chamber. This being so, then the virtues by which nobility should be measured were those which governed rank in these brighter regions, and not the mixed conditions of the lower portion of that Kingdom, as interpreted by the world.

For that they killed Him; and today there is remaining too much, as we see it, of their sentiment, both in the Church and in the world outside. And until men do realize us our presence, and our right of consideration as fellow-members of this same Kingdom of the Father, and not until this come to pass, shall men make much advance in the discerning between the light and the darkness.

Blind guides there are too many, friend; and they displease us much by their arrogant sniffing at our work and commission. "Had they known they would not have killed Him—the

Lord of Glory." No, surely; but they did kill Him withal. Did these present know that we who come to earth on our loving enterprise were angels, they would not have reviled our work of communion and those who rise above the ruck that we may make our whispers heard. No, but they do revile us and those our friends and brethren. And they shall plead their unknowing and their blindness with like effect as those who killed the Master Christ.

Zabdiel, this is no doubt all quite true and just. But I think you are, perhaps, speaking with some heat. Also, it was St. Peter who pleaded for the Jews, was it not, and not the Jews themselves?

Aye, friend, I do speak with heat somewhat, in indignation. But there is another heat more generous, and that is the heat of love. It is not true to think of us as always placid and unmoved. We sometimes are angry; and our anger is always just, or it would soon be corrected from those who are over us and see with eyes more clear than our own. But we do never avenge ourselves—remember you that, and remember it well. Nevertheless, in justice, and in love of our friends and co-workers on the earth plane, we do mete out punishment, and that of duty, to those who deal with them unkindly. But I see you do not favor me in this. I will defer to your inclination, therefore, and leave this matter for this time. But what I have said is true every whit, and worthy to ponder well of those whom it shall be seen to touch.

As to that matter of St. Peter's pleading. Yes, so did he. But keep in mind one more thing also. I speak from this hither side the Veil, and you hear me through it on the earth side. Now, we have here, as you have there, records of history—the history of these realms—which are carefully kept.

And from these records we know that in their judgment here those His accusers did plead this blindness, and to little avail. Light was as darkness to them, and darkness to

them was as light, because they were themselves of the darkness. They did not know the Light when He came to them,
for this same reason. Very well, they were blind and did not
know. Now, blindness here in these spheres is not the effect of
the shutting off of the outer light, but proceeds from deeper
cause. It is not outward but inward, of the essence of a man's
nature. Because, therefore, they were blind, to the place of
the blind were they sent; that is, to the regions of gloom and
anguish.

This age is one of great activity in these regions of light.
Much energy is being directed on the earth in all its parts. There
is scarcely a church or creed unstirred. It is the light being directed into the darkness, and it is a matter of very great responsibility to those who are still in training in the earth sphere. Let
them be curious and very brave to see and own this light. This
is my warning, and I give it with solemn thoughts. For I speak
after much experience in this school where we learn much,
and more quickly than by the use of a material brain. Let men
search humbly and find out the truth of these matters.

For the rest, we do not sue on bended knee. That let them
also keep in mind. We do not proffer gifts as slaves to princes.
But we do come and stand by you with gifts which gold of earth
cannot buy; and to those who are humble and good and of a
pure mind we give these gifts of ability to understand the Truth
as it is in Jesus, of certain conviction of life beyond and of the
joy of it, of fearlessness of disaster here and hereafter, and of
companionship and comradeship with angels.

Friend, I leave you now, and beg you bear with me if I have
said what you have less willingly recorded than at other times.
I have not unwittingly thus impressed you. At another time I
will endeavor your compensation in messages of brighter hue.

Peace and joy be in your heart, my ward. Amen+

5

The Science
of the Heavens

Tuesday, December 2, 1913.

DEAR friend and ward, I will tonight speak to you of certain matters which connect with the question of transmutation of energy. Energy, as I now employ the word, is to be understood as that intermediary which couples up the motion of will with the effect as displayed to the minds of men. We here are trained to this end that we may, by the motion of our wills, transmit, by what we may call vibration, our thoughts through the intervening spheres, or states, into the earth plane. It is this movement in vibration which I call energy.

Now, you must understand that in using earth phrasing I am employing a medium which is not adequate to express, either exactly or fully, the science of these spheres and realms. It is necessary, therefore, that I qualify my terms, and when I use the term vibration I do not speak merely of oscillation to and fro alone, but of movements which are sometimes elliptical, sometimes spiral, and sometimes a combination of these and other qualities.

Transmission of Spiritual Power.

From this point of view the atomic system of vibration, which has but of late been revealed to men of science, is to us one with the movements of the planets of this solar sphere, and of other systems far away in space. The motion of earth round the sun, and the motion of the molecules of the atom are vibrations. It matters not by what degree you measure them, or what the diameter of their orbit, they are one in kind, and in degree only do they differ each from other.

But transmutation brings into any such system a change of movement, and the quality of movement being changed, there is also, and of necessity, a change of result. Thus we, acting always in perfect obedience to laws laid down by those higher and wiser than ourselves, concentrate our wills on the movement of certain vibrations, which become deflected and transmuted into other qualities of vibration, and thus change is wrought.

Usually we do this work slowly and gradually, in order to obtain the exact quantity of divergence from the original quality of vibration intended.

It is by this method that we deal with the actions of men, and the course of nature in all its parts. There are manifold classes and companies who have in charge the various departments of creation—mineral, vegetable, animal, human, terrestrial, solar, and stellar. Beyond this, also, the stars are grouped together and dealt with by hierarchies qualified for that great task.

It is by this same method, then, of the transmutation of energy that systems are gradually developed into worlds, and these worlds furnished with form, and then enabled to produce vegetation and animal life. But, this being so, you will note that all life, and all development, is consequent on the operation of spiritual energy obeying the dictates of the will of spiritual beings. This once grasped, blind force disappears, and intention takes its place—intention of intelligent and powerful spiritual workers of various grades operating according to certain fixed laws but, within the bounds of laws free and mighty.

The Relation of Spirit to Matter.

Moreover, matter itself is the result of the transmutation of spiritual vibrations into those of grosser sort, and these latter are now being analyzed by scientists who have come to the knowledge that matter is indeed the result of vibrations, and that no article of matter is still, but in ceaseless movement. That is correct, but not conclusive, for it does not pursue the matter to the end of it. It were truer to say, not that matter is in vibration, but that matter *is* vibration, the result of vibration of a quality more refined, which is found, not in the phenomenon of material things, but in those spheres proper to its quality.

Thus you will see how little it matters that, when the time comes for you to cast off the body of earth, you stand discarnate. Your earth body was a body of vibrations and no more. Very well, you now have a body of vibrations more substantial and enduring, because of a higher quality, and nearer to the energizing Will which brought it into existence, and so sustains it. That body will serve you while you sojourn in the lower spheres and, when you have progressed, that body will be transmuted into one still more permanent, and of quality more sublime. This process will be repeated as the ages go by and you proceed from glory to higher glory in the infinite reaches of progress before you.

It follows also that, as those in the lower spheres in this spiritual realm are not normally visible in the earth sphere, so those of the higher spheres are not normally visible in those lower spheres, and so on in like order as we rise from sphere to sphere and pursue our way along this glorious road of light and high endeavor.

So it is then, friend and ward, and when you come hither one day you will be the better able to understand. For although you do now employ this same method of which I have spoken in your own daily life, and so does every man, yet you little understand the manner of its working. Did you so it were well that all men be of one mind with us who try to use our powers for the glory and worship of God; for the weapon, to be used for good or evil, which man would then find to his hand would pass in might and strength all his present knowledge; as that exceeds the mental endowment of the fly or little ant.

It is well that we are able to coordinate the progress in knowledge and in holiness that they journey together. For this is so—not, perfectly, but within certain boundary lines, wide but sure. Were it otherwise the world would not be what it is today; nor order rule comparatively.

This, however, is one aspect of our care for the human race; and what the future holds I cannot say. For I cannot see so far as to conjecture how far men will go in this new knowledge, the threshold of which they now have crossed. But things will be well ordered by those who watch with jealous care, and wisdom very great; and all will be well while this is so.+

Wednesday, December 3, 1913.

It may be well to pursue our subject in hand a little further in order that my meaning may be made more explicit. Know then, my friend and ward, that what I have said already in respect of the transmutation of energy is by way of defining, rather than explaining in detail, the use of my terms.

Consider the Heavens.

If you will look out into the display around you of God's life manifest in the elements of your sphere you will observe several points of interest.

First you would not be able to use the sense of sight to help you to understand His working were it not that light, which is external to you, were poured upon your planet. But light also is merely vibration, and also is not consistent in its vibrating quality from first to last. For you observe the sun to be visible, and the source of those vibrations. But outside the atmospheric envelope of the solar sphere those vibrations are transmuted by the variant medium into which they have entered. Thus the stream of light passes through regions of darkness, and so continues until it approach another atmospheric zone, such as that which is about the earth, when once again that energy is transmuted as to its quality, and becomes once again what men call light. Yet one entity alone is that stream from sun to earth, a stream of light energizing from its source, passing through a vast region of darkness, and emerging once again its native quality wherever it strikes upon a planet in its course.

You will remember the words, "The light shineth in the darkness, and the darkness does not comprehend it." This, then, is more than an analogy merely. It is the mode of working which God adopts in His universe both of matter and spirit. And He is One; and His Kingdom is one.

It is obvious, therefore, that certain conditions are necessary in order that light may become operative to reveal things to men. Those conditions are the environment upon which light acts, and by which it is also affected by reflex action.

So is it in respect of spiritual environment. It is only when a genial environment is found that we spiritual ministers are able to become operative. And that is why to some we are able to reveal things in measure greater, and with greater ease, than to others whose environment is not so congenial. Whatsoever makes manifest is light, whether the thing manifest be material or spiritual.

And I tell you of another similitude. This is that, as over the intervening region of darkness the light is directed from the sun to the planet far away, so from higher spheres is the light sent over the spheres intervening, and is received in the earth plane as direct, in a manner, as the earth itself receives the sun's light.

Now, look on another field. Far away beyond the farthest star you see from earth is a zone of wondrous beauty where suns have evolved to a much more conclusive system than those you observe. It is seen here that light is measured in proportion as heat is decreased; which would point to the fact that heat is by evolution of ages transmuted into those vibrations which constitute light. The moon is colder than the earth and reflects a greater light in proportion to its bulk. The older a system becomes the colder it grows, and more brilliant withal. This is as we believe in my sphere; and I may tell you that no observed fact has to this present time been found to oppose our conclusion.

The Web of Light.

I once observed a very beautiful instance of the transmutation of energy here in my own land.

There was a company of visitors from another sphere, and they were about to return to their own, their mission having been finished. A party of our own, of whom I was one, went with them to the large lake over which they had come to us. Here they embarked in boats, and were giving us their parting words of thanks and goodwill, when one of our Princes was seen approaching with a company of attendants, from behind us. They came through the air and hovered about us and the boats while we, knowing their habits, but not their present intention, waited to see what manner of thing they—or rather, he—had in his mind to do. For it is a delight in these realms to give pleasure, each to other, by exercising such powers as we possess, and that in varying combinations by which effects are differently produced.

Far up in the heavens we saw them, as they moved slowly, circling about the Prince from whom to those in circle went threads of vibrations of different quality, and so of different color. These he of his will sent forth, and those his subordinates wove into a network of curious design and very beautiful; and where two threads crossed there the intensified light shone like a stone of brilliant hue. And the knots were of many colors owing to the varying combination of threads entering into their construction.

When this was complete the circle widened out and drew away and left their Prince alone in the midst. And he held the net by its middle in his hand, and it floated out around him like a many-colored spider web. It was very beautiful.

Now, that net was really a system of many qualities of vibrations woven together. He loosed it of his hand and it began slowly to sink as he rose through it, until it was level with his feet. Then he raised his hands and descended with it. And as he came he looked through the net at the boats below; and he made slow movements with his hands in their direction.

Then they began to move on the water as of themselves, and so continued until they floated in a circle. Then the net descended and settled over them, and we saw that they were all within its circumference, and also that, as it lighted on them, they passed through it and it sank and rested upon the water. Then the Prince, standing on the net and on the water, in the midst of the boats, waved his hand in greeting to them. And the net slowly arose from the water, lifting the boats with it, and floated upward into the air.

So away over the lake they went together, and the company of our sphere closed in around them, and sent up a song of Godspeed as they floated away towards the horizon over the lake.

It was merely one of those little tokens of love which we here delight to show our brethren of other spheres of labor— nothing more. My reason for relating this—which was, in display, much more beautiful than I am able to show you thus writing—was to illustrate the effect of the will of a powerful Angel Lord concentrating on the forces to hand and transmuting them in quality.

Beauty is not alone the minister of pleasure to the sight. It is rather a characteristic of these realms. For beauty and utility go together here. And the more useful a man becomes the more beautiful is he in person. The beauty of holiness is literal and real, friend; and it were well if all men could accept that truth.+

Thursday, December 4, 1913.

Having now explained, somewhat briefly, some of those principles, which are found in operation in your own sphere of earth, as also of these of more rarefied substance, I will continue in slightly different vein. For although it is not of your ability, nor helpful, to speak of those things which exist in these higher spheres alone more properly; yet a man must look ahead as he journeys; and the more he is able to understand of that land for which he is set out upon the road, the more sure will be his stepping onward, and less strange will appear that land on his arrival.

Beginning, then, at this point, it is one of the first tasks we have to learn here—having passed through the veil of flesh into the clearer realms of spiritual life, and having first to make familiar to ourselves the conditions here found existent, and that accomplished—to hand on to those who come on after us that same knowledge.

Spiritual Reality.

One matter which causes much distress and distrust to many souls is the fact that all they see here is real. You have already been shown this; but so strange it is and, contrary to all rational expectation, that I would fain add to what you already have received a little more. For it is of primary import to every one that he realize that the existence before him is no dream, as a man would say—but not we—but that it is indeed the fuller life developed, and the life for which the earth life is both a preparation and beginning. Why do men imagine that the sapling is of larger strength than the full-grown oak, or that the spring is of more reality and power than the river? The sapling and the spring are of your present earth life; the oak and the river are here.

The body you now wear, and the trees and rivers and other of material substance, which you call real, are not so enduring, nor so real, as their counterparts in these spheres. For here is found the energy which comes to your systems, and is as the electric dynamo to the single lamp as to its power and intensity.

When, therefore, men think of us as whiffs of smoke, and of our environment as drifting shadows, let them pause and ask if there is any sound reason to bottom their view. Nay, there is no reason in it whatsoever, but, on the contrary part, it is foolishness, and unworthy thinking beings of spirit estate.

The Reality of Heaven.

Let me describe you a scene in one of these spheres, or regions, as I will say to make it more natural seeming to you, a scene and an incident, by way of showing you what kind and manner of life you will take your part in one day soon. For when you step over into the sunlight, and think backward of your earth life, it will surely stand out very vivid and plain, and the reason of things you now discern but in part will be seen to be both ordered and wisely beneficent. Nevertheless, how short a day will your present life then seem to you when around you unfolds ever one infinitude after another, and eternity begins to be of your life, which now you reckon day by day.

Far away a light is rising in the sky which overlaps the horizon like a violet-tinted veil, and seems to drop behind it, curtaining the further distance from my sight. Between that horizon and the high rock on which I stand to view is a wide-stretching plain. Here at my feet, far down below, I see a temple which, in its turn, is still high above the City which stretches round the base of the mountain.

Domes and halls and mansions surrounded by lawns of emerald, and flowers flashing and sparkling like gems of many colors I see, and squares and statues and fountains; and many people, whose robes outshine the flower beds and outnumber their colors, move about in groups. One color is seen to be dominant over the rest, however, and that is gold, for that color is the principal of this City.

The City by the Lake.

High walls stretch, crescent-wise, along the outer part and embrace the City as the horns bend in towards the mountain on either side. On these walls are watchers—not against foe, but to give tidings of what is forward out on the vast plain from time to time, and to welcome friends who journey hither from regions far away.

The walls are lapped by the waters of a lake which is in extent as a sea or ocean on earth would be measured. But yet it is possible for those who are trained to watch to see, beyond it, the land on the farther shore where the light is growing, and is seen kissing the sails and flashing oars of the ships as they go, some in one direction and some in another, upon the bosom of the gently swelling sea.

And now I descend and stand on the walls to watch what is enacting. Presently I hear a rumbling as of thunder coming from the direction of that violet cloud of light. This grows in volume and rhythm, and gains in pleasurable tone, until it has become one sustained chord of music.

Then from the temple above me I see emerge a great throng who wear white glistering robes, with golden bands about their middles, and each a fillet of gold upon his head. These take hands upon the platform of rock before the Temple and, looking upward, seem to be lost in adoration. They are really gathering power to answer the salutation of the party who are traveling towards us beyond the horizon yonder.

Then another man comes forth and stands before them, looking towards the violet cloud of light. He is of larger build than the rest, clothed like them of white and gold, but more beautiful and bright of face, and whose eyes are like a flame of quivering light.

Presently, as they stand thus, a cloud begins to gather around them and, as it thickens, we see it in movement revolving, until it takes the shape of a sphere, and is in color golden, but full of many-colored lights. It enlarges until at length it hides the Temple from view. And then a very notable thing ensues.

The sphere, revolving and sending out flash after flash of light-gold, crimson, purple, blue, green and other, slowly rises into the air, and higher still it goes until it is level with the topmost peak of the mountain behind and above the Temple. Higher still it rises, and its light radiates far afield. And I notice that the platform where stood the party of Temple-dwellers is bare of them. They have ascended in that globe of living light and flame. This is not possible but for those who have developed in training to endure that intensity of spiritual power which generates such phenomena as this. Higher still rises the sphere until it rests suspended, and the brilliancy of its flashing is increased.

Then I notice a shadow stealing from out its midst, and settling and spreading over that half of it which opposes itself to the region behind; but, the front which is toward the violet light in the horizon is naked, and its brightness is increased by so much that I may not look at it, but only at the rays as they travel high over the plain in answer to that message coming from afar.

Then, too, we hear a humming noise, like that of bees, which comes from the sphere of light; and this increases like the other, like a chord of great orchestras, as it swells out, high in the heavens now, and floods the plain and the sea both with light and music—for here these are often made to go hand in hand, blended in condition and effect.

Our friends are seen and heard by those who come towards us from far away, and the two streams gradually approach, and so do the two strains of harmony, and all blend together in wonderful beauty. But they are not near together. That which in these realms answers to distance in yours is immense. These two in opposition are as if one of the stars you see from earth should salute a sister star billions of billions of miles away, and send her music to her in greeting, receiving answer in like responsive light and sound together blended. Then, could these two stars leave their moorings in the ends of space, and begin to come nearer each to other along the heavenly road, century after century, approaching at awful speed and, for greeting sending out from time to time floods of radiance and music, as throwing kisses by the way, ahead of their meeting—so imagine this approachment of those two spheres of the spiritual universe, and you do not overestimate either their beauties or powers of movement thus displayed.

I leave them thus, and go about my business, and all the time the light increases, and the people of the City tell the news, and hazard who it is who comes for this time, and remember one to another he meets, who came last, and what it was transpired then of glories new and not before seen in that city while they had been citizens.

So each goes about his work in happy expectation, for all visitors here bring joy, and joy receive in themselves of their hosts, and take it back to their own people when they again depart.

Now, I would that I might describe for you the meeting. That I am unable, for it is of those things that are not possible to utter in words of earth. Even thus far I have been much hampered, and have only found it possible to picture the scene hereto by lopping and chopping off all the more beautiful parts and giving you just a skeleton frame to hang your imagination upon. If the glory of it all in separation be tenfold more glorious than I have been able to indite, what shall serve me of language to tell you of the blending of those two glories when they were come together? The heaven was transformed into a blaze of light, and thousands of beings flashing hither and thither, with many species of transport animals, and wagons of different construction, and banners and devices, and flashing, radiating, shimmering lights and colors, and voices which were like instruments of music falling upon us below, as they wheeled and circled in the heavens above, like showers of golden rain mingled with violet flowers and diamonds.

Rhapsody? Yes, friend, to those who would measure heaven by earth's drab pageants, tawdry and tinsel in their trappings, and enacted in an atmosphere which to this of our own land is as fog to sunlight. Yet in the midst of all the dull dampness of earth and earth life, you yourselves are not of earth but of those heavenly Spheres potentially and by reason of your destiny. Be you, therefore, not so sordid to grovel about with nose to earth smelling for gold which decomposes itself, and is not of lasting and persisting quality. Use what things you have, and be glad that your world is so wisely ordered and so wonderful as it is, but do not rate this land by what you find normal in that lower sphere.

Look onward, friend and ward, for this is yours; and all those beauties and delights we hold in trust for you. Stretch forth your hand in faith, and I drop into it just one small gem of all these heavenly treasures. Open your heart to us and we will breathe into your being some of the music and love of your own future home.

And so, be you content awhile, and do what you find at hand to do. We keep your inheritance sure and safe for your coming, and, so you do your work as faithfully and as well as you are able, you and all such shall come to us as Kings and

Princes of the Blood—of the Blood—which is His Life for all who love holiness as He loved it and, because He loved its beauty, did not flinch to do His Father's Will—at Whom men scoffed, and for which they crucified Him.

Tread in His way, for that way led Him to the Throne, and shall lead you thither, you and all who do their parts nobly and with love.

Of such He is their King.+

Monday, December 8, 1913.

And now, my friend and ward, I am of a mind tonight to continue that of which I made a beginning when last I impressed you.

That violet cloud of glory and the one of my own sphere were commingled and, as I looked up at the sight, I saw, as I told you, the movement of those who were within. Then the glory settled down upon our City, and all the buildings and trees and people and all things therein were bathed in that violet-golden shower, and took on a more lovely aspect by reason of the baptism.

For you will understand that it was from a sphere more advanced than my own from which these our visitors were come; and none come so but they bring a blessing in gift to leave behind. Thus when they had departed we had received that which enabled us nearer to our next step onward, and the whole city glowed with somewhat more of sublimity than heretofore.

Now, it chanced that I had business in the Temple at that time, and thither I made my way along the mountain path. It was a long ascent, but usually I went afoot by way of meditation and preparing of myself for whatever I had in hand on such occasions as this.

Old Comrades meet.

Here and there along the path ascending are shrines, set a little off the way, like those in many lands of earth. And as I stood before one of these, a little removed, I covered my eyes with my hands, and stood thus awhile to commune with Him Who of His Life gives strength to us to follow after Him in the Heavenly road. Thus it was that I did not hear when some drew nigh me until their steps were present with me on the path behind. Then they ceased and I, having finished my offering, turned and saw those whose light showed me of their degree that it was not as mine, but higher in the spheres. So I bowed myself to them, and stood with eyes to look upon the ground, and waited for them to tell out their will and purpose with me.

But I stood for long and they did not speak to me. So, making bold from the silence of them, I raised my eyes and looked upon them, first at the girdle of their robes to understand of what order they might be. Thus I understood that they were of those messengers who attended their Chief on his journeyings, both. Such they were as you shall call them aides-de-camp to their Leader.

Then, they still continuing in silence, I looked on their faces. They were aglow with smiling; and amusement was not lacking in their smile. So I steadfastly gazed upon them, and at first I could discern little, for it was no easy matter that I should penetrate through that radiance shimmering around them then, to see their features whether I knew them or no. But, catching some of their power, as is the manner at such times, I did at length come to a knowledge of their countenances. Then I understood. They were two old comrades who, when we did service nearer to the earth plane, had fought for souls and won them out of the darker regions into the light of the Presence. And I had been their minister then, and their companion.

They came to me, when they saw the dawning recognition in my eyes, and, taking each a hand in his, we went together up the hill ascending, and on towards the Temple plateau, they kissing me first on either cheek, and so imparting to me further of their strength, to be and to converse with them.

Oh, the bliss and the great pleasure of that walk, when they who had been advanced beyond my present estate spoke first of old times and service together and, gradually leading, came to present times in this my own sphere, and then spoke, in sequence, of their own more bright and glorious, to which soon, perhaps, I should be called.

The Temple and its Sanctuary.

So we came to the Temple, and the way seemed not so long by much as at other times for the beauty of their presence and the entrancement of the talk they gave me of the added glory of their Home

They bore a message to the Temple-keeper that their Chief and Lord would sometime soon come, with our own Ruler, to bless the Temple and to offer worship there, both for his own retinue and himself, and for the City at which, for the time being, he was guest.

Will you describe the Temple to me, Zabdiel?

What I am able in your words at my disposal I will give you.

There is no wall between the facade and the edge of the precipice, so that the Temple is seen most clearly from the plain a little out from the City walls. It rises sheer from the platform of rock, one arch topping another, and mounting upward in perfect harmony, and in color growing lighter as the higher arches are reached. The dominating color I cannot tell you, for you have no such on earth. If I name it a combination of pink and gray that is all I can do; and it does not give you a very exact idea of its aspect. But let that suffice, and indeed I come little nearer in my description of the architecture itself.

There is not one great porch alone, as in most of your cathedrals, but there are five. They are of different build and hue, and are so constructed for the accommodation of those who come hither to worship. For were all to be admitted through one gate, those of lesser power would experience an enervation which would take from their ability to worship when within. So these five doorways are made to lead them into that nave where they may recover to be strengthened. Here they pay their first vows and devotions. Then they pass on into the great central hall of the Sanctuary, where they all mingle together without discomfort.

There is a square tower over this central space, open to the top and to the sky above. And over the tower hangs a moving, luminous cloud, which is like the Shekinah of old, the Dwelling Place from which, at certain times, descends into the Temple, and upon the worshippers, an access of His Life and blessing.

On the farther side of this space there is another nave; and here are angels who come to meet with those who are called. These minister to us by teaching of those Mysteries which are of the Higher Realms, and only those who have progressed much may receive their teaching, for it is both very high in wisdom of Divine things and powers, and also it is given sparingly, for, as a moth is destroyed of the flame it seeks too eagerly, so it is not with impunity that the higher Wisdom may be either had or given.

Into that inner Sanctuary I never yet have looked, for my time is not yet at hand to do so. And when it comes I shall be ready. I shall not be bidden thither before I am fully prepared. Yet before I am advanced to my next sphere onward I must pass through the learning to be had there, and there alone. Towards this I am at present endeavoring.

I have told you somewhat of that mighty Shrine, but falteringly, for it is too glorious to put into your words. Of such a theme St. John of the Revelation strove to tell to those his brethren who had been less favored than he. But he could but tell them of precious stones and pearls and light and crystal and—no more. Well, that is my present case, my brother, and

I am at pause. So let me leave it there with some sorrow that I can do no more than this which falls so short of the glory which crowns and suffuses all that Temple which stands on that Heavenly Mountain in the Tenth Sphere of these long reaches of progress in knowledge and wisdom and power and strength and blessing towards Him Who is the Source and Spring of them all.+

Zabdiel, I feel it rather a strain to come on succeeding days. Would you rather that I came on every other day; or on every day I can, as at present?

As you will, friend. Only remember this: that the power is here now, and it may not continue. I will sustain you for so long as I am able, and when that fails by reason of your limitations then I can no more. I will make my journal so completed as I can, however, while you are in this state of receptivity. But do as you think well. If you decide to continue daily, then do not task your mind with other writing more than is necessary for your dutiful fulfillment of your obligation to your people and friends. Take exercise and recuperation without-doors, as you feel it helpful. And I will give you what I can of my strength and sustenance. But my ability to give is greater than is yours to receive. So, if you feel able, come daily, or as nearly so as your duties permit. We have not once failed hitherto on any day, and may be able so to continue.

6

Summerland of God

Tuesday, December 9, 1913.

S O you come to me, my ward, as I desired you. I think you
will find my endeavors none too feeble but that I shall be
able to say some little thing which will be of help to you, and
to others, tonight. For there are forces on hand which will enable you when you do not know it, and I use them to put my
thoughts in order before you. So do not falter in your distrust
of your own faculty to reproduce them. When you are no longer fortified to do so I will inform you and we will close up our
book for the time being and give our minds to other matters.

Now give me your mind that I may continue on my way,
for I will that tonight you should be given to know a little further of our doings here in this Tenth Sphere. Only remember
always that I am constrained, and that of necessity, in my narration, to model my description, in some measure, on the conditions as they are found in the spheres lower than this of mine,
even as, once again, these pictures are further reduced within
the compass of the language and imagery of earth. This of necessity, I say, for it is not competent to put a bushel of wheat

into a pint measure, nor to confine light within the darkness of a leaden casket.

"Teach Me Thy Way."

The Temple-shrine of which I spoke is of use not for worship alone, but for instruction of those competent to receive it. This is the High School of the sphere, and only those who have passed through the lower forms may come here for their final learning. At various points in that region are other schools, or colleges, each for some special class of instruction in wisdom, and some few for the coordination of some of these branches together.

The City itself has three of these colleges, where those who have passed through what I will call the provincial schools come to learn the relative value of the various teachings they have received, and to combine them together. In many spheres this line is followed. But each sphere is both continuous, and also in advance of, the sphere inferior to itself. So that from the lower to the higher spheres there is a graded system of progress, and every step onward implies an added capacity, not alone of power, but in enjoyment in the using of it.

Instructors are mostly of those who have qualified for the next sphere in advance, but who elect to stay in order to teach those who, in their turn, shall succeed them when at length they go on into their own proper place of abode. From time to time these preceptors do make their journey into the sphere above, and then return to continue their task. For they are enabled to bear its enhanced glory, while those who are of less degree are not able to do so.

And also there come once and again those of the higher spheres into the lower for friendly intercourse and conversation with their fellows who teach there; and then they nearly always are willing to condition themselves according to the environment of that same lower sphere, in order that they may impart some loving words of encouragement to the pupils.

When a spirit from one of these spheres descends to your earth, it is necessary, in order that he may make contact with you who dwell there, to condition himself in like manner, and this in more or less degree. So it is here between the higher and lower conditions obtaining in the spheres of various quality and elevation.

But it is easier for us to commune with some of you than with others, and that according to your degree of advancement spiritually. So again, is it here in the spirit land. There are those in the Third Sphere who know of the presence of those of the Fourth or Fifth or even higher spheres, by reason of their advancement spiritually beyond their fellows. If to these latter such visitors wish to become visible and audible they must the more completely condition themselves to the environment of that sphere, and this they do.

This description is in outline, and you will see that what seems at first to complicate life here really serves to its orderly arrangement. The leading principles which govern the communion of saints on earth with those passed higher are produced hither, and continued on into the higher places upward in orderly sequence. And if you wish to know what regulates our own communion with those above us, then reason it out by analogy, and you will have as fair a knowledge of it as is possible to you while still on earth incarnate.

Thank you. Would you describe a little more in detail the City and the country of the Tenth Sphere?

Yes. But first as to the name "Tenth Sphere." That is what we name it by way of brevity. But in every sphere other spheres are found to touch it. What we will call the Tenth is the dominant note: but the harmony of the spheres is one and blended. For this reason a man may aspire to that above him, and is lifted up by reason of the contact of that higher zone interpenetrating his own.

But also, having progressed to, let us say, the Seventh, he is initiate into all those spheres below, through which he has passed. Thus, as others come down to him, so he can go down to others, so he condition himself always according to that sphere into which he goes. And he may from his own sphere reach forth his power to those in the spheres below. This we continually do, even from our own projecting our cognizance, and power to aid, into the earth for those with whom we have established contact. We do not always leave our own home when we help you; but on occasion we do so, as necessity compels.

Where are you now—in your own, or here in the earth sphere?

I am now calling to you from near by. For, although I count little of bricks and mortar, yet, on account of your incarnate condition, and your inability to rise far hitherward of yourself, needs must I meet you on the way. So I come to you and stand within call of you, or you would produce my thoughts, but not in the order and manner I wish.

And now to answer your inquiry of this land which is my own. Bear in mind the words with which I began tonight, and I will tell you.

The Glade of the Statue.

The City stretches round the base of the mountain. Between the walls of it and the lake, are mansions and their grounds which extend left and right, and most of them approach the Lake itself. We embark on the water and take a straight course ahead and, landing on the opposite shore, we find it is wooded with trees, many of a kind only found in this Sphere. Here also we find paths set out and, taking the one before us, we go a long journey inland, and at length emerge into a glade.

In this clearing there is a statue. It is that of a woman who stands looking upward into the heavens above. Her arms hang down against her sides, and her dress is a plain robe without ornament. The statue was placed there long ago, and has stood gazing upward for many ages.

But you are spent, my brother, tonight. So I must leave this theme and review it, if I may, at another time.

Look up, as the face of that statue does, and you shall receive a baptism of light upon your eyes that you may see some of the glories which are there.+

Thursday, December 11, 1913.

To continue:

The glade in which the statue stands is one where we often meet to receive direction from those above us who, from time to time, find it convenient to call us away from the throng of our brethren in order that they may commend to us some line of special study to be done. Here we meet and they come to us and in that beautiful glade are more beautiful than the setting in which they shine.

Flora of the Tenth Sphere.

Out of the open space lead several paths. We take one to the right of the further side, and pursue it. On either hand as we go we see flowers blooming, some of the daisy family, and the pansy, and others standing aloft as if rejoicing in their beauty of foliage and coloring, like the dahlia and the peony and the rose. All these, and more too; for we in this sphere know no flowers in their seasons, but all bloom together in the perpetual, but never-wearying summertime.

Then, here and there are other kinds, and some are of great diameter, a veritable galaxy of beauty, like great shields of flashing light, and hues all beautiful, and all giving forth delight to the beholder. The flora of this sphere is beyond description to you, for, as I have already explained, there are colors here which earth knows not, by reason of its grosser vibrations, and also because the senses of the human body are not enough refined for their perception.

Thus, to digress a little, there are colors and sounds about you ever which are not cognizable of your senses. And here we have these, and more added, to help the gorgeous display of loveliness and to show us some little of what the Beauty of Holiness must be like nearer to the Central Bliss where the Holiest dwell in the Heart of the One Alone.

The Sanctuary of Festivals.

Presently we come to a river which bisects our path, and here we turn to the left, for we must visit a colony which will be of interest to you. And what, think you, do we find here at the edge of the forest which bends away from the river and leaves an open plain to view? Naught else but a Sanctuary of Seasons or—shall I say?—Festivals.

Now, you in the earth plane have small wit of the nearness of us who seem to you so far away. Why, not a sparrow falls but your Heavenly Father knows and marks it. So all you do is open to us, and scanned with interest and much care, if perchance we may be able to throw into your worship, from time to time, some sprinkling of heavenly dew which shall tincture it and you with thoughts of Heaven.

Here, then, in this colony are curious [zealously careful] ministers who seek to weigh your Festivals on earth as they come round year by year; and these add their own offering to that of those [spirit attendants] who attend your worship to strengthen them in their helping of you as to that particular bent of mind which directs your thoughts and aspiration at the greater Festivals of your cycle.

This is not of my own special work, so that I do not speak expertly. But I know that all those ideas which with you do cluster about such as Christmas and Epiphany and Easter and Whit and the like are reinforced from such colonies as these.

I have heard, moreover, and believe it true, that those who worship the Father God by other rules than the Christian are likewise tended at their great Festivals by their own special guiding, watching angels.

Thus it is that you will note at such times an added fervor in the worshippers at their Shrines of grace, and much of it, I believe, is the result of streams of spiritual power directed from these schools, and flowing into the hearts of the congregations on earth united in praise and worshipping of God.

You would like something to be told of the buildings of the settlement. There are many, and most of them are lofty. And they assemble around a dominant structure which rises on many arches and is storied far and high into the space above. The top of this is spread out and hangs, with liplike festoons, over the houses below it, as it were a lily opening ever but never quite fully in bloom. It is of blue and green, but shaded in its folds with rich brown, like gold intensified. It is lovely to look up to, and speaks of worship unfolding heavenward, like a flower whose perfume ascends while the very heart is expanding itself to the gaze of those above, and to the Heavenly Creator and Lover, Who is over all, and yet sees and knows and finds pleasure in the breathing of the heart's life back to Him Who gave it and sustains it unceasingly and for ever.

We leave this beauteous flower to hover like a bird with mother-wings above her brood of clustering dwellings which fondle one another below and seem safe in the protection, as it were, of their mother Sanctuary and Shrine. We leave these and continue.

After a long journey up-river we begin to ascend, and continue. Thus we come to the Mountainland; and here we look far away into the distance. This is on the borderland between our Sphere and the one next in ascent. Some of us are able to see farther and in more detail than are those who have not attained to develop themselves so far. What I see I tell you now.

A Heavenly Vista.

We are on the summit of a mountain, which is one of many. Before us is but a little valley and then rises range after range of higher peaks and summits; and the farther you move to focus your gaze the brighter is the light which bathes them. But that light is in nowise still. It moves and shimmers and dazzles and darts among those far mountains as if they lay within an ocean of heaving crystal or of electricity. That is the aspect, and I can no more than that for you.

Streams and buildings there are, but these are far away. I know that among those mountains there is grass, and there are flowering plants and trees and meadows and gardens and mansions of those who dwell in that Sphere. But these are not to view for me, who can only see the outstanding landmarks.

And over all, and throughout all, I see the Love of God and His most exceeding and excellent comeliness and beauty: and my heart leaps forward to rejoice me on my way. For thither I am going, and, when I have fulfilled my task here as it is given me to do, and not until then, I know that some fair denizen of that enchanting land will come and call me, and I shall leap in joy to hasten thither.

Ah but, my brother, is it not thus with you also? What that farther sphere is to my own heart, the next of your advancement should be to you, and as lovely by comparison.

I have told you but only a very little of this sphere, but enough to give you zest and appetite to urge forward on your march.

I would now recur to the glade and bid you keep your eyes full steady gazing upward. Nay, your foot shall in nowise stumble because your eyes are not groundward bent. For those who look aloft look in the way they are going; and we look downward to keep your stepping sure.

So all is well, my ward; yea, all is well for such an one, for, because he trusts us who serve our Lord, on Him his heart is stayed; and none shall make him stumble.

So be it, then. The world is dull and wearying, times and oft, yet there is beauty, too, and love and holy aspiration. Take of these and enjoy them. Give of them freely to others, and the gloom will seem less gloomy, and the light beyond will dawn more clearly and brightly, and the sons of the morning will lead you on into their own more lovely Summerland.+

Friday, December 12, 1913.

The Meeting at the Valley of the Peaks.

Standing on that high peak radiant with the light which strikes it from the realms behind me, and bathed in the greater light of those before, I commune with those of both spheres and, through them, with the spheres beyond. Such moments are of bliss too great for utterance, and open the eyes of spiritual understanding to see things glorious and mighty, and infinitudes vast, and all-embracing love.

Once I stood thus, with face turned towards my future home, and closed my eyes, for the intensity of light as it moved before me was more than I could bear continuously. It was there I first was permitted to see and speak to my guide and guardian.

He stood upon the summit over against me opposite; and the valley was between. When I opened my eyes I saw him there, as if he had suddenly taken on a visible form for me, that I might see him the more plainly. And so it was indeed, and he smiled on me, and stood there watching me in my perplexity.

He was clad of glittering silk-like tunic to the knees, and round his middle was a belt of silver. His arms and legs below were bare of covering, and seemed to glow and give forth light of his holiness and purity of heart; and his face was the brightest of all. He wore a cap of blue upon his hair which was like silver just turning into gold; and in the cap shone the jewel of his order. I had not seen one of this kind before. It was a brown stone and emitted a brown light, very beautiful and glowing with the life which was all about us.

At last, "Come over to me," he said; and I was thereupon afraid, but not with any terror, but rather abashed of awe. In that way I feared, not else.

So I said, "I know you for my guide, sir, for my heart tells me this much. And I delight to look upon you thus; for it is very lovely and sweet to me. In presence you have been with me often on my heavenly road, but always just before, that I have not been able to overtake you. And now that I am given to see you thus in visible form I am glad to thank you for all your love and tending. But, my lord and guardian, I fear to come to you. For, while I descend into the valley, the brightness of your sphere will dazzle me and make my feet unsure. And when I should ascend to you I think I should faint by reason of the greater glory which is about you. Even here I, from this distance, feel it scarce to be borne for long."

"Yes, for this time," he replied, " I will be your strength, as many times before I have been, not always of your knowledge; and at times again when you have known me near but only in part. We have been so much together that I am able now to give you more than hitherto. Only be strong, and with all your courage to the fore; for no harm shall fall upon you. It is to this same end that I have impressed you to come to this place, as often I have come to you."

Then I saw him for awhile stand very still indeed, as he might have been a statue very well. But presently his form took on another aspect. He seemed to be in tension as to the muscles of his arms and legs; and I could see, beneath the thin gossamer-like garment, that his body there was in like manner exerting its every power. His hands were hanging at his side, and turned outward a little, and his eyes were closed. Then a strange thing happened.

From beneath his feet there came a cloud of blue and pink mingled; and it moved across from him to me until it was a bridge between the two summits, and spanned the valley below.

It was in height little more than that of a man, and in breadth a little broader. This gradually came upon me and enveloped me, and when I looked I could see him through the mist, and he seemed very near.

Then he said, "Now come to me, my friend. Tread firmly forward to me, and you shall have no hurt."

So I began to walk to him through that shaft of luminous cloud which was all about me, and, although as I went it was elastic beneath my feet, like very thick velvet, yet I did not sink through the floor of it into the valley, but continued my way uplifted with great joy. For he looked on me and smiled as I went to him.

But although he seemed so near, yet I did not reach him, and yet again, he stood still and did not retreat from me.

But at last he held out his hand and, in a few steps more, I had it in mine, and he drew me on to firmer footing.

Then the shaft of light faded and I found I stood on the further side of the valley, and looked across on my own sphere. For I had crossed over by that bridge of heavenly light and power.

Then we sat down and communed together of many things. He called to my mind past endeavors, and showed me where I might have done my task in better ways; and sometimes he commended me, and sometimes did not commend, but never blamed, but only advised and instructed with love and kindliness. And then he told me something of the sphere on the borderland of which I then was; and of some of its glories; and how the better to sense his presence, as I went about my task to which I should presently return to finish it.

And so he talked, and I felt in very good fettle of strength and delight, and of greater courage for the way. So did he give me of his larger strength, and of his higher holiness, and I understood a little more than hitherto of man's potential greatness, in humility, to serve his Master the Christ, and God through Him.

He came back with me by way of the valley, with his arm about my shoulder to help me with his power; and we talked all the way down and across, and then, as the ascent of the hill on the other side began, we slowly fell to silence. Instead of words we communed in thought and, when a little way up returning I looked upon him, I noticed that I could not see him quite so plainly; and began to be sad at that. But he smiled and said, "All is well, my brother. Always it is well between you and me. Remember that."

Still he grew more faint to my sight, and I was minded to turn back again for that reason. But he impelled me gently and, as we ascended, he surely faded away from my sight. I did not see him thus again. But I knew him now as I did not till that time. I felt him in touch with me all the time I lingered on that summit. I turned and looked into the brightness of his sphere across the valley, but I did not see him on the other side.

Just as I was turning to depart, however, I looked again, and I saw a form speeding over the mountain peaks beyond; not a solid form, as his had been, but one almost transparent. Like a ray of sunlight he went away from me visibly, or partly so; and that sight, too, slowly faded. But yet I felt him present with me, felt that he knew of me, and what I thought and did. And I turned to descend with much joy, and greater strength to do my work awhile.

As from that brighter sphere such of blessing is given to me, shall I not in turn hand on some little to those who need it as greatly as I do? And this we do, my charge, through those heavens below our own; and even to you on earth we come and minister with much gladness. For it is very sweet to do to others our brethren what so bountifully is done to us.

I cannot make a bridge for you, as he did for me; for the variance of degree between the earth sphere and this is, at present, too great to be treated so. But there is a Way by which to cross at the appointed time, as He has said. And His power is greater by far than that of him who made the road for me across the Valley of the Peaks. Of Whom I am a very lowly servant. But what I lack in degree of holiness and wisdom I strive to supply of love; and if we do both serve Him as we are able, He will keep us in peace, being stayed on Him across the depths from glory to the greater glory which is beyond.+

Monday, December 15, 1913.

I left that spot uplifted for the work I had to do before that time when I should be called hence to be as he is. Oh, the beauty and high peace of that place, and of him who is my guide. If the people of that farther zone are but half so beautiful and so lovely as he, then indeed a blessed race is that to whom I am on my way.

But now, my brother, it is upon me to help you hither on your way. And this I would, but by little or by much, so I add something to enable you and others on the road I sometime trod myself. Reach me your hand, then, and I will, on my part, what I am able.

I left that place, I say, uplifted, and from that time my own environment was the more plain to me, in that I had viewed it from on high afar to see the outstanding matters in their right proportion, and from time to time I do this now when some problem more vexed than others perplexes my understanding of it. I view it as from the high places nearer that farther sphere, and things resolve themselves more orderly-wise, and become more plain.

This do you, my ward, and life will then appear not quite so much in a tangle; but leading principles will take their place of right, and the Love of our Father be more plainly seen. In order thereto I will continue to describe for you more of this sphere in which my present work is cast.

Descending, I turn to the right hand from the river and, taking a road which bends around the wood some little distance away from it, and through a plain bordered on the right by mountains, I go my way alone in meditation.

The Meeting with Harolen.

Presently I meet a company of those who have their dwelling farther ahead, and these I will describe to you. They are some afoot, and some on horses, and some in wagons, or chariots, open vehicles they are, of wood, and with gold about them for a binding and bordering, and also devices on their front parts which tell of what realm and order the riders are. The garments of the throng are of many colors, but the dominating one is mauve deepening into purple. There are some three hundred men of them, and I receive and give salutation and inquire whither they are bound, and on what manner of business.

The one I speak to falls out of the line to answer me. He tells me that word has come to his city that a number of those of the Ninth Sphere are about to receive their initiation into this the Tenth, having qualified by their conversation thereto. On hearing this I beg that he will speak to the leader that I accompany them in order to see what is agait yonder, and also that I may add my welcome to their own. On this he smiles, and tells me to walk with him and he will vouch for my acceptance. "For," adds he, "he you call the leader walks side by side with you

At this I turned and looked on him, greatly surprised; for he wore a purple tunic, truly, but it was without ornament, and the fillet on his head was also a purple band with but one red jewel in it, and no device. Others were much more richly clad, and to look upon more comely and princely. I did not say so much, but he was of development greater than I, as I had already begun to suspect, and knew my thoughts without their utterance.

So he smiled again and said, "These newcomers shall see me as I am at this time; for some among them, I am told, are hardly ripe for much display of radiance. So they shall be as glorious as I, and they will not be dazed. Have you not lately had an encounter, my brother, as will serve to show you that too much glory may possibly impede instead of help?"

I confessed this to be the truth, and then he said, "You see I am of that sphere to which your guide belongs, and stay here in order to finish my task as I myself elect to finish it. So I condition myself in such wise that those our brothers and sisters who come hither shall feel the homeliness of home till they be ripe for the glory of the Court. So come, my brother, and we will overtake those yonder before they reach the river."

We did so and crossed the river with them, swimming it, men and horses and wagons, too, and came to the other side. We left my city on the right, and went on to the pass which goes between the mountains where the scenery is very large and massive. Rocks rear themselves with much stateliness on either hand, like spires and towers and domes, and they are of different colors. Here and there vegetation grows and now a plateau is seen stretching away between the shoulders of two hills, and on it rises the chief city of a colony of happy people, who come and look down on us from aloft, and wave their salutation, and throw flowers to us as love tokens.

To the Gate of the Sea.

So we pass along and at length emerge into a valley which opens out on either hand, and very beautiful it is here. Groups of trees cluster about fair and stately mansions, and some, of the more homely kind, of timber and stone; and lakes there are and streams falling with sweet music into the river which runs onward from the mountains round which we have come into the distance before us. Here the valley closes again, and we see two giant pillars of natural rock through which the road must pass side by side with the river.

We emerge through this Gate, which the Valley people call the "Gate of the Sea," and before us we see the open ocean, into which the river falls from a great height, and is very lovely to see as it falls, like many thousands of kingfishers and hummingbirds making their many-colored flight down the mountainside, flashing and sparkling, into the waters below. We descend by pathways and stand on the shore; but some still remain behind to watch for those who shall come over the sea. We are well timed, for our leader has powers which are of the sphere beyond, and is able to use the forces of this zone with by so much the greater ease. He has so arranged that, but a few moments after we have taken up our station on the shore, a shout is raised by our watchers above that the company is in sight far out at sea. Then round the bend of shore beyond the river come a company of our ladies who, as I learned when I asked, had their habitation in that district in order that they might join those who came to that shore from distant lands.

Great was the rejoicing of us all to greet them, and theirs to receive and give greeting in return.

Then high upon a rounded summit, below which their home was, we saw their Mother standing. She was robed from head to foot in silver gossamer, and shone through her robe like a beautiful glittering diamond or pearl endowed with life and fresh vitality. She looked intently at the party on the sea, and then began to make a weaving movement with her hands.

Presently we saw a large bouquet of flowers was taking shape between her hands. And then she changed her movements, and it began to float out and stretch itself into a rope of flowers which went out into the air, high up across the waters, and at length it rested over the people who were on the sea.

Then it drew itself inward, and began to form a flat spiral, and circled above their heads awhile, and then gently settled down upon them, and broke up into a shower of roses and lilies and other kinds of flowers, which fell upon them and about them. As I looked I saw their faces change from inquiring expectation into glad smiles of happiness, for they understood the token they had received, and knew that love and beauty awaited them in this new sphere to which they had journeyed far to come.

Now I was able to see the fashion of their ship. Indeed it was no ship at all, but a raft. How shall I speak of it simply? It was a raft, indeed, but it was no bare structure, for there were upon it couches and beds of soft down, and instruments of music; and of these the chief was an organ on which three men were now beginning to play at one time—all these and other things of comfort. And at one side I noticed what looked like an altar of offering, but in detail I cannot speak of it, for I do not know the use of it explicitly.

Laus Deo.

Now the organ begins to sound, and the people afloat break forth into an anthem of praise to the All-Father, to Whom every knee bows in adoration, for from Him only is Life, and all are through Him enabled. The sun shines forth His life to earth, and the Heavens are as chambers within the Sun for light and warmth of love. To Whom, and to all those Gods Who owe Him birth and due allegiance, be our duty paid in offering of a pure heart and will of loyalty.

Now, these words were of a strange tone to me. But when I heard them, and the music which bore them through the air, I looked once again at the Altar, for I thought to find in it an answer. But this I could not. There was no sign or emblem upon it by which I might interpret this thing. It was but later that I was able to come at the meaning of it.

But you grow towards the end of your powers for this night, my ward. Therefore we will cease now, and I will take up my theme again tomorrow, if you will. Tonight God give you His blessing, as ever. So, goodnight. Zabdiel is with you in thought and communion through the day and the night.

Remember this and you will understand whence come many thoughts and suggestions. . . . No more now. You begin to tire.

ZABDIEL+

Wednesday, December 17, 1913.

And so we now proceed on to the further account of the coming of those from the far land across the sea. For their voyage had been a long one by way of preparing them against their taking up residence in this their future home.

Now, they had disembarked upon the shore, and all were gathered beneath the high headland which stood above like some giant watchtower. Then their leader looked among us for our Chief, and at last espied him, and knew him. For they had met before. So he came to him and the two greeted each one the other with warm love and blessing.

They conversed together for some time, and then our Chief stepped out and spoke to our new brethren, somewhat thus: "My friends and brethren, children with us of the One All-Father, Whom all adore according to that light he has, I bid you welcome to your new home.

"You have come far to seek it, and it will not disappoint you when you explore its beauties. I am but a humble servant here, but as it is to the Colony over which I am set that you will be led to begin your manner of life here, I am sent thus to welcome you.

The Altar on the Raft.

"As you well know, and have learned by a long course of training, the faith you once held was but one single ray of the whole sunshine of God's great Love and Blessing. In the course of your instruction and development you have come to understand so much as this and more. One item alone of your own peculiar manner of worship have you retained—the Altar I see upon your vessel. But inasmuch as the distinguishing device has faded from its pedestal, and as I saw no smoke of incense rise as you neared the shore, in offering of thanksgiving and adoration, I think that, as a token and badge, your Altar has lost some, or all, of its meaning to you. It is for you to choose whether you will bring that with you, or leave it aboard to return it to the land from whence you came for the use of others less progressed than yourselves; or whether you will land it, and convey it with you into your new life here. Will you, of your courtesy, consult together, and tell me?"

Then they held a conference, but not for long; and their spokesman said, "My lord, it is even as you say. There is now little meaning left to us in that which once was of aid to know and worship God our Father. For we have, by much teaching on the part of others, and our own meditation, come to know that all God's children are of one birth and race, as children of the One Father Alone. The time is now when it helps us no more to remember aught which divides, even though it be in love and general tolerance. We would, therefore, send it back; for yonder are those who perhaps remember more of the details of that religion which we have now progressed beyond.

"And now, my lord, we follow you to learn, of your goodness, and that of our brethren who serve under your guidance, what more we may of the Brotherhood of all mankind in the light of this brighter land, and those realms which lie beyond."

"You have very well said it," replied the Chief, and it shall be so. Had you chosen else it would have pleased me; but this choice pleases me the better. And now, my brothers and sisters, come, and I will lead you into the fields which lie beyond this Gate, and into your Home."

So saying, he mingled with them, and kissed every one upon the brow; and I noticed that, when he did this, their countenances became of a more luminous aspect, like our own; and their clothing became more radiant also. And the Mother descended from her station aloft, and did as he had done. They were so happily met with us, and we with them, that we did not hurry to depart. Also their leader came some way with us for company; and we set off through the Gate, while the Mother and her maidens sang a hymn of Glory to the Highest, and to us a welcome and farewell in one. So we took our way inland along the valley.

Now, you will wonder at that Altar, and at the meaning of the speech of our Chief—

If I might interrupt you, Zabdiel, why do you avoid telling me his name?

I will tell you his name as you may put it into these letters, but cannot render it to you in its essential manner. Moreover, that is not permitted me. I will call him Harolen. That has three parts in speaking it, and so has his; and it will serve very well. So, to proceed.

He was much in occupation among the throng until we had passed the valley and river and were well into the country, the aspect of which I have not described to you hereto, for it was beyond that spot where I first met him. Then, when I noticed he had leisure, I approached and asked him who these were, and what worship they and he had spoken of on the shore. Harolen answered, in effect, that they in the earth life had been worshippers of the God Whose Name was wrapt in the Fire and in the Sun, and Whom the old Persians reverenced.

"One Lord, One Faith."

Now, I must add to that, of my own knowledge, this ensuing. You must know that, when people first come out of the earth life into the first stage of their life eternal on this side, they are as they left the earth. This much you know. They who have any serious religion at all continue their worship and manner of life and conduct according to that religion as to its main and leading principles. But as they progress there is a winnowing, and the chaff is blown away, one fistful after another, as they go on from sphere to sphere. Yet, while some shoot ahead, the bulk linger and go more leisurely onward; and those who have left them behind come back to them, from time to time, to instruct them.

So they go on from age to age, and realm to realm, and sphere to sphere; and all the while they approach nearer to the Universal idea of the All-Father. Brethren they still are together; but they learn to welcome, and then to love, brethren of other modes of religious thought and belief; as these others do also. And so there is a constant and increasing intercourse between those of varying creed.

But it is long before most will merge together in absolute unity. These old Persians still retained many of their own peculiar ways of looking at things, and will do so long hence. Nor is it to be wished for otherwise. For every one has a character of his own, and so adds of his own to the commonwealth of all.

But that party had made one more step onward during that voyage on the sea. Nay, rather I would say that during that voyage they had been brought to realize that they had already progressed that one stage in advance. Thus it came to pass that while certain of their phrases, and the way they made their adoration, gave it, to my mind, a distinctive tone and turn, yet that was more of the outer than the inner. And when the test was given them they decided to leave that Altar behind them, and to go onward themselves into the wider Brotherhood of God's Household of the Heavens.

It is thus we leave to float away into the mists behind us one after another of those minor helps which on earth seem so wonderfully important. It is thus we learn here what Love and Brotherhood really mean.

You are troubled, my charge; for I can both see and feel your mind and self at variance. Let it not be so, my brother. For know and be well assured of this: whatsoever is real and good and true will endure. Only what is not as these will fade away. And He Whom you serve is indeed the Truth, but did not reveal to you all truth; which was not possible to be done for those who are subject to the limitations of the life as you live it incarnate on earth. But He said you should be led into all the truth; and that is seen proceeding in the spheres beyond the bounds of earth. Of such I have even now been telling; and this leading continues I know not into what eternities of existence, or into what infinities of expansion in wisdom and love and power sublime.

But this I know—I who, as you, did worship and homage to the Christ of God and of Nazareth, and who pay my reverent devotion now as you are not yet able—this, I say, I know, my ward and fellow worker in the Kingdom, that He is still on before a long, long way. The light that would blind me is to Him in His holiness as the twilight is to me. Beautiful He is, I know, for I have seen Him as I am able, but not in His fullness of glory and majesty. Beautiful He is, aye, and lovely as I cannot find words to tell. And Him I serve and reverence with glad devotion and great joy.

So do you not fear for your own loyalty. You will not take from Him by giving reverence to our brethren of other faiths than ours. For they are all His sheep, if they be not of this fold. Who is, and was, the Son of Man, and so Brother of us all. Amen.+

Thursday, December 18, 1913.

The territory through which we passed was hilly but not mountainous, and on every side were green knolls, and here and there a dwelling. As we went Harolen became slowly changed in aspect. He grew brighter of countenance, and his robes began to assume a more luminous appearance. By the time we had progressed past the woodland on our left hand he was come into his normal beauty and appeared thus. On his head a symbol of light appeared, as it might be a crown of jewels of red and brown, which sparkled and shone forth their rays, and between the rays and about there hovered an emerald radiance. His tunic fell to his knees, leaving bare his arms; and a gold belt he wore about his middle, clasped with a jewel of pearl-like substance, but in color green and blue. His cap was of like color, two-tinted, and on his forearms were zones of gold and silver interwoven.

He stood in the wagon, which had two wheels and was very beautiful in wood and metal, and drawn by two horses, white and brown. I noted that brown seemed to be in evidence throughout, but not so much as to give distinction to that color but, as it might be said, to underlie every device, in a way that its presence was seen, and yet its aspect was subdued.

Symbolism in this land is of much interest and greatly used. I, therefore, seemed to read in this of his colors the fact that he belonged to an order and realm in which brown was distinctive but, serving in this lower sphere, while present of propriety, yet those other colors which are more familiar among us in this sphere were given a place about him who had elected to serve here some time longer than of necessity he might have done.

But as I looked on him, thus so simply garbed and yet so altogether beautiful, I felt his great power. For in his eyes there shone clear holiness, with dignity to command, while his brow, over which his brown hair parted and curled backward about his temples, seemed to woo humility and gentleness as a sister more beloved. Yet he was such as no one of lesser estate might willingly dare in opposition, while none would fear him, so that one be simple in his good intent and loving withal. One he was whom to follow his lead was joy, and in whose protection and guidance implicit trust might well be placed. For he was a Prince, with a prince's power, and wisdom to use it aright in gentleness and love.

A Heavenly Transfiguration.

So we journeyed on, not much conversing together, but drinking in all the beauty of that place with much gladness of heart, and peace and rest about us. Thus we came at last to the place where the newcomers should pause to stay awhile until they had become familiar with their new environment. Then they would proceed farther inland to one of the settlements, and perhaps would go some to one and some to another, according as they were the better fitted for this or that in the work and service of this sphere of the Kingdom of God.

Arriving here Harolen called a halt, and asked for silence for a little space, as he had a message to bring to them from his chief city, which lay ahead beyond the rising hills and out of sight.

So we kept silence and, presently, a great flash of light shot through the heavens from some point beyond the hills in front. It struck upon us and we stood all bathed in a flood of brightness; but no one was startled or afraid, for the light had joy in it. But if it clothed us, then about the chariot in which the Prince stood was a very glorious thing to be seen.

He stood there quite still, but the light about him became focused and concentrated; and he appeared no longer as he had been hereto, but, as it were, transparent and all aflame with glory. How shall I make you to have some small idea of what I wish to tell? Try to picture him made of alabaster, but living and glowing and irradiated through with a beauty of glorious light, itself alive and rejoicing. Every jewel and ornament became suffused with it, and the chariot itself was glowing as with flames of fire. And all about him was glory and the majesty of life and energy. The horses, also, did not so much absorb as reflect the radiance. And the circlet about his head shone forth with a sevenfold intensity.

Yet he did not rise into the heavens, as well he might have done, so translucent and sublimated had he become in appearance. He stood there still, his eyes looking straight into the light and reading it as a message, as if he saw what we could not see, and that, too, not there but far away ahead over the hills, at the place from which that light was sent.

The next we knew surprised us all greatly. Instead of compelling some wonder or miracle of power, he quietly knelt down in his wagon, and bowed his face into his hands, silent and still. And yet we all felt that he was not afraid, but master, of that light, and of even higher majesty. We knew he bowed to One of greater might and in holiness higher than he. So we, too, knelt and bowed to worship Whom he worshipped, knowing a Power was present, but in whose Person we did not know.

The Son of Man.

As he knelt thus we presently heard music and voices chanting some very beautiful theme, but in words we none of us could interpret. Still kneeling we looked up and saw that Harolen had descended from his wagon, and stood upon the road in front of us his company. Walking down the road towards him was a Man, clad in white from head to foot. One circle of light crossed His forehead and girded His hair behind. No jewel did He wear, but over His shoulders two bands, which were crossed between His breasts before, and were held in place with a belt. They and it were of silver and red mingled. His face was calm, and with no majesty save that of love and kindness; and He walked with slow and thoughtful step, as if He bore in His heart the weal and woe of some great universe. It was no sadness we saw, but something near akin, and yet I cannot name it, so unfathomable was that quiet all-embracing calm which was about Him.

He came to where Harolen still knelt, and said some word to him in a tongue we did not know; and also His voice was so subdued that we felt He spoke rather than heard Him. The Prince looked up then into His face and smiled; and his smile was lovely, as everything about him was lovely. Then the Other bent down and folded him in His arms, and raised him up, and stood by his side and held his hand in one of His own. Standing thus He raised His right hand and, looking on us, He blessed us and spoke words of cheer and encouragement to proceed in our work which lay ahead of us.

He was not eloquent, but rather were His words those of a mother to her children setting forth on a journey. No more than this, and spoken so quietly and so simply, and yet in such wise that they gave us confidence and joy together, and all fear was taken away. For at the first we were somewhat in awe of Him before Whom our Prince had bent the knee.

Standing thus, the light all gathered itself together and enveloped Him, and while He held the hand of Harolen He became more and more invisible, and then was gone from sight where He had stood. And the light was gone, as if He had absorbed it into Himself, and had taken it with Him when He went.

Once again our Prince knelt down upon the road, and bowed himself awhile. And then he arose and in silence, waving his hand to beckon us onward. He mounted his wagon in silence, and in silence we followed him round a hill till we came to the place near by where these should abide.+

7

The Highlands of Heaven

Friday, December 19, 1913.

Zabdiel's Tour of Inspection

"A CCORDING to your faith be it unto you." This stands a promise of power today as when first He said it; and it may be claimed with full assurance of fulfillment. Only that faith must be present, and then the present enablement will be manifest, in ways diverse but with no uncertainty of cause and effect.

Now, this is not alone to you, but to us here in these spheres progressed and progressive. It is the acquiring of faith in exercise that we study to compass and, that gotten, we are powerful to help others, and ourselves to enjoy. For it is delight and pleasure to give, more than to receive, as He said.

But do not mistake the nature of faith in the using of it. In the earth life it is of indefinite quality as mostly understood—something between trustfulness and a right understanding of what is truth. But here, where we study all things as to their essence, we know that faith is more than this. It is power capable of scientific analysis, in a measure in correspondence with the progress made by any man.

In order to show you my meaning the better I will tell you of one incident in which this is seen.

At the Children's Home.

I was making a visitation of certain homes at the instance of my Superior, to see how they did who lived in them, and to help by what advice I might, and to report on returning. So I went from one home to another, and came at length to a cottage in a woodland part, where there dwelt a number of children with their guardians. These latter were a man and his wife who had progressed, in the latter period of their ascending, side by side. These had the care of the children, boys and girls, who had been either stillborn, or who had died at birth or soon after. Such are not, as a rule, taken to those Homes in the lower spheres, but brought higher for their development. This is because there is little of earth to do out of their natures; and they also need more special care than those who have, even by a little, fought and developed in the earth battle of life.

The guardians greeted me, and the children came, at their beck, to pay me their welcome. But they were very shy at me, and did not easily respond to my talk to them at the first. All these children are very delicate in their beauty who come over here so, and I was much given to loving them, these little lambs of our Father and His Son. So I enticed them, and at length they became easier of manner.

One little man drew near me and began to play with my belt, for its brightness pleased him, and he was inquisitive of its metal. So I sat on a little grass bank, and took him on my knee, and asked him if he would choose what pretty thing the belt should bring him. He was doubtful o f my meaning at first and, following, of my ability. But I repeated my invitation, and he replied, "A dove, please you, sir." That was very polite of him, and I told him so, and that when little boys asked in such ways, trusting and believing, then they always got their will, if that will was wise and pleasing to our Father.

A Lesson in Creative Faith.

This saying, I placed him on his feet before me, and put out my will to the end he desired. And presently the form of a dove was seen in the plate of metal which fastened the belt, and this grew in distinctness, until at length it expanded beyond the plate, and then I took it, and it was a live dove which stood on my hand and cooed, and looked at me, and then at the boy, as if wondering which was the parent of its being. I gave him to the lad, and he took him into his bosom, and ran to show the others what had come to pass.

Now, this was no more than a bait to hook more fish. Surely they came, by one and two, until a little crowd of eager faces looked up into mine, not daring so much as to ask, yet longing to be brave enough to do so. Still I waited and said naught, but only smiled them back their smiles; for I was giving them a lesson in the power of faith, and their acquirement of it demanded some initiative on their part.

It was a little maiden who first braved to utter the wishes of herself and companions. She stepped forward and took the border of my tunic in her little dimpled hand and, looking up to me, said rather tremulously, "If you please, sir—" and then broke off and colored with confusion. So I hoisted her to my shoulder and told her to ask her will.

She wanted a lamb.

I told her that orders were coming in, in some good style, and growing in bulk betimes. A lamb was rather a bigger pet than a dove. Did she believe that I could give her a lamb?

Her reply was very naive. She said, " If you please, sir, the others do."

I laughed heartily, and called them nearer, and they said, Yes, if I could make a dove with feathers, I could make a lamb with wool on it (but they called it fur).

Then I sat down again and spoke to them. I asked them if they loved our Father, and they said, Yes, very much, for He it was Who made all this beautiful land, and showed people how to love them. I told them that those who loved the Father were His true children, and that if they asked Him for anything wise and good, believing He was present in His life and power, they would be able so to make their wills use that power that the thing desired would come to them. So it was not needful that I should make any more animals for them, as they could make them themselves. But, as this was rather a difficult case to begin with, I would help them.

Then, at my bidding, they all thought of the lamb they wished to have, and then willed that it should come to them. But nothing came of it apparently; and I restrained my power within certain limitations, of a purpose. After trying awhile I told them to pause.

Then I explained that they were not powerful enough yet, but when they grew bigger they would be able to do even this, if they continued to develop their faith, in prayer and love, and continued, "For you have that power, only it is not yet large enough, except to do small things. And I am going to show you that you have some of that power in you now, so that you will continue to learn your lessons from your good guardians. You have not yet sufficient power to create a living animal, but you have enough to influence one already alive to come to you. Are there any lambs on this estate?"

They said there were none, but there were some on an estate rather a long distance away, where they had gone on a visit a short time before.

"And you," I said, "by your faith and power have brought one of these lambs to you."

I pointed behind them and, turning, they saw a little lamb feeding on a path among the trees a little distance away.

They were too much surprised at first to do aught but stare at him. But some of the older ones recovering, broke away and ran, with cries of delight, to the place where he was and, seeing them, he ran sporting and prancing to meet them, seeming as joyous as they to find playmates to sport with.

"It's alive," they cried, and turned to beckon the laggards on; and soon that poor lamb was smothered with fondling and caressing, as he might have been a child of their own begetting. I do think they had for him a considerable sense of mother-hood and proprietorship.

Now, this may seem more or less casual, according to the bent of him who reads. But it is essentials which matter. And I tell you that the pretty little lesson thus given was the spring of what will eventuate, perhaps long ages hence, in the creation of some cosmos, as it might be that of which your planet is a small member. It is thus the Principalities and Powers began to train for mightier things. What they had seen me do was an act of Creation. What they had themselves done, with some little aid from me, was the beginning of such evolvement, which should lead them on to do what I had done, and then to progress, as we in these spheres do, from power to power greater still, as faith is added to, little by little, as we use it in the service of Him Who gives it us to enjoy.

This is faith, and, unseen by you, or not so clearly seen, your faith it is which, sanctified by prayer and high motive, brings to pass its own fulfillment. Use it, then, but with care and circumspection and all reverence, for it is one of the great trusts which He has confided to you—and to us in greater trea-sure—and that is no mean mark of His great love. Whose Name be blessed for the free bounty of His giving. Amen for ever.+

Monday, December 22, 1913.

At the Village of Bepel.

Thus far, then, of the children's home and schooling. And now to other matters of that tour.

I entered a village where some small number of houses were grouped, but each in its own small domain. Here were there several miniature communities of people who had in hand occupations dissimilar in detail only, but in general on the same line of development. The head man of the place came to meet me at a bridge which spanned the stream which well nigh circled this village and passed onward, eventually emptying its waters into that river of which already I have spoken. Our greetings made, we passed on together. As I went I noticed the neatness of the gardens and dwellings, and remarked on it to my companion.

Could you tell me his name, please?

You may write it down: Bepel. Let us continue.

I came to one, however, which had not so much wealth of aspect, and on this I also remarked, and asked the reason why; for I was not acquainted with what reason it might be which, in this sphere, should arrest the progress of any.

Bepel smiled and replied, "You know the man who lives here, he and his sister. They came over from the Spheres Eight and Nine some good while ago together. Here they progressed and, from time to time, have returned to the Fourth Sphere, where they have loved ones and, in especial, their parents. This they have done in order to help them onward. Lately they have come to be some little less at their case in these surroundings for the love they bear to those behind. It would seem that these are making their progress very slowly, and it will be long before they reach this estate. These two, therefore, await the coming of someone who has authority to permit them depart to take up their abode with those they wish to help, in order that their more continual presence should be at the disposal of them to enable them onward."

"I will see these two," I replied, and we went within the garden.

Now, you may be interested to know how such a case as this is dealt with here, and so I will proceed, in more or less detail, to describe what followed.

I found the brother in a small coppice to the side of the house and accosted him, inquiring for his sister. She was within, and we went to seek her. We found her there in deep meditation. She was engaged in communion with her parents far away in that other sphere. Rather would I say that she was sending her help and uplifting strength to them, for "communion" implies a mutual action, and the others were little able, if any, to return their thoughts to her.

So I talked with them awhile, and gave them my conclusion after this fashion: "It would seem that the strength required to build up your own progress in this Sphere is being drawn upon by those in the Sphere some degrees behind. You are held back by the love of those who are yonder, and slow to progress. Now, if you go to that Fourth Sphere, and there take up your habitation, you will be able to help them a little, but not much. For when you are at hand why should they stretch forth to come beyond their own present degree? It is not well, therefore, that you go to them in such manner as that. Yet love is greater than all else, and as it is found both in you and them, it will be of great might to prevail when obstacles which now obstruct have been removed. I would advise that you do not relinquish your degree of this Sphere, but that you come with me to our Chief, and I will ask that he will give you other work to do by which your own progress will be ensured, and that of your loved ones not hindered."

When I departed they came alone with me and, after consultation with our Chief Lord, I was glad to find that he, in the main, approved of what was in my mind. So he called them, and gave them words of approof for their great love, and told them that, if they would, they should become of those whose mission it was from time to time to go to the spheres behind and, there appearing (by conditioning themselves to the environment of the sphere in which they should be), deliver what business he should have to communicate. On such occasions he would request that their parents should be permitted to see and talk with them. By so doing they would be lured onward and upward to join these their two children in those higher realms.

He further counseled great patience, for that this thing might in no wise be forced ahead, but must progress by natural development. To this they assented with much joy and gratitude of heart. So the Chief Lord blessed them in the Name of the Master, and they departed to their new home well content.

So you will see from this, my friend and ward, that in the higher realms of progress problems arise which feature those of the spheres just ahead of the earth plane. For many there, too, are held back by their love of such on earth who do not so progress that they may come into communion with their spiritual lovers and helpers did these ascend many degrees removed above the state of those incarnate laggards.

But others there are, also incarnate, who, by their own advance do but by a little, or not at all, hold back their spirit guides, advancing after them by strenuous endeavor, with humility of heart and holy aspiration, that they help the rather, often, and hinder not at all.

Keep this also in your mind with the many other things you have learned. It is possible, nay, inevitable, that you incarnate on earth do help on or pull back your good friends on this side.

Joy and Sorrow of the Angels.

In which light think of the Angels of those Seven Churches to whom the Christ sent word by the hand of John. For those each, by the virtues or sinfulness of the Church he had in charge, was judged in person, as through that Church accountable to Him Who assessed each in its exact value, and awarded praise or blame to the Angel-guardian of each Church according as it merited the one or the other. As the Christ, the Son of Man, identified in Himself the character of the children of men, and held Himself accountable for the salvation of His brethren according to the flesh before the Father, so is each Angel-guide accountable for, and identified with, the one, or the community, over which he is placed to serve. He enjoys with them, and suffers with them; he rejoices over them, and mourns over their shortcoming. Remember what He said, for this I have seen, not once, nor two nor three times, but many, "There is joy of Angels before the Presence of God in the Heavens when a sinner repents." And I add to you, my brother, the bright Angels do not always laugh—though laugh they do, and that in constant. But Angels, too, can weep tears—weep and suffer for your sorrows and sins who fight the fight below.

This will not be in tune with the thoughts of us in many minds. Never mind, write it down. For by what reasoning do we joy, if we may not also mourn?+

Tuesday, December 23, 1913.

For all that it is so plainly written that men and angels work together in the one service of God, yet men find it hard to believe this to be true. It is because they give too much thought to the things of earth, and too little to the origin of material things. This is not of those forces which come immediately into contact with matter to shape and use it, but beyond, where they use those forces as a potter uses clay to make his jar or vase. This has, in some degree, already been given to you to write down. Tonight I will tell you some narrative of their doings as we see them at their work from this side the borderline.

Not all are progressed evenly in any one of the spheres, but some are advanced beyond others. Those of whom I last told you were of the least in this Tenth Sphere. I will now tell you of some who have risen to greater life and power.

Into the Highlands.

On my way, as I journeyed after leaving the village where the brother and sister dwelt, I paid my visit of inspection to many other settlements. One of these lay among the mountains towards the zone which marks the beginning of the next Sphere superior to this—not that spot where I met my guide, but at a similar altitude, and some distance away. Hither I ascended by a winding path which led to the highlands among the summits of the mountain range. When I began to ascend the grass was very green and the flowers large and profuse. Birds sang about the velvet path among the leafy trees of forests deep with purple lights and shadows, and many spirits of the woodlands sported or worked with bright smiles as I passed them, giving and receiving greetings of blessings, and adding joy to beauty by the way.

Then the surroundings began to change, and the trees became more stately and statuesque, the forest less dense and leafy. Whereas before glades of flowers and arbors of foliage had been, there now appeared lofty cathedrals of pillars and arches, as the trees stood up and bent their heads to make them. Deep and lovely still were the lights and shades, but more like those of a sanctuary than of a bower. Of large proportions were the avenues, as I passed them, stretching away on either hand. Here, too, there was a sense of meditation and greater power than away below. And I was aware of spirits in the colonnades who were beautiful with a grander and holier beauty than those I had left behind about the first rises of the hills. This also, as I went, gave place to scenes more awful and inspiring. Gradually the tree country was left behind, and about the white, gold and red of the summits played lights which told of presences from the higher realm descended on some business, to linger among these heights awhile.

So I came to my destination. I will describe it as I am able. There was a flat space, perhaps a mile in square each way, paved with alabaster stone, which appeared of flame color, as if it were a floor of glass stretched over a realm of fire whose rays played about it, and glowed through, tinting the air for some hundred yards above. There was no fire of such sort, But this is in what aspect it appeared.

The Highland Watchtower.

On this level space was one building. It was of ten sides, and each side was diverse in color and in architecture from all its fellows. Many stories it had, and rose a glittering pillar whose top caught the light which came above the peaks of the mountains, some far, some near—so high was this tower, as it stood there, a sentinel among the mountains of heaven, a very beautiful thing to see. It covered some eighth part of the square, and it had porches on each side. So there were ten ways to enter, and one facing each of ten ways. A sentinel in truth it was; for this is the watchtower of the highest regions of that sphere. But it was more than this.

Each side was in touch with one of the first ten spheres; and those who watched there were in constant communication with the Chief Lords of those spheres. There is much business passing between these Heads of the different spheres continually. Here it was gathered up and coordinated. If I might descend to earth for a name, I would call it the Central Exchange of that vast region comprised in all those spheres stretching from that which borders on the earth zone, over the continents and oceans and mountains and plains of the second, and then of the third, and so onward to the Tenth.

Needful it is that those who serve here be of very high development and wisdom, and so I found them to be. They were different from the ordinary inhabitant of this sphere. They were always courteous with love and kindness, gentle, and anxious to help and gladden their brethren. But there was a stateliness of absolute calm upon them which never gave place to the slightest agitation whatever news came to them there of the doings and strenuous life they held in direct contact with themselves. They received all reports, information, requests for solution of some perplexity, or for help in other ways, in perfect quietude of mind. When something more tremendous than usual burst upon them, they were unmoved and ready always, quietly confident in strength to cope with their task whatever it might be, and with wisdom to make no mistake.

I sat within the porchway of the side which was in communion with the Sixth Sphere studying some of their records of past events and their concern in them. As I read, a quiet voice whispered over my shoulder, "If you are not too much interested, Zabdiel, in that book, you would perhaps enjoy to see what we do within." I looked round and up at him who spoke, and met his quiet beautiful smile with a nod of assent.

How Messages are Received there.

I went within. There was a large hall of triangular shape and, high up, the floor of the next apartment. We went to the wall, where it met in angle, and there my friend bade me stand awhile and listen. I soon heard voices, and could discern the words they brought. These were being dealt with in a room above us, five stories aloft, and were transmitted downwards, passing through the floor into the ground below, where there were other chambers. I asked the reason of this and he informed me that all messages are received by those who had their station on the roof of the building. These extracted what words they needed for their part of the work, and allowed the residue to proceed downwards into the chamber below them. Here the message was treated in like manner, and again handed on downwards. This was repeated again and again until what was left passed down the walls of this ground-floor room to be once again sifted and the residue passed on below. In each room there was a great multitude of workers, all busy, but without haste, going about their task.

Now, you will think this a strange way to go to work. But the reality was stranger still. For when I say I heard the words, I only tell you half. They were audible visibly. Now, how shall I put that into your tongue? I can no better than this: As you gazed at the wall (which was treated in different metals and stones, each vitalized by what principle here answers to electricity with you) you saw the message in your brain rather than optically and, when you were sensible of its import, you heard the voice which uttered it in some region far away. In this manner you were aware, in your inner consciousness, of the tone of the speaker's voice, of his aspect and stature and manner of countenance, of his degree and department of service, and other details of help to the exact understanding of the meaning of the message sent.

This dispatch and receipt of messages is brought to high perfection in these spirit realms, and in this Tower of Vigilance to the highest perfection I have encountered. I was not competent to translate what I saw and heard, for the communication had come through the conditions of all those spheres intervening, and had become more complex than I could unravel. So he explained it to me in simple.

It was to the effect that a party had been sent from the Sixth Sphere into the Third to help in the construction of some works there proceeding. Those who had designed them had been of high development, and had included in the apparatus and structure to contain it, a somewhat more advanced scheme than it was possible to construct successfully out of the substance of that sphere. I might put the problem to you thus: If you were to endeavor to build up a machine for the manufacture of ether, and the conversion of it into matter, you would find no substance to your hand on earth of sufficient sublimity to hold the ether, which is of a force greater and more terrific than any force which is imprisoned within what you understand as matter.

It was a somewhat similar problem they had to encounter now, and wanted advice as to how best to proceed in order that the scheme might be carried out to as large an extent as possible. This is one of the simpler problems these high ones are given to solve.

Now, I will tell you more of this at another time. You are spent now and I cannot find words in you to say what I would.

My blessing is upon your life and work. Be assured thereof and go forward bravely.+

Christmas Eve, 1913.

I have spoken of the science of that High Place and it would not be much of help to you were I to continue in that vein; for the wisdom and duties there are of a degree you would understand but little. It would confuse you, and seem not over-wise, what I could give to you. I will, therefore, briefly add what I may, and get on to another theme.

I went up to the storey next above, and found it and the rest full of business, with workers at it in plenty. The walls of these large halls are all utilized in the sifting of messages and other like work. They are not flat walls, such as you know, but all shimmering with varicolored radiance, and embossed with devices, and otherwise relieved. All these are instruments of their science, and all are watched, and their effects recorded and considered and handed on to their proper destination, whether to others within that settlement, or to spheres higher or lower, as the business in hand demands.

A Horizon of Glory.

My kind guide took me to the roof of the Tower, and here I was enabled to view the country far afield. Below me I saw the woodlands by which I had ascended. Further away stretched range on range of high mountains, all bathed in the high celestial light, and glittering like jewels of many colors. About some of those peaks there played a shimmering beauty which reached them from the Eleventh Sphere; and they seemed to be alive and responsive to the presence of high beings whose nature was of a degree so refined that their forms were just beyond the circumference of visibility to one, like myself, of the Tenth Sphere.

Yet I knew that these were come over from their own brighter region, and were on some work of love engaged in this my own. At that I rejoiced very much for the knowledge of the love and power beneficent all about me, and my only speech was silence, which spoke more eloquent than words of mine could do.

At last, when I had feasted long my spirit on this great beauty, my companion gently laid his hand on my shoulder, and said, "Now these, my good brother, are the highlands of this heaven. The solitude is such as, in its beauty, fills you with reverence, awe and holy aspiration. For you now stand at the summit and boundary of your present attainment; and you have here found an environment into which, of your own strength, you are not able to penetrate. But it is given to us, as a sacred trust, and to be used sparingly and with discretion, to unveil the veiled, and look on that which is invisible to our normal sight. Would you that this, for a few moments, be given to you, that you look into what is around you unseen till this present?"

At this I paused, somewhat afraid, for what I saw was as much as I had strength to endure. But, while considering the matter, I resolved that where all was love and wisdom, no harm should be able to strike me. So I entrusted myself into his keeping; and he said it was well.

Then he turned from me and went into a Sanctuary which was upon the roof of this Tower, and was absent awhile, as I told myself, in prayer.

Presently he came forth, and he was changed greatly; for his robe was not upon him, but he stood naked before me but for a circlet of flashing gems upon his brow. How beautiful he was as he stood there bathed in that soft penetrating light which intensified about him and moved and lived, until his body was like liquid glass and gold, and shone forth increasingly till I looked downwards and shaded my eyes from his exceeding brightness.

Walls of Light.

Then he spoke to me and told me to stand before him, while he would keep to my rearward, using his power upon me, but not blinding me with his radiance. Thus we stood, his hands upon my shoulders, and the light from him enveloping me also, and, streaming forth on either side of me, it shone far out blending into the distance with those other lights far away about the peaks. Thus a lane appeared in front of me where I stood, its either side bordered with a wall of light, and the space between not dim but of lesser brightness.

I could not penetrate those walls with my vision, as they swept away across the deeps and heights of the mountaintops, opening out as they went, on either side in such-wise that, while I stood, as it might be, in the angle where the two walls of living flame met just behind me, yet in front it was a space of great breadth between the walls where I could see them far away.

Then he spoke again and told me to watch this space. I did so, and there grew a vision very wonderful upon my gaze, so that I who have beheld many beauties and marvels have never seen aught so entrancing as this.

The two rays struck one on either side a mountain peak which rose into the sky, a sharp needle with lesser spurs about it below. As I looked it began to change, and I saw a large Temple emerge into my view, and about it were a host of high angels in robes of light, moving here and there. There was a high porch and upon it stood a great Angel who held a cross aloft, as if he showed that symbol to some congregation of people in some other far-away sphere. On each arm of the cross stood a child, one in rose-pink garments, the other in green and brown. They sang some song I could not understand, and then, as they ended, each laid his hands upon his breast and bowed his head in worship.

Motherhood Enthroned.

But my guide now turned me about to the right and another vista came into my range of vision. Upon a hillside far away I saw a Throne. It was of light and fire mingled, and there sat upon it a woman who looked in silence into the far, far distance unmoving. She was clad in gossamer which sparkled like silver as her body shone through it; but over her head was a robe of violet-colored light which fell upon her shoulders and behind her, framing her beauty in such-wise that I thought of a pearl hung against a velvet curtain.

About her, but below her Throne, were her attendants, both men and women. They stood there before the Throne and on either side, silent and waiting. They were all of much more brightness than I, but none was so radiant as she who sat there serene in all her loveliness. I noted her face. It was full of that carefulness which is born of love and pity, but her eyes were dark in their depth of high wisdom and power. She rested her two arms upon the arms of the Throne, and I noted further that all her limbs told of strength, but such strength as is mingled with the gentleness of motherhood.

Then suddenly she stirred, pointed with her hand here, beckoned there, waved to others, as she issued, in no haste, but briskly and incisively, her commands.

All suddenly the crowd was in movement. I saw one party rise and fly off like a flash of lightning into the distance. Another went in other direction. And other troops I saw bring forth horses, mount and ride away into space. Some wore flowing robes, and some were girt with what looked like plated armor. Some parties were of men, others of women, and others of men and women both. In, as it were, a moment's time, the sky was dotted with diamonds and rubies and emeralds, as these appeared flashing on their heavenly way; and the dominating color of the group shone back to me, as I stood to gaze in awe and silence.

Thus the lane of light was moved from place to place the whole horizon round and, at each pause, something new to me I saw. Each scene was diverse in character, but of equal beauty with the rest. In such manner I saw some of those who were of higher degree than any I had yet beheld at work in the service of the Father. And when I saw, by the changing light, that my friend had withdrawn once more into the Sanctuary behind me, I sighed for bliss too great, and sank down overcome with the glory of the service of God as I had seen it in operation among those who watched us as we, too, worked, and took account of our needs.

It was thus I came to understand, as never before, how that all the inferior spheres are included within those above, and not lying sharply defined, away each from its fellows. This Tenth Sphere included in itself all those below and was, in its turn, included in those above, together with the others below the Tenth. This is well understood here, up to our own degree. But as we advance, this inclusion of spheres becomes more complex and wonderful, and there are things to understand in it which are unfolded but by little and little. This I have come to see, and am all agape for the further advance when I am ripe for it.

Oh, the wonder and beauty and wisdom of our God! If what I know be but a little of His scheme of love, then what must the whole be like, and how tremendous! Veiled are even the lower glories of the Heavenly Lands from mortal eyes, which strain to see them. Brother, be content to go slowly in these things. Such things are veiled in love and mercy. For, could they burst upon you in their fullness, your mind would give way before it all, and you would for long, long ages fear to go ahead lest worse befall you. I see it now as once I could not. It is wise and good—all wise and altogether good. And He is Love indeed.+

Saturday, December 27, 1913.

The Crimson Glory of the Christ.

Now, it was very wonderful that I should thus be permitted to see these wonders of those spheres beyond my estate. I thought upon it afterward, and found I could understand some of the principal intention and motive of what I had seen; but there were many things else I could in nowise fathom unaided. One was in this manner of appearance.

The whole heaven between the two ends of the light-rays, which formed each a wall on either hand of my prospect, was flooded crimson. Deep, deep and intensely deep was the region, on which I gazed, with crimson light. It seemed to be some gigantic volcanic upheaval, for clouds of this luminescence heaved and swayed one upon another, and lifted up great hunks of itself on high, and swept to one hand or other hand, and sank and met other banks of cloud. All was commotion as of blazing and consuming catastrophic fury. So awful did that red maelstrom seem to my soul that I trembled very much in fear of it.

"Turn me away from it. Of your love, sir, turn aside to some scene less awful. For this is of mystery too terrific for me to uphold myself before its overbearing grandeur."

Thus I besought my friend, who replied, "Rest you awhile, my brother, and you shall see it is not terrific any more. You are now looking toward the onward Spheres, the first of these being Sphere Eleven. In what sphere that light shines I cannot tell you, unless I afterward read the record of it, and this is not taken in this college, but in one some distance from here. For this you behold is far beyond our duties to deal with. It may be Sphere Thirteen, or even Fifteen, upon which you now look so much afraid. I know lot. But this I know—the Christ Passes there, and the Crimson Glory you see is the aura of His communion with His loved ones there in love. Look steadfastly upon the sight, for it is not seen so well but rarely, and I will try to enable you to penetrate some of the details therein."

I felt him intensifying his energizing upon me, and strove to raise myself to meet his endeavors. Success did not come, however, for this was beyond me, as I soon found out. All I could see, more than I have told you, were some vague shapes of beauty moving in the midst of the crimson, fiery glory; no more. So I besought him again, rather piteously as I fear, to suffer me to turn away. And this he did. But I could no more thereafter. I had no heart for aught else. All seemed very pallid as matched against what I had beheld; and I was rather sick at heart awhile that I might not go yonder, and be as they must be who endure so much beauty and yet enjoy to live. By and by I recovered and, when he had come forth of the sanctuary again, in normal guise and raiment, I could so far as to speak to him in words of thanks for his very large bounty in giving to such as I what he had given.

Now, what may I tell you more of the doings upon that lofty perch? For you will keep in your mind that only a little of our life and actions here are you able to understand, and that only in part. So that I have to choose very carefully what items I show you; which are such that in some degree I may reproduce in your mind and earth phrasing. One more I think I may essay.

A Colony with a Problem.

When the larger visions were ended, we stayed awhile up there upon the roof, and looked upon the country round about us. I noticed, some distance away towards the Ninth Sphere, a large lake bordered with forest-land and, here and there, an island, with buildings nestling among trees or peeping above them. Also in the forest ashore was there, now here and now there, a turret to be seen. I asked of my guide what colony was that; for a colony it seemed to be, it hung together so well, and seemed one settlement.

He told me that a long time ago a difficulty arose in dealing with those who arrived in this sphere from other regions, who had not yet progressed in all directions as in some of the branches of heavenly science—I am not satisfied with that; I will try to make it more clear.

There are some who progress evenly in all the faculties which are theirs; but others do not develop all their faculties equally all along their way of progress. These, none the less, are very highly developed spirits, and come to the Tenth Sphere in due course. But had they developed their neglected powers in the same proportion as the others, they would have arrived here much earlier.

Moreover, arrived here, they are at just such an altitude that what served in spheres behind them will serve no more in future. They must henceforth become more equalized in their faculties, and so of more equal balance.

The problem which gave rise to the establishment of that settlement was no other than this. And there they abide doing their work of help to others, and self-training the while. You may wonder wherein is the difficulty. If you do so wonder, that is by reason of the much more complex perfection of the conditions here prevailing than is the case with you.

It arises from the fact that these people are really of the Tenth Sphere in some portion of their character, and of perhaps the Eleventh or Twelfth in other portion. And the difficulty is this: They are in some ways too large in power and personality for their present environment, and yet unable to proceed into the next sphere, where their inferior parts would suffer damage, and catastrophe would ensue which would probably throw them backward many spheres behind, where they would be as ill at ease as ever.

Now, have I made their case clear? If you lift a fish out of the denser water into the rarer air it will have disaster. If you take a mammal from the forest, and plunge him into water, he will die also of the denser element. An amphibian is able to live if he have both water and dry land, but place him altogether on dry land, and he will sicken. Put him altogether in water, and he will sicken likewise.

Now, these of whom I have been telling are not quite like any of these, yet the analogy will suffice to help you to understand their case. For them to be here is like a bird caged. For them to penetrate higher would be like a moth flying into a flame.

And how is their case dealt with?

They are there to deal with it themselves. I believe they are only in the course of finding the best solution to the problem. When they have done so they will have rendered a service to this sphere which will be carefully recorded for future use. This is continually happening in various branches of study. I think they at present have been able to classify themselves according to their leading traits, and are working on a kind of reciprocal system. Each class endeavors to foster in the others that virtue and power which it has and they lack. So does each, and there is a very complicated system of communal education arisen, which is too intricate even for those who dwell in the Highlands to analyze. But something will come of it which will, when finally ripe to be given forth, add to the power and influence of this region, and that, I think, in some large measure.

Thus it is that mutual service is rendered; and the royal delight of progress is to help others forward in the way, as we go. Is that not so, my friend and ward?

And so, my blessing, and Goodnight.+

8

Come, Ye Blessed, and Inherit

Monday, December 29, 1913.

OF other things which I saw there I speak not now. It is easier to describe in your earth language the scenes and people and the doings of them which are of those spheres nearer to that of earth. But the higher you go the more of difficulty comes in between, and this sphere is somewhat exalted comparatively; and this that I have but just written is of the Highlands of this sphere. So, as before I told you, I am but able to give a very foreshortened and inadequate view of this land and its glories. So let me to matters of more immediate importance to you, and no less helpful.

Zabdiel's Mission to the Fifth Sphere.

I come to a time when it was laid upon me by the Chief Angel Lord of this Tenth Sphere to take my journeyings into the Fifth Sphere of a special purpose, which I will now explain.

I was to go to the Capital City of that region and, presenting myself to the Chief, to inquire of the reason for which I had come thither. This he would tell me, having already received word of my coming. Nor was I to go alone, but with me went three brethren for my company.

When we arrived at our destination I found the City very easily, inasmuch as I had known it in that time I was a sojourner in that sphere. But how different it appeared now to me after this long time and my many experiences. Bethink you, friend. This was the first time I had come hither since my advancement from that estate into the Sixth Sphere; and through this and the others I had worked my upward way until the Tenth was reached. Then, after all these stages, and each with its busy life and many incidents to change and develop me, I come back to this sphere wherein, moreover, I had not stayed so long as in any of the others. It was strange, but very familiar, even to detail. The strangeness lay in that when I had first come here from the Fourth Sphere, the glory of it had seemed too great for my apprehension. It dazzled me. But now my eyes had labor to conform to its dimness and want of light.

As we passed through the spheres intervening we conditioned ourselves to each, but went swiftly. When we reached the confines of the Fifth, however, we descended and went afoot slowly from the higher into the lower lands, in order that we might grow into its condition by little and by little. For we should, mayhap, be here for some time, and so would the better be able to endure, and do what work was ours to do.

It was interesting, as an experience, that descent from the mountainous country into the low lands. There was, as we went down, a continual dimness increasing ever, and yet we were continually accustoming our eyes and bodies to its condition. The sensation was strange and not unpleasant; and to me it was quite new at that time. It exhibited to me the wonderful wisdom which is throughout all and every necessary detail of these realms, this co-adjustment between light and less light, as we went from one onward into the other.

If you understand anything of my narration, then try further to imagine what it means to us when we come through those other less enlightened realms into your own, to speak thus with you as I do now. Then you will not wonder, I think, that at times we find much to do to get into touch with you, and often altogether fail. Could you see things from this side of the Veil you would not marvel at this—the marvel is afoot the other way about. Now to tell you of the City.

The Capital City of Sphere Five.

It was on the plain near the middle parts of the region over which the Angel Lord ministered to rule it. It had no walls, as most such cities have; but there were the usual series of watchtowers, and there were some out on the plain standing solitary, and some within the city, here and there, in carefully chosen positions. The House of the Chief stood foursquare at the edge of the City, and had a large gate.

Now I will tell you not as it appeared to us who came from a higher place, but as it is in the eyes of those whose normal environment is that same sphere, the inhabitants, that is, of Sphere Five.

The Great Gate of this Palace is of liquid stone. That is quite literally to be read. The stone was not solid, but in flux; and the colors of the gate changed from moment to moment, affected both by what went forward within the House, and also by what was agait upon the Plain before it. It also was affected from the Watchtowers on the Plain; but only by those on this side, not by others on the other side of the City, which were in touch with stations on the other sides of the Palace. It was very beautiful to look at, that gateway, massive on either side and blending into the wall of the main structure, solid above the square arch, and changing in beauty as the colors changed. One part only was constant, and that was the great keystone, in the middle above, which always and ever shone red for love.

We passed within and found many roomy chambers about the gateway, in which were recorders who read the messages and influences coming at the Gate, divided them into their own proper groups, and sent them whither they should go. They had expected our coming, and two youths were waiting in the roadway beyond the Gate to lead us to the Angel Lord.

We passed down the broad street, whereon went people happy of face, as ever people are hereabout. I simply write it down for you who sometimes and often do not smile for contentment within. For us it is as we should tell you the sky today is blue in Egypt in the summertime.

Then we came to the chiefest building within the Palace walls, which was the Chief's own quarters.

We ascended the steps before it and passed beneath a porch which ran along its front, and through a door into the central hall. It was also square, built with high pillars of liquid stone, like the Gate; and these were also changing continuously in hue, but did not all wear the tint of color at any one moment as the Gate did. They were diverse. There were twenty and two of them, and each was different. Seldom were two of them of the same color at one time; and this gave a very pleasant aspect to that hall. They were also made to blend together their beauties in the large dome of crystal above, and that was a sight even more lovely, and one you must try to imagine, for it is beyond my power to describe.

We were bidden to rest within this hall, and lay on couches near the walls to watch the play of color. As we did so the effect seemed to invade us and give us a peace and ease which made us feel quite homely at last in this old-new environment.

Presently we saw a light flash out of one of the corridors which gave on to the Hall. And then the Chief came to us and bowed and took my hand, and saluted me very kindly. He was of the Seventh Sphere, and conditioned to the Fifth, as is necessary to rule it.

He was very kind, and did all he could in love to enable us in every way; and then we went to the Presence Room, where was his Chair of Estate, in which he sat me, with my companions about me, and himself near by.

Word was given, and a company of women came into the Hall, and greeted us with courtesy. And then the Chief expounded the nature of my visit to me and to my companions, while the women stood before us in their pretty white and blue robes; but their jewels they had left behind, for this occasion. Yet they were very sweet in their simplicity of attire, which was, moreover, becoming to them in the demure demeanor which was upon them in the company of us who were some few spheres removed from them.

It amused me much, and so I asked that he would permit me awhile before he continued. So, descending to the floor, I went and blessed each one, my hand severally upon the head of each, and added kindly words. Whereupon their shyness was abashed instead of them; and they looked up and smiled at us, and were altogether at their ease.

Now, of the audience which ensued I will tell you when next you sit with me. I have been full in telling what I had to tell, that you might understand the conditions and customs of these parts. So let us leave it there for this time. I blessed them with words and a touch; and they blessed me with their happy smiles. And so we both were blessed, one of the other. That is the way with us. So let it be with you below. It is better thus than otherwise.

And so also with blessing I leave you now, my ward, for this time, and asking not your thanks for it. For when we bless it is our Father blesses through us, and His blessing, passing through us, leaves somewhat of its benediction in us in its passage. Remember this also, and you shall know that he who blesses his fellow is blessed himself in the doing of it.+

Tuesday, December 30, 1913.

To continue:

They stood there before me and I tried to find the reason of my coming, but could not. Then I turned to the Angel Lord for guidance in this matter, and he answered me well:

"These our sisters are brought here together, who have worked so, in one band, for these three spheres last past. None of them would go before to leave the others behind; but if one should make her progress faster, then she remained to help those who lingered some little, and together they came on until this place was opened to their entry. Now they have progressed to merit their further advancement, if you should judge it fitting so to be done to them. They await your wisdom to that end, for they have come to know that, were they too soon to go forward into the heaven next ahead, their progress would be the more retarded."

Being thus at length enlightened, it came to me that I too was on my trial. This thing had been withheld from me by my own Ruler in order that, with no premeditation, I should be found face to face with a problem, and my wits be put to hazard in the resolution of it. This added to my joy, for that is the manner with us in these realms, that the harder the task. the greater the pleasure, knowing our Leader's confidence that we are able if we will.

Zabdiel's Test of the Faithful Women.

So I thought a little space, and rapidly, and this is how I measured it. There were in all fifteen of these faithful, loving souls, who had so come their long road together. So I divided them by three, and sent five each way into the City. I bade them each bring me a little child, one to each party of five; and the child should tell me the lesson which they should impart to him, as being what most he should have needed to know.

By and by they returned, and with them were three sunny little children. Two were boys and one girl.

Now, they came in nearly together, but not quite. By this I knew they had not met with one another by the way, or they would have joined forces, and not parted again, for their love together was very great. So I bade them stand the children before me, and to the first boy I said, "Now, little one, tell me what lesson you have learned from these kind ladies."

To which he replied very nicely, "If it please you, bright sir, I came hither without knowing God's earth, for my mother gave up my spirit into the heavenly land before she gave my body to earth. These lady-sisters, therefore, instructed me, on the way, that I must know that God's earth is the cradle of these brighter spheres. In it are little boys fostered by much rocking to and fro; and no peace is known, as we know it here, until the earth is left behind. Nevertheless, it is of the same Kingdom of our Father's Love, and we must pray for those who are being rocked about unkindly, and for those who rock them too hardly."

And then he added, in perplexity at receiving this one last injunction, "But, my lord, this we do always, for it is a part of our school lessons so to do."

Yes, it was a very good lesson, I told him, and one which would bear enforcement at other lips than those of his own teachers; and he was a good boy to have given his answer so well.

Then I called the other little mite, and he came to my feet and touched them with his soft little hand and, looking up to me very sweetly, he said, "May it please you, kindly-looking sir—" But at this I could forbear no longer. So I stooped down, and caught him up to my lap, and kissed him, tearfully for the joy of love, and he gazing at me in submissive wonder and pleasure mingled. Then I told him to proceed, and he replied he could not with ease and perfection were I not pleased to set him down on the steps again. This I did, I wondering now, and he continued.

He laid his hand again upon my foot exposed from beneath my robe, and said very solemnly, taking up exactly where I had broken him off so short, "that the feet of an angel are beautiful to the sight and to the touch—to the sight, because the angel is good, not of head and heart alone, but in the way he goes on the service of our Father; to the touch, for they tread softly ever, softly where men feel their weight in rebuking for wrongdoing, and softly when he takes up in his arms the sorrowful, to bear him away to these brighter lands of comfort and joy. We shall be angels one day, not little boys any more, but big and strong and bright, and having much wisdom. And then we must remember this, for in that day some one of great degree will send us also to earth to learn and teach at one time; for there are many there who will need us as we do not need who came away so soon. Thus the lady-sisters instructed me, sir angel, and I know it is as they have said since I have seen you here."

Now, the love of little children is always so very sweet to me, it unmettles me in a way, and I do admit to you I lowered awhile my head, and looked within the folds of my lap, while my breast uplifted and sank in its almost painful ecstasy. Then I called all three, and they came—very gladly by their faces, but warily by their feet—and knelt one on either side my thighs, and the little girl before my knees. And I blessed them very earnestly and lovingly, and kissed their sweet bended heads of curls, and then sat the lads on the step beside me and, taking the little maid upon my lap, bade her tell me her story.

"May—it—please—you,—sir," she began, and she said each word so carefully separated from its fellows that I laughed right out; for I knew she had omitted the "kind" or "kindly-looking," or other such endearing adjective, fearing further disaster, and wishing, in her maidenly modesty, to avoid all such.

"Young lady," I said to her, "you are more in wisdom than your years or size, and bid fair to become a very able woman some day, who will govern well where you are set."

She looked at me doubtfully, and then round at the company, who were all enjoying this interview in no common measure. So I bade her, speaking softly, to continue. This she also did, as the boy had done, taking up where she had left off, "that girls are God's dams to nurture His lambs in their bosom, but not until they have grown in love and wisdom, as their bodies grow in stature and in beauty. So we must ever keep in mind the motherhood that is in us, for our Father put it there when we slept in our own mother's womb, before our angel awoke us, and brought us away into these blessed Homes. And our motherhood is very sacred from many causes, and the best cause of all is this: that our Savior, the Christ Lord (here she crossed her little dimpled hands upon her breast and, with fingers interlaced, bowed very reverently, and straightway continued so), was born of a woman, whom He loved, and she loved Him. When I am grown into a woman I will be told of those who have no mothers as we have here but know no tender love of mother like ours. And then I shall be asked if I would wish to be mother to some of those not borne by me, but needing some such one as I very sorely. Then I must stand up straight and strong, and answer, 'Send me forth of these bright places into those that are more dim for I am wishful to suffer with them, if I may perchance help and foster those poor little ones; for they are lambs of our good Shepherd Who loves them; and I will love them for His sake as also for their own.'"

I was much moved by these three answers. Long before they were complete I had come at several points which showed me that these women must go onward, and together, into higher places; for they were worthy.

So I answered them after this fashion. "My sisters, you have well done in this matter; and your scholars have done well for you. I perceive, among other things, that you have learned what is here to be had for the learning, and that you will be of service in the sphere next beyond. But I have learned also that you will do well to go together as hitherto, for, although you instructed these tiny philosophers each apart from the others, the trend of their answers is the same—love of those in the earth life, and their duty to them. So I see you are of such a concord in purpose that you will be of greater service together than apart."

Then I blessed them and told them they should journey back with us when we should be ready to go shortly.

Now, several points I did not note for their instruction then, but kept them back for our journeying together, when I could expound them at my leisure. One was this: so utterly at one were these fifteen loving souls that, in their several instruction of the children, they had fixed on one phase of duty and service alone. All these three children and, by implication, all those who had come over here from stillbirth, were to be sent back to help those on earth by tending and guarding them. They had altogether lost sight of all the other manifold duties allotted to such as these; and the further fact that but a small proportion of those who come hither in the manner they did are ever sent back to do mission work on earth, for the reason that the very refinement of their natures fits them for other work the better.

But I will no further now, so bid you God's Love and blessing, and on your own lambs, too, and their own dam. Believe me, my brother and ward, those of the Kingdom here look with tender eyes on those who keep their sacred charge in love, and fit them the more for this Realm of great love when they come hither. Keep this in mind and be glad that it is so, and within the power of every father and mother among you so to do.

Wednesday, December 31, 1913.

The Constitution of Sphere Five.

Before proceeding further I will describe the City at which these things were done, for the Fifth Sphere, as I know it, has certain points which are peculiar to itself. Most of the spheres, but not all, have one City in Chief; but Sphere Five has three, and there are three Chief Lords who minister there to rule.

The reason of this threefold dominion is found in that this Sphere stands at that altitude, which having attained, a choice has to be made as to the particular way to be followed thereafter. It is a kind of sorting-room, as one should say, wherein are the inhabitants, in the course of their sojourn there, classified into their proper groups, and proceed onward in that special branch of service for which they most properly are fitted.

These three Cities stand each near the borderland of a very large flat continent, and a line drawn through them would form an equilateral triangle. For this reason the broad roads of each City spread out from the largest square, where stands the House, fanlike through the City and onward in right lines across the open country. These communicate with the other two Chief Cities and the settlements of the plain. But in the middle of the triangle there is a Temple of Worship and Offering, which stands within a large circular glade in the midst of a forest. With this Temple all the roads are linked up by other crossroads, and hither, at certain times and seasons, come deputies from the Three Cities and settlements under their charge, to combine their worship of God.

Thousands, and tens of thousands, come at one time from all quarters of that sphere, and it is a very wonderful sight to see. They come in parties, and meet together in the glade, which is a large plain of grassland. There they mingle together, and all the different colors of that sphere, mingling also, make a pretty show to behold.

But more lovely than these is the sense of unity in diversity. Some are beginning to progress onward in one direction, and some in another; but over, in and throughout that vast assembly the one vibrant note of deep love pulsates; and all know that this is enduring, and, whatever be their future destination, can enable them to come at one another in whatever part of God's large domain they be forever. So there is no foreboding of coming separation. We know not any such here. For where love is what you know as separation, and its sorrow, cannot come. Even on the earth this would be so now had not man sinned, and so gone away from the right path of development. It will be hard for them to regain this now; but it is possible, for the faculty remains, if it sleep unawakened, except in very few.

Into the Sixth Sphere.

Now we must away to the next stage of my journeyings, when I should take my enlarged company into the Sixth Sphere, and there deliver the women to the Chief of that land.

Arrived there we were met, some way from the Capital City, by a company of welcome. For I had sent the message of our coming from the highlands of the borderland of the Fifth Sphere. They came, and among them were some who had known these women, and the friendship was taken up anew with much joy and many benedictions.

When we had arrived at a town where was to be their home for awhile, the citizens came forth in bright attire, both men and women and some few children. They came along the lane, where we were at that time, to meet us. The trees which grew on either side met overhead in some places and, choosing one such spot, the oncoming company came to a halt and awaited our coming. The scene was very like the inside parts of some cathedral, with leafy roof studded with gems of light and the people were the choir and worshippers.

They brought garlands of plants and flowers, and beautiful raiment and jewels for their new sisters. These they arrayed them with, and their less radiant garments melted away and vanished before the new robes proper to the Sphere into which they were now come. Then, each amidst her friends, all happy to welcome and be welcomed as to home, they who had come turned about and struck up a sweet marching air, with instruments of melody, and sang as we went forward towards the town. Here the townspeople thronged the walls and towers and gates, and cried greetings of welcome to add joy to joy already great.

Thus it is that initiates are made to know their welcoming, and, when two or three spheres have been passed through, none fear any longer that strangeness of new scenes and faces shall ever mar their progress onward; for all is love, as they very soon come to know.

The Initiation in the Sanctuary.

We went within the gate and into the town, and came to the Sanctuary. It was a large oval building of very nicely proportioned architecture. The whole, in scheme, was, in significance, that of two circles joined. They symbolized, the one love, and the other knowledge; and the blending of these beneath the central tower within was very nicely and cunningly arranged. Here the light was never still, but ever changing, like that of the Hall of Pillars I lately described. Only there were two dominant colors here, the one rose-red and the other violet with green and blue in it.

The women were led within, and a large congregation gathered thither. Then they were taken to a raised place in the very middle of the Sanctuary, and made to stand there awhile. The keepers of the Sanctuary, with their leader, then made their offerings of praise and, when the worshippers joined with them, a cloud of bright mist gathered from them around the women initiates, and bathed them in the conditions of their new sphere.

When it passed away from them and floated upward, forming a canopy above, they all stood, in a deep and silent ecstasy, watching the beautiful cloud as it rose and spread out until it covered the space above the other people also. Then came a sound of music, as if it was far away, and yet within the building. It was so sweet and soft, and yet so full of power, that we all felt ourselves to be in the Presence, and bowed in worship, knowing He is ever near.

That music melted away, and yet was with us still; for it seemed to become a part of the cloud of light above us. And, in a way you are not yet able to understand, this is indeed the truth of it. So that cloud of color and melody of love sank gradually upon us, and was absorbed into our bodies, and made us all one together in the blessedness of holy love.

There was no further Manifestation that they could see at that time. But I, whose faculties have been in longer training, saw what they could not, and knew of those who were present to them unseen; and also from whence the voice came I knew, and the sort of power given in blessing.

But they went away, all very content and very happy together, and the fifteen not the least of them all.

And, Zabdiel, what were you doing all this time? For I suppose you were the highest in degree there, weren't you?

It ill becomes that I should tell of myself who did but minister in a work of very happy service. The principal of interest were those fifteen. There were three and myself from our own sphere, and none others from any sphere above that one. And to us all the people were very friendly and very kind and loving; and we had much happiness of them by reason of this. Before they would suffer their friends to lead them away to their homes, moreover, those fifteen dear women needs must resist, to come back to us, and thank us, and say very nice words to us in gratitude. We gave them our own in return, and promised that we would come again in awhile to inquire of their progress, and perchance give words of counsel. This at their own desire; in which also they showed wisdom rightly named. For it will be helpful to them, I know, and a help not usually given, because not often asked.

So you see the rule here is, as it is with you, as He said, "To those who ask it shall be given." Which word my brother and good friend, I leave with you to think upon, with my love and good word of benediction.+

Friday, January 2, 1914.

Back in the Tenth Sphere.

I will that you now come back in your mind to my own Sphere, for there are doings there which I would tell you of. By so much as we progress to learn of God and His ways of wisdom, by so much do we come to understand how simple, and yet how complex, are His forces in operation. This is paradox, yet true nevertheless. Simplicity is found in the unity of forces, and the principle on which they are used.

For instance, love strengthens, and less love weakens, in ratio to its lack, every stream of power which comes from the Supreme Father for our use in His service. They who have come so far as to this sphere are able, by what wisdom they have come at, to absorb into their own personalities, to see the trend of things. We see, as we get towards the Unapproachable Light, that all things are tending towards one central principle, and that is Love. We see Love at the Source of all things.

Perplexity is found as from this Source and Center we proceed outward. Love still runs onward but has, of necessity, to become adapted, by reason of the lower wisdom of the personalities by whom the service of God is done, and is, therefore, not so clearly seen. When these vibrations of spiritual activity, sent forth by innumerable workers in the one great Scheme, reach the cosmos of matter, the perplexity of adaptation and coordination is very much increased. If, then, even on earth, His Love may be discerned by those who themselves are loving, in how much greater degree is it manifest to us.

But yet the wisdom we have before us to attain, if more simple in one sense, is inversely much more intricate, because of the vaster regions over which our view is given to range. As you go from one sphere to another you meet with those whose providence is concerned with ever wider systems of planets and suns and constellations. These you must consult, and from them you must learn ever more widely of the constitution of the Father's widespread realms, and the children of those realms, and His dealings with them, and theirs with Him.

So you will see that we do well to be careful in our stepping forward, that a thoroughness of understanding be had, step by step, for the duties allotted to us become ever wider in their effect, and the consequence of our decisions and actions are fraught with greater solemnity, and have responsibility to wider reaches of space and its inhabitants.

I do not deal, however, with other than your own planet in these messages which I have given you, for the time is not ripe by far for such extended knowledge. What we have now in hand, I and my fellow-workers, is to help the people of earth to a higher wisdom in respect to their duty in love one to another, and unitedly to God, and of our ministry of help to such as, in love and humility, are willing to work with us—we from this side the Veil, and you on earth being our hands and eyes and ears and the words of our mouth to speak forth, as we help you, that men may know themselves as God made them, glorious potentially and, for the time of the season of their earth sojourn, toilers in a world where the light has been permitted to grow dim.

Now let me tell you of those things of which I spoke.

The Temple of the Holy Mount.

On a large plain in this Sphere Ten there is a high mountain which stands sheer up from the grassland and dominates its fellow-mountains like a king on his throne among his courtiers. Here and there about the steep ascent, as viewed from the plain, you see buildings. Some are shrines open to the view on every side; some are sanctuaries in which worship is offered, and on the summit the Temple itself, which is over all, and to which all minister and lead. From this Temple, from time to time, Manifestations of the Presence are given to assemblies gathered on the plain below.

Is this the Temple of which you told me before?

No. That was the Temple of the Capital City. This is the Temple of the Holy Mount. It is higher in degree and of different use. It is set here not so much for worship within, but for the uplifting and strengthening and education of worshippers who assemble on the plain. Keepers and officers there are, who worship within the Temple, but these are very high in degree, and few go in with them until they have progressed some spheres onward, and return on some duty to this Tenth Sphere.

It is a Colony of Powers who are advanced beyond this Tenth in their persons, but who visit this High Place on missions of help and judgment from time to time. And there are always some of them there. The Temple is never left without its complement. But I have not been within, and shall not until I have attained to higher power and sublimity in spheres beyond.

On this plain were gathered a very vast number of people, called thither from all parts of this wide Sphere. From some half a mile—as you would say—from the mountain's base they stretched out far across the country, group after group, until they looked like a sea of flowers in gentle movement, their Jewels of Order flashing as they moved, and their garments of many hues ever shimmering from one combination of colors into another. High up on the Sacred Mount stood the Temple and, from time to time, they looked that way in expectation.

Presently there emerged upon the roof a company of men whose shining garments told of their high estate. These came and stood upon the Porch of the Temple, above the chief Gate, and one lifted up his hands and blessed the multitude on the plain. Every word he said was clear and loud to the furthest group. They who stood afar both heard and saw with as great ease as those who were nearer. Then he told them the purpose of their coming together. It was in order that certain might be presented before them, who shortly should be advanced onward into the Eleventh Sphere, inasmuch as their progress had been judged to warrant their safe journey on that upward way.

Now, none of us knew who these new initiates were to be—whether oneself or one's neighbor. That was left to be told. So we waited, in some sort of silence, the next that should happen. Those on the Porch stood silent.

The King of Kings.

Then from the Gate of the Temple came forth a Man, clad in simple white, but radiant and very lovely. On His head was a fillet of gold, and gold sandals upon His feet. About His middle was a belt of red which shone and sent forth rays of crimson here and there as He moved forward. In His right hand He carried a golden cup. His left hand was upon His girdle, and near His heart. We knew Him at once, the Son of Man, for none else is like to Him Who, in whatever form or Manifestation seen, ever blends two forces perfectly in Himself: Love and Royalty. There is always a simplicity in His grandeur, and a majesty in His simplicity. Both these you feel come into you and blend with your own life whenever He manifests Himself, as now. And when the Manifestation is over, the blessing so received does not pass from you, but remains a part of you always.

He stood there beautiful altogether, and sweet beyond my telling—sweet and lovely, and with just a tincture of sacrificing pity, which did but add to the joyful solemnity of His face. That face was a smile itself, but yet He did not smile in act. And in the smile were tears, not of sorrow but of joy to give of His own to others, in love. His whole aspect, and what His form expressed, was so manifold of powers and graces in combination as to make Him One alone among those others who attended Him there, and to set Him above all as King.

He stood there gazing not at us but beyond us into the realms where we could not follow. And while He stood thus rapt, forth from the Temple, by its several gates, came a long company of attendants, both men and women, whose sublimity was seen in the delicacy of their faces and forms.

One thing I noted, and will tell you as well as I may. Each of those blessed spirits had a well-defined and powerful character written upon the countenance, and in the gait and actions of each. No two had the same virtues in equal parts and combination. Each was a very high Angel in degree and authority, but each a personality in himself or herself, and no two alike. And He stood there, and they on either side, and some on the lower ledge before Him. And in Him, both face and form, were united, in sweet blend and communion, the beauties and qualities and powers of them all. In Him you could see each quality of theirs distinct, yet all blended together. Yes, He was Alone, and His Aloneness lent added majesty to His appearing.

Now, think of that scene, and I will tell you more tomorrow, if you find opportunity for my company. Blessing and glory and beauty are where He is, my dear friend and ward, as I have seen, not once nor twice, but many times since I left the earth life. Blessing He brings and leaves with His brethren. Glory is about Him and links Him with the Throne in the High Places of the Heavens of God. Beauty sits upon Him as a robe of light.

And He is with you also, as with us. He comes not in figure but in fact, into the dim earth plane, and brings there also His Blessing and Glory and Beauty. But there they are unseen, except in part and by a few—unseen by reason of the dark cloud of sin about the world, as we see it, and lack of faith to look, believing. Still, He is with you. Open your heart to Him and you, as we do, shall have what He brings to give you. +

The Power and the Glory.

Awhile He stood in rapture, silent, still and beautiful altogether to look upon. Meanwhile, in the throng of bright ones about Him a movement began. Slowly, and with no haste, the multitude rose into the air, and took shape until there was an oval of light round behind and on both sides of Him. Those in rear were higher than His head, and those in front were lower than His feet. So a frame was made and, as it took shape, their brightness increased until we scarce discerned the forms of them by reason of the brightness of their glory. They shone golden about Him, but He was more radiant still than all other beside, as they stood still now, and shining. Only before His feet was there no arc of light, but a breach was made, so that the oval was not complete but gapped at its lowest part.

Then He moved. His left hand He extended and stretched forth towards us in benediction. With His right hand He tilted the chalice towards us, and from its bowl poured forth a thin stream of many-colored light which fell upon the rock before Him and flowed down the face of the mountain towards the plain. And as it flowed it increased in volume, until it began to lap over the plain towards us, still expanding. It reached us a broad river of light; and in it were seen colors in all their hues, from deep purple to pale lilac, from deep red to faint pink, from orange-brown to gold. And all these mingled, here and there, in streams of green or other composite hue.

So it came to us, and among us, as we stood there wondering both at the thing done and all the beauty of it. Now it swept onward until it had covered all the ground on which stood that vast multitude of people. But they did not stand in the liquid lake, for it did not rise upon their feet, but formed a sea beneath them, and they stood upon it. Nor could the eye penetrate to see the grassland upon which it rested as upon a sea-bed. It seemed to lie there beneath us very deep, a sea of liquid glass, rainbow-tinted, and upon that sea we stood as on firm ground. Yet it was all in motion, here and there in little waves, and here and there in rivulets of red or blue or other color, flowing among us underfoot, very strange and very pretty to see.

But in a while it was noticed that it did not serve every one equally. There was one here, and another at some little distance, and this repeated throughout the throng, who became conscious of a change in them; and this made them to be silent and in very deep meditation. This change also soon became apparent to their near neighbors. For this is what they saw: the flood of light about him who was thus changed ran yellow-gold, and lapped first his ankles, and then, rising like a pillar of liquid glass, all radiant, bathed his knees, and then still rose until it was about him a pillar of light, and he in the midst of a golden radiance. Then upon his head, in place of jewel, or chaplet, or whatever he wore, there appeared eleven stars. These also were of gold, but of a brilliance greater than the stream, as if it had become concentrated into eleven jeweled stars to crown the chosen one. On each of those so dealt with that fillet of stars rested upon his head near his forehead, and clasped his head on each side behind his ears. Thus it rested, and shone, making the wearer more beautiful, for the light seemed to invade his countenance and all his body, and uplift him above his fellows.

Then the Son of Man tilted back the cup, and the stream ceased to flow. And the rock became visible once again, where before it had been hidden by the river of light falling. Presently the grassland about the multitude began also to be seen, and at last all the sea of colors had melted away, and we stood on the plain as afore we had done.

Only there remained those who had become enveloped. They were enveloped now no more. But they were changed for aye, and would never be as they had been ever again. Their countenances had become of more ethereal appearance, their bodies also, and their robes were of a brighter hue than those of their fellows, and of another color. Also the eleven stars remained to crown them with their light. Only the pillar of radiance was no more about them to envelop them.

Now another man came forth of the Temple on the Holy Mount, and cried, with a very strong voice of great sweetness, that those who had the stars should come forth of the crowd and stand before the Mount of Blessing. So they came forth, and I among them—for I was one of those so called—and we stood before the Mountain-foot, and before Him Who stood aloft before the Temple.

While we stood there He spoke to us in this wise, "You have well done, my children very much beloved, in what duty has been given into your hands to do. Not perfectly have you served the Father and Me; but as you were able so you did your work. I ask no more than you do after this manner in the wider sphere of service into which now I call you. Come up to Me, therefore, My beloved, and I will show you the path into that higher place where your houses await you all ready, and many friends to welcome you whom you will find there. Come up to Me."

Then we saw that before us arose a broad stairway whose bottom rested on the plain just before us, and the top at His feet, far above upon the Mountain-top. So we all went up that long high flight of steps, and we were in number many thousands. Yet when we were well above the plain and I turned to wave my hand in loving farewell to my group of companions who stood looking after us among the multitude below, it seemed that no less number remained than had come thither to the meeting. So great was that assembly.

When we were all come upon the platform before the Temple He spoke good words of cheer and blessing to those who remained on the plain. If any had been in sorrow that they too were not called along with us, no trace remained upon their faces as I looked upon them then. In the Presence of their Savior Lord none could sorrow, but only rejoice in His great love and the benediction of His Presence.

Then upon the stairway certain angels descended from the place where we now were, and stood upon the steps, from the topmost until halfway down, or thereabouts. They, being assembled, raised an anthem of Thanksgiving, praising God in High Heavens of His Glory. On the plain the multitude made response in alternation with those on the stairway. So they sang, and made an end.

The choristers once again ascended, and stood with us above. The stairway now had gone away—how I do not know. It was not to be seen there any more. He raised His hands and blessed them, they keeping silence with bowed beads below. So He turned and went within the Temple, and we followed after Him.

* * *

Zabdiel's Farewell

And now, my friend and brother and my ward, I do not say farewell in parting, for I am ever with you to help, to hear and to answer. Count me always near by, for, although my home in proper is far away, as men would reckon far and near, yet, in a way we know to use, I am ever near by you, in touch with you, in what you think, and in what you will, and in what you do. For of these things I have, from time to time, to give account on your behalf. Therefore, if I have been aught to you of friend and helper, remember me in this, that in my reckonings may have joy of you, as you, if faithful, shall have joy of yourself. Remember the Angels of the Seven Churches, and deal well with me, my ward. Remember, moreover, that one day you also, as I now, will have a charge to keep, and lead, and watch and help, and to answer for his life and how he uses it.

And now my blessing. It may be I shall find means and permission to speak with you again as I have done in these messages. It may be in this way, or it may be in ways more plain even than this. I do not say. Much rests with you in this. But, whatever betides, be strong and patient and in sweet simplicity, with humility, and in prayer.

God bless you, my dear ward. I lack the will to bring this to an end. But so it must be.

Remember, I am ever near you in the Master's Name and Service. Amen.

Zabdiel+

BOOK III

THE MINISTRY
OF HEAVEN

Poem: Creation

Where spaces spread their acres broad
　　Stands many a mighty Angel Lord,
With ear attent to catch the tone
　　Of whispers wafted from the Throne.
They weave them into light and shade,
　　And lo, a Universe is made.

Anon a Voice, "Lords Delegate
　　Of My Omnipotence, Create!
Unmoved, yet moving everything,
　　Like golden rain their thoughts they fling.
The cosmos stirs uneasily,
　　And sentient Life begins to be.

Diverse and lovely, at their urge,
　　A myriad living forms emerge,
As they on bird and beast and tree
　　Impress their personality;
While He from Whom all things began
　　Becomes articulate in Man.

Then speaks the Eternal Sentinel,
　　"We have done all things very well.
It is enough. These sons of Mine
　　Shall know their origin divine,
Assume their heavenly dignity
　　And lead Creation back to me."

February, 1921.

* * *

Note: Subsequent to the reception of the portion of the script which is included in this volume, I received the verses above as the keynote of the general theme.—G.V.O.

1

The World's Unrest

Saturday, September 8, 1917. 5:10–5:35 P.M.

I AM speaking through your mind, so put down what thoughts I am able to suggest to you and judge by the result. Afterwards we may be able to write direct, without my thoughts coming into contact with your own. Let us begin then by saying that, although many take in hand to write thus, yet not many continue, because their own thoughts clash with ours and the result is a medley of confusion. Now, what would you say if I were to tell you that I have written before by your hand, and that many times? For it was I who came with your mother and her friends and helped them to give you those messages which you wrote down a few years ago, and, in doing that, I also prepared myself for further work of the kind with other people. So let us begin tonight very simply, and you and I will progress together by practice.

Have you noticed the truth of the words "All things work together for good to them that love God"? It is a truth which few people realize to the full meaning of it, because they take only a limited view. "All things" include not the earthly alone, but those of these spirit realms also, and the end of "all things" is not seen by us, but is produced into realms higher still than ours and is focused on the Great Throne of God Himself. But the working is seen, in small measure truly, but plainly nevertheless. The phrase includes the angels and their duties as they go about to do them both here and on the earth plane and, although the working out of those commands which come to them from those High Ones who supervise God's economy seems often to clash with man's ideas of justice and mercy and goodness, yet the wider view of them who stand above, nearer the mountain peak, is fair and serene in the sunlight of God's love, and seems to them, as it does to us in lesser measure, very beautiful and very wonderful in its working.

At the present time men's hearts are failing them for fear, because it seems to many that, somehow, things are not working out quite as God would have them. But when you are in the valley the mists are so heavy and thick that it is hard for you to see in anywise clearly, and the sun can penetrate to your regions scarce at all.

This Great War is, in the eternal councils, but a heaving of the breast of a giant in his sleep, restless because on his torpid brain is impinging rays of light his closed eyes cannot see, and music he does not hear is beating upon him, and he heaves a sigh of restlessness as he lies down there in the valley—the Valley of Decision, if so you will. Only gradually will he awake and the mists will clear away, and, the carnage over—wrought madly while he slept—he will have leisure then to think and wonder over the night past with all its frenzy, no less than all the beauty of a world flooded with the light from over the mountain's peak, and then he will at last understand indeed that all things do work in love and that our God is Father still and His Name has been Love ever, even when His Face was hidden by the surging mists and cold winds and miasma which had lain like a pall over the valley's bottom. It was a pall to cover all there is of death in the world, and out of death life comes, and life is all beautiful because the Source and Fountain of all life is He Who is beautiful altogether.

So remember that God's ways are not always the ways man would design for Him, and His thoughts are not circumscribed by the enclosing hills, but come from the Realms of Light and Gladness; and thither lies our way. This, then, for tonight.

It is a little ray of brightness on ways at present dark for many a poor erring soul.

May God keep that giant in His keeping, and in due time give him the heart of a little child, for of such is the Kingdom of our Lord. And the giant, sleeping, blind, deaf and restless, is the Humanity He came to save.

KATHLEEN

2

A Haven of Rest
in Sphere Six

Tuesday, November 6, 1917. 5:20 P.M.

"PLANTED by the water-side." Those are the words which, if you think of it, seem to have a twofold meaning. There is, of course, the more manifest meaning of the plant or tree drawing its fertility from the river or canal near which it is planted. But we in these realms understand how every earthly truth has a spiritual significance, a significance that is as natural in these heavenly spheres as that which the outer truth conveys to you on earth. Whether the writer of these words had any knowledge of these heavenly conditions to which his phrase is applicable, I do not know. But it seems likely at least that his Angel Guide meant to convey something more than an earthly fact by those words to those who have ears to hear. I will amplify this according to my own rather limited knowledge helped by those who have more wisdom in heavenly science than I. The water-side I have in mind is not a river, however, but a very broad lake which, in the earth plane, would be called an inland sea, so large as to form a separative boundary between two large tracts of country in Sphere Six.

The shore is varied, being in some places rocky, even precipitous, and in others sloping down to the water's edge in grassy lawns and park lands. Nor have I in mind so much a tree as a whole forest of trees belting the blue-gold waves of the sea and sweeping up over hills and highlands and fringing cliffs with their leafy verdure. Near to the lake side stands a grove, and in the grove a mansion. It is a place of rest for voyagers across that lake whence they come, some very tired from their long journey over land and sea to this haven of rest. Some are newcomers into Sphere Six, and rest here to condition and acclimatize themselves to their new environment before penetrating further inland to explore their new homeland. Others are residents in this Sphere who have gone forth over the sea on some commission into the spheres inferior, some even passing onward, as I have now done, down into the sphere of earth. Returning, they often, but not always, rest here, and gather strength before proceeding to report to the Angel Lord or one of His commissioners how they have fared on their errand.

Others again simply return here and recuperate, and, their business being of urgency, do not go inland at all, but dive down across the lake and disappear into the less bright horizon toward the sphere where their task has been left not quite complete. Occasionally, and indeed not seldom, a visitor from one of the higher Spheres passing on his way to or from your earth, or some sphere intermediate, will spend some little season here in the Grove of Rest, and gladden the guests with the brightness of his personality. Yes, dear friend, we know what it is here to enter into Rest—it is one of the sweetest pleasures, this rest, after some enterprise of high adventure for the sake of those who are in need of such help. And there planted, just where it should be, by the water-side, is the grove-embosomed Home, where the fruitage of many a sowing far, far away in the dimmer spheres is brought, considered and put in order for presentation to the Angel Lord. Many a trophy, too, wrested for the Lord of Love by blows given and taken, both hard and keen, is brought here for refreshment and careful tending, living trophies for which the Christ Himself has fought, and, fighting valiantly, won.

You grow weary now, my friend. More practice will enable me to use your hand with less strain and more facility. May I say, accept my love and thanks and goodnight.

3

Water of Life

Thursday, November 8, 1917. 5:15–6:00 P.M.
Kathleen writes at the instance of others.

AND now, dear friend and fellow pilgrim, let us take a journey inland from the Home of Rest and see what chances by the way to those who journey so. For we are both pilgrims, you and I, and are on the same road to the same brightness still beyond and away over the high mountains which border this sphere and that one next ahead.

We leave the grounds and gardens of the Home behind us and take our way down a long high colonnade of trees which leads to the open country, and as we go we notice that the way goes not straight onward but follows the line of the valley beside the river which comes down by this way to the sea. Let me now before proceeding explain some of the qualities of the waters of this river.

You have read of the Water of Life. That phrase embodies a literal truth, for the waters of the spheres have properties which are not found in the waters of earth, and different properties attach to different waters. The waters of the river or fountain or lake are often treated by high spirits and endowed with virtues of strengthening or enlightenment. Sometimes people bathe in them and gather bodily strength from the life-vibrations which have been set up in the water by the exercise of some group of angel-ministers. I know of a fountain situated on the top of a high tower which sends forth a series of musical chords of deep harmony when it is set to play. This is used instead of bells to call the people of the surrounding lands together when some ceremony is forward. Moreover, its spray disperses itself over a wide radius, and is seen to fall around the gardens and homes spread out over the plain in the form of flakes of light of different colors. These flakes are so constituted as to bring to those on whom or around whom they fall a sense of the general nature and purpose of the meeting about to be held, a kind of glow which suffuses the whole being and brings a sense of comradeship and communal love which makes the recipient the more eager to be away to the gathering. Also by this process is borne through the district a sense of the time and place of meeting, and often, too, the knowledge of some Angel Visitor who is to address the assembly or to transact some business as deputy of the Lord of his Sphere.

The chief property of the waters of this river whose banks we now follow upward is that of peace. In a way far beyond all earthly understanding all the qualities of its waters infuse peace to him who strolls beside its waters. Its various colors and hues, the murmur of its flowing, the plants to which it contributes fertility, the shape and appearance of its rocks and banks—all, in a very intense measure, bring peace to the soul who needs it. And there are many who need that peace among those returning from the lower spheres across the great lake, for it is a strenuous life we lead at times, my friend, and not at all the deadly monotonous existence so many earth people imagine. So that there are times when it is necessary to lay the burden down for awhile, and for our future operations regain that calm and strong quietude of spirit so necessary to the adequate carrying out of our allotted work.

You must also understand that there is in everything here a permeating personality. Every forest, every grove, every tree, lake, stream, meadow, flower, house, has a pervading personality. Itself it is not a person, but its existence and all its attributes and qualities are consequent on the sustained and continuous volition of living beings, and their personality it is which is felt by all who come into contact with each and any of these, and that in a degree in ratio to their sensitiveness in the particular direction of the resident personality. Some, for instance, are more sensitive to those beings whose activity lies in the trees; others to those of the river. But all seem to sense the qualities of a building, especially when they enter within, for these are erected mostly by spirits more nearly of their own quality and degree, while most of what we might call nature spirits are of a state and manner of existence and of function much more removed.

Now, what obtains in these realms is usually found true in your earth sphere also, only in a lesser degree of intensity as sensed by the ordinary individual, consequent on his deep immersion in matter at this present stage of evolution. It is only less apparent, it is not less true.

For some minutes a question has been forming in your mind. Ask it, and I will try to answer you.

I was thinking that all this is very unlike the thoughts which usually occupy the mind of a lady. You said it was you who wished to write by my hand, Kathleen. Are you writing this?

Yes, my inquiring friend, it is I who am writing. But you did not suppose I imagined for a minute that you would be satisfied with my own small talk, did you? Anyway, I provided against any such disaster by bringing a few friends with me who use me much as I am using you. They are not all men;

some are women, and they act together with one consent as one voice, one message, so these words I write are a blend of varied mentality, and we have managed a fairly good blend too, if we are able to control your restiveness a little better. Aid us in this and we will do our best on this side, too.

And now goodnight, and may we progress well as practice lends its aid.

4

Angel Visitors to Earth

Saturday, November 10, 1917. 5:15–5:55 P.M.

"**P**ARTAKERS of the heavenly calling." You and I, my friend, are such partakers, for while I call to you, I in turn am called to by those further removed, and they by others of still higher degree until the line of callers finds its source in Him Who Himself was called of God the Father and sent on His mission to your poor darkened sphere in time long past. It is in the fact of this "calling" by those superior to us in strength and in their faculty to impart that strength to those of lesser rank and power that we find our sure confidence.

It is no light matter, I do assure you, to receive the command "Go forth downward." For as we proceed earthward, both the brightness of our environment and of our own persons also grows less and less, and by the time we reach the neighborhood of earth we can but with difficulty see about us.

This at first; but by and by our eyes become attuned to the coarser vibrations impinging on them, and then we are able to see. This also comes more readily by practice. But it is a blessing only in that it enables us to do our work among you, and not by any means to be desired of itself alone. For the sights we see are mostly such as do not give us cheer, but much heart-rending to take back with us into our brighter homes. Such places as that I described to you planted by the water-side are therefore not only convenient and desirable, but absolutely needful to our work. For I must tell you another function they serve. From such Homes of Rest are sent forth streams of life-power generated from Spheres above, stored in those Homes, and given forth as required. When we call there, on our way earthward, we set forth again bathed in such a stream of strength and vitality.

As we approach the earth, the effect of it is not so apparent to our senses. But it is about us, nevertheless, laves us, penetrates through us and permeates all our being, and by it we are sustained, as the air tube sustains the diver on the ocean floor, where the light from the wider freer atmosphere above is dim and he goes heavily by reason of the denser element in which he moves. So it is with us, and when we find difficulty in speaking so that we be heard of you, or make mistakes in our wording or even in the matter of the message, then be patient, and do not ever be thinking that some deceiver is at hand. For, bethink you, friend, how difficult it would be for one diver to speak audibly to another, both helmeted and with water between them, and then you may realize how much of patience and steadfast endeavor on our part is needed, and will perchance, more readily, give us a more patient hearing on your own.

But when we, our labor done here below, face us about toward the upper reaches of the heavens of God, then we the more readily feel the stream of life flowing from the distant Home of Rest and Refreshment.

We feel its laving once again; it beats upon our tired brows refreshfully; our jewels, whose lights, like the virgins' lamps, had burned most dim, once more take on their luster as we proceed heavenward.

Our raiment glows into a brighter hue, our hair becomes more burnished and our eyes less tired and dimmed, and best of all, perhaps, in our ears we hear, increasingly more plain, the melody of our Calling, bidding us back from the harvest field to the Harvest Home with whatever sheaves we may have gathered ripe for the Garner of God.

Now, friend, I will not longer detain you, for I know you have business afoot which must be done and brooks of no delay.

Only this further: Your old doubts have been once more between you and us who call to you. Yet this message is not of your own making.

How can I know that?

Only by patience which will ensure progress and progress conviction. Goodnight, friend, and all Peace.

Kathleen and her users send you this.

5

Music

Monday, November 12, 1917. 5:25–6:10 P.M.
Kathleen the organist is going to practice; that will not hinder you, will it?

SO far from hindering, it will help, and perhaps, à propos, I might say to you this evening some few words about the music of the Spheres. Yes, we have music of a like nature with yours of earth.

But—and there is a large But here—your music is but the overflow from the reservoir of Heaven's music. You do get gleams of the glorious harmony we have here, as it comes through. But it is muffled by reason of the thick veil through which it all has to pass, even the finest of earth's masterpieces.

Listen, my friend, while I try to explain how you receive your music from these lands, and you will be able then to give your imagination rein and stint it not at all, for you will not overdo your imagining.

Eye hath not seen, nor ear heard—ear of earth could not hear—the heavenly harmony in its pulsations and liftings and failings, and the strong harmony of its foundational bed of deep-toned glory.

Nay, while in the body material, with brain of matter as both receiver and interpreter, it cannot enter into the heart of man to conceive, much less to bring forth, any worthy image of the dulcet beauty of our harmony.

What music formed the Spheres, we here, in these of lower estate, are unable to measure, as you of earth are not competent to measure ours.

This, and almost this only, do we know, or think we know—it passes for knowledge with us in any wise—the Heart of God is the Source of harmony in music—not so much the Mind of God as God's great Heart. From Him flow forth the love-strains of His melody, and those spheres which are most near to His attunement receive those Divine harmonies, and by them, with other influences combined, become more and more attuned to Him Who is the Source of all that is Lovely and Loveable. Thus, as the eternities glide on, they who inhabit those far high Spheres blend within themselves more and more of attributes awful and sublime, and compass, each within himself, more and more of Divinity.

That, however, is far too high for us to tell of adequately. Our business with you at this time is to tell as best we may, in what few words suffice, some of that we take note of as this same stream descends upon us and passes onward, broadening as each molecule of tone expands of itself and thrusts its fellows outward, until by the time that stream impinges on your boundary it has become much grosser and more coarsened in its texture, and so suited to those almost tangible vibrations available in your sphere.

This stream from above us finds a receptacle here, and more than one receptacle. This is used as a reservoir, and the music is molded into airs and melodies and started forth once again as a small but intense stream earthward. Immediately, it begins to expand as I have already told you, and what you receive therefore is not sterling essence but the attenuated expansion of the original creation. It is like a small hole in a shutter of a darkened room. Through is streams a small jet of sunlight, but when it reaches the opposite wall it is much thinner in quality and the stream is filled with dancing motes which only tend to obscure the brightness with which it enters through the small aperture.

Well, but even so, your music is both lovable and uplifting. Oh, bethink you, then, my friend, what must the music of these Spheres be. It ravishes us with ennobling pain and pleasure, and each becomes in himself an accumulator of energy to give forth again what he has received, interpreted and molded, by his own personality for the benefit of those who are not so progressed as he. So is the exquisiteness and potency tempered by those among us whose special aptitude is of such a kind, in order that it be not too fine in nature for the comprehension of those higher souls of earth who catch, and in some degree retain, what thus reaches them from the Master of Music here aloft.

I would we might lengthen out our account, but you cannot well receive more now. We would put it in brief then, that as in other so in this matter the broad, grand truth holds true, from the Father in orderly retrocession down to the humblest of men: "As the Father has life in Himself so has He given to the Son to have life in Himself"—not life alone, but life in all its phases—of which music is one.

As the Son dispenses that life received from the reservoir of His being, giving life as from Himself, so His servants do in lesser degree in ratio to their capacity—not life alone, as parents to the child, but love, beauty, high thoughts and heavenly melody.

My love to you, my friend. Kathleen, for those others who use me to give their thoughts to you, who am nearer to you than they.

6

Inspiration
from the Spheres

Tuesday, November 13, 1917. 5:25–6:20 P.M.

WE have spoken to you, friend, of the life-stream of the Father's love, of water and its uses, of music also. And now, tonight, a few words as to the coordination of forces to any certain and particular end purposed by those whose duty and responsibility it is to issue into these Spheres inferior such commands as are decreed in those above. Know you, therefore, you who dwell in one of the uttermost of these Spheres, that such duties as are assigned to you have all been worked out as to their class, and the end to which they tend, by those who dwell in realms far above you. These schemes of allotted service are transmitted downward until they reach you, and are made known to you sometimes in one manner, sometimes in another, and to one more plainly, and to another less watchful, not so plain. Nevertheless, all who run the race of the earth-life may read the scroll if he choose, and persevere still to will that light be vouchsafed to him as to what his life shall be and to what end he has been guided.

But to few is given to know or glimpse the future far ahead. "Sufficient unto the day" is the rule, as He once said, and this suffices, so your trust be firm and quiet all the time. Not because the future is not known, but only because it is competent alone for those of high capacity and estate to view the distant course of life's grand purpose; and our capacity is sufficient for just a little view, and that of man in average scarce for any view ahead at all. As such schemes are given through so many spheres descending, it is therefore of natural consequence that they be tinctured by the dominant character of each of those spheres through which they filter downwards, and, by the time they reach you, they partake of a nature so complex in design that the ultimate issue is very hard to discover, even to us, times oft, who have some practiced skill in the matter. This is one purpose and use of faith, to be able to realize one's duty and no more, and on that conviction to go forth and do valiantly, nothing doubting that the end is seen by those who compassed the design. If those who are instrumental in the working-out of such scheme be faithful and diligent, those who conceived it have the power to attain. But not unless, for every man is free to choose, and no man's will is overruled in the matter of his choosing. If he choose to go faithfully onward and with trust, then the end is sure. If he choose to go out of the way designed, then he is not let nor forced. Guidance is offered then and gently. If this be refused, he is left to go alone—yet not alone, for others will be his companions, and that in plenty.

In order to illustrate our meaning. A book will be projected whose need is seen. We will say that those in a sphere whose dominant note is that of science will conceive the outline of the book. This is handed on to another sphere whose note is love. Into the scheme will be infused a softening, rounding-off effect, and the scheme handed on. A sphere where beauty rules will add some illustrations which will give harmony and color to the theme. Then it will come to such a company as they who study the different traits dominant in the races of mankind. These will study very carefully the theme itself, and look for the nation most fitted to put the venture forth in the world. This decided, they will carefully select the next sphere to which it shall be entrusted. It may need an infusion of historical precedent, or a poetical vein, or romance perchance. And what started out a framework of hard scientific fact may issue into the earth-plane as a scientific treatise, an historical resume, a novel, or even a poem or hymn.

Read some of those hymns you know best in the light we have now given you and you will glimpse, if even faintly, our meaning. "God moves in a mysterious way" might be re-written as a scientific exposition of cosmic philosophy, or even science. So also "There is a book, who runs may read."

"0 God, our help in ages past," might form the basis of a very informing work of Divine Providence as historically considered, and very possibly in its first conception may have been cast on those lines in some high sphere whose tone partakes of that disposition. For you will readily understand that such schemes are originated not all in one sphere but in many, and do not pass all from one sphere into another in identical order. Also, what may originate as a book may, before it reaches you, have been so much transfigured as to become an act of Parliament, or a play, or even a commercial enterprise. There is no finality to the ways and means. Whatever eventually seems to commend itself to the group of companies concerned in the production of any scheme in the service of God and on behalf of man is pressed into service. Thus it is that men work out the work of those who watch and guide them from on high. Let such, then, realize what great host of helpers they have behind them, and go forward bravely, nothing doubting, never faltering in their way, for they are not alone.

* * *

To these thoughts which I have handed on to you, good friend, I would now add a few lesser ones of my own, Kathleen.

What has been given by those who know more than I concerns men who are busy about the world's business of various kinds. But what I know of myself is that their words are also applicable to your own case, for no work of anyone is left unguided or without support from these fair realms.

Take this little gift of mine in parting, therefore, dear friend. It is but a small one, but it is Kathleen's own.

7

The Cobbler

Thursday, November 15, 1917. 5:15–6:30 P.M.

MEN used to say in those times when we lived among you of earth that they who chose the better way of life should rue it soon but later triumph. That some of us at least have proved and found not wanting in wisdom. For they who choose so have an eye not on time, which is short, but on eternity, which is long. From these spheres now we look backward, and, seeing our journey in view foreshortened and flattened out like a picture, we are able the better to mark the salient points which the canvas holds, and shape our future course in harmony with what lesson we there may read.

And how different is that picture, as the white light of Heaven shows it to us, from what it seemed when we were in the midst of the making of it and gathering the materials for the composite work. Do not you who are doing this today as we did it then, be careless too much of how you value the different elements of human life and living. Now we see that those great enterprises in which we took our parts were mostly great because we looked on them in bulk. But our part in them was individually but minute, and only motive mattered, not the part we played, to us. For, dispersed over all who came within its influence, each great enterprise thins out so much that each has only a little part to play. It is the motive continuously operative with which he plays that part that matters. The whole is for the race—the individual gets his share of benefit of result, but each share is only small, while, if his motive be high, it matters not how much the world takes note of his doings; here he is given what part to play he has fitted himself for in the battle of the earth life.

This seems a bit involved. Could you give me an instance by way of illustration?

We could give you many, friend. Here is one.

A cobbler who earned just enough to pay his dues and had naught over when his burial fees were paid came over here many years ago, as you say it. He was received soberly by a small group of friends, and was well content that they had borne him so much in mind as to come so far as to earth to show him his way to the sphere where he should go. It was one of those near earth, not a high one, and, as I say, he was well content. For there he found peace after much toil and weariness and his battle with poverty, and leisure to go and see the various interesting sights and places of that sphere. To him it was Heaven indeed, and all were kind to him, and he was very happy in their company.

One day, to use your earth-phrasing, a Lord from a higher sphere came along the street where was his home and went within. He found the cobbler reading out of a book which he had found in the house when he was taken there and told it was his home. The Angel Lord called him by his name of earth—I do not remember what—and the cobbler arose.

"What read you, my friend?" the Angel asked him.

The man made answer thus, "It is naught of much interest to me, sir, that I read. It is but just within my comprehension, indeed, for it was evidently written not for people of this sphere but of one much higher."

"To what end was it written?" the Angel asked again, and he replied, "Sir, it tells of high estate and enterprise, of the ordering of great companies of men and women in those spheres above us in the service of the One Father. These people, I find, were once of nations and faiths diverse one from another, for so the manner of their speech would seem to show. But to the writer of this book they do not seem diverse any more, for they have, by long training and much progress, come together as a band of brethren, and there be no longer any divisions among them to divide them, neither in affection one for another, nor in reasonable understanding. They are at unity of purpose and service and desire. By that I judge that the life herein written of is not of this sphere, but of one far above this. The book, moreover, is of instruction, not even for that bright company, but rather for the guidance of leaders among them, for it tells of statesmanship and of high rule, and of the wisdom required of those who lead. For this reason, sir, it is not of interest to me presently, but it may be in some long distant age. How the book came here I cannot tell."

Then the Angel Lord took the book and closed it and handed it to the cobbler silently, and, as he took it from the Angel's hand, his cheeks flushed red in great confusion, for, blazing upon the cover, were gems of ruby and of white whose order of spelling flashed back his name to him in light and fire.

"But I did not see it, sir," he said. "I did not see my name thereon until but now."

"Yet it is yours, as you see," the Angel said, and so, for your instruction. For know you, my friend, this sphere is but a resting-place for you. Now you have rested you must begin your work, and that not here, but in that higher sphere of which this book tells and in which it was written."

The cobbler faltered in his speech, for he was afraid, and shrank back and bent his head before the Angel's words. This only could he say, "I am a cobbler, sir; I am not a leader of men. And I am content with a humble place in this bright home which is Heaven indeed for such as I."

But the Angel said, "Now, for that saying alone you should have advancement. For you must know that true humility is one of the surest shields and safeguards of those who stand in high places to rule. But you have more weapons than this shield of humility, which is protective in a passive way.

Weapons of offence also you have been tempering and sharpening in that life on earth. When you made boots, your thoughts were to make them so that they would endure long wear and so ease the purse of the poor buyer of them. You thought more of this than of the price you would be paid. That, indeed, you made a rule; that rule grew into you and became part of your character. Here such a virtue is not lightly esteemed.

"Again, though hard pressed to pay your dues, yet from time to time you gave an hour out of daylight to help some friend to gather in his harvest, to plant his plot of ground, to thatch his roof or rick, or perchance, to watch some sick man by his bedside. The hours thus given you restored by candlelight, for you were poor. This also was noted from this side by reason of the growing brightness of your soul, as we can see the world of men from our vantage point, where the light of the spheres, sweeping over our shoulders from behind, strikes on those in the earth life and is reflected back by the virtues in men, and finds no reflector in their vices. So the souls of those who live well are lightened, but dark and somber show the souls of those who live ill lives.

"Other things I could tell you of what you did and why. But let these for the time suffice, while I tell you now my message. In the sphere of which this book tells, there awaits you a company of people. They have been trained and organized. Their mission is to visit a sphere near earth from time to time and to receive from the hands of those who bring them the spirits who have lately come over. Their task is to study these newcomers and to allot to each his proper place and to send him there by a band of helpers who attend for that purpose. They are ready to start at any time and have only been awaiting their leader. Come, good friend, and I will show you the way to them where they await you."

Then the cobbler knelt down and put his forehead upon the ground at the Angel's feet and wept and said, "If I were worthy, sir, for this great service. But, alas, I am not worthy. Nor do I know this company, nor whether they would follow me."

And the Angel Lord replied, "The message comes from Him Who cannot err in choice of person. Come, you will not find a band of strangers there. For often when your tired body slept you were led into that same sphere, aye even in your earth life this was done. There you, too, were trained, and there you learned, first to obey, and later to command. You will know them well when you see them, and they also know you well. He will be your strength, and you shall do valiantly."

Then he led him forth of the house and down the street and up the mountain pass beyond. And as they went his dress became brighter and lighter of texture, and his body gained somewhat in stature and very much in luster, and, as they went ascending, so the cobbler was gradually left behind, and the Prince and Leader emerged.

After a long journey and a very pleasant one, much drawn out in order that the change might be the more gently wrought, they came to the company. He recognized them, one and all, and they, on their part, came and stood before him, and he knew he could lead them well, for the love-light he saw in their eyes.

8

The Importance
of Kathleen

Friday, November 16, 1917. 5:14–6:16 P.M.

MUCH of what we say to you, friend, no doubt seems strange to your ears, who have not heard nor seen what we have been privileged to hear and see. But if aught perplex you, be you well assured of this: that what clouds of mist you now endure we also once encountered before you. We, therefore, are not strangers to your difficulties and your doubts, and do not marvel at your frequent hesitancy. Nevertheless, put down what comes into your mind; later read it critically and perchance you will admit the sum of the result as worthy of the labor, lacking in perfection as it may well be, both in body and in raiment. The body is of more importance than raiment, remember, and interior to both is the soul. Get down to that of our discourse, for if there be any worth in what we give you it is there it may be found.

Your phraseology is a bit antique. I suppose you find it easier than modern English. Is that it? I have frequently been about to write a phrase in a more modern way, and immediately some quaint bit of wording seems to have come into my mind and thrust it out.

You go not far out of the way, my friend. For indeed we find it more of ease to us to use what comes into our mind of past manners in words and their use and arrangement. But if you would rather, we will endeavor so to use your brain as to employ what we find there of more modern style. We will try if you wish it so.

By no means. I merely remarked on it as being not quite in the ordinary course of things. For instance, when I am preaching, the friend who helps me then does not make me use old-time phraseology.

No, there are many minor differences in the method by which we do our work. It would come more easily to him, no doubt, to lapse occasionally at least into the way of speaking which he learned when on your plane. But by practice he has managed to clear this and use your own stock of wording, lest the strangeness of his perplex your hearers and give them cause to question whether the pose be yours and unworthy a preacher of simplicity and meekness. On the other hand, we speaking thus for you to write have words and groups we cannot use unless we force your mind and then you in your perplexity would falter and we should go astray together from the purpose of our theme.

How do you manage this business then?

Well, only in part are we able to make in any wise clear to you the method we are employing in this particular case. And that we will so far as we be able. First then, here we stand a group tonight of seven—sometimes more, at others less. We have already broadly settled what we will say to you, but leave the precise wording till we sight you and sense your disposition of mind and also what store for the day your mind has in hand.

Then we take our stand a little distance away, lest our influence, the emanations of our several minds, reach you in detail, and not as one stream but as many, and so confuse you. But from the little distance at which we stand they merge and mingle and are focused into one, so that by the time our thoughts reach you there is unity and not multiplicity of diction. When you sometimes hesitate, doubtful of a word or phrase, that is when our thoughts, mingling in one, are not quite perfected into the special word required. You pause, and, continuing their blending together, our thoughts at last assume unity, and then you get our idea and at once continue on your way. You have noticed this, doubtless?

Yes, but I did not know the cause.

No. Well, now to continue. We think our thoughts to you, and sometimes they are in such words as are too antique, as you say, for you to grasp them readily. This is remedied by filtering them through a more modern instrument, and it is of this which we now would speak.

That instrument is your little friend Kathleen, who is good enough to come between you and us and so render our thoughts available for you. This in more ways than one. First, because she is nearer to you in status than we, who, having been longer here, have become somewhat removed from earth and the ways and manners of earth. She is of more recent transplanting and not yet so far away as when she speaks you cannot hear. For a like reason also she comes between; that is, the words that form her present store. She still can think in her old tongue of earth, and it is more modern than our own—though we like it not so well, since it seems to us more composite and less precise. But we must not find out faults with what is still beautiful. We have, no doubt, still our prejudices and insularity. These are not of recent growth, and when we come down here we cannot but take on anew some of those traits we once had but gradually have cast aside in our onward course. When we come back thus, we renew their acquaintance, and it is not altogether irksome; there is more than a little pleasure in it. Still, the little lady Kathleen is nearer you than we are in these respects, and the stream of our impelling we direct on you through her for that reason. Moreover, we stand a little apart from you because the presence of us combined would overmatch you. Aura is a word which we can use—we do not much affect it, but it must serve us now. Our blended auras would so affect you that you would indeed have experience of us which would be to you most pleasurable—a kind of ecstasy. But you could not write it down, and our purpose in coming is to give you such narrative of words as you and others may read with intelligence and perchance with benefit also.

You glance at the dial of your timekeeper. You call it a watch. Why? That is one little instance of our preference for our older way of speaking. Timekeeper seems to us more explicit than the other word. But we do not press on you our opinions, lest we seem to fail in courtesy. And the meaning of your glance is clear, whatever we call the thing on which it fell. So we bid you goodnight, good friend, and God's fair blessing for you and yours. Goodnight.

* * *

May Kathleen add a word, please?

Yes, of course.

These good friends are now speaking together, for they usually linger awhile, as if for old times' sake, Before they go away. I always know when they are going, because the last thing they do is to turn to me and call out their thanks and farewell. They are a very bright and nice lot of gentlemen, and sometimes they bring a lady with them. I think that is when they are going to talk about some subject which the mere masculine mind can't grasp altogether. I don't know who she is, but she is very dignified and beautiful and kind-looking. Goodbye for the present, my dear friend, I shall be with you again soon. Thank you very much for letting me write with you.

Goodbye, Kathleen, my dear. But I think the thanks should come from me.

And yet you were reluctant to begin, weren't you?

Yes, I was. I have so much to do just at present. Also, I do not forget the strain when I wrote those other messages four years ago.

And yet the time for sitting for us has been arranged, hasn't it? Have you noticed that? And the strain is not so great as you expected. Isn't that so ?

Correct in both items.

Well, the latter item is correct, as you put it, because your unworthy little friend Kathleen has made it her business to come in between. So don't think me in the future of no account, will you? Goodbye, and thank you once again. Ruby would say "and kisses," but that is the privilege of being your daughter, you see. So I will just say goodbye, with love and good wishes.

KATHLEEN

9

Difficulties of Communication

Saturday, November 17, 1917. 5:35–6:30 P.M.

BY reason of many intricate complications we find sometimes, when we read over what message we have given,
that much which we tried to impress is not apparent there, and
some lesser quantity of what we had not in mind appears. This
is but a natural consequence of the intervention of so thick a
veil between the sphere from which we speak and that in which
the recorder lives his life. The atmosphere of the two spheres is
so diverse in quality that, in passing from the one to the other,
there is always a diminution of speed so sudden and so marked
that a shock is given to the stream of our thoughts, and there
is produced, just on the borderline, some inevitable confusion.
It is like a river tumbling over a weir into a lower level where
the surface is a span of ruffled water. We try to get in beneath,
where the stream is not so disturbed, and then our message
comes through more clearly. But this is one of the many difficulties we find.

And here is another. The human brain is a very wonderful instrument, but it is of material substance, and even when the stream of our thoughts reaches and impinges upon it, yet, because of its density, the penetration is impeded and sometimes altogether brought to a stop. For the vibrations, as they leave us, are of high intensity, and the fineness of their quality is a hindrance to their effecting a correspondence in the human brain, which is gross by comparison.

Once again there are many things here for which there are no words in any of the earth-languages to express their meaning. There are colors which your eyes do not see but are present in your spectrum; and there are more colors which are of higher sublimity than could be reproduced by the medium which shows both the earth-colors to you and registers those invisible to you but present withal. There are also notes and tones of sound of like nature and too fine for registration by the atmosphere of earth. There are forces also likewise not available with you, nor able to be expressed to you who have no experience or knowledge of them empirical. Sometimes it is said these constitute the Fourth Dimension. That is no true way of expressing the fact as it is, but it is perhaps better than leaving it unsaid utterly, and that is not to value such explanation very highly after all.

These and other matters there are interpenetrating all our life and forming our environment. And when we come to speak of our life here, or of the causes we see in operation, of which you behold the effects alone, we are much perplexed, and strive continually to find just how to say it, so it shall be both understood of you and also not too wide of the target as known to us.

So you will see that we have a task to do in speaking into your sphere from this of ours which is by no means easy. Still, it is worth the doing of it, and so we essay our best and try to rest content.

This might be made more easy were men more prone to believe our presence and comradeship than at present is the case. Were belief more venturesome and lively, and more simple the hearts of men and more trustful, then your spiritual environment would be so much raised in tone and texture as would make our task more readily accomplished, and more pleasure would be given to us in our efforts to aid you.

It is easier to speak to the Hindu than to you, because he gives more entrance to spiritual matters than you do. To you here in the West the science of organic things and inorganic things—as you suppose them to be, and wrongly—the things of substance and also the science of exterior organization, which is the business of your state politic, are the things which have seemed of more urgency. And that work you have done very well, and it was a necessary work to do. It was necessary also that your greater efforts be concentrated on that aspect of the world's affairs. But now the thing is almost complete, so far as this present age is concerned, and we await your turning your mind into a higher channel upward towards the spirit-life. And when this shall have been done, then those who watch for opportunity to speak with men will find it and will not let it pass. That time is well-nigh here, and much that is helpful may be looked for and expected. For we have seen that the hardest battle before us is to conquer the materialism of the West, and we rejoice in a hard fight, as you do, and moreover we do not weary so soon.

We will not pursue this further now, as you grow weary. So goodnight, friend, and God's peace to you.

10

Preparation for Writing

Thursday, November 22, 1917. 5:18–6:80 P.M.

IF you can give your mind to us for a little while, good friend, we will try to explain to you further regarding our method of work and of service to men. You will understand that, these regions being of vast compass and the inhabitants of the spheres uncountable, methods of work vary in different places and according to the evolution of organization proceeding in each. We speak therefore, at this time, but of our own and not of others. This we might do, for one community is given to the study of the proceedings of others, both for edification and also for co-ordination sake. But we will confine ourselves to our own now.

There are many things to hand for humanity's help which are committed to us as our own peculiar task in the sphere from which we come. These duties are divided and a more especial task allotted to bands of workers. Of these bands we here present, to the number of seven, form what you would call a section or detachment. We have been deputed for this work we have now in hand, which is the giving of a series of messages through Kathleen, your little friend, and then through you in order. The band to which we belong varies in number from time to time, as new members are initiated or progressed members are called into the sphere next above. At the present time the total number of the band is thirty-six, and we work in detachments of six with a leader, in ordinary, but sometimes more and sometimes less, according to the nature of the work we have to do. The reason why we work in numbers and not singly is not alone for reinforcement of strength and greater power, but also for the combination of influences to be exerted as a blended whole. This we have already explained to you. This blend, to be effective, must harmonize with the personality or personalities through whom we work, otherwise the effect would be of uncertain quality and liable to error of greater or lesser degree. There are services other in kind to which this does not apply, but we leave them for the time and speak of our present work.

There are but two personalities we have at present to consider: that of Kathleen and that of yourself. We speak but of two, for our interpreter—you would so name her—is one of us. You two we have had under observation for many months past. First we found you. We came to know you by your writing for the lady, your mother, and her band, and later for my lord Zabdiel.

Can you tell me anything of him?

Most assuredly, friend, and so we may at some more fitting time, but not tonight.

We therefore studied and analyzed your mentality and what you had stored there in the years of your earth-life, and your soul—that is your spirit-body, so we employ the word here in these writings—and its health, and in what members health required perfecting the more; and also, so far as we could, the quality and the character of the facets of you, the spirit himself. These we put through the spectrum which we use—not much like one of which your scientists speak, but which is applied by us to men and their emanations as your scientists do to a ray of light. Thus were you, unknown to yourself, searched and tested with much care and closeness. We made our diagnosis, carefully writ down in details, and then we compared it with that one which was made when my lord Zabdiel used you, and also the more crude, but fairly full, record used when first your mother came to you and with her companions impressed on you their thoughts.

These three records showed your progress. In some things you have—would you that we tell you of yourself, friend?

Yes, please.

In some things you had progressed and in others you have fallen back, mostly by reason of the much service of your time and thoughts given to work made by the present war. On the whole balance, I think, we may say we found you a little inferior as an instrument than you proved a few years ago. We agreed that we would be able to use your mentality almost as completely as they did before. But it was in the deeper things you were found to be lacking—those which make for spiritual flight and ecstasy, and enable us to work on the imaginative faculty, which is what might be termed an inner clairvoyance, and also on the inner hearing. Nevertheless, we found in you an instrument which might be used and might perchance improve with use, and we were content to use you.

Other than this, we discovered that the lines of progress up and down did not meet always in continuous right lines when we placed the three records end to end in sequence. There were discrepancies and those which concerned the two last records, ours and the one before ours, were found to belong to our own account, not to those who made the record for my lord Zabdiel. This is not to be wondered at if you could understand our method employed. For your progress, not being all of the same direction, lines intercrossed and became involved one with another, and confusion resulted. But the mistakes were all our own.

We will cease here and hope to continue this same subject on the morrow of tonight, for you have had interruptions more than one and much more than enough, and you are not so facile to use tonight because of them. We must endeavor a better arrangement, if we can, so that such shall be avoided hereafter. We will try. Goodnight, friend, and God's blessing on the way you go.

Friday, November 23, 1917. 5:20–6:10 P.M.
We will continue, friend.

The chain extending between the composite of our mentality and the pencil and paper by which you hand on this stream of thought-matter to others is now growing towards completion. Having searched in regard to your own personality and traits peculiar, we had to find a link between us and you—one who could receive this same stream of our minds united, refract it, in certain measure transmute it, eliminate from it those elements which in a spectrum are not of utility to the human eye, nor with effect on the retina, and transmit the residue to you. What comes to you from us, therefore, is not the sum total of what we send initially. It is analogous to what you call the visible part of the spectrum, that is, it is all that can be made visible to the human eye—that light made up of the ray—vibrations which are not ultra either end. This in itself is an explanation of many difficulties of communication which seem often so unreasonable at your end of the chain. Now, all laws cohere and have certain points of likeness. It is so in this present. For as that white light by which you see is not unity, but unification, so it is with us. The white light unifies in itself more colors than one which, combining, produce a stream of light of one color, and that one a neutral. So we, our minds combining, produce to you, not each its own element separately, but one stream coherent as if from one mind alone. This illusion is helped also by reason of our transmitting this stream through our most excellent little friend and medium of transmission Kathleen. Mark also that these elements must be blended in due proportion, and each in its proper quantity, or the effect would be marred, even as the light would be not white, but tinted, were one color to predominate over its due proportion in the blend of them all.

We are collecting our materials for the pudding, see you, but it is not yet ready for the pot. One very important element we have but lightly treated. We found the little lady Kathleen, and that by reason of her friendship with, and affinity to, one of your own blood.

You mean Ruby?

Even so—who else? Your daughter Ruby is to Kathleen both friend and instructor. Very well. We treated her as we treated you, in more or in less, and then we came to a very delicate and pretty problem on which the success of our service and venture greatly hung. We six were men, and Kathleen woman. Now sex dominates much of our science here as it does with you. We could the more easily work through a masculine brain even as these of ours. So, not to hang too heavily on your patience, let us say that we found one whose mind on the one side could correspond with ours, and on the other, with a mind of feminine order. This is the lady who acts the office of interpreter. She is one of us in sphere, and is also one of our band, and, therefore, much practiced, and for long in our company. She is in tune with us as one of our band, and in tune with Kathleen as to womanhood. She it is who summarizes and blends the sum of our mentalizing—thinking—and transmits it to you through Kathleen. In these messages you will find that they mostly have the masculine flavor of thought and expression. That is by reason of the predominance of the masculine element in the composition of this detachment of the band. But at times you will be able, perchance, to detect the feminine element in prominence. That is when the subject is such that it is the more convenient that a woman's mind lead on and we poor men but follow, applying our rougher strength to the wheels, and so increasing the dynamical element in the venture. Even Kathleen will at times peep out on her own business, and no doubt will be charming to you, as she is to us, in her naive sweet way.

You speak as if you intend this series to be rather a long one. I don't wish to seem ungracious, but that other lot was rather a strain, I found.

Nay, friend. Be no more alarmed. We have been at some pains to prepare this enterprise—a minor enterprise it is. You will cease to write for us whenever you will. But I do not think you shall find yourself so willing to give up our company. Already you have found it somewhat pleasurable to come and be near us and to listen to our message. This will continue, as I think it. But, for your comfort, I will say that our purpose is none so large as to give what my lord Zabdiel gave, but somewhat which will be not so strenuous in nature but of profit, we hope, nevertheless.

Sometimes you say "I" and sometimes "We." I suppose that is because there are two aspects of your message: the one stream and the various elements which go to form the stream, the seven of you speaking sometimes in the plural and sometimes as one. Is that so?

It is not a bad explanation, friend, and it is partly true, but in part only. When we say "I" we speak as in the name of the leader[1] of the whole band of thirty-six, as at present numbered.

---

[1] On the Wednesday subsequent to the above Mr. Vale Owen was asked the following question through the planchette used by his wife: "Will George be in Church tomorrow quite by himself? Because Leader likes him to be quiet; not pressure put on him by people coming in to speak with him. I shall be coming tomorrow quite early to prepare him for a willing Leader.— Kathleen." G.V.O.: "Do you mean that the Leader of the band who comes with you is is willing?" K: "Yes, we always call him Leader." *Note:* Mr. Vale Owen decided after the above planchette message to attribute all the unsigned messages in this volume as coming from Leader. [H.W.E.]

When I say "We" I am speaking for the moment on behalf of the other six of this detachment. And now there is something for you to think on: how unity and diversity, how the singular and the plural can be so interchangeable and with such ease as in these messages is seen.

Friend, there is a depth here which you will fail to sound while in the flesh, try as you will, for it is an outer ring of the innermost sanctuary where is the sublime Mystery of Three in One.

11

Building a Temple in Sphere Five

Tuesday, November 27, 1917. 5:25–6:50 P.M.

WE have our subject ready to hand, friend, and we ask you to give us your mind, in order that we may tell you of an incident which lately happened in the sphere where we often take our stand in order that we may supervise a work which is there toward.

It is the erection of a temple-like building, the purpose of which when completed will be the coordination of energies to the end those in earth-life may receive the more readily our thoughts than heretofore. This building has been slowly coming into being for some time past and is near completion. We will describe, as well as we may, first the material of which this structure is built, and later the use to which it will be impressed anon.

The material is of various colors and of various density. It is not put together in bricks nor blocks as of stone on earth, but grows of a piece in one together. When we had settled on the design of it, we went to the place already chosen where it

345

should stand. That place was a plateau between the lower and the higher lands of Sphere Five. Note you, that we here in these messages follow the line which Zabdiel laid down in the numbering of the Spheres. Others sometimes adopt that method, and others again form another of their own. But you are familiar, more or less, with this way, and so we use it. And it is, moreover, a more convenient system of gradation than some others, which are often rather complicated, or else too general. My lord Zabdiel chose a kind of mean, and so let it stand here and now.

We assembled, therefore, and, after a silence by way of harmonizing our personalities into one endeavor, we concentrated our minds creatively on the foundations, and, gradually and very slowly, raised the stream of our willpower from the ground upward and higher until we came to the dome-like roof, and there we stayed while the Angel-Lord, the leader of us, gathered the whole of our energies into his own, and gently rounded off our endeavors by diverting the will power stream into space the while we began to stay the current pulsing from ourselves, each one.

Now, this may sound strange in your mind, friend. But the reason of it was this: we as a company are well trained, and for long have exercised to act in concord. Nevertheless, in the finishing of the first stage of that fragile structure, it needed that a far more powerful personality control the forces we had set in operation, or the building would have been either marred in shape or wrecked in structure, and our efforts would have been for naught. Further reason we find it hard to come at, so as you should be able to understand our words. Mayhap, in thinking on the matter, you will be able to see the reason of it, if not the method. Think it out on the lines of severing of the cord umbilical, and also the other cord vital at death, or the too sudden shutting off the conduit by sluice-gate, or somewhat of a like nature, and you may glimmer what we fain would tell but for lack of words to tell it.

So the first stage was the outer building in completeness, but faint in outline and of transient duration. So, resting a space, we set once again to our task, and starting at the foundations as afore, we strengthened each pillar and gate and tower and turret as we ascended slowly, until the dome again was reached. This we did many times, and then left the structure standing, the outer shell alone, but still completed in form. What was lacking was, in principal, depth of coloring, rounding off of the finer ornamentation, and, when this should be done, then the solidifying of the whole, until it should be so strong as to endure many ages.

We went for long time and oft, as our forces were renewed, to the process, and most delightful and blissful was the work of beauty. For the Temple was of much majesty, both of proportion and size and also in design—a thing of much beauty, ever growing more beautiful as we gave each of our own to its generation. Buildings are not ever thus raised in the spheres; there are many methods of their erection. But when they are so made, they become not so much the work of the builders as our children much beloved, because they be of our own vitality and of our own idealizing. Such buildings as these also are more responsive to the aspirations of those who come after as workers within them, for they have a certain life, not perhaps completely conscious life, but most certainly they are endowed with sensation. I think we might put the matter thus: That while such a house as this shall last, its function is to us, its creators, as the human body is to the spirit who uses it, both waking and sleeping. We are always in touch with the work therein proceeding through its sensitiveness. And in whatsoever spheres, at any future time, the company who created it be dispersed, they always have in that building a focus of communion real and vivid, and the joy of it all is only such as you will know when you attain to creatorship in these spheres, if that be the line of your ascent in the Kingdom of God.

Now, when the outer part was done and confirmed, there remained the work of greater detail within: the fashioning of the chambers, halls and shrines; the setting of the pillars in colonnades; the waters of the fountains to bring forth in perpetual flow, and many other matters of detail. First we stood without and concentrated on the supporting pillars and walls of partition, and when these were placed, we went within and viewed our handiwork, as you would say, but our hands did not much and our heads and hearts were the builders.

So we took up our abode within, and, as you would speak it, daily went about from chamber to chamber, hall and corridor, and fashioned each, little by little, after the original plan and scheme, till all was done and finished off by beautifying the whole.

Then what a wonder of delight was it to us, when our Great Director descended from his own high realm once again to view the work and to approve our endeavors. Many little details he corrected, mostly by the exercise of his own creative will. But some he bade us finish and remodel for our own training.

And there came a day when all was ready, and he returned with another—a mighty Lord, whose status was of sublimity higher than his own, and whose powers were what would in Israel be called as those of Aaron, and of them who followed him; and by the Greeks, Hierophant; and by the Christians, Archpriest. The process he came to enact was what you would name sanctification.

Consecration?

That word will serve very well. It is what links on a building in any sphere—earth or other—to those who dwell in some higher realm for protection, and also for the mediumship of grace and power for those who use the place hereafter.

On earth your temples are but a very faint model of these in our realms. But they are, in esse, of the same purpose and use. In Israel the cloud showed the communion between the two spheres of earth and Jehovah's abode. In Egypt the cloud was also used in early days. In Greek colonies the temples were of less vitality in response, but not without vibrations. Islam seems to lend itself least of all to this special aspect of help and uplifting from these realms. I have visited the spheres of Islam here and find this particular work of communion and grace is administered in other ways principally. So is it in the Churches of the Christ, but in great diversity of degree. In some of the temples consecrated to the Christ His Presence and that of His Servants is all but visible, and I think will shortly become visible to those who will.

So on earth you have the principle at work, and it has been for long ages past. But here it is much more powerful in effect and more visible in operation, and very beautiful and fraught with much blessing to those who are climbing the steps of the Heavenly Highlands from sphere to sphere.

What is the particular use of this Temple?

It is now beginning to be used for the storage of energy into which those will be baptized who come from the different parts of Sphere Five, and also from those spheres below, from time to time. They are immersed in its vibrations of color, laved in the streams and fountains of water which are within, or swathed in web and woof of music, the while, their natures responding, they are strengthened in the parts where strength is lacking, or enlightened in those other parts where intellect is dimmed. But, mark you, it is not a sanatorium merely, but of, shall I say, higher quality. Its use will be both for body and for personality, to fit the spirit for the journey onward, not alone in bodily strength, but also in intellectual clarity, by which he may the more readily and the more greatly profit by the knowledge it is his to come at. But also himself is attuned to those whose love and life are focused on that Glorious Temple, and who await the pilgrims coming to their own higher places.

Do all have to pass through that Temple in their ascent upward?

Nay, not all, friend, but most of those of Sphere Five. It is a sphere where some, nay many, stay long. It is a critical sphere where attunement has to be made in a man's various traits and all unharmony done away. A difficult sphere for many to pass, and where many delays are constant to be found. It is therefore that we raised the Temple, for the need was great. It is still new, and we have yet to find how it will serve, and doubtless, as experiment continues, modifications in detail will be made.

But some there are who come and look round them and find naught for them here to learn or to compose within themselves. These quiet, strong ones pass onward, blessing as they go, and the way they take is brighter for their passing; and those who are at hand are gladdened and take courage from the sight of them. It might be otherwise on earth. But those who come so far aloft as to Sphere Five are of no mean grace, and to such the beauty of a spirit more beautiful and strong than they but adds grace to their grace, and certifies to them the reality of the Brotherhood of All.

12

The Sign of the Cross

Wednesday, November 28, 1917. 5:20–6:45 P.M.

Its effect in hell

MAKE the sign of the Cross when you feel at all doubtful of our presence with you. It will help you both to realize our protection and your own freedom from all intrusion of those who would prevent us by coming in between. Not bodily, but by projection of their thought—influences which make a mist to obscure. You will mind, friend, that in degree they come nearer to you than we do, and have there a vantage ground which we want.

How does this sign help?

Because of the reality it signifies. When you ponder on it, much is wrought by signs, not because these signs have aught of dynamic value in and of themselves, but by reason of the potency of those persons or forces they represent.

For example?

For example, the letters which you are at the moment writing are but signs, yet they who read them with sympathy and love will lay by a store of fitness in themselves to progress the more readily when they come here, than had they not seen these signs at all. The name of a king is but a sign of him for whom it stands. Yet he who lightly uses it upon his lips, as also he who disregards a command written under that name, is not lightly to be dealt with in any orderly state. Otherwise the progress of that state would be much hindered because of the disorder and lack of unity ensuing. Names are, therefore, had in reverence, not alone in economies of earth, but in these heavenly realms also. For he who names a great Angel Lord compromises that person with whatever work he has afoot to do. This is so ordained; and the highest of all, His Name, must be had in deepest reverence as in your own sacred law it is also enjoined.

The Sign of the Cross is but one of the signs of Holiness which we know and have in past and present made known to the children of earth. But it is, at the present stage of evolution, the sign more powerful than any else, for it is the sign of life from the Living One, poured out for earth's progression. And as other ages have been periods of God manifest by other— write it, friend, do not hesitate—Christs of God His Majesty, so this age is a peculiar of that Christ of God Who, coming last of that high band, is Prince of All, Son both of God and Man. They, therefore, who use that sign use His Sign—manual writ in blood, which is the Life, and before it even those our brethren who do not own His Sovereignty nor understand His Love must bow, because they know and fear His power.

Even those in the hells, then, know His Sign. Is that so?

Most truly and terribly so. Let me for a few moments dwell on this matter, for there be many, as we know, who on earth do not reverence that sign overmuch, because they do not understand. I have been in the darker regions times and oft, but when I go there—I have not just of late been there, having other business toward—I use that sign most sparingly, knowing the agony it flings upon those poor souls who have agony within themselves more than a little already.

Will you tell me of any instance in which you used that sign?

I was once sent to search for a man who had, strangely enough, been brought, on passing from earth, into the second sphere. But he was not fitted to dwell there and gravitated to the spheres below. I will not pause to explain this matter in particular. It is rare that such a thing comes to pass—not unknown. Such mistakes are made here and there by guides of lesser knowledge. Their zeal outruns their powers of discernment and of penetration, and, when a difficult and entangled personality comes over, mistakes are sometimes made. I descended into the spheres of gloom, therefore, and when somewhat conditioned thereto I began my search. I went from city to city, and at last I came to a gate where I felt his presence within. You will perhaps not readily understand that I have but just given you. Let it pass, you will one day. Passing within I came by the murky glimmering of light prevailing to a square wherein a large crowd was gathered. The air seemed ruddy of hue, like a smith's working-house, flickering and faltering as the crowd were uplifted or depressed, grew angry or grew weary. Standing on a stone block was the man I sought. He spoke to the people in a harsh voice earnestly, and I stood behind them and listened awhile.

He was telling them of the Redemption and of the Redeemer—not by name, mark you, but by allusion. Twice or thrice I saw the name upon his lips, but it never came forth, for whenever it happened there, I saw a wave of pain sweep over his face and his hands gripped inward on themselves, and he became silent a space and then proceeded. But of Him of Whom he spoke no one there could doubt the Personality. For a long time he urged them repent, and told them what the lack of spirit-leaning had done by him, bringing him down, willy-nilly, from his short glimpse of Heaven and light into the thick gloom of these underworlds of pain and remorse. What he was urging them to do was this: he said he had come hither with open eyes, and had marked the way well enough to go back upon his steps and reach the light at length. But the way was long and of painful ascent and very gloomy. He therefore called upon them to be willing to make their departure with him, and all together, as a flock of sheep, for company and mutual aid, and they would come to rest at the end. Only let them not go astray by the roadside, for ravines and rank forest lands they must pass beside, and those who should stray might lose the track for ages and wander lonely whither he could not tell, but always in darkness and peril from the cruel who lurked in those regions to wreak their frenzy on any who came within their power. So let them follow the Banner he would bear before them and they should then have naught to fear. For the Banner he would make for them would be a symbol of great strength to them for the way.

That is the burden of his speaking to them, and they seemed not without a wistful readiness of response. He stood there silent some time, and then there came a voice from one in the crowd who cried, "What banner do you speak of? What arms will you emblazon on it, so that we know whose leadership we follow?"

Then the man who stood upon the stone in the middle of the square lifted his hand on high and tried to force it downward to make a line, but could not. He tried to do this many times, but his arm seemed palsied whenever he tried to move it downward deliberately. Then, at length—it was a very painful sight to me who knew him—he heaved a sigh loud and full of tears of agony, and his hand fell of itself and hung limp by his side.

Soon he started, and stood erect once again with determination on his face. He had realized that he had made a vertical line through the air, and lo, there shone along the path which his falling hand had taken a faintly luminous streak standing before him. So with much effort and caution he once more raised his hand, stretched away from the line and somewhat above the middle of its length, and sought to approach and cross through it, but this again he could not.

I could read his mind and what was in it. He was trying to give them the Ensignment for the banner they should follow—the Sign of the Cross. So in pity I pressed forward, and at last stood by his side. I traced first the vertical line still visible. I traced it slowly, and as I did so it shone out with a brightness which lighted the square and the faces of the crowd assembled. Then I made the cross-piece, and there it shone before us, and we, hidden by its luminous radiance, stood behind unseen.

But I heard a wild cry and a great wailing and looked out again. The Cross had grown more dim, and I saw the multitude were prostrate and writhing in the dust of the great square, seeking to hide their faces and blot out the memory of that sign. It was not that they hated it—these were come through that stage of remorse—but it was the very progress they had made towards repentance that caused their present pain. Remorse was blending into sorrow for sin and ingratitude in these, and that progress added bitterness to their sorrow.

The man beside me did not grovel as the others, but knelt down with his face covered with his hands, and his hands on his knees-bowed double with his agony of repentance.

Now I saw I had been too much in haste, and what I had meant for their comfort had been their undoing, so I had much labor to restore them once again to their proper mood of calm on which I might, taking the office of my friend upon myself, begin to play the tune he had begun. At long last I was successful in my task, but I made my resolve, then and there, to be more restrained in the use of that potent sign in these dark realms hereafter, lest I should cause more pain to those who already had so much of their own to bear.

You called the speaker your friend?

Yes, he was my friend. He and I had taught philosophy in the same university when in earth-life. He was of a right life, and not without generous impulse on occasion. Brilliant, however, rather than devout, and—well, he is on the upward way now, and doing much good among his fellows.

They had their banner after all, as I sought to tell you. But it was not of very excellent workmanship—merely a couple of tree-branches, much twisted and gnarled, as trees grow in these dim quarters—but they strung them together and called it a cross, but the cross-piece tilted sometimes up and sometimes down, and it was grotesque but for the earnestness of them and what it meant to them; for it stood to them for the power it signified, and for Him from Whom that power flowed, and so to them it was indeed a Sign most Sacred and to be followed bravely, but in silence and in awe. And the strip of red cloth which they tied about the intersection flowed out like a stream of blood. And they followed where they saw it go before them on the long, long journey, often weary and footsore, but ever towards the Uplands where they knew they would find the light.

Thank you. Before we stop I would like to ask you a question. That temple you spoke of last night. In the first part you said the purpose of it was to help people in the earth-sphere. But you afterwards mentioned a purpose quite different? I am not quite satisfied. Could you please explain?

What we said, friend, was true enough, although not so clear as we would have said it. Your mind was somewhat heavy last night. And now also you are fatigued. We will explain what was in our mind when next you sit for us, so God's blessing and goodnight.

13

The Temple
in Sphere Five

Thursday, November 29, 1917. 6:20–6:45 P.M.

Obstacles to communication

WE promised to explain to you your difficulty of the Temple. There is little of difficulty really. You will mind we said that it was for the purpose of service to be rendered to those of Sphere Five and the spheres inferior. Included in those is that of earth, which is not diverse from what you distinguish by the name spiritual spheres, except in its outer manifestation. The influences projected from that building go far through the spheres downward and into that of earth. We were not explicit very much, not because of our haste, but your limitations, both of leisure and of receptivity, the one greatly dependent on the other. For they who lack leisure for quietness and peace are not able to respond to the thoughts of us who come from realms so different, and coming, bring with us, even to the verge of your plane, much of what calm strength we had in us when we started on our journey. Not all of it is dispersed from us into the spheres as we come hitherward; and of what remains we always seek to impart to those of earth who respond to our seeking, and who need so greatly what peace we have to give. When we, too, become deplete of our grace and of the power to impart it to you, what little is left to us, then we return homeward to replenish the cistern in the free, clear air of the Heavens of God, from which all strength and peace go forth.

This has bearing on the matter of the Temple, for that is one of its uses: to be a reservoir in which shall be accumulated such power and blessing from the higher realms for use as occasion serves to those of earth and the spheres next in order of ascent.

As the work shall develop, other uses for it will also be found, and coordinated with the work presently afoot there.

Now you have been hindered in coming to us tonight, and before the next engagement with your people shall take you away once again, the time is not very long. So we will be brief tonight and say but a few words more, and that on a matter which you do not quite clearly understand.

When we come to earth, we children of the Heavens, we have much difficulty at times to get into touch with those who await us and listen for our coming. You yourself are an example of this. For oft we have noticed you almost awake to our presence near you, and, having listened, end in doubt at best, and sometimes you conclude it is but your own fanciful imaginings and not the breathing of your spirit friends you feel and hear. Now, the reason of these failures on our part to give, and on yours to receive, is chiefly the lack of courage to believe. You have thought of yourself that you have this courage, and in some things it is true. But in this matter of spirit communion you are often too fearful of error to be useful in the work of truth. It is not too much to say if we put it thus. At all times, whenever you feel us near you, that is the effect of some cause. The cause may or may not be such as you desire or as you feel you discern. But cause there is, and if you at such times will but be quiet and listen, then the nature of the cause will grow further clear. It may be you think a certain friend is at hand, when it is not he, but another. But who it is will be made clear in the process of the transmission of his thoughts. So, when you feel yourself to be cognizant of some one near you, cease, as far as you may, from doubts, and entirely from fears of error. Receive what is given to you, and on the matter so received sum up your judgment of the affair.

No more now, for you have to go to other work. May our Father be with you in it and in all you do from day to day.

Friday, November 30, 1917. 5:20–6:25 P.M.
Repairing a defective tower.

Whatsoever is beautiful is always true, and that is one of the laws which stand out in front of others in these bright realms. Conversely also, whatever is ugly and ill-favored in form outwardly, will, on closer study, be found lacking in the grace of truth. Truth, as we use that word, means that which is consonant with the Mind of the Ultimate Whom you call God and Father. All that flows from Him is orderly and in harmony with the highest and fairest aspirations of us, His offspring. And what answers to this quality is beauty, for beauty is that which pleases; and harmony is a garment of love which is always pleasing to them who in their nature respond to love's endearments. It is only those in whom there is some tincture of love's opposite that have no relish for such a feast as Love alone can spread. And, mind you, Love is not alone of God, but God Himself.

So all the beauty of landscape and of the waters and the comeliness of a face or form we know to be such a manifestation of Him from Whom they derive their beauty, and, as truth is only what is in concord with the thoughts of Him, so we say that whatsoever is beautiful is true, and whatever is true must manifest itself in beauty.

It is where some cross-current of opposing forces enters into the mainstream of God His Life and power, that the water there becomes fraught with murk and mire. This is as true of humanity as of things in concrete, for disharmony in a family or in a State is not of its own origin, but has its rise from that far source of power which is erratic from the purpose and will of the One Supreme.

But so wonderful is He in His operative energy, that these things He wills to turn to good account in total, and also to extract from each such opposing manifestation of His Life-force wrongly used, some help for the betterment of the race both of men and angels.

I don't know whether I have got this right; anyway, could you, please, try to give me something a little more explicit and less involved in expression?

We will try, friend, to describe to you a little more the Temple of which we have already written. We can use your inner sight in this as well as your hearing, and that will be simpler for us to give and for you to take a hold of. Tonight you are not quite so quiet in mind as we would wish.

There was one corner of the Great Tower which we could not understand. The Tower stood on a corner of the building, and was a foursquare Tower. One of the corners was not as the other three. But, strangely enough, we could none of us, comparing them, tell what was amiss and in what it was diverse from those others. As I looked at them it seemed to my mind as if the defective corner was in shape and proportion as its fellows. But when I looked at the others, and then back at it again, going round the base from time to time, it always struck me as not in harmony with them. I will not dwell on this, but tell you at once what was found wanting. It was not one of our architects who discovered the nature of the defect, although we had several to look at the tower. It was one from a sphere above, who was passing through Sphere Five, who explained to us the matter. He was one of those whose business it is to descend into the darker realms on occasion when any certain locality is seething so much with dissension and tumult as to affect painfully those in the spheres next in advance and adjoining. Such effervescence throws off a kind of distressful influence which, rising up to the sphere above, hinders what progress is there proceeding, and pulls back those not very robust spirits whose lot is cast in that dim place, so that they lose heart and cease for the time being from their struggle to continue their way out of the gloom toward the light of the upper spheres. This is not so powerfully felt by them as to bring upon them the discouragement of despair, except the tumult below them be of extraordinary vehemence. When that happens, then the one I have spoken of with others descends and soothes the poor restless ones into such stupor that their distress does not affect those who have won a little way ahead in ascent.

It was because he was, by much and long service, become skilled in this business that he was able to help us in our perplexity of the Tower. Having very carefully examined and tested all four walls, he went to a long distance away, and, ascending a hill, he turned and sat down and looked very steadfastly and for a long time, at the far-off Tower. Then he came back to us, and, assembling us in the plain, he told us what was amiss in some such words as these:

"My brothers, when you were building this Temple, you left this Tower until all the other halls were formed. Then you gave all your energy to the making of this Tower so strong as it was possible for you to do out of the strength you had. But there was one thing you overlooked in your eagerness for the finishing of it. You had taken no care that an equal number should be on all four sides of it. And also, when the Tower was raised then, from far away, the light, striking on its uppermost part, deflected the wills of those who stood below, and they left the parts not so brilliantly in the light exposed to whatever currents of will power should at the moment be passing. Now, at that particular time there was a band of us coming from service in the regions dim and gray, where we had found much ado to achieve the purpose for which we were sent there; so that, passing over this plane, we were much depleted of our strength, and gathered it as we proceeded. So it came about that, because of the unequal force applied to the Tower on its four sides, without our seeking to do so, we absorbed some of the vitality from that part which was least protected. This is the corner which is defective, and you will find the defect not in the shape or proportion, but in the texture of the material of which the corner is made. Look again, this time, with the knowledge I have given you, and you will detect a darker tint where the damage lies than in the other parts of the Tower. That is because the vitality we extracted left it lacking in luster, and therefore its appearance is deformed, while in itself it conforms in shape to the other corners."

This we found was true and the remedy simple, for we gathered the same band of builders as we had afore, and set to work again. And, as the energy streaming from our wills was directed on those darker parts, they grew lighter in hue and took on an equal sheen with the other parts, and, when they were exactly matched, we ceased, and, on looking on it, we found it quite right and in perfect harmony.

You will see, friend, that what had done the mischief was in reality the influence brought to bear, all unwittingly, upon our still uncompleted work by those whose vitality had been expended in the darker spheres. No evil is positive in nature, but only negative. It is the negation of good. All that is good is strong. It was the strength of these good angels which had been absorbed by those who lacked strength in the region to which they had made their way. Re-accumulating strength as they passed by us they, by their unconscious action, brought to bear on our work what was really the influence of those darker spheres, and the result was lack of harmony, which means lack of beauty, which brings us back to our first word, like a cat curled before the hearth with its head to its tail in a circle. And with that picture of contentful repose we leave you with our blessing.

14

Methods
of Communication

Monday, December 3, 1917. 5:25–6:20 P.M.

WHEN we come to earth, friend, we say one to another by the way that we are going into the land of mist and twilight, that we may, in the interior world which we find there, shed abroad somewhat of our light and warmth. For, indeed, that these be much needed we are able to sense, even in those far spheres from which we come. You may wonder by what process of chemistry or dynamics this is made possible to us; and, indeed, it would not be possible for us to explain the method in detail. But we are able to give you a somewhat epitomized account of this affair, and so we will, if it would be of interest to you, and those who shall come to read what we give to you.

Thank you. Yes, I should like to hear your explanation of it.

Then we will try to make it as simple as we can. You will readily understand that the first and grand necessity of communication is already to hand—that of a universal principle which bathes us all, you and us, in one and the same ocean. I speak of spirit life, and force and energy. This spirit life is to you as it is to us, and as it is also to those above us, so far as we are able from this sphere to stretch our minds in reasoning and imagination before us. For that spirit-life is the cause of the life-phenomena, obtaining in the sphere of earth, you will readily consent to. As you progress upwards this coupling of cause and effect becomes more emphatic in each sphere as you ascend. It is, therefore, reason to conclude that this constant intensification proceeds into the higher spheres of all. It may there be so sublime as to find perfection in unity. But we think that in such Unity will be found, by such as are able to penetrate into those High Places, the principle of cause and effect in its most intimate form of all.

So when we speak of the one ocean of spirit-energy, we are touching on what to us is no mere speculative theory, but a tangible fact to be taken and used in any process of communion we should put our hands to it to devise. That is the first thing to realize.

The second is this: As you proceed away from earth upwards there is no void between any two spheres. We know of the abyss of your Holy Book. But that is no void. There is a bottom to it. Also, it is not between your earth and our sphere, but lies aside in the off-way, and comes not into the line of ascent.

Each sphere as you progress is blended into the next by a kind of Borderland. So there is no shock to those who pass from one to another. Albeit, you will mark that each sphere is distinct in itself. Nor is the borderland between two spheres a neutral land. It partakes of the qualities of both. There is, therefore, no void, but a very real and continuous gradation all the way. From these two premises you will deduce quite comfortably the fact that we are in direct communication with you potentially. Now we must apply ourselves to explain how this medium of communion is put to use.

There are many windows to this house, and every one is used. But there are three which serve to evidence the rest.

There is the method of continuous posting, wherein those workers nearest you hand on messages and reports to those in the sphere above, and they continue the operation until the message comes to its destination where it is to be appropriately dealt with. This is done swiftly—and yet in the flight of any message through the spheres it is sifted in each and that extracted which is proper to the workers of that particular sphere to undertake its answer. Also, messages from workers and prayers from the earth are filtered and made suitable for transmission into higher realms. Were this not done their earth grossness would weigh them down so heavily that what was in them of sublimity would not be competent to rise and come to the sphere where it is appropriate it should find destination. I will not pursue this further—'tis a bare outline I give, but I must go on to the next method.

This we may call the direct method. There are those of you who have guides in the spheres for special work and guidance. Some of these guides are very high and bright angels, and their proper home is far above those spheres bordering on the earth. They may not ever be coming down to those of their charges, for, high as they be, they are not all powerful, and to descend to earth is expensive of energy, by reason of the necessity of conditioning themselves to the spheres through which they pass, and in each sphere there is a new condition for them to achieve until they come to earth. This is done from time to time, and, indeed, not seldom, when such work is afoot as to warrant such undertaking. But we are ever careful of waste, who have so much to do for others' help, and do not spend lavishly, even of that which is infinite in its supply. We can do our work better, as a rule, by the method of direct communion.

In order to establish this we devise a kind of telephone or telegraph—to use your own speech—a cord of vibrations and pulsations between us and you, and it is constructed of the blended vitality of the guide and the guided. I use here words

I like not overmuch, but I cannot find other in your brain to use, so they must stand. I refer to such words as "construct," "vitality," and such as these. Sympathetic intercourse is by this means rendered continuous and sustained.

It is like the system of nerves between the body and the brain: it is always potentially operative, whenever need arises of help to be given. Whenever the charge turns to his far-away guide in thought or longing, that guide himself is at once aware and gives answer in the way he judges best.

There is a third method, but more complicated than either of these I have summarized. It may, perhaps, be given such a name as the universal, which is bad enough, but must serve. In the first process the stream of thought passing from earth to spheres more or less remote is handled and modified in each sphere as it travels on its way, like a continuous post across continents—only there is no change of horses nor pause on the way. In the next, the line is ever open and ever charged, like a telephone with electricity, and is direct in a line from the man on earth to the guide in his own proper sphere.

In the third the process is distinct from either of these. It is that by which every thought and action of man is reported in the heavens, and may, by those competent to do so, be read from time to time. These records are real and permanent, but the aspect of them and their method of constructure it is not possible for us to explain. Words have been very strained to serve in the first two descriptions. Here they fail in total. I will say but this, that every thought of every man has a universal application and effect. Call it ether, or what you will, the fluid which fills these spheres is of so sensitive and so compact and continuous a substance that if you touch it with a sigh at one end of the universe the effect is registered at the other end. Here, again, "end" is not a proper word to use, for in the sense you use it there is no significance here. But that of which I now try so lamely to come at, so that I may show somewhat of its wonder to you, is that which the Savior Christ had in mind when, wiser than I, He did not name it with any name, but spoke of it only as it is found to be in operation thus: "Not a hair of your head is hurt, not a fledgling falls from its nest, but the Father of All is notified."

15

The Sacrament

Tuesday, December 4, 1917. 5:20–6:30 P.M.

Of the Body and the Blood of Christ

BE content, friend, to write what we are able to put into your mind, and do not question that it comes from us. For, on the one part, we keep a somewhat close hold on you when you write thus for us, and, on the other part, we disallow others taking up our tale on their own behalf. We are enabled to do this by the long preparation of you and of ourselves before ever we made known to you our wish by the help of our little friend Kathleen.

Tonight we would speak to you on the matter of the Sacraments, which are in use in Christendom, and which should be of much note and concern to those who profess the Name of the Christ their Master. That of His Body and Blood is the one which is continuous in the life of a Christian. It has many phases, both of help given and also in its teaching, and on that Sacrament we wish to say something now. First as to its founding:

You will remember from your records remaining that there is much more left unwritten than that which has come to

369

you down the ages past. A cursory reading will show this. Also those accounts, in essentials agreeing each with the others, are not clear as to the lesser points. You must know that these records are but a few of many. The others have been destroyed, or have been lost for the time being, and will one day find their way into the light of day once again. We have all the records here and have studied them, and on that study we now base our words.

The Master Jesus was about to change His state from the incarnate to the discarnate. Knowing this, He, being assembled with the Twelve, gave to them a Rite of Remembrance and of Communion by which they and those who should follow them might be able from time to time perpetually to intensify their contact with Him, and so draw from Him that Life of which Himself is the reservoir. Cast your mind back to the three modes of communion which we have given you, and you will be able to see that so sensitive is the quivering and pulsating life-stream coming down from Him to you that the very slightest disturbance in the system of vibrations, obtaining in their own special and peculiar quality throughout that radius which is His Kingdom, will cause an effect at the Center and Source of it of so manifest a nature as to ensure some immediate response. For there is nothing in the economy of your earth-sphere of such enormous intensity and momentum that we may apply as a type by which to make in any way clear our meaning. It must satisfy you and us that we remind you that the greater the velocity of any series of particles in motion, the greater the disturbance to their arrangement and direction given by any intruding influence.

That is what we would imply in speaking of this stream of vital force proceeding from the Father, arrested in the Christ, tinctured with His quality of life, and projected outward in radiating waves towards the circumference and boundary of His Kingdom. Such a disturbance is created by the willful offering of the Bread and Wine, with invocation of words, in that Rite of Communion which He gave. On the elements displayed before the assembly there is, at the words of prayer, directed this vital stream, and they are interpenetrated with the Life of Him and become, as He said, Body and Blood of Him. That form of prayer you use is not alone of the nature of invocation, but also is the assent of those assembled to the receiving of Life from Him. For without such assent no blessing is ever thrust upon men. It matters not if the assent be silent. It is the spirit which is the source of those responsive pulsations which leap forth to meet the flowing of His Life earthward and, meeting this Christ-stream, like those who came from Salem to meet Him when He rode to the city over Olivet, are commingled and, by reason of the greater momentum of that stream set forward by Him, are turned back and together, as one stream, they fall plashing upon the congregation from which the initial impulse of pleading came.

So the blessing is threefold. First, the communion of spirit with Spirit—that of the worshippers with their Master and Lord. Second, the quickening into greater health and vigor of their spiritual covering, the soul. And third, the natural effect of those operations, still proceeding outward, namely, the transfusing of the inner vitality into the over-clothing, which is the body material.

This is the phase which we may name the vitalizing or quickening of the whole Body of the Christ in its singular members, each and each, by the communicating of the Life of Him from the Source and Center through the mass to the circumference.

There is another aspect of this Sacrament we will treat of at this time, but with brevity. For it were not of any use to endeavor to give you a full account of its significance in whole. You would not understand our words that we should use, and there are none of your own which would serve us. This thing reaches far beyond where tongues of earth are remembered, and is spoken of, in its inner mystery, only in those forms of language proper to the Spheres far removed in sublimity, and near that of the Christ.

As He said, those two common things of earthly origin, the Bread and the Wine, do come to be His Body and His Blood. They are therefore a part of Him Who spoke those words. Men have asked how this could be when on that first occasion of their utterance Himself was present in Body of flesh and bones and blood. But yet, every man—without ceasing, all his life, and sustainedly—does communicate of himself to things without himself. No coat he wears but, flung aside, is marked with the impress of his personality. No thing he touches, no house he inhabits, but he leaves his quality there indelible to be read by those who are so endowed.

As He gave of His vitalizing force to the sick and halt in Judea and Galilee, as He breathed of His spirit power upon the Apostles and they became inspired of His Life, so upon the Bread and Wine did He pour of the life-stream of Himself and they did in verity become His Body and His Blood.

And so it is today. For He did not offer so great a thing to snatch it away so soon as that meal was ended and His Body given to the Tree. No, the Source of that vital river operative on the Bread and Wine or on the persons of the Apostles or on the bodies of the multitude was not that Body of flesh He wore for so short a time and then laid it by like a cloak past wearing. Nor was it the Body of spirit substance, through which it did but flow as through a conduit from the Reservoir into the cisterns of a town. But it was the Spirit Himself, the Christ, Who was and is the Source, and that, too, whether in the Body of flesh or out of it. For that little matters in things of spirit force and power, except by way of manifestation. The thing manifested is unaltered in itself whatever form the manifestation take.

So it is true to say that the Bread and Wine at the last meal of theirs together, at His wish and will, became depository of

His life-force, and so were made His Body and His Blood. And so, far from the present lack of that Body material hindering now a similar operation on His part, it would almost be true to say that now the way is made more easy and direct by the absence of one medium. At least, it is entirely true to say that such absence of the Body of flesh forms no hindrance to the flow of life from Him to these elements of Bread and Wine.

When therefore the Ministrant, the Priest, takes up the consent of the congregation and, laying the Body and Blood upon the Board, pleads the Sacrifice of Him Who lives today very highly exalted, he in essential places his hand upon the bosom of his Lord and, looking into those realms which are the abode of Angels, and of Angels who rule, looks towards the Father's face and pleads the Love and allegiance of His Son for poor humanity's sake that they be made all beautiful as He. And if he be of simple mind and in heart a little child of the Kingdom he shall feel within that Breast beneath his hand the quiet strong beating of the one constant Heart in Christendom today, and shall know that what his weakness will not bear to do shall have reinforcement of the Life which wells within, and that what pleading is his with the Father goes not unaided into that bright Sphere of awful purity, and holiness so still, but as He promised so He keeps at hand to perform, and out of His Heart goes forth a sighing prayer, and your prayers are acceptable for His sake.

16

The Sacrament of Marriage

Wednesday, December 5, 1917. 5:15–6:10 P.M.

WHAT we gave you last night, friend, had reference in chief to that one Sacrament which stands pre-eminent among its fellows. We now will tell you of some of those lesser ones and what to us their meaning seems to be and their efficacy in the lives of those who have adopted the Christ their Leader and Sovereign. We use here the word "Sacrament" not in the narrow ecclesiastical sense cut down to its littlemost, but in the way we should use it here in these Realms where we are able to view the outgoings of power and vitality from a standpoint nearer their Source.

We speak first to you of Marriage as of the union of two personalities in creative faculty. The people take it as quite in the ordinary course of things that sex should be, and also that sex should be complete in blend of male and female. But it was not of essential necessity that this should be, humanity might have been hermaphrodite. But far away beyond the beginnings of this present eternity of matter, when the Sons of God were evolving form, in its ideal conception, they took counsel together and afterwards decreed that one of the laws which should guide their further work should be, not so much a division of the race into two sexes, as you and earth philosophy have it, but rather that sex should be one of the new elements which should enter into the further evolution of being when being should shortly enter into matter, and so take form. Personality was before form was. But form endowed personality with individuality, and so the element personality, by evolution of concrete form, issued in its complement of persons. But as from one element persons came, so sex is unity composed of two species. Man and woman form one sex, as flesh and blood form one body.

So far as we can penetrate, the reason for this decision on the part of those High Ones was in order that humanity should know itself the better. It is a great mystery and we do not possess the key to the whole of it even here. But we understand that in the creation of the two elements, male and female, the process was made more simple by which the human race might understand at last the element of Unity, out of which it came and towards which it will once more turn when it has fully entered on the upward way from matter towards spirit.

Two great principles which are included in the Unity of Godhead were made to appear as two separate things in order that those two principles might be studied in detail by those who were not competent to study them as One. But when the male considers the female he is but getting at a more clear understanding of a part of himself, and so when the female reasons on the male. For as they were not separate in the eternities of development which went before this present eternity of matter and form, so the two elements shall become one again in those eternities which shall come after.

In order that the essential unity of being obtaining in those far reaches behind us be carried forward into those which are still to come, it was necessary that both elements be included in each individual who should form an item of the whole race. So marriage was evolved, and in marriage we have the turning point of the destiny of the race.

From the time when, from the Heart of the Ultimate, came forth the first fiat of that movement which has resulted in a series of eons of development, the one keynote of the whole has been a development into diversity, until there came forth, one after another, into the ocean of being the principles of personality and individuality and form. The last and most extreme act of diversity was the creation of two aspects of the faculty of reproduction, which you call sex. That was the outmost point of extension of diversity in principle and act.

Then came the reflex impulse, given to the onward urge of evolution when the two were blended into one again and the first step retraced towards Unity of Being, which is God.

So of the blend of the two elements, spiritually as bodily, there is born a Third Who within Himself unites these two elements in His one Person. The Lord Jesus was the perfect Son of Humankind and His nature, spiritually considered, is a blend of the male and female virtues in duly equal parts.

Bodily also this great law is true, for upon his breast the man bears the twin insignia of his erstwhile womanhood, and physiologists will tell you that a like correspondence is not wanting in the other half which, with himself, makes one whole unit of humanity.

By this experience of the two in unity, the perfected human being, ages hence, in other higher worlds of onward press towards the state of Being consummate, man shall have come to the knowledge how it is possible in loving other and giving to other by denying of self he is loving himself the more and but the more bountifully giving to himself by that same denying of self, and that the more he hate his own life the more he will find it in those bright spheres eternal—you know Who taught it, and He did not speak of a strange thing nor of some principle on trial. You and we, friend, are still learning this very sublime lesson, and far ahead lies our road before we learn it in its fullness. But already He has attained.

17

The Sacrament of Death

Thursday, December 6, 1917. 5:15–6:20 P.M.

W HAT we have already written, friend, we have written in brief and not expansively. For it were not possible to tell you all even of what we might, for that would serve only to make the bulk the bigger, and also would do disservice by leaving you not enough room for the exercise of your own mind in penetrating into the real meaning of things. We give you just enough corn to make your cake. If the eating be found to be good, then grow more corn for yourself, thresh it, grind and knead it and you shall the longer retain what you thus get, to the larger benefit of yourself and others who shall read what we have written. So to our further words.

When we said that marriage was the turning-point of the evolutionary cycle of being we spoke of the matter in mass and not in detail. Now we turn to detail more especially and speak of that outcome of marriage, the human unit, male or female as the case may be.

He is born, you will note, of fourfold element. There is the male and female element of the sire, and also the female and male element of the dame. In the father the dominant expression is that of masculinity, in the mother that of femininity. By the incorporation of these four elements, or rather four aspects of one element, or more nearly still these two aspects and two other sub-aspects of one thing, in the one person of the offspring, there is first multiplied and then unified once again some of these variations which are the outer expression of the inner principle of sex.

So he begins to live his own life, this child of the eternities past, and to look forward to the eternities of the future.

You are waiting for us to speak of Baptism, and its complement the Laying on of Hands. Free your mind, friend, and let us go on our own way with you and, by your good leave, we will perchance be able to help you better than did you lay down the course we should sail. We have our chart all pricked and ready. So write what we give you and do not be getting ideas into your mind of what is afoot tonight or on the morrow. We will that your mind be free that we may have no headlands to round nor straits through which to pick our way precariously. We shall do better on our own course, and not so well on yours.

Sorry. Yes, I was certainly expecting you to speak of Baptism next. You seem to be rather erratic in your order of the Sacraments—Holy Communion, then marriage. Well, Sir, which is the next one, please?

The Sacrament of Death, friend, which surprises you. Well, what would your life be without surprises, for these are as seasons of the year and serve to emphasize the fact that inertia is not progressive. And progression is the one grand object of the Universe of God.

You would not have given such a name to Death. But we look upon Birth and Death both as very real Sacraments. If Marriage be rightly so, named, then Birth follows naturally in the same group, and Death is but Birth progressed into consummation. In birth the child comes forth out of darkness into the light of the sun. In death the child is born into the greater light of the Heavens of God—no more, no less. In birth the child is enfranchised in the Empire of God. In Baptism he is incorporated in the Kingdom of God's Son. By death he is made free of those Realms for which he has been trained for service in that part of the Kingdom resident on earth.

In birth he becomes a man. In Baptism he realizes his manhood in taking service under the banner of his King. By death he goes forth on wider service, those who have done well as veterans tried and found loyal and good, those who have done better as officers to command, and those who have done very well as Lords to rule.

Death therefore ends nothing but carries forward what has been begun and, as it stands between the earth phase of life and the life of the Spheres, so it is a sacred thing enshrining a transaction blended of both, and so a Sacrament, as we use and understand that word.

So we have spoken of Baptism, after all, and, if we do not dwell on it, believe me, it is not because we do not understand its great moment in the career of the servant of the Christ, but it is because we have other things of which to tell you that we do not dwell on that which you the better understand. So, a few more words on the Sacrament of Death, and we will cease for this time, for we note you have other work toward.

When a man comes near that hour when he shall change his sphere, there occurs in his being a reassembly of such elements as have been gathered and engendered during his life on earth. These are the residual particles of those experiences through which he has passed—of hope and motive and aspiration and love and other expressions of the true value of the man himself within. These are dispersed through the economy of his being, and are ambient about him also without. As the change comes near they are all drawn together and gathered up into his soul, and then that soul is carefully drawn from the material envelope and stands free, as being the body of the man for the next phase of progress in the Heavens of God.

But death sometimes comes of shock and in a moment of time. Then the soul is not so far completed as to be of full health and strong to go forward. It is necessary to delay the onward progress until those same elements have been withdrawn from the body material and duly incorporated into the body spiritual. Indeed, until this has been done well and fully the man is not well-born into the spirit. It is like a birth before the full time into the earth life, when the child is like to be weakly, and only gradually to grow strong as he gathers to himself what forces he lacked when he came into the light of the sun.

So we say that Death is a Sacrament, and indeed it is a very holy thing. Some few of your race—and more than you wot [are aware] of, by the way—have disrobed of their bodies of earth without passing through that disintegration more slowly which stands for death in the eyes of men. But the essential act is identical in both. And in order that death might be paid due Honor in its more usual form, He Who is Lord of Life did not scruple to pass that way from life to the life of ages, and by the manner of that His death He showed that, whatever be its form and value in the eyes of men, it is an act normal to the journey of humankind as it presses onward toward the upper reaches of the River of Life which comes from the Heart of God.

18

The Wall
of the Borderland

Friday, December 7, 1917. 5:20–6:55 P.M.

The two young comrades, arrival and meeting

OUT of the gloom which hovers over the earth sphere, and through which those who would come to you from these brighter realms must penetrate, emerges continually a stream of people who have passed through the Vale of Conflict into these fair fields of sunshine and of that peace which is rarely known among you of earth. We speak now not of such as fail to realize their high destiny, but of those who, striving to understand and fathom the meaning of Being, and of their part and lot in it, have shaped their earthly course by the compass of His Love. These have known that over all this gloom and beyond all perplexity of twilight, the sun which shines is the sun of Righteousness and of Justice and of Love.

So they come hither somewhat prepared for the righting of what has seemed to be wrong and with trust in those who have helped to guide their faltering steps lest they stumble too greatly or lose their way on their pilgrimage to the Heavenly City.

This much surely. And yet few there be, or almost none at all, who do not lift their eyelids in surprise and wonder at the greater beauty and serenity of peace which is to their imagining as the living person is to the picture which, in flat limning of light and shade, strives in vain to emulate the pulsing life of the original.

Yes, I can well believe all of it, Leader—that is what you are called, so Kathleen tells me. But could you, please, give me a specimen instance of it? Something individual and definite, I mean.

Among so many it is hard to choose. Yet, we will tell you of one of those who came here lately. It is not of the duties of our band at the present stage to go near the border and bring those who come over to their proper places. But we are ever in touch with those whose business it is to do this, and their experience is for us to draw upon. He was a youth who came through the wall but lately, and was laid on the grassland by the roadside.

Would you mind explaining what you mean by the wall?

In your realm of matter a wall is, we will say, of stone or brick. The stone of which the wall is built is not solid in the sense of being coagulate absolutely. Every particle of which the stone is made up is in motion, as your science has but recently found. And the particles themselves are also constitute of denser motion than the ether, as you call that element in which they float. Motion is consequent on will, and will is set in action by personality. It therefore results in this, as considered inversely: A person or group of persons concentrate their will on the ether which is set in vibration, and out of that vibration particles are the resultant. These also by the operation of the will of other groups—hierarchies, if you will—cohere in more or less dense formation, and the result is water or stone or wood. Every kind of matter, therefore, is but an outer manifestation of personality, and varied in composition and density according to the order of the personality, acting singularly or in concert, which continuous exercise of will-force produces, such manifestation as is to their own class appropriate.

Here obtains a system of operative law very like this we have detailed to you as obtaining between the spiritual Realms and your economy of matter.

The Wall we spoke of is produced and sustained in position by will power resident and operative in the sphere of earth. This is met on this side by the will power proper to and operative in the Spheres above the earth and, being beaten back, it becomes condensed and welded into a wall of thickness and substance quite palpable to us who are of nature more sensitive and refined, but which to you incarnate in bodies of grosser substance is cognizable only as a mental state of impenetrable density, and of which you speak as a cloud of perplexity or spiritual gloom or some such like name.

When we say it is produced by the wills of you of earth we speak in literal sense of the creative faculty of spirit. All spirit is creative and you in the flesh are spirits, and each a focus-point of the Spirit Universal, even as we. This cloud of vapor, therefore, which comes against our Boundary from earth is of spirit creation, even as that which proceeds against it continuously from these higher Realms, and keeps it constant in its own place. It is not a difference in nature or kind but only in degree. It is the meeting of the higher and the lower and, in ratio, as one or other rises or falls in intensity, so is that wall produced forward or thrust back earthward. But it is fairly constant to its place and is never found far away from its mean position.

You set us a task, friend, by your question. It was to tell you in earth wording of one of those matters which are still ahead of science as you understand the term among you today. Some day when your science has enlarged its borders hitherward, some one of yourselves will be able, perchance, with words more familiar to you in their usage, to make plain more easily what we have found it somewhat hard to set down.

I think I catch the general drift of it. Thank you for your effort, anyway.

So they found him lying on the turf near the gateway through which he had entered, borne of those who had brought him hither. Soon he opened his eyes and looked around him in much wonder, and when he had accustomed his sight to the new light, he was able to see those who had come to lead him on the second stage of his journey to his new home.

His first question was a quaint one. He asked them, "What about my kit, please? Have I lost it?"

One of them who led the others replied, "Yes, my boy, I fear you have. But we can give you other and better kit in its place."

He was about to reply when he noticed the aspect of the landscape and said, "But who brought me here? I don't remember this country. It was not like this when I was hit." Then his eyes opened wider, and he asked in a whisper, "Say, sir, have I gone west?"

"That's what it is, my boy," was the answer, "You have gone west. But not many realize that fact so soon. We have watched you all the while, watched you grow up, and in your office, and in your training camp, and in your work in the army till you were hit, and we know you have tried to do what you felt to be right. Not always but, on the whole, you have taken the higher way, and now we will show you your home."

He was silent for a time and then said, "Can I ask questions, or is it against rule?"

No, ask your questions, we are here to answer them."

"Well, then, was it you, sir, who came to me one night on sentry and spoke to me about going west?"

"No, it was not any of us here. That one is waiting for you a little further up the road there. If you are strong enough we will take you to him. Try to rise and see if you can walk."

He arose quickly and stood to attention, from the habit he had formed, and the leader smiled and said, "My dear boy, all that is past. Discipline here is quite different from that which you have known hitherto. Count us as your friends, and come along with us now. Commands you will be given, and you will obey, but not yet awhile. When that comes to pass, such commands will be given by those who are higher than we, and you will obey them, not from fear of reprimand, but out of the greatness of your love."

He simply said, "Thank you, sir," and went forward with them along the road, silent and in deep meditation on what had been said, and on the strangeness of the beauty of his new surroundings.

They ascended the roadway and passed over the brow of a hill, on the other side of which was a coppice of very large and beautiful trees, with flowers growing by the roadside, and many birds singing amidst the green-gold foliage. And on a mound there sat another young man who rose as they approached him.

He came towards the group and, going up to the young soldier, put his arm around his shoulders, and walked beside him in silence, the other keeping silent also.

Suddenly the young soldier stopped and, removing the arm of the other, turned and looked at him intently. Then a smile suffused his face, and he took both hands in his own and said, "Why, Charlie, who would have thought of this! Then, you didn't manage it after all."

"No, Jock, I didn't, thank God. I went west that night, and afterwards they let me come and stay with you. I went with you pretty well everywhere, and did what I could for your comfort. Then they told me you would soon be coming over here. Well,

I thought you ought to know. I remembered what you had said to me when you tried to get me out of it, and back to the lines again, after I had got it in the neck. And so I waited till you were quiet, and by yourself, and then I tried all I could. I knew afterwards that I had managed to make you see me, and partly hear what I had said to you about your coming west."

"Ah, yes, it's 'coming' west now, not 'going,' isn't it?"

"That's the size of it, old fellow. And now I can thank you for what you tried to do for me that day."

So these two friends went on ahead of the rest, who slowed their pace that this might be so and, in homely language such as their wont had been, made their friendship for each other articulate.

Now we have chosen this incident in particular to show you several things, among them these:

No kind act is ever passed by without note in these spheres. The one who does the act is always thanked here by the one to whom the benefit has been done.

Those who come over still use the language and manner of earthly speech. Some of you would be greatly shocked to hear the rather forcible phrases which drop from the lips of really bright spirits when first they meet their friends of earth. I speak now more especially of the soldiers who have fought in the war, as these two had done.

Rank here keeps pace with true inner worthiness, and is affected not in the least either by earthly rank, or by earthly education. Of those two, the one who came over first had been a laborer before enlistment, and of poor parentage. The other had come of a family not poor in worldly affairs, and had for some years been in an office of business in preparation for a responsible position in his uncle's house. Their respective status was not of much account when the one had led the other wounded away from the enemy trenches. Here it was of no account at all.

So do friends meet here and begin their onward way. For they who are faithful in their duties of earth are made welcome when they come hither into these fields of beauty and rest where no sound of war is heard, nor wounds nor pain can penetrate. For this is the Realm of Peace where the weary find sanctuary from all earth's troubles, and many joys of life abound.

19

In the Second Sphere

Monday, December 10, 1917. 5:28–7:05 P.M.
The arrival of a minister of religion.

SUCH incidents as that of which we told you at our last coming are not rare in these realms, although to you it may seem somewhat strange to hear of a scene from the battlefields of earth being reproduced in these acres of calm and peace. But it is of such small things that the web of life is wrought, and here life is life indeed. Those two friends are not the only two who thus have met, and have in these bright lands renewed the friendship which first they made amidst much hurry of business and stress of earthly endeavor.

Let us now go forward a little and we will tell you of another meeting by way of enlightening those who dwell below the mist which lies between us and you, and through which for the present time their foreshortened vision cannot penetrate. It will not be so ever, but, for the time, until their eyes become more quickened, we must strive in this less direct way to help them in their seeing.

There is, in the Second Sphere from earth, a house where those who are newly come over await their sorting-out, to be forwarded, each with his guide, to the place where best he may be trained in the beginnings of the heavenly life. It is a very interesting Home to visit, for here are to be found together many varied types of character, and some who, being of good report as to their earth probation, yet are not quite so settled in convictions on this or on that as to be able readily to be classified. Not, mark you, by reason of the lack of skill in such a matter on the part of the workers of these Realms, but because it were not well to move any newcomer forward on a definite road until he first very plainly and fully be able to understand himself, and where he lacks, and where he excels, and of what content his character be. So in this Home they rest quiet and in congenial company for a while until they shed some of the fever and unquiet which they have carried over from earth, and be able to take stock of themselves and their environment with deliberation and more certainty.

One of our band not long ago went to this Home and sought out a man who had come to such a forward state as this. On earth he had been a minister of religion who had read somewhat of what you call psychic matters, and the possibility of speaking one to other between us and you, as we do at this present. But he could not come at the thing in thorough, and was afraid to say out even so much as he in his own heart knew to be true and good. So he did what many of his fellows are doing. He put the matter aside from him. He could find other ways in which to help his fellow-men, and this other matter might await the time when it was more and more widely understood and accepted of men, and then he would be one of the foremost to proclaim what he knew, and would not shirk his duty in that time.

But when others came to him and asked him first whether it was possible to speak with their dear ones who had come over here; and second, whether it were God's will so to do; he put them in mind of their Christian belief in the Saintly

Communion, but urged them that they be patient until the Church should have tested and sifted and should have issued guidance for those who were of the fold. And while he waited, lo, his time on earth was fulfilled and he was carried over here into this Home where he might rest awhile and come to some decision on what attitude he had assumed on divers matters of his calling, and of the use he had made of his opportunities.

The worker of whom I spoke—

Why not tell me his name and save words?

It is not "his" name, my friend, for the worker is feminine. Let us call her "Naine," and it will serve.

She went to the Home and found him walking in a pathway through a wood, a pathway of greensward very beautiful with foliage and flowers and lights and colors and shades of softer hues, very peaceful and quiet and, at that spot, lonely. For he sought to be alone, so he might think more clearly of what was in his mind.

She went to him and stood before him, and he bowed and would have passed on, but she spoke to him and said, "My friend, it was to you I was sent, to speak with you.

And he replied, "Who sent you to me?"

"The Angel who has to answer to our Master for your life-work while in the earth sphere," she said.

"Why should he have to answer for me?" he asked her. "Surely every one must answer for his own life and work—isn't that so ?"

And she said, "That is surely so. Yet, to our sorrow, we here know that it is not the whole of the matter. For naught you do or leave undone ends with yourself alone. He who had you in charge made effort, time and again, for your welfare and, in part, succeeded, but not in whole. And now the earth period has been closed for you, he has to sum up your life, and answer for his charge of you, to his joy and also to his sorrow."

"This seems hardly fair, to my mind," he answered her. "It is not my idea of justice that another should suffer for one's failures," Naine said, "And yet, that is what you taught the people yonder—it was your understanding of the doings at Calvary, and you handed it on to them. Not all you said of it was true, and yet it was true in part. For do we not share joy on behalf of another's joy, and shall we not also share in his sorrowing? This your Angel does for you even now. He both joys and sorrows over you."

"Please explain."

"He joys in that you did good work in charity, for your heart was much bathed in love for God and man. He sorrows for you in that you were not content to do what you taught was done for you on Calvary. For you were not willing to become scorn for men, and to be withered with their disapproval, for you valued the praise of men more than God's praise, and hoped to be able one day to buy more cheaply your reward for having spread light upon the darkness when that darkness should begin to pass from night into the twilight of the dawning day. But you did not see, in your weakness and lack of valiant purpose and of strength to suffer shame and coldness, that the time for which you waited was the time when your help would be not needful, and the fight all but won by others of more stalwart mettle, while you stood with the onlookers and viewed the fight from a fair vantage ground, while those others fought and gave and took blows good and strong and fell forward in the battle when they would not surrender their cause to those who opposed them."

"But why all this?" he inquired. "What is your reason for coming to me at all?"

"Because he sent me," she said, "and because he would that he also might come to you, but is not able until you are of a mind more clear of purpose, and until you have mastered and acknowledged the various elements which made up your earth life in their true values and appraisement."

"I see, partly at least. Thank you. I have been in a cloud all this time. I came here, away from the others, to try to understand it all better. You have said some pretty straight things to me. Perhaps you will add to this service by telling me how I am to begin."

"That is my mission here and now. It is the one thing with which I was charged. I was to probe your mind, to make you look inward upon yourself and, if you showed any will to progress, I was to give you a message. This will you have now shown—not very heartily, however. And this is my message from your Angel guide who awaits you to lead you on when you have trained yourself some little more. You are requested to take up your quarters in a home, which I will show you, in the First Sphere. From there you will, from time to time, visit the earth plane and help those there in their communion with their friends here in these spheres of light, and also aid them in speaking comfort and encouragement to those who are in the darker spheres, that they may progress into the light and peace of His Presence. There are even among those to whom you ministered, several who are trying to do this good work for those in anguish, and also to give and to get gladness by their speaking with their loved ones here. They sought your guidance in this matter and you had no courage to give it to them. Go and help them now and, when you are able to make known to them your personality, unsay what you then said, or say what you lacked courage then to tell them. In this you shall have some shame, but they will have much joy and will deal very kindly with you, for they have scented already the fragrance of love from Realms higher and brighter than this in which you have been resting. But the choice is still for you. Go or go not, as your heart inclines you."

He stood with bowed head, silent for a long time, while Naine waited. He fought out his struggle, and it was no little one for such as he. And then he failed to come to any decision, but said he would think it over in all its bearings and decide later on. So his old failing of fear and hesitation clung to him like a mantle and hindered the freedom of his going forward even when he would. And Naine returned to her own Sphere, but was not able to bear back with her the joyful answer for which she came.

And—what did he do, what decision did he come to?

When last I heard he had not come to any decision. The whole happening is a recent one, and is not finished yet. Finished it cannot be until he decides of his own free will to do what he has to do. There are many who visit your Communion gatherings who are such as he or very like.

By Communion gatherings do you mean the Service of the Holy Communion, or séances?

What if we will call them of like nature? Truly in earth estimation they be much diverse, each from other. But we here judge not by the standards of earth. Those who go to the one or to the other go for a purpose identical—communion with us and our Master the Christ. That suffices us.

But of our minister: It is in your mind to ask why a woman be sent on a mission such as this, and to a minister of Theology to reason with him on his conduct and life-work. We will answer what we note in your mind.

It is simple enough, the answer. He in his early life had a small sister-child of only a few years, and she died and passed on, while he stayed and grew to manhood. This woman was that little child. He had loved the little one very well, and had he been all attuned to the higher part in him, he would have known her again, for all her beautiful and glowing maturity of womanhood. But his eyes were holden and his sight dimmed, and so she went away unknown.

Truly we be all of one family in joy and in sorrow pooled together for us, and we must drink the cup perforce, even as He did Whose cup was the sins of the world, and the love in the world, of joy and sorrow mingled.

20

Communion Between Earth and the Spheres

Tuesday, December 11, 1917. 5:20–6:52 P.M.

A manifestation of the Christ

WHEN we come to speak with you, as we are doing, there is between us and that sphere in which our normal "Habitat" lies a lifeline, as we may so call it. It has taken some time in the fashioning of it, but it is well worth any labor we have given for its construction. When we first descended into these realms we had perforce to be very gradual in our descent. We had to travel slowly downward from sphere to sphere and, as we came, we evolved in ourselves that condition of progress in spirit which is suitable to the environing conditions of each sphere through which our journey lay.

This traveling to and fro we made many times, and each time we made the journey it became easier for us to readjust ourselves constitutionally and we were able to go more quickly from state to state than at first was possible to us. And now we may come and go almost with that ease with which we travel from one place to another in the sphere in which our dwelling is. So that to come from there to you we count not time at all, for we come on the instant by one continuous effort of transposition instead of efforts several and repeated as we approached each self-conditioned sphere. Thus have we established the life-line of which we spoke, and which we use in descending hither and in ascending yonder from time to time.

What is your normal sphere, please?

As Zabdiel numbered them to you, ours is the Tenth. It is that of which he briefly told you and from which he later went to that above next in order. Few, and that not often, come from any sphere of higher degree to this of earth. It is possible so to do, and it has come to pass many times, if you count the ages in the sum of them. But when that happens some great purpose is toward and one which it is not competent for us who live in the Tenth or lower spheres to understand so well as to be the chosen messenger. Such was Gabriel who stands in God His Presence, ready to do His behest in the Heavenly Realms, both far and near. But even he has come to the lower regions about the earth but seldom.

Now as it is possible that we should come to you, so it is also within the economy of the heavenly wisdom that others of higher degree and estate should come to us from time to time. And for a very like purpose, which is that we should be given to know, in our bliss of service in these spheres of light and glory, of the greater glory and bliss of higher service and wisdom to know of the Ultimate which lies ahead of us in the great advance from strength to strength from one estate to another of more sublimity.

Thus are given to us, as to those of you who will receive the boon, glimpses of the way ahead. Thus we be not altogether strangers in those farther lands towards which we go ascending ever. And as it is with you, we also, time and again, are permitted to visit those higher glories for brief space and, returning, to tell our fellows of how they, our brothers, fare in those intenser spheres ahead of us.

So is the economy of God but one, and what is afoot in the lower spheres is found to serve in those of higher degree. And as you who accept our mission of enlightenment look forward with longing to your future life and ways, so having attuned ourselves to the estate we now enjoy, we also look still ahead to those realms which await us when we, by Grace and our own quiet endeavor, shall have enriched ourselves in such qualities as shall fit us for our further pilgrimage.

And there comes in these ways to our knowledge the life of the realms above us where those who dwell there be so near to the Christ and His own Abode, that in their face and form are seen to be the form and the lineaments of the Christ Himself.

About these realms supernal and sublime in their silence of potential energy the Christ moves freely, while to us He comes in what has been shown to you as Presence Form. In that way, too, He is altogether lovely, as well I know. And if this be so, then what suns of splendor must His eyes be like and what rosy glory must his raiment soften to the gaze of less than He, so they be not too much in amaze at His Present beauty.

You have seen Him then, Leader?

In that form, yes; but not in His naked loveliness, as I have lastly told.

More than once?

Aye, friend, and in spheres more than one. In this way He can and does penetrate even to earth and there He is not seldom seen. But then only by the young or those who have carried in their hearts their child-likeness, or those who in great anguish need Him very sorely.

Could you tell me of one of those occasions on which you have seen Him, please?

I will tell you of that time when there was some stir in the sphere where they come to be sorted out and classified, the sphere of which I told you at our last sitting to write. Many had come over at that time and the sphere was rife with much business and some perplexity. The workers there were hard put to, to know how best to help those many who were still not classified. And the mixture of good and ill in the multitude was causing some effervescence amongst them, for they were chafing and ill at ease and feeling that they were not being dealt with in justice and wisdom. This does not often happen. But I have known it to be so more times than one.

Mark you, they in that sphere are not bad, but godly people. They did not openly complain. In their hearts they know that all was well done to them. But their confused mixture of cloud and light prevented them from understanding. And while they did not openly murmur, yet they were sad at heart and began to lack courage for their task of self-knowledge—a hard work, too, mark you—for those who have neglected the thing in the earth life. It seems harder to be come at here, than in your sphere. But I will not pursue this further now.

The Angel Lord of the Colony came forth of His House and called to the multitude and they came with sad faces, many with their glances bent on the ground, with no heart to look upon the fairness of his beauty. When they were assembled before the high flight of stairs on which he stood outside the portico of his dwelling, he spoke to them in quiet tone of voice and told them not to be of poor heart for One before them had felt as they did now and He had won through because when clouds came between Him and His Father's face He still held on and would not distrust, but called Him Father still.

And while he spoke, one after another they lifted up their eyes to him and saw his majesty and his glowing, for he was of a higher sphere, he who had in charge this very difficult colony. And gradually as he still spoke gently to them with words of penetrating wisdom, they saw a mist begin to come about him and envelop him and slowly his form seemed to dissolve in the cloud of mist which, condensing, clothed him as with a mantle cast about him. At length they saw him no longer, but lo, upon the steps where he had stood another form began to appear, the form of One of lovelier countenance and brighter radiance than he. Brighter He grew and then there emerged into view about His brow a thorny chaplet with blood-drops beneath and on His breast, as if they had but now fallen. But as He grew brighter those thousands of tired eyes grew brighter too and they became lost in amaze at His exceeding glory of loveliness. The crown became changed into one of gold and rubies, the red drops upon His breast were gathered together into a clasp upon His shoulder to hold in place, and the robe he wore beneath His mantle glowed with the gold light of His radiant form beneath, which shone within its gossamer like molten silver with a tincture of sunlight in its texture. And the face of Him I cannot limn to you, for it is not possible in your words of earth more than to say that the majesty of the all-conquering Redeemer was there. His brow was the brow of a Creator of worlds and cosmoi and yet with the frail beauty of a woman's brow where the hair fell apart in the center. The chaplet spoke of Kingship and yet there was no pride of rule in the softness of the wavy hair, and His long lashes rather called upon our tenderness, while His eyes made us both love and reverence Him, but in awe.

Well, slowly the vision of Him melted into the atmosphere—I do not say faded away—for we felt that as He became more and more invisible to sight, yet His form was becoming vaporized as the air became more and more enforced with the very Presence of Him.

And then at last He was gone from our sight and where He had been we saw once more the Angel Lord of the Colony. But now he stood no longer, but with one knee aground his forehead rested upon the other and his hands were clasped about his forward foot. So still he was in rapture of communion that we left him there and went our ways. Only now we stepped with lighter tread and hearts uplifted. We were weary now no more, but ready for our task, whatever it should be. He spoke no word while we stood looking upon Him, but in our hearts "I am with you in all the ages," sounded very clear. And so we went to our work in great content and resolute.

21

Descent of the Christ
into Matter

Wednesday, December 12, 1917. 5:24–6:30 P.M.

IT is not that we are far away from you, that you must think
of us. We are very near by. You have it in your mind that,
because Kathleen writes with you directly, we who speak to
you through her are calling from a distance. That is not so.
Being that we have compassed the difficulty of descent by
readjustment, we come well into the sphere of earth and,
that being so, we find no difficulty in attuning our minds
so that we be very near to you. For there are degrees of estate in the earth sphere, as there are in those more advanced.
It were very difficult, if possible at all, that we should come
into the near environment of those who spiritually have not
risen much higher than the animal state. But with those who
seek to aspire towards us we, on our part, may bend down
to them and meet them at the highest point they can mount
to. And so we do with you. Does this rest your mind in some
measure, friend?

Well, I have felt as you have described, certainly. But if your further explanation be true, what need of Kathleen at all?

That, in part at least, we have explained before. We add a little now. You must bear in your mind some few facts— as these: Kathleen is more of your own period than we who mostly lived on earth some long time ago. She is nearer you in estate, normally, than we, and, while we can come into touch with your innermost self, she finds it easier than we to play upon that outer part where speech and motion of your fingers have their seat, that is the brain of your material body. Also, in the transmutation of our thoughts into words she plays a good part between us. But for all these, yet you and we are quite in tune and in touch together.

May I ask a few questions?

Most surely—but you hasten forward with some zest for knowledge, friend. Ask one and if there be time for more we will have them also.

Thank you. About the Descent of the Christ: when He descended from the Father's Home to become incarnate, I suppose it was necessary for Him to condition Himself to the Spheres, one after another, until He reached the earth sphere. Coming from so high a place, that would take Him a long time to do, wouldn't it?

So far as we have been taught, friend, the Christ was present in the earth Sphere when it was without form, that is when it was non-material. When matter began to be He was the Master Spirit through Whom the Father wrought into orderly constellations the material universe, as now you understand it. But, although He was present, yet He Himself was also formless, and took upon Himself, not material form but spiritual form, as the universe became endued with its outer manifestation, and so took form of matter. He was behind the whole phenomena, and the whole process passed through the Christ as the ages went along and matter grew from a chaos into a cosmos. That were not possible except for some dynamic entity operating from outside and superior to the chaos, and working downwards and into that chaos. For order cannot come out of what is lacking in order except by the addition of a new ingredient. It was the contact of the Christ Sphere with chaos that resulted in the cosmos.

Chaos was matter in potential state. Cosmos is matter realized. But, this being so, matter as realized is but the phenomenal effect of that dynamic energy which, added to inertia, produced motion.

Motion itself is the sum of the activities of will considered potentially. Will, passing from the potential state into its realization, becomes motion regulated according to the quality of that particular will which is its creator. Hence the Creator of all, working through the Christ, produced, after ages of continuous urge, the cosmos.

Now, if we have in any degree been able to make clear to you what is in our minds, you will see that the Christ was in the material universe from its inception and, that being so, He was in the earth sphere also while it gradually assumed first materiality and then form and last became, in its own turn interpreter of the meaning of the work of the ages which had become articulate, at length, in Earth's genesis. That is, it reproduced from itself the principle of creation and gave it expression. For from Earth came forth mineral and vegetable and animal forms of life expression. See you, friend, in what this eventuates? It means no less than that Earth and the whole Cosmos of matter is the Body of Christ.

The Christ Who came to Earth?

The Christ Who was One with the Father and, being One with the Father, was of the Father's Selfhood. Jesus of Nazareth was the expression of the thought of the Father, incarnate as the Christ for Earth's salvation. Bethink you a little, for I see a slight disturbance in your mind. On the other planets of your System are beings not unlike men. On planets of other systems are beings not unlike men also. In other constellations there be those who are related reasonably to God and His Christ and can commune with their Creator, as also do men. But they are not of human form nor of human method of thought-communion which you call speech. And yet to them the Creator and His Christ stand in the same relation as they do to you. And it has been, and still is, necessary that their Christ become manifest to them from time to time, in the form themselves have evolved. But then He goes to them not as Jesus of Nazareth, in human form, which to them would be less helpful than strange. He goes to them in their own form, and with their own methods of communion, and uses their own rational processes. This were obvious except to such as they who, having thrown into the void of space behind them the geocentric theory materially considered, have still bound that theory about them spiritually, like mummy wrappings, so that they scarce can move or see beyond their small world that there be other of as great import to the Creator as is this small earth of ours.

So that we say to you, the Christ Who came to Galilee was but the Earth-expression of the Christ Universal, but true Christ withal.

Now let us come to an end, albeit we have told you not a tithe of the glorious and splendid tale of the rhyme and rhythm of the eons and their birth and marriage and their bringing forth of suns who smile upon their own lesser children today.

The Christ, then, descended with matter as matter descended—by precipitation, if you will—out of the energizing of spirit dynamics. He was embodied in mineral life, for by Him all matter consists. He was embosomed in the rose and lily, and all vegetable life was the life of Him by means of Whom their beauty and wonder came forth of matter moving onward towards reason, but, at the highest, only touching the hem of the garment of rational activity. And He became manifest also in the animal life of the earth, for animals, as man, are of His evolving. The highest expression of His will was mankind. And in due time He came forth of the invisible into the visible world. He, Who had made man, was Himself made man. He, by Whom man came to be and to persist, thought forward into matter, and His thought took on expression in Jesus of Nazareth. So He Who was the Anointed Agent of the Creator for the making of man, Himself became the Son of Man whom He had made.

It is enough, friend. Your further questions will await our further coming. God and His Christ, Who united to bring you forth as man, friend, have joy of you in that you realize, and help others to realize, the splendor of their sonship and their destiny.

22

The Ascent of the Christ

Friday, December 14, 1917. 5:20–6:50 P.M.

The Kingdom of the Child.

WE have spoken to you, friend, of the Descent of the Christ into matter, as you inquired of us. Now let us pursue the normal road in continuance of what already we have given you. That road is now not downward into the womb of the material cosmos, but upward into the spiritual and toward that state which eventuates in the spiritual perfected which you have called by the name of the Home of the Father. That is the boundary of the present content of the universe of man's imagination. Further than that he cannot go in his forward gaze into what he conceives to be the possibilities of Being.

And yet we here have come to know that Spirit, sublime as it is in essence, is not the sum of Being. As beyond the realm of the material stretches the spiritual, so beyond those far and distant heights of light impenetrable, and holiness in awful purity towards which we think our way, there lies Being which is not Spirit alone, but which into Itself absorbs all that Spirit is at its whitest sublimity, and encompasses the sum total of spirit resultant in a universe of sublimity higher still.

As the light of a planet is but a small part of the outgoings of the central sun, and reflects back that light tinctured by its own planetary quality, so matter receives of spirit, and, in like manner, contributes its own small ingredient to the qualification and enrichment of the spiritual universe. As the Sun, in his turn, is of a system much greater than himself and but one unit of a constellation of suns, so Spirit is but part of a universe of Being of magnitude and sublimity beyond our ken. And even a constellation is in itself a unit of a vaster aggregation—but we will here cease to apply the analogy lest we become lost in wonderment, when we would rather find our way along the road of reason and understanding.

Let us therefore follow the Christ on His heavenly way, remembering that, being lifted up and exalted, He draws all men after Him, trailing His myriads along the heavenly road among the glories of the spheres towards the Home from whence He came, that where He is they might also be one day.

As the ages blend into ages yet to come, so the glory of the Christ intensifies, for every new recruit coming into His army adds a spark to the luster of His shining Kingdom, which is viewed, so we are told, by those who stand aloft on the dizzy heights of the Realm which is most distant and lofty of all, as in the realm of matter you view a distant star. In the ocean of spirit all the Spheres of the Christ are gathered into one great Star, and can be viewed exteriorly by those who dwell on high. That is not possible for us adequately to comprehend, yet we may get some small idea of its meaning thus:

From the earth you are unable to see the Solar System as a unit, for you are in the midst of that system and a part of it. But one standing aloft on Arcturus would see one small sphere of light, and in that sphere would be comprised your Sun and his planets and their moons. So do you view Arcturus and the other millions of the stars you see from Earth. So the Kingdom and Spheres of the Christ are viewed from the Realm afar, and age by age that System grows in brightness as the races which go to make up the whole evolve more and more out of the material into the spiritual. In this I speak of the whole spiritual economy as one star, and Those Who are placed to view it are They Who dwell on those far steppes of Being which are beyond the realms of Spirit in the great Void of the Unknown and Incomprehensible.

So far ahead are Those of Whom we speak, that we who have progressed ten spheres in Spirit can count ourselves no nearer to Them than you of Earth. The distance from you to us in progress, divided into that from us to Them, would be so infinitesimal as to be beyond all reckoning.

Yet as the whole of the constellations of suns march onward in orderly formation towards a sure if distant goal, so the Spheres of Spirit march onward towards their destiny, when the pilgrimage of Spirit shall blend into that which is beyond, and find there its consummation.

To this end the Christ, bending down from His Father's Bosom, touched humankind with the tip of His finger, and man became electrified with that Life Divine which pulses within his soul with onward urge, that in the train of the Sovereign Prince he may keep his rank with those of other planets, who together march forward as the one Army of the Father under the Vice-regency of His Son.

There is one thing I am not quite clear about. Our Lord said of little children, "Of such is the Kingdom." What you have said seems to imply that as we grow older we become less of the Kingdom, in the sense of childlikeness. Indeed, this seems to agree with our experience. But this would mean that we progress backward, with a kind of inverse development. Yet again, if our progress is only the first stage of the journey, and is continued in the Spheres, the child-like standard seems to be rather anomalous. Can you explain my difficulty?

The child is born into the world endowed with certain qualities and powers. But these are in childhood quiescent and undeveloped. They are there, but sleeping. As the mind enlarges in its capacity, it is able to call upon these powers, one after another, and to employ them. In so doing the man is continually both enlarging his sphere of action, and also coming into contact with new forces which impinge upon his environment, as that environment, enlarging its circumference, contacts, one after another, the spheres where these forces reside. Such forces I speak of as those which are creative and unifying and spiritualizing, and are apprehensive of the knowledge of God. On the manner in which he employs these means of larger strength depends his development as a spiritual being. The child is of the Kingdom in so far as he opposes not his will against that of the Father. Let the man, as he grows in capacity, keep that in his mind, and such child-likeness in his heart, and his enlarging powers will be used in consonance with the one grand purpose of God in the evolution of the race of men and other races who are of the one great family of the Creator. But if he, growing in years and in powers, fails to carry along with him on his way that quality of trustful obedience which is so marked in the child, then he will be found to be at variance with the Creator's mind, and friction will ensue which will clog the wheels of his chariot, and he will begin to lag behind till he come nearer and nearer the outlands of the Kingdom, and less and less in harmony with that company as he nears the boundary-line. But they who lose no portion of their child-like trustfulness, and to that add other virtues in their measure as they go along life's way, do not progress inversely, but more and more become children of the Kingdom. Jesus of Nazareth was such as this for, being the Son of His Father, to that Father His heart ever inclined in perfect unison, as in the Book of the records of His life you may read quite clearly. When He was a boy it was His Father's affairs which filled His mind to be busy about them. It was His Father's House which claimed His protection from worldly passions of self-centered men. In Gethsemane He sought to maintain that unison of purpose with His Father's will. Upon the Road He turned to see His Father's face, which the density of the world's miasma arose to obscure for the moment. Yet He did not fail to hold His heart God-ward, and when He left the Body of flesh it was towards the Father that His way was set. On Easter also He must still make that the pole-star of His heavenly voyage, as He told the Magdalene He must do. When the Seer of Patmos met with Him in the Heavenly Temple, He gave announcement that so much at one with the Father had He proved His will to be, that into His hands had been given authority to act in the Heavens as in the Earth, with plenitude of power. And who shall not see—who look upon His brief life of earth, or who have looked upon His Person here, as have we who now speak to you of Him—who shall not see in Him the Child unspotted but blent with the dignity of strength and of developed Man, and crowned with the Majesty of Godhead.

Yes, friend, it is only one who has come to great place in the Kingdom of the Father who may understand the Kingdom of the Child.

23

Temple
of the Holy Mount

Tuesday, December 17, 1917. 5:18–7:00 P.M.

The seer dismisses Leader and his party on their mission.

IN the preceding messages we have told you, as we ourselves
have learned, somewhat of the mystery of creation and progress of the Universe of matter, and, in a lesser degree, of that
of spirit. There are reaches there far surpassing any imagining
of ours, or of your own, and these will be made clear to us
as we in the ages which are ahead put on state after state of
more perfection. So far as we are able to project our minds into
that far immensity of life and being we cannot see any end to
our onward going, for, as a river viewed from the mountain in
which it takes its beginning, so is the life eternal. The stream
broadens, and into its volume absorbs more and more those
other streams which come from lands diverse in character, as
in soil. So is the life of a man, as he, too, gathers into his personality many side-currents of divers quality, and in himself
blending them in unity makes these one in and with himself.
As the river is seen still to broaden until it passes out of it-

self and ceases to be distinctive as a separate entity, so man, as he himself broadens out beyond his initial state, passes into that great ocean of light where we cannot follow him in his further progress from our viewpoint on the mountain of his birth. But this we have learned, and few there are who doubt it, that as the water of the ocean does not change the substance of the river from water into that which is other than water, but only enriches and modifies its quality, so man will still be man when he emerges from between the banks of individuality on the one hand, and of personality on the other, and blends the richness of his accumulated qualities with the infinitude of That which is the beginning and the consummation, the outgoing and the incoming forces of the whole cycles of Being.

Also, in the river fishes and water-animals have their habitation, but the wider and deeper realms of ocean make room for things of life of grander bulk and power than these, so those who in unity disport their immensity in person and in power must be of magnitude of glory beyond our ken.

We, therefore, glance ahead toward those far brothers of our own and know that they are not unmindful of us who, if we be much removed from their abode, yet have our faces set toward their quarters. It is from the Ultimate through such as these that life comes forth and bathes in love these lesser worlds of us and you. It is enough. We take our sip of the chalice of our destiny, and go forward much refreshed and strengthened for what duty lies to hand.

Would you like to tell me of some of these duties, please?

But they are manifold in number, and in diversity as great. We will tell you of a task we but lately were set upon and how we carried it to an end.

In the sphere from which we come to you there stands a Temple aloft upon a hill.

Is that the Temple Zabdiel told me about—the Temple of the Holy Mount?

The same. It is the Temple of the Holy Mount. It is so called because of the Beings who descend thither on various missions of blessing for that sphere and those inferior, and also because from that place they go into the higher sphere who in holiness and wisdom have become so qualified as to be capable of living in that sphere without discomfort, being conditioned to the more rarefied atmosphere of the place by long training, and also by visiting that Temple and the plain below from time to time where the conditions prevailing in the Sphere Eleven are brought about, while they bathe in that environment which will one day be their permanent one, and so qualify themselves for their new abode.

We went to the plain, and ascending the pathway round the side of the Mountain, approached the porch before the principal gate.

Were you qualifying for further advances?

Not in the way we have but presently described to you. No; that intensified atmospheric condition is not perpetual there, but is brought about at those seasons when they are to approach who are near their advancement.

We came to the Porch and waited awhile, and then there came without one of the bright residents of that Holy Place, a Keeper of the Temple, and bade us come within with him. This we hesitated to do, for none of our band had entered that shrine hitherto. But he smiled, and in his smile we read assurance and went with him without fear. There was no ceremony toward at that time, and so we were in no danger of coming too nigh powers which would be to us as naked sunlight to the eyes of a man who dares to gaze into the sun's disk at noonday.

We found we were in a long colonnade, and, on either side, the pillars supported a beam running from the porch to the bowels of the Temple itself But above us there was no roof, but the void of infinity itself—the vault of the heavens, as you say. The pillars were of great diameter and height, and the beam atop much decorated in its plinth and facade, but with symbols which we were unable to unravel. Only one factor of the pattern could I personally recognize, and that was the tendril and leaf of the vine, but of fruit there was none, which to me seemed quite right in such a place which was but the passageway as was the whole of that Temple from one sphere into another, and was not a place of fruition. At the end of this long and wide passage curtains were hung, and we were halted before them while our guide went further, and then returned to bid us enter. Even when we had passed through into the place beyond, we found we were in no wise within the great hall itself, but only in an ante-chamber. This ran across our path and we entered it, not at one of its ends, but in its side-length. It was of very large size in area and also in height, a square of the roof open in the middle before the door where we entered. But all the other part was covered with the roof.

We turned to the right and went to the end of this apartment, and then our guide brought us to a halt before a throne or chair and spoke to us in words such as these: "My brothers, you have been called hither in order that you receive commission to do a work which is required of you in the spheres yonder below. Will you of your good will await the coming of our brother, the Seer, who will give you to understand further what is required of your band."

As we stood there waiting, there came from behind the chair another man. He was taller than our guide, and around him as he moved there seemed to be a mist of blue and gold, set with sapphires. He came forward and took each of us by hand, and as we touched his fingers we became aware (as we told one the other afterwards) of the proximity of a sphere, within the Sphere Ten, which was a kind of concentrated essence of its condition, so that, entering within the circumference of that inner sphere, we were in touch with all that was going forward in the whole of that wide realm and in all its parts.

We sat down on the steps about the Throne, and the Seer stood before us facing the Throne. He talked then of things which I could not help you to understand in whole, for they are not of your experience, and even to us were of those things which we were but then advancing to understand. But then he told us some things which we can tell you profitably.

He told us that when Jesus of Nazareth was upon the Holy Rood there stood among those who beheld Him the one who had sold Him to his death.

Do you mean he stood there in the flesh?

Yes, in the flesh. He could not bring himself to keep away and stood not very near, but near enough to see the features of the dying Man, the Man of Sorrows. The Crown had been removed, but the blood-drops were upon His forehead, and His hair was here and there stained with blood. And as the betrayer looked upon the face and form of Him, there came into his soul a voice which mocked and said, "As you would have gone with Him into His Kingdom and there have taken high place of power, go now into the Kingdom of His adversary: there you may have power for the asking. He has failed you. Go now where He will not be at hand to reward you as you have served Him."

So voices came about him, and he strove to believe them and to look into the face of the One on the Cross. He was eager and yet in fear of those eyes into which he never had been able to look with comfort at any time. But the sight of the dying Christ was all too dim and He did not see Judah [Judas Iscariot] there. And still the voices hummed on and taunted him and cajoled him more gently, and at length, in the gloom about the place, he rushed away and let out his life in a place where he found solitude and a tree. He took off his girdle and hung himself to death on a tree. So they two died on a tree both on the same day, and the light of earth went out for them both at the same hour.

When they entered the spirit-spheres both were conscious, and they met there once again. But neither spoke then—only as He had looked on Peter, so He looked on Judah now, and left him for a time in his sorrow and anguish till that should do its work when He might come again with pardon.

As He did with Simon, when He went forth into the night to weep, so He did now, with Judah, who turned and stumbled away from Him with his hands to his eyes into the night of the hells.

And as He did with Simon in his penitence and sorrow and his sore need, so He did with the one who had failed Him in his loneliness, as Simon also did. He did not leave him comfortless all his days, but sought him out and gave to him the blessing of His pardon in the bitter anguish of his sorrow.

This was what the Seer told us, and more than this withal. And he bade us stay awhile in the Temple and Shrine and meditate on the things he had told us, and also gather power to go forth at length with the story, telling it—with others which he told us—wherever it were needful that sinners should hear of it, who in the darkness of despair had lost hope of the forgiveness of their Master betrayed, for a sin is betrayal.

But in what manner our task was done we will tell you at another time, for you now grow spent, and we have had some ado to carry you on even thus far.

So may the Savior of sinners, the Compassionate One, be with all who are in the darkness, brother, for there be many in earth as in spirit who need His comforting very sorely. His graciousness be with you also.

24

In Sphere Five

The pear-shaped hall.

FROM that High Place we went forth from the Audience Chamber wherein we had received the words of the Seer. More than I have told you he said to us in much love, and strengthened us for our mission. We went forth beneath the Porch and stood to view the wide expanse before us. Beneath us lay the plain of grassland, and it stretched very far forward to either hand. Then rose the encircling hills from which the streams descended into the plain and gathered into a lake to rightward of us as we stood. To left they opened, and beyond the gateway between them we could see the mountain range which rose between the Sphere Ten and that next in order inferior. And as we stood the Seer stood in our midst, and by his power enveloping us we were able to envision what was beyond our normal sight and to see into those spheres where lay the road we had to take. Bright and less bright they appeared before us, and then dim and still more dim, until into the mists they went, where from our vantage-ground we could not penetrate. For those most dim were they which were about the earth and also those below that state in average, and from whence they who would come to earth must ascend, while they who, having lived their lives on earth unrighteously, go by natural attraction downward into the places where they most will benefit by their environment. These you call the Hells. Well, such they be, my son, if hell means anguish and torment and soul-rending remorse.

So having taken our stock of things and what sort of task lay ahead of us in the business we had afoot, we knelt and he blessed us and we went our way. We took the leftward steep and came beyond through the gap and bent forward on our long journey. The first few spheres were traversed by aerial flight, going over the breasts of the mountains, and not descending until we came to the Fifth Sphere, and here we stayed awhile and told our story in most fitting words such as would help in the resolution of what difficulties they who there abode had most at heart.

Before going further, you might tell me how your mission was received in Sphere Five, if you will.

It was the first of our series of gatherings and the first sphere where our work began. We were the guests of the Chief Lord, the Governor of that Sphere, because he was himself of a higher estate than Sphere Five, as the custom is. But we stayed in the College of Praetors who were well versed in the study of the perplexities arising in the minds of those who tarried there and who could point out to us where to look for ground to work upon and what points to make to stand forth in our teaching.

Those gathered an assembly to the Great Hall of the College. It was a very great hall and in shape an oval, but one end was compressed more than the other.

Like a pear?

But that is a fruit we had forgotten, well-nigh, to name it. Yes, it was like a pear in ground-plan, but not so pointed. The people entered at the narrow end which was covered without by the Great Porch of the building. The rostrum was equal in distance from the other end and right and left walls. And here we took our stand.

A song of the Cosmos.

We had a singer with us and he first gave voice to a very magnetic air which he had made for the purpose. Low he began to sing, and his theme was Creation. He told us in rhythm of those things some of which we have told you—how, by the Ultimate His power projected, love first had its birth, and was found to be of sweetness so perfect that the Sons of God bathed in love, and of their contact came forth beauty. That is why all beauty is lovable and all love is simple and unalloyed, and in whatever phase it be manifest is full of beauty. But when the will of those who were given to act and bear their part in the development of the Realm of Being ran counter to the main stream of Beauty impulsed by love, then ensued an element which, being born of will acting not in consonance with original holiness, beings were evolved who were beautiful but not altogether beautiful, and their impetus once being blended with the ever-flowing stream of developing chaos, there also evolved others who were less and less of beauty, but none altogether lacking of some dim strain of beauty much overlaid and hidden from the eyes of those who continued in the broad onward road in a downward right line from their source.

So he sang, and the large number of people were very attentive and listened to his words, for the music of them seemed to come from where beauty and love had taken birth, and the words themselves were such as showed that the Supreme and Ultimate was Unity and not diversity in Himself, and that what diversity had come about was only permitted to be by way of fulcrum, where resistance might be found that, being expressed in multiple, might be levered higher and toward Unity once more.

Well, he being finished, a great silence fell upon them and they were very still. They stirred little, and those who had been standing on their feet so continued, and those who had been sitting upon the benches and stools remained thus in silence, and those who reclined aground, they still lay to case. I noted this, and that no one altered his posture of place because the spell of the song with its far-off origin in mighty upheavings of might and pulsations of life and energy held them and made them try to resolve all into focus with present environment and cosmic science.

In a while I, who should speak to them, began. The singer had begun in tone repressed and dulcet, but as the ages began to travail in the birth of the worlds his voice swelled in travail too, and the mighty upheavals of force and energy seemed to be in his soul and to come forth in painful grandeur of volume. And then, when the chaos was shaping itself out of itself to become the Cosmos and the manifold offspring of the one Creator's imagining, the stately rhythm of his voice and phrasing, in orderly sequence of progression, gradually poised itself on a level note, until he ended in monotone, as if he would leave the theme suspended in mid-Heaven to show that the presence of eternities was but begun and not ended.

A speech by Leader.

So I paused before I followed him, to give them space to gather their thoughts to arm and to bring them out of the luminous cloud in air and to wrap them about them as a cloak, that I might see and mark what each one wore over his heart and understand each his character and his wants and of what I could best give to his helping.

So I began and spoke to them altogether, but to each in his turn the while, and yet to them all as one continuously. And I told them of the re-assembly of these diversities and the gathering together of the scattered sparklers of love into one great sun of beauty which should absorb and give forth the glow and light from the Ultimate Who was altogether Beauty and altogether Love. Thus I told them of the traitor Simon and the traitor Judah and of their repentance, one in the earth-life, where he lived his brief hell to such good purpose that the remorse of a thousand years was squeezed into a month of days and claimed its own, which was, as it is today, forgiveness and reinstatement within the orderly family of the Father, And also I told them of that other whose repentance did not come about until the One he had stabbed so hastily in his frenzy of despair was sold to death, and how he, hasty ever, and of desperate temper always, plunged out of the world where naught had happened as he had planned, and how he came to no repentance until the Christ-Manifested, Jesus of Nazareth, went after him and others into those deep ravines of the dark mountains of hell, as after a strayed sheep, and told to those who there dwell in the gloom and tangible darkness of the Redemption wrought, offered and accepted of Him Who was Light and Love, and Who, through the Anointed, projected His love-beams into void spaces of immensity beyond the understanding to measure them and even into those same hells of night. And as they looked, their eyes were enabled to see the first light which some had seen for many, many years, until they had well-nigh forgotten what light was and what the look of it was like. But He was clothed with a dim, soft, sweet radiance, suitable to them in their present state to see, and one and then another crawled to His feet, and their tears sparkled as they fell like diamonds of dew into the sunlight, as they received the light from Him. And I told them that among these came the traitor Judah and was forgiven, even as Simon was later told of His forgiving love also.

So, my son and friend, they listened, and began to see how I was telling them of the incomings into unison with God His Love and Sovereignty, of those outgoings from obedience to

Him which had been so fruitful parents of the many perplexities which had troubled the children of men.

Then in silence I ended, and in silence we left them there, and we went about to leave the hall and college and to go on our journey. And so we did, and the proctors sped us with words of kindly gratitude and we answered them with our benediction. So we departed from them.

25

Leader's Problem
in Sphere Five

Wednesday, December 19, 1917. 5:30–7:10 P.M.

WE went gently now and with no haste, for we began to come near to those regions where we were not of ease very much to abide therein, until we should have attuned our condition to theirs. And so we at length arrived at that Boundary Land where begins the Second Sphere, as reckoned from your earth, which we will count zero for the purpose of reckoning.

Leader, before you continue, might I ask you a question? Was it not in Sphere Five that you stayed rather longer than in the others, because you had some kind of perplexity which held you back? I mean, in the earlier period—that of your ascent?

You would like me to explain the problem which vexed me and held me there awhile. It was this:

I knew that all men came at last to understand that God is Lord, and that all who came from Him told that to those who dwelt further away from His Throne and Sanctuary. Yet, if this be so, why were there so many myriads left behind us in those darker spheres, where misery and anguish surged and seemed to belie all love, and to counterplead its presence universal?

That was my problem. It was the old crux of the existence of evil. Well, I could not understand nor reconcile these two opposing forces, as they appeared to my mind to be. If God was almighty, why, then, should He permit evil to be, even for one moment and in the minutest degree?

Long I brooded upon it, and was much troubled because the distrust which came of such contradiction within the realm of God took away from me all confidence to proceed towards those dizzy heights ahead, lest I lose my balance and come to grievous hurt by falling into depths far deeper than I had hereto plumbed.

Its solution

At length I was ready for the help which is always given in its own season. Unknown to myself, I had been led in my reasonings all the time until I was ripe for enlightenment, and then the vision was given to me which swept all my doubtings away into oblivion, never to return to trouble me again.

One day, as you would say, I sat in a bower-like hollow of the trees upon a bank of small red flowers. I was not thinking of my chief perplexity, for I had many more things to think on more pleasurable than it. I was drinking in all the beauty of the woodland—its flowers, leaves and birds, and the songs they sang one to another—when I turned to see sitting by my side a man of grave and very lovely aspect. His mantle was of rich purple, and underneath he wore a tunic of gossamer through which his flesh shone like sunlight reflected from the heart of a crystal. His shoulder-jewel was of deep green, and the one upon his forehead was of green and violet. His hair was brown, but his eyes were of no color of which you know.

So he sat there looking before him and I looking upon him and his great loveliness for a long time, and then he said, "My brother, this seat is a very cozy one, and pleasant to rest upon, think you?" And I replied, "Yes, my Lord," for I had no more words than those.

"And yet," he said, "it is a bed of flowers on which you set your mind to lie upon." And to that I could not give any answer. So he continued, "Think you, friend, that these little red beauties of the flower family which are filled with budding life and comeliness, such as little children have, were made for such purpose as this to which we put them?"

And all I could reply was, "I had not thought of it, sir?"

"No, that is after the manner of most of us, and it is strange, too, seeing that we be, every one of us offspring of One Who is thinking all the time, and Who does naught that is not in agreement with reason. And it is within the ocean of the Life of Him we swim from age to age, and never out of it. It is strange how we can act unthinkingly, who are children of such a Father as He."

He paused, and I glowed red with shame. Yet His voice and manner were not of severity a whit, but gentle and winning, as a maid would mother a man. But I began to think now, if not before.

Here I was crushing beneath the weight of my body, all heedlessly, these tiny blossoms which were so pretty, so full of life, and yet so helpless in their meek loveliness. So at last I said, "I see the quarry of your arrow, sir, and you have shot deep. It is not well that we sit here longer, for we smother these poor flowers with weight of body."

"Then, let us rise and walk onward together," he said. And so we did.

"Do you much frequent this path?" he asked, as we went forward side by side.

"This is my favorite walk," I told him. "It is hither I often come to think out matters which perplex me."

"Yes," he said thoughtfully, "this is a sphere of perplexity beyond its fellows. And, coming hither, you often sit down upon some bank and think things out—or do you rather think yourself in deeper into your perplexity, I wonder? But let that rest awhile. Where sat you last when you came hither to think?"

He stood still to ask the question, and I pointed to the bank before him and I said, "It was here I sat when I came hereabouts last time."

"And that but recently?" he asked, and I said, "Yes."

"And yet," he said, "I see no mark of your body's shape upon this moss or its blossoms. They have very soon recovered themselves of any untoward pressure they received."

For it is so in these realms. It is not as on the earth. These flowers and mosses and the greensward quickly recover their seemliness, and it is hard, even on rising, to see where you have lain. It is of Sphere Five of which I speak. It is not so in all spheres, and least in those near earth.

A manifestation of the Christ sorrowful and glorified.

But he continued, "Yet this is the concern of the All-Creator equal in value and appraise with the bruising of the souls of men. For whatever work is His is His indeed, and His alone. And now come, brother, and I will show you what you have not been able to see for lack of faith. You now begin to doubt the wisdom of your own imagining, and in that doubt lies the nucleus of faith in the goodness of Him Whose Realm is Love, and the Light of that Realm His Wisdom."

Then he led me through a by-path of the wood and to a hill, which we ascended until we stood higher than the top of the woods below and I looked over the landscape into the distance. And as we looked, I saw far away upon the plain beyond the Temple of the Sphere, and there arose through the openings of the roof bright shafts of light, and these united in one about the central dome. These were sent up by the spiritual exercises of those who were met within.

At length there arose in the midst of the dome the figure of a Man, Who ascended until He stood upon the top of it. It was the figure of the Christ, clothed all in white. The garment He wore came from His shoulders to His feet, but did not hide them. And as He stood there, a rosy hue began to flood His garment, and this deepened in tone until, at length, He stood there enrobed in deep rich crimson, and upon His brow a circlet of rubies red as blood, and His sandals upon His feet were enriched with rubies, too. And when He held His hands stretched outward I saw that on the back of each one great red stone sparkled, and I knew what the vision meant to me. He had been lovely in His whiteness. But now He shone with crimson loveliness, and rich deep beauty which made me gasp for ecstasy as I looked upon Him.

Then, as I looked, about Him gathered a golden cloud streaked with sapphire and emerald. But behind Him, from above His head downward, stood a deep, broad, blood-red band. And another band, of equal depth of color, crossed the upright band behind Him as high as His breast, and He stood before it in all the regal splendor of His coloring.

Out upon the plain below we saw the people thronging to get a sight of this glory. And upon their faces and their robes there shone the light projected from His body, and it seemed to breathe of some call to sacrifice and service which needed trust to undertake it, inasmuch as those who should offer themselves for the work must go forth and suffer, yet without knowing quite all the mystery of suffering. But there were many who knelt and bowed their heads to earth in answer, and these He took, and told them to meet Him within the Temple and He would give them their word of mission. Then He faded downwards through the dome into the building, and I saw Him no more.

I had forgotten the man beside me and was not mindful of his presence for a time after the vision had ended. And then I turned and looked upon him, and I saw that on his face suffering had been traced in lines both many and deep. And yet they were not of the present, but of the past, and they but made him the more lovable for their afterglow.

But I could not speak to him, and so stood by in silence. And then he said, "My brother, I have come from a place much brighter than this sphere of yours to bring you hither that you should see the Man of Sorrows in His glory. Those sorrows He came forth freely to gather to Himself and make them His own. Without them He would lack some loveliness which is His today. And those sorrows which give to Him so much of gentleness are they which, in their crude and undeveloped state, flood earth with pain and the hells with torment. These are but for the moment for each who passes beneath their shadow. We cannot penetrate, my brother, into all the great Heart of God. But we can, as we even now have done, get at times a glimpse of the reason shining through it all, and then perplexity loses some of its more sinister aspects, and the hope arises that some day we may be able the better to understand.

"But till that day dawns for me, I am content to know that He Who came forth of the Father's Heart came white and pure, and, with steadfast purpose, faced the task ahead, where His path lay amidst the turgid clouds of sin and hatred which gather about the planet of earth. Nay, into the very hells He went and sought out those who suffered there, and because of their anguish He suffered also; so the Man of Sorrows returned to the Steps of His Father's Throne, His task accomplished. But not as He had gone forth did He return. Ile went forth white in purity of holiness. He came back again the Crimson Warrior Prince and Conqueror. But the blood He shed was not that of another, but only His own. Strange warfare this, and new in the world's stranger history, that the warrior meeting his foe should turn the blade towards his own breast, and yet come forth conqueror by reason of his blood he shed.

"So, adding those rubies to His crown, and to His person the rosy tint of sacrifice, He came back more beautiful than He went forth. And now that tragedy of His Descent into matter is but as a moment's pressure of the moss on which you lay unthinking, and which is unhurt in its perennial freshness of growth and blossoming.

"He, coming whence He does, from those high Realms of Light and Power beyond our measuring to tell us of the grandeur of the sacrifice of self—He is my warrant for God's good wisdom.

"As for the tragedy of sin and frenzy of Hell's rebellion— well, they who have traveled those dark ways bring back something, too. Because of the love He and His Son have shown, in bringing out of the darkness those who had left the highway of obedience and had sought another ruler in Self, something is added to them which is precious to them and sweet, for it binds them so close to Him. Yes, my brother, you will understand one day more of that wisdom. Be patient until then. It will be a long time yet before you can come to understand. It will not come to you so readily, nor so soon, as it did to me, to fathom this deep mystery, because you did not sink into those deep caverns of remorse and agony. But I have dwelt there, for I came that way."

26

Changes in Sphere Two

Thursday, December 20, 1917. 5:10–6:17 P.M.

The three roods on Calvary

SO we came to Sphere Two, and went about to find the place where they mostly gathered, for since my sojourn there changes had ensued, so that I had perforce to renew my knowledge of the ways and manners obtaining. For know you, friend, that in those spheres nearer earth there is more of change in minor things than in those spheres more remote and progressed. In Sphere Two the progress of earth-knowledge and intercommunion of peoples are still felt in their development from generation to generation, for the one sphere intervening but little modifies these, and earth-manners of thought and prejudices have still much influence in that sphere, which influence but gradually is neutralized as the spheres are traversed. Even in those well progressed there linger traces of these things, but not so intensified as to arrest development, nor to mar the Brotherhood of the children of God. They become, these differences of earth-life, varieties of type which add to the interest and charm of such as Sphere Seven and onward, and have no taint of division, nor belittling of other

431

opinions and creeds. Those who have proceeded so far into the light have by that light learned to read the lessons written in the Book of the Acts of God, and there is but one Book for All who speak one tongue and are all one great family of the Father there. Not, as in earth-life, out of mere passive and constrained toleration, but with hearty co-operation in work and in friendship—one in love.

But now we speak of Sphere Two and our business therein.

There the people were gathered into groups, as it pleased their choice. Some sought to consort with those of their own race. Other groups were formed of those to whom Creed was of higher appeal than blood. And even political circles were not absent. And those from these groups singly would from time to time attend the assembly of other groups which were to their mind in part. A Moslem would pay a friendly visit to a group of international socialists, or an imperialist would attach himself to those who worshipped God according to the Christian faith. Much diversity was there in the grouping of the people, and much interchange in the composition of the groups. But for the most part they remained and continued in what faith they had ever been, and of what political party and of what blood.

But the coming of a mission from Sphere Ten was soon known throughout that region, for not so much bitterness remained to divide them as in the earth-life, and much good will was there. They were learning the lesson as we had learned it time agone, so, although at first they seemed a little bit slow to come together in general, yet we told them that this must be so, if they would hear us, for we could not speak to groups and parties, but only to an assembly of all as one.

So they came and stood in a part where small knolls and dips of turf-land stretched out from a hill, not very high, but higher than the other hills around. We stood upon the hillside halfway up, where we could be seen of them all, and behind us was a rock of great height and flat of surface.

Then when we had praised the One Father together, we sat about the ledge of rock, and one of our number, who was more in touch with them of this sphere, spoke to them. He was of Sphere Seven, but had been lifted up to the Tenth, in order to receive with us the commission and strength for the way.

Now he had great skill in the matter of word-grouping, and he lifted his voice and flung it forth over that widespread company, diverse in coloring of raiment as in opinion of what truth is. His voice was strong and sweet, and this is in substance what he told them.

Down on the plane of the earth there dwelt one family, which had been divided into many sections, and, seeing the evils of such division, there were many who would confederate them once again. Even in this sphere was to be seen that same stubbornness of pride which said, "My race and my creed are more to the Father's mind than those of others." It was for the reason that such must be done away before advance could be free and unimpeded that we had brought them altogether as one family to deliver the message we had from the One Father, through the only Christ.

At this there was some uneasiness among them, but no word was said amiss, for when they saw that our brightness was of luster beyond their own, they gave us heed, knowing that once we thought as they thought now, and that only by the releasing of some of our opinions and the remodeling of others had we come to be brighter of form and countenance than they. So they gave our speaker heed.

He paused awhile, and then took up his theme anew: "Now hear me patiently, my fellow pilgrims on the royal road of progress to the City of the Splendor of our King. On Calvary there were three Roods, but one Savior. And there were three men, but only One who could make the promise of the place in the Kingdom, for one only of the three was King, and although the darkness fell and with darkness comes repose, yet only One there could fall on sleep—and have you reasoned why?

It was because no other there was of compassion so tender, nor of love so great, nor of spirit so pure, as to be able to understand the purpose of the Father in the creating of man in his own fashion, and of the tremendous forces which surged through the ages tearing asunder the Kingdom and the Family of God. It was the knowledge of the magnitude of that long sustained warfare and the crushing burden of the enemy's hate which wearied Him so sorely that He fell asleep. Into matter had He gone to plumb the deeps of divergence from the Highest. Now He left the body material and began His ascent back to those High Places once again. And His first captive was the one who had pleaded with Him upon the Tree, and another was he who for thirty pieces gave his Lord to die.

Here, then, is a strange trinity of persons. Yet, as in that other Trinity the Three find Unity, so in these three is unity to be found.

"For the robber sought the Kingdom of the Christ, and Judah had sought the Kingdom of the Christ, and the Lord had sought and found, that He might present it to the Father. And only He had found what He came to seek. For the robber, he had not come to understand that the Kingdom was not of the earth alone, until he saw before his dying eyes the regal mien of One Who was just on the threshold of the spirit. The other, the Betrayer, had not found that Kingdom until he had passed through the gate into the darkness without and beheld the King in the budding beauty of His native comeliness. But He Who came and found told out what sort of Kingdom it was which the Father would approve. It was both of the earth and of the Heavens. It was within them while incarnate. It was there ahead where they were going. So it embraced the heavens and the earth, as it was in the beginnings of things, when forth from the Mind of God came earth and heavens.

And so I speak to you and ask you to consider each for himself his brother. Consider the diversity of these three upon the Trees of Calvary; or these Three, the Perfect One and His two first-redeemed in the beginning of His life triumphant. Yet they show the will of God to be that, from one end of earth to the other, all people of all degrees shall be one in the Christ, and one in Him Who is greater than His Christ. So now I ask you to find among you any such diversity as that between Jesus of Nazareth and the Iscariot, or one of those on either hand. And thinking thus, my brothers, you will see that He, by Whose permissive wisdom men were divided, shall bring them once again within the Household in the Heavens of His Glory, for the greatest of all His glories is the glory of His love, and love unites what hatred would divide.

27

At the Bridge

New Year's Eve, 1917. 5:15–6:25 P.M.

In the land of darkness.

OF our descent hereto we have spoken in brief, but now we come to those spheres where the light grows more dim, and of which not so much has been told by those who have come earthward to show to men what awaits humanity when they cross the borderline and become vibrant with the quicker life as it pulses in these realms of spirit. So we would presently be more discursive for the sake of those who would the rather attain to an equal knowledge of what is of light and shade, and those who are of the weaker sort, and who desire and need the buoyancy of joy and of beauty, may turn about and leave us to cross the chasm alone, awaiting our return to the spheres where light is dominant over all, and little of shadow there is to sully the fairness of the life abounding.

So, having passed through that tract where people come on leaving earth, and of which we have already spoken in brief, we passed on into the darker realms. And now we felt increasingly that pressure of soul which needs stout hearts and wary feet to combat.

For you will mark that we were not to pursue that method by which the higher ones may sustain their contact with those in the darkness, yet be to them unseen. We were to condition ourselves, as hereto, to the environment of the spheres inferior to our own, so now to those of even lower estate, so that we become of body not indeed so dense and gross as the inhabitants in proper, but yet so nearly approximate as at times to be able to be visible to them at will, and quickly, and even that they might, on occasion, be aware of our touch upon them and that they might also touch us. So we went but slowly and afoot, and all the time in-breathing the condition which was ambient about us to this same end and purpose. And we thereby also got at some sympathy of feeling with those among whom our labors were now to be.

There is a region which is still in the sunlight, but ends in a steep descent, where the bottom lies in darkness. As we stood there to view, we looked across the deep valley, which seemed to be filled with gloom so gross that we could not penetrate it from our standpoint in the light. Above the murky ocean of mist and vapor a dull light rested from above, but could not sink beneath the surface far, that ocean was so dense. And down into that we had to go.

The Bridge of which your mother spoke to you runs right across the valley and lands on a lower elevation beyond. Those who front the depth climb up that side, then rest a period at the further end, and come across the great causeway to the hither side. There are rest-houses here and there along the way where they who are too weary still to make the journey at one stage may stay and refresh themselves from time to time. For even after gaining the Bridge, the journey across is a painful one, inasmuch as on its either side they see the murk and gloom from which they have but lately come, and hear the cries of those, their sometime companions, who still linger beneath, way down, in the valley of death and despair.

Our purpose was not to cross this Bridge, but to make our descent into the depths from this side.

What is beyond the "lower elevation" you spoke of, and on which the further end of the Causeway rests?

The Causeway rests on a ridge not quite so high as the Rest-Land which leads to the regions of Light. That ridge is but a short one, and runs in parallel with the precipice where the hither end of the Bridge finds issue. So that ridge stands as a mountain, in shape an elongated oval, with the valley beneath it and between it and the Rest-Land. Beyond is a vast plain on a level with the valley's bottom, but unequal of surface and broken up into cavities and ravines, and beyond there is a dip into regions lower still, and of darkness more gross. It is up that mountain that they perforce must climb who would reach the Bridge from that side. The mountain ridge is short only as compared with the vastness of the region in whole. But it is so great, notwithstanding, that many lose their way and return to the valley time and again. It depends on the degree of their vision, which again is in ratio to their quality in repentance and will for the better life, how soon they find their way of escape.

So we stood awhile and pondered, and I turned to my companions and said, "It is a murky place, my brothers, and it does not call us with much sweetness. But thither lies our way, and we had best be agait to make it."

And one replied, "I feel the chill of the hate and despair from the bottom of the pit. We can do but little in that ocean of anguish. But such little as we can do cannot wait the doing, for the while we wait, they suffer."

"That is the word to say," I answered him, "and it is the spirit of Him who went beforetime. We have followed Him into His Light. Let us now go into the darkness, for that, too, is His, since He claimed that also as His own by His going."

So we took the path downward, and as we went the gloom became more gloomy and the chill more full of fear. But we knew we went to help, and not to fear aught, and so we did not hesitate in our steps, but went warily withal, and looking this way and that for the right path, for our first station lay a little to the right-hand as we went, and not between the Rest-Land and the Ridge, and it was a colony of those who were weary of the death-life they had endured, and yet who lacked the strength to break away, or the knowledge which way to take, if they should leave their present desperate anchorage. As we went, our eyes became more attuned to the gloom, and we could see about us, as on a night one might see the country outlying a city by the ruddy flares on the watchtowers thereof. We saw that there were many ruined buildings, some in clusters and some solitary. Decay was all about us. It seemed to us that no one had ever made whole any house, once it began to fall into disrepair. Having built it, they left it to build another elsewhere at the first sign of wear, or, having tired of it before it was finished, had left to build another. Listlessness and want of endurance was all about us in the air—the listlessness of weary despair and the despondency of doubt, both of their own strength and of their neighbors' purpose.

There were trees also, some very large, but mostly leafless, and those with leaves not comely, for the leaves were of dark green and yellow, and spiked with lance-like teeth, as if they, too, took on the aspect of enmity from those who had lived near them. Here and there we crossed a waterway full of boulders and sharp stones and with little water, and that water thick with slime and stinking.

And at long, long last we came within sight of the colony we were seeking. It was not a city, but a cluster of houses, some large and some small. They were scattered about, here and there, and not in order. There were no streets in the city. Many dwellings were merely mud-huts, or a couple of slabs of stone to form a shelter. And there were fires about the open spaces to give light to the inhabitants. Round these, many groups were gathered, some sitting in silence looking at the flames, others loudly brawling, others wrestling in their anger, one with another. So we drew near, and, finding a silent group, we stood by waiting and looking upon them with much pitifulness in our hearts for their hopelessness of spirit. And, seeing them, we took hands one of another and thanked our Father that He had given us this present work to do.

28

The Sometime Magistrate

Thursday, January 3, 1918. 5:18–6:45 P.M.

A Lesser Christ from the Fourth Sphere.

WHEN we had come upon the group, they had been sitting and lying round the flickering fire in sullen silence. Now we stood behind them and none looked up. Had they done so, they would not have seen us, their eyes not being attuned to our state, which was not quite modified to their own in degree. So we took hands one of another and gradually merged ourselves into visibility; the while they, one and another of them, began to shift about ill at ease, sensing as they did some unknown presence not at tune with them. This is ever so, and it is the same sense of irritation and uneasiness, when they begin to seek to aspire, which holds them back so often. The upward way is ever an arduous way, full of difficulty and failures recurring. The reward is well worth it all in the end of it. But this they do not know very clearly, and what they do know is by report of those who come to them as we did then.

At last one arose and looked about him in the mist and gloom uneasily. He was a tall, gaunt figure, with knotted joints and limbs, bent and bowed, and his face was pitiful to see, such lack of hope and fullness of despair was there upon him, and found expression throughout his frame. Then he came with shambling gait to usward and stayed a few yards distant and looked upon us inquiringly. We knew then that, although but dimly, yet we could be seen by some at least of those who lived in that dark place.

At this I stepped forward and said, "You look full weary, my friend, and much disturbed in mind. Can we befriend you in any way?" And then we heard his voice. It was like a long-drawn sigh sent through a tunnel underground, so weird it was. He said, "Who may you be? There are more than one of you, for others I see behind you. You are not neighborly to this land. From what land do you come, and why do you come to us in this dark place?"

I looked upon him now more intently, for even in that ghost of a voice I seemed to find somewhat familiar to me or, at least, not strange altogether. And then I knew. He and I had lived near one to the other on earth. Indeed, he was Magistrate in the town near by my home, so I said his name, but he did not start as I had expected he would do. He looked at me confused, but not with comprehension, so I named the town, and then said the name of his wife, and at length he looked down aground and put his hand to his forehead and tried to call to memory. First he remembered the name of his wife, and looked up to my face and repeated it again and again. Then I said his own name again, and he caught it from my lips quickly and said, "Yes, I remember—I remember. And what of her? Do you bring me news of her? Why did she leave me thus?"

I told him that she was in a higher sphere, and could not come to him until he had begun his journey ascending toward her home. But he only half understood me. So dazed are they in the dark spheres, that they mostly do not realize where they are, and some do not know that they have passed over from earth-life, for only occasionally does a flash of memory of their former course on earth come upon them, and then dies away again leaving a blank behind. So they be for the most part uncertain whether they have ever lived in other places than these hells. But when they begin to grow weary of the torment, and restless to be gone to some place less gross, and to live among people less debased and cruel, then remembrance dawns back again into their dull brains, and they begin their agony of remorse in earnest.

So I repeated my answer and began to explain. He had loved his wife, in his own rather selfish way, when in the earth-life, and I thought to pull him back to her with that string. But he broke in upon me, "Then she will not come to me now I have fallen on evil times." "She cannot come all the way," I said. "You must go your way to her and she will meet you." And at that he cried out in anger, "Then let her be damned for a proud and hard-cased wench. She was ever the fine lady-saint to me and moaning over my little lapses. Tell her, if you come from her parts, she can stay in her spotless mansion and gloat upon her husband's state. They be here in plenty more pleasurable than she, if not so comely. And if she will descend from her high estate we'll have a rousing rout for her reception. So good-day to you, sir." And sneering he turned away and laughed to the crowd for their approval.

But there arose one other of them who came and took him aside. This one had been sitting among them, and was drab of dress as any of them. Yet there was a gentleness in his movements and somewhat of grace withal which was to us surprising. He spoke to him awhile, and then they came back to me, and this companion said, "Sir, this man did not quite understand the purport of your words, nor that you did really come to comfort and not to taunt. He is some little repentant that he spoke to you in words such as were unseemly. I have told him that you and he were not altogether unknown each to other once. Of your kindness, sir, speak to him again, but not of his wife, for as yet he cannot endure her desertion, as he names her absence."

I was very much surprised at this speech so quietly uttered, while the brawling noises came from all around us and shrieks and curses intermingled from the groups by the fires upon the plain. But I left him with a word of thanks, and went to the man I had known. I felt my business was with him in chief, for I had a sure conviction that could I impress him we would through him be able to concern his companions in their future course, for he seemed to be dominant among them and of consequence.

So I went up to him and took him by the arm, and spoke his name and smiled, and we took a walk apart, and gradually I led him on to talk of his earth-life, and his hopes and ventures and his failures, and, at last, of some of his sins. These he did not admit very readily, but before I left him he did allow me to blame him in two matters, and he admitted I had the right to my side. This was a very great gain, and I asked him to think on it all, as I had put it before him, and I would seek him out and speak with him again, if he would wish it so. Then I gripped his hand in a good, stout grip, and left him. I saw him sit down and draw his knees up to his chin and clasp his arms about his shins, and so left him gazing into the fire in deep introspection.

But I would not go forward until I had sought out and spoken with the other, who seemed to me to be ripe for his journey out of that region into one more in tune with his repentant mind. I did not find him for some little time, but at last came across him sitting apart on the bole of a fallen tree in talk with a woman, who was listening very intently to what he had to tell her.

Seeing me approach, he stood up and came towards me, and I said, "My friend, I thank you for your good offices, for I have, through your timely help, been able to impress that unhappy man, as otherwise I had not done. You be more familiar with the natures of these your companions than I, and have used your experience to good effect. And now, what of your own life and future?"

"I thank you, sir, in turn," he replied. "I ought not longer to delay the discovery of myself to you. I am not of this region, sir, but of the Fourth Sphere, and I am here by choice to do service, such as I am able, among these poor darkened souls." "Do you live here constant?" I inquired of him, amazed; and he replied, "For a long time, yes. But when depression becomes too heavy, I return for a little while for replenishing to my own home and then come hither once again." "How often?" I asked him. "Since I came here first," he said, "some sixty years have gone in earth-time, and I have returned to my home nine times. Several of those I knew on earth came here in the first early period, but none of late; they all be strangers now. Yet I still contrive to help them, one by one."

At this I marveled greatly and ashamed.

Here my party came on tour and thought it a virtue so to do. But the one who stood before me brought to my mind Another, Who laid His glory aside and emptied Himself that others might be filled. I think I did not realize in fullness until then what it meant that a man should lay down his life for his friends, aye, and those friends such as these, and to dwell with them in these regions of the shadow of death. He saw me and understood some of what passed through my mind, and taking my own shame upon himself, he said wistfully, "So much He did for me, sir—so much—and at so great a cost."

And I said to him, taking his hand in mine, "My brother, you have read me a lection of the very Book of God His Love. The Christ of God is beyond our understanding in the Majesty of His Beauty and His Love so wide and sweet. Him we may not comprehend, but only worship with adoration. But since this be so, it is something of profit to consort with one who knows how to attain to be a Lesser Christ. And such, methinks, I have found in you."

But he only lowered his fair head, and as I, of reverence led, kissed him where the parting of his hair was, murmured as if to himself. "If I were worthy—if only I were worthy of that Name."

29

Into the Greater Darkness

Friday, January 4, 1918. 5:30–7:55 P.M.

The City of Blasphemy

FROM that colony we went further into the regions of gloom. We had done what we were able, going from group to group where houses clustered or where fires burned, and ministered comfort or advice to those who would receive us. But they were not of much readiness for the most part. Some few would be able to retrace their steps upward from that place, but the many would have to descend lower into the misery of the further regions before their hardness should give place to despair, and despair should return into longing, and a glimmer of light should glow in those poor lost souls. Then would come repentance and amendment, and their toilsome journey towards the Valley of the Bridge. But that time was not yet at hand. So we left them, for we had our orders, and in our minds the map of the country by which to find our way to those places where special work awaited us. For we did not go at random into those dark places, but of purpose, set for us by those who sent us thither.

And as we went we felt about us a growing power of evil. For, you must mark, there are degrees of Power, as of evil, in the different colonies there, and also diverse notes of evil dominant in its several regions. And, further, the inequality of forcefulness obtains there as in earth. They are not all of one type and pattern in evil. For free will and personality are there, as elsewhere, and by the persistence of these, some be great ones and some of less account in power, even as in earth and in the brighter spheres.

Thus we came to a large city, and entered through a massive gateway where guards marched to and fro. We had relaxed our will to visibility and so passed within unseen. We found the broad street beyond the gate was lined with great houses of heavy build like prison fortresses. From several of the wind-holes lurid flickering of light fell into the roadway and across our path. We went on until we came to a large square, where there was set up a statue on a high pedestal, not in the middle, but toward one side, where the largest building stood.

The statue was that of a man who wore the toga of a Roman noble, and in his left hand he held a mirror, into which he looked, but his right hand held a flagon, out of which he poured red wine which plashed into the basin below—a travesty of nobility. The basin was ornamented with figures here and there around its border. There were children at play, but the game they played was the torture of a lamb by flaying it alive. At another part there was a rudely carved woman who held a babe inverted to her breast. The carvings were of such like nature, all of mockery, blaspheming the virtues of childhood, maternity, valor, worship, love and other, an obscene and motley crowd which made us near despair of good result by any appeal to nobility of those who lived in that city. Filth and mockery was rife all around us. Even the buildings in their plan and ornamentation shocked the eye whichever way we turned. But we were there for a purpose, as I say, and we must stomach what we met, and go forward on our errand.

So we willed ourselves into such a condition as that we should be seen of the inhabitants, and entered the gate of the dark Palace of Evil before which the statue stood. We passed through a large dungeon-like entrance, and, traversing the passage beyond, found ourselves at a doorway giving on to a balcony. This ran around a lofty hall, halfway up between floor and roof, with flights of steps here and there descending. We approached the balustrade and looked over into the hall below, from which a voice, strong and piercing, came to us. We could not see for a while from whom it came; but when our eyes had suited themselves more to the ruddy light which filled the great space below us we saw and knew what was toward.

Opposite us there rose a great flight of steps from floor to balcony. All the crowd which filled the hall sat around and faced it. Upon the lower steps and halfway up there were coiled, in different attitudes, all unbeautiful, men and women in loose and scanty clothing, which, nevertheless, made pretence to grandeur. Here and there a gold or silver belt, or chaplet, or silver brooch of jewels, or bejeweled buckle or clasp appeared; but all were false, as one could see: the gold was tinsel, and the gems were counterfeit. Upon the stairs, just above them, stood the speaker. He was of giant stature, bigger than they all, as he also dominated them in his wickedness. He wore a spiked crown and a long mantle of dirty gray, as if it once had been white but lacked the luster of whiteness, and had taken on its neutral tone from the wearer. About his breast was a double girdle of false gold, which crossed and was gathered at each hip by a belt of leather. Sandals were upon his feet, and lying on the steps beside him a shepherd's crook. But what sent through our company, as we watched him, a pang of unutterable pain was the crown. The spikes were the thorns of a bramble done in gold, which, circling his dusky brow, was wrought into a crown.

We would have turned away, but our task was set, and we must listen to his speaking until he had finished. It is painful for me to give, as it is for you to take, his story. But it is well, my brother, that they still in the earth-life should come at the knowledge of what life is in those dark spheres, for there the mixture of the good with the bad no longer holds. The good go up, the evil sink into their own lower places, and the tempering of evil with the good is not of the economy of those infernal regions. So evil left together with evil works blasphemies which are not possible in the composite society of earth.

He preached to them of the Gospel of Peace. I will give you a few periods of his discourse, and from these you will judge the rest:

"And so, my brothers and sisters, we all in meekness come together in our worship of the Beast who slew the lamb. For if the lamb be slain for us, then he who slays the lamb is the active benefactor of our being but the passive instrument—to the end we may come to blessedness and survive the damnable ills of the cursed. It is, therefore, meet, my brothers, that, as the Beast so curiously sought out and found the lamb, and out of its harmless uselessness brought the blood of life and salvation, so you, on noble actions bent, should seek out and find the lamb's counterpart and so do as the Shepherd has taught us. By your shrewd tempers, out of lamb-like inertia shall be brought forth life in all the fever and frenzy of your rapture. And what so like the harmless timid lamb as is a woman, my brothers, the more comely, if more foolish, counterpart of man. And in your ears, so attuned to ribald delicacy, my sisters, I would breathe a word of counsel also. Children do not come hither into these great realms over which you have done me the honor to elect me Governor. But, nevertheless, to you I would say, look upon me in my meekness and look upon this crook, as I take it in my hand, and count me your shepherd to follow me. I will lead you to those who have children too many, children to spare and to cast away from their motherly breasts as once they cast away the immature life which had begun within them, but which they of the plenitude of their pity sacrificed upon the altar of Moloch before they came forth to a life of toil and pain upon the earth. Come, fair ladies, you shall join these poor ones who lament the slain, while they shrink from and strive to cast away the all too life-like memories of their loved, their murdered little ones."

Other words he said, too wicked for utterance now, nor would I ask Kathleen to speak them to you, nor you to hear. But these I have given you, that you and others may glimpse the evil mockery and the sneering meekness of that man, who is in turn but a type of thousands in these realms. He who assumed so gentle a character, and with so ill a grace, was one of the fiercest and most cruel despots of all that region. Truly, as he said, they had elected him Governor, but that was in fear of his great power of evil. And now that he called those poor misshapen, half-frenzied men noble, they applauded him in their servility for the self-same reason. Those poor hags, the women in their squalor of finery, he called fair ladies, and bade them follow him as sheep their shepherd, and in fear they, too, cheered approval and arose to go with him as he turned to mount the great flight of stairs.

But as he began to ascend, placing the staff upon the step next above that on which he stood, he stopped and drew back and slowly descended step by step, until he reached the floor; and the whole crowd crouched about the hall breathless with wonder, blent of hope and fear. The reason of this was the vision they beheld atop the stairs before them. For we stood there, having assumed so much of our native radiance as we were able in that environment. A lady of our company stood some half a dozen steps below us. Her chaplet of emeralds shone fair upon her brow as it bound her brown-gold hair, and the jewel of order upon her shoulder shone bright and true of her own virtue. About her middle was a belt of silver. And all these showed in relief against those tawdry jewels of the crowd before her. And in her arms she held a bundle of white lilies. She stood there, the presentment of pure womanhood in all its perfect loveliness, a challenge to the late speaker's ribald cynicism of her race.

Then, when a long time they had looked upon her, both the men and the women there, one of them sobbed and tried to smother the sound in her mantle. But then the others gave way before the returning upon them of their sometime womanhood, and the hall was filled with the wailing of the women— oh, so hopeless to hear in that place of misery and of bondage, that the men also began to cover their faces with their hands, to sink upon the ground, and to press their foreheads in the thick dust upon the floor.

But now the Governor took himself in hand, for he saw his power at hazard. He began to stride in great anger over the bodies of the women to get at her who first had set the pace to their weeping. But now I came down to the lowest step and called to him, "Stay your hand and come hither to me."

At this he turned and leered at me, and began to say, "But, you, my lord, are welcome, so you come in peace among us. Yet these poor cravens be too much bedazzled of the light of that fair lady behind you, and I do but seek to bring them to their reason, so they shall give you proper welcome."

But I said very sternly to him, "Cease and come hither." So he came and stood before me, and I continued, "You have taken upon you to blaspheme, both in speech and also by your trappings. Take off that crown of blasphemy and lay down the shepherd's crook, you who dare to mock at One Who claims these His children whom you hold in your bond of fear." These things he did, and then I spoke to some men standing near, and I said to them more gently, "You have been cowards too long, and this man has enslaved you, body and soul. He shall be taken to a city where one stronger in evil might than he rules. Do you, who have served him hereto, do now my bidding. Disrobe him of that mantle and that girdle which he has donned in his mockery of Him Whom even he shall own some day his Sovereign Prince and Lord."

And then I waited, and there came forward four of them and began to unbuckle his belt. He turned in fierce rage upon them, but I had taken the staff from him, and this I laid upon his shoulder, and at the touch he sensed the power within me and strove no more. So my will with him was done; and then I bade him go forth of the hall into the darkness without, where guards awaited to take him into that far region where as he had done to others it should be done to him.

Then I bade them sit about the hall and, when this was done, I called to the singer of our band, and he lifted up his strong voice and filled that vast chamber with his melody. And as he sang, the hearts of those people began to beat more freely, not being held in leash now by fear of him whom they had seen to be so helpless in our hands. And the light began to lose its ruddy glow and became more mellow, and a more peaceful sense of being invaded the place and bathed their hot and fevered bodies in its refreshing breeze.

What did he sing to them?

He sang a song of merry joy and romping—of the spirit of the spring, of the morning breaking through the prison bars of night and liberating song and melody of birds and trees and babbling streams. He sang no word of holiness or God-like qualities, not there and at that time. The medicine needed first was to stimulate their individualities that they should realize their freedom from their late slavery. And so he sang of pleasure of life and joy of comradeship. And they became not joyful, but less despairing. Later, we took them in hand, and gave them instruction, and the day came when that hall was filled with worshippers of Him to Whose blaspheming they had listened once in their listlessness of fear. It was no such service of worship as would be of help to people of higher life in goodness. But their poor voices, lacking harmony as they did, yet had a note of hope which was very sweet to us who had labored with them in their doubts and terrors.

Then others came who took our place to strengthen them and hearten them till they were fit to travel on the journey, long and trying, but ever towards the dawn-light of the east, while we went our way toward our next destination.

Were they all of the same mind?

Well nigh, friend, well nigh. A few there were who were lacking. And I will tell you a thing which you will think strange and unlikely. Some elected to follow their Governor into his abasement. So much at one with him had they become in his wickedness, that they could find nothing in their own characters on which to stand of their own accord. And they followed him in his fall as they had served him in his lurid glory of power. But only few went thus, and other few went elsewhere about their own business. But the great crowd of them stayed and learned again of those truths they had so long forgot. And the old story was so new and wonderful to them it was pitiable to see.

What became of the Governor?

He still remains in that far city where his guards led him. He has not come forth yet, being still of evil intent and very malicious. Such as he, my friend, are hard to move to higher things.

You spoke of his guard. Who were they?

Ah, there you touch one of the difficult matters to understand until you learn more of the ways of God His Wisdom, and His Sovereignty. In brief, know you, friend, that God is

Sovereign not in Heaven alone but in Hell also, and in all the Hells He rules and He alone. The others dominate locally, but He rules over them all. The guards I spoke of were men of that same city to which we sent the man. Evil men they were, and did not own allegiance to the Creator of them all. But knowing not whose judgment delivered this one more victim into their hands, nor knowing it was for his ultimate salvation, they did our will without ado. You may find the key here, if you go beneath and deep enough, to much of that which happens on your earth.

Evil men by many are thought to be outside the pale of His Kingdom; and evils and disasters to be faulty manifestations of His dynamic energizing. But both are in His hand to use, and even evil men, unwitting, are made to work out his plans and purpose in the ultimate. But this is too large a matter to treat of now. Goodnight, and our peace be yours, friend.

30

The City of Mines

Tuesday, January 8, 1918. 5:16–7:42 P.M.

A S we went about those parts on our business of help and mercy we found our prearranged plan had been very curiously made for us. Each colony we visited gave to our store of knowledge some experience a step in advance, so that, as we ministered to others, we ourselves were ministered to through them by those who watched over their welfare and our schooling. Wherein, my brother, you may and you will discern another phase of the principle we have already told you of, namely and to wit, the using of those who are in rebellion in the loyal service of their true King.

Without their permission?

Without their opposition. They who be even very far gone away into the darkness, so they do not oppose their wills to the influences sent upon them by those who watch them from their habitations in the Realms of Life and Light, are made of service to the King. And when they turn about to retrace their steps once more towards the sunshine of the Great Day, and their reckoning is made, then this also shall be placed to their good account, inasmuch as, although unknowing, they were found so much in tune with holiness as this, that they, in this and that little, did not sustain their habit of rebellion against their God His Will.

But the Governor of whom you told me at our last sitting was not one of these apparently. Yet he was used in a certain degree.

He was used, yes, for in his discomfiture it was shown to his sometime company that there was a power greater than his own. Also it was shown that, by soon or by late, yet evil-doing goes never always insolent, but the scales are weighted on the other beam to match, so the balance in the end sets equal, and justice is thereby declared and quitted. But that governor will not count that among his assets, for his will was not with us, but was overborne to his discredit. Nevertheless, inasmuch as punishment was meted to him then, in part, for the crimes of him, that shall be taken from the total sum of his debt to pay, so, in a negative way, you will mark it, that also shall be put to his good account.

Yet your question has some bottom in it, friend. That governor was dealt with truly against his will, but that was by way of restraint when his work of evil had gone so far as to be enough for the purpose of those who permitted him in his evil doing up to that point. It was, therefore, we were sent and were guided to that hall at that moment. We knew naught of this at the time, but acted, as we deemed, on our own judgment of the circumstances we found afoot there. Yet it was all planned by those who sent us.

And now, if you will, we would go forward with our narrative to tell you of some of the places we happened on, and of the people, their conditions and their doings, and what we did by them. As we went about we found many of those settlements where people of like mind sought to consort together. It was sad to see them who wandered from town to town in search of that companionship which should ease their loneliness, and finding shortly that agreement one with another was not to be had in any enduring measure, would wander again into the deserts to get away from those whom they had thought to offer some chance of case and pleasurable company.

The captain of the gate.

We found that in nearly every colony there was one master-mind—and here and there more than one nearly equal in forcefulness of character—who dominated the rest, and enslaved them by the dread he sent forth upon them. Here is one whose city we came to once after a long journey through a very desolate and forsaken country. The city itself was built about with a strong wall, and it was large in area. We went within, and were challenged by the guard at the gateway. There was a company of ten there on guard, for the gate was principal and large, with double wings. These men were all of giant stature, having much developed in their wickedness. They called upon us to stay, and questioned us, "Whence came we last ?" "From going on our ways about the wilderness," we gave answer to their captain. "And what business do you purpose here, good sirs and gentlemen?" he said, for he had been of culture in the earth-life and that burnish still was upon his manners, but it was now tinctured with some malice and with mockery, as is the manner of most in those sad places.

To this question we answered—I for the company, "We have a mission to the workers in the mines where your master enslaves them."

"A very engaging end for your journey," he said with pleasant accents, seeking to deceive us. "These poor souls work so hard they be ready for any good friend who should take stock of them, their existence and their troubles."

"And some," I said, "be also ready to depart hence free of the yoke of your lord, which, each in his degree, is bond upon you all."

At once his face changed from smiling to one dark frowning, and his teeth showed like the teeth of a hungry wolf. Moreover, with the change of his mood there seemed to descend a darker mist and settle about him. He said, "Do you say I am enslaved also?" "A very slave and bond for your master, a slave himself and a driver of slaves." "That he shall make you as one of us, for you shall come to be shortly of those who dig for the gold and iron for our lord.

With this he turned about and bade his guards seize us and take us to their ruler's house. But I stood a little nearer to him and laid my hand upon his right wrist, and the contact was agony to him, so that he let go his short sword which he had drawn quickly upon us. I still held him while the auras of him and me made disturbance about his soul, to his agony, but not to mine, for, being of the greater strength in force of spiritual power, I went unscathed, while he was anguished. Spiritual dynamics, this, to be studied, if you choose, among your own incarnate neighbors. The principle is of universal application, as you shall find if you search it out. Then I said, "We are not of these dark spheres, sir. We come from a place in sunlight of the Presence of Him of Whose life you have partaken, and violated it to evil purposes. For you it is not yet the time to win freedom of these walls and the tyranny of cruel masters here."

Then he broke down through the thin shell of his lordly bearing and cried piteously, "Why may not I also go free of this hell and the devil who lords it here? Why others, if not I?"

And I replied, "You are not yet accounted worthy. Watch what we do in this place, do not oppose your will to ours, help us in what we have in hand to do, and, when we have gone hence, then ponder on it well and long, and perchance even you will find in us somewhat of blessing."

"Blessing," he sneered, and laughed, with naught of music in his laugh. And then he said, a little more soberly, "Well, what would you have of me, good sir?"

"That you should lead us to the mouth of the mines."

"And if I do not lead you?"

"We will go alone, and you will lose a benefit."

To the mines.

He paused awhile, and then, seeing there might be op-portunity for self-serving and benefit, he cried, "And why not? If there be benefaction to be had, why not I who first came upon the hazard of it? And he shall be damned the deeper in his damnation if he do but show himself against me to hin-der me this time in my doing." Then he began walking on and we followed him, he murmuring to himself the while, "He is ever at variance with my plans and schemes. He is ever alert to thwart me of my will. He is not satiated with all he has hitherto compassed of malice against me," and so on, until he shortly turned him round to us and said, "I ask of you your pardon, gentlemen. It is the way with us here that we are oft bemused when our minds should be most clear. Climate probably, or overwork, perhaps. Follow me, by your courtesy, and I will take you where you will find what you are seeking."

Levity and cynicism and bitterness were in his speech and bearing; but since my grip of him he was more subdued and did not oppose us now, and we followed him. We passed through some streets where single-storied houses were placed in no regular line or pattern, but gaps were in between, and waste places where grew no herb or vegetation, or only coarse, dank grass, or shrubs with stems and branches blasted as if by the sirocco breath which came about us, now we were within the city and its high enclosing walls. It came in chief part from the mines which we were now approaching.

These were the hovels where the slaves took rest of short duration, with long periods of labor in between. These we left behind us, and shortly came upon a place where there opened out to us a large cave-mouth which led into the bowels of that region. We drew nigh, and there came forth, in gusts, a wind of odor so foul and hot and fetid that we drew back and paused awhile to call for strength. This done, we steeled our hearts and went within and downward, the Captain still leading, now in silence and in much oppression of spirit, as we could tell by the forward bend of his shoulders, even while descending the pathway.

Seeing this I called to him, and he halted and glanced back and upward at us, and his face was agonized and gray. So I said to him, "Why are you become so sad, my guide? You have put on a sorry aspect since you drew near the mouth of these mines."

"Sir," he answered, and meekly now, "I was once of those who work with pick and spade within these hell furnaces, and the fear of it comes upon me now."

"Then search into your inmost soul for a grain of pity for those who work there now where once you suffered so sorely."

He sank upon a boulder by the side of the path, overcome of weakness, and replied to my words with stranger words of his own, "Nay, nay, 'tis needful I be pitied by them, not they by me. Their lot is hell, but mine is hell ten times doubled."

"How, since you have escaped their slavery and come forth of the mines into a better state of service to the one you call your lord?"

"I thought you were some one great in wisdom," he replied with a bitter smile, "and yet you do not understand that to fly from one state of servitude to another of higher degree in authority is to put off a hair-shirt for one with thorns and brambles for web and woof."

And then I took shame to myself that I had but just learned that lesson on top of others gathered of our experience in those dark tracts of hell. They who live there in the darkness of death are ever reaching out after an easier fate, and grasp any chance of escape from servitude by promotion to some post of authority. And when advanced to that post, they find the glamour fade away into the miasma of fear, being more nearly in contact with the archfiend, who by his brutality and remorseless malice has seized the chief power. Yes, the glamour dies, and hope dies with illusion.

And yet they keep on in their grasping after advancement, and, gaining their ambition, writhe more in their despairing frenzy of agony than before. Well, I knew it now, for it was embodied in the man who sat there all unnerved and limp before me in his misery of many memories of that awful place.

So I said to him, being very pitiful to see him thus so greatly suffering, "My brother, is it worthy of manhood, this life of yours?" "Manhood," he replied, "I put off that when I entered service here—or it was stripped off by those who thrust me in. I am no man today, but a devil whose pleasure is to hurt, and whose wealth is to add one cruelty to another, and to see how others endure what I have endured."

"And does that pleasure you?"

For a long time he was silent, and at last said, "No."

Then I laid my hand upon his shoulder, this time not opposing my aura to his, but in sympathy, and said, "My brother."

At this he started up and looked at me wildly and cried, "Did you not say that word before? Are you also mocking me as others mock me and as we mock each the others?"

"Nay," I said, "you call the one you serve here your lord. Yet his power is but hollow as your own is hollow which you have received, at his hand. Remorse is just at your door now, but in remorse there is not much merit, save that it be a door giving into the chamber of sorrow for sin. When we have done our work here and have left you, think on all this that has been afoot between you and me, and that, knowing all, I claimed brotherhood with you. If you in that time cry for me, I will send to help you—that is my promise. And now let us go down, even further down into the mines. We would get our work done and go forth again. It oppresses us to be here."

"Oppresses you? But you cannot suffer; surely you do not suffer who come freely of your choice, and not in the wake of your crimes."

And then I gave to him the answer which would help him if he would receive it: "Believe me, my brother, who have seen Him. While one of you down here in these dark prisons of Hell do suffer, One there is who wears a ruby on His shoulder, red as blood. When we look upon that token, and from it to His eyes, we know He suffers, too. And we, who do, in our own degree, go forth on His enterprise of salving men, are glad that He gives leave that we should be one with Him at least in this, that we may suffer too, though not acquaint with grief as He. So do not marvel that your sorrow should be our sorrow, or that I call you brother now. He, by His love, outpoured upon us all in one great sea, has made us so."

31

The Mines

Friday, January 11, 1918. 5:25–6:45 P.M.

SO we continued our descent, the Captain going before us some little, heartened by my words to him. And now we came to a stairway cut into the rocky earth, and at the bottom of it a heavy gateway. He knocked upon this with the handle of a whip, which he carried thrust into his belt, and through a grid a hideous face appeared and demanded who stood without and knocked. It was a human face, but with much of the savage animal in it, large mouth, enormous teeth and long ears. Our guide gave some short answer, speaking as one to command, and the gate was opened inward and we passed through. Here we found ourselves in a large cavern, and, before us, an opening through which a ruddy, murky glow came and but barely lighted the walls and roof of the place in which we stood. We went forward and looked through this opening and saw there was a steep dip without, about the height of six men.

From our vantage point we looked about, and, as our eyes became more used to the gloom, we saw that before us there lay a large stretch of territory, all underground. We could not see how far it reached, but there were passages leading off the main cavern, here and there, which disappeared in what seemed black darkness. Figures went hither and thither, to and fro, with furtive tread, as if afraid some horror should start up in their pathway when they were most unaware. Now and then the clanging of chains came up to us, as some poor fellow shuffled on his way in fetters; then a weird cry of agony and often a mad, wild laugh and the sound of a whip. All was sad both to hear and see. Cruelty seemed to float in the air as one sufferer gave vent to his agony by torturing another more helpless. I turned to our guide, the Captain, and said, "This is the place of our destination. By what path do we descend?"

He quickly noted the stern tone of my voice and answered, "You do well so to speak to me, and it is not to me so painful to bear that you use so hard a manner as that you call me brother. I have been of those who have labored down yonder, and then of those to whom a whip was given to make others labor withal, and then at length, by my hardness, I became Chief-Overseer of a section beyond yonder doorway. You cannot see it from this point. It gives on to workings lower and deeper still than this, which is but the first of a series. Then I came to be about the palace of the Chief, and after that Captain of the guard of the Principal Gate. But as I look back now, I think, if there be aught to choose in it, I suffered less as a lost soul in the bowels of the mines than in the place of authority to which I have come. And yet, I would not go back again—no—not again—no—"

He was lost in agonized thought, and fell to silence, disregarding our presence until I said, "Tell me, my friend, what is this large place first before us?" And he answered:

"This is the department where the metal, having been smelted and prepared in those galleries beyond, is made into weapons and ornaments and articles for use of the Chief. These finished, they are hoisted up through the roof into the outer region and taken where he commands that they should go. In the chamber next in order, the metals are rolled and trimmed; in the next they are smelted and molded. Farthest and deepest is the mine itself. What is your will, sir? Would you descend?"

I said we would descend and see what was toward, by nearer viewing of the chamber first below us. So he led the way to a trap in the floor of our present chamber, and we went down a short flight of stairs and along a short passage, emerging a little way from beneath the whole through which we had been at view. We passed on through this first chamber, whose floor sloped downward as we went, and through those of which he had told us, until we came to the mine itself, for I was resolved to fathom the misery of these dark regions to the uttermost.

These chambers intervening were all as he had told us, and of immense range in height and length and in breadth. But the many thousands who worked within them were strictly prisoners, and were taken under their guards at long intervals, and in small gangs, without and above ground. It seemed to me that the motive was not that of mercy, but rather of cruelty and utility. First, it most surely enhanced their despair on their return below. But also it was held out as a reward to those who slaved most hardly and were obedient. The air was fetid and heavy, wherever we went, and a dullness of hopelessness seemed to sit upon the shoulders of those we met, whether overseers or workers, for they all were slaves.

At last we came to the mine itself. A large heavy gateway gave on to a plateau. Here I could see no roof. Above us was blackness. We seemed to be now not in a cavern, but in a deep pit or ravine, the rocky sides rising up until we could not follow them, so deep were we below the land-surface. But tunnels here and there penetrated deeper still and most were in pitch darkness, except where at times a light flickered and went out again. There was a sound as if a wind blew about us, the sound of one long-drawn and perpetual sigh. But the air was not in motion. There were also shafts sunk into the ground into which men went, climbing down the vertical sides by steps cut in the rock, to fetch the ore up from tunnels and galleries deeper still, bored in the rock far below the level on which we stood. From the plateau there sloped down paths towards other openings which in their turn led to workings far away, either in the ravine itself, or through corridors cut into the sides of it. It was a very large region, a region deep below the level of that dark land, which itself lay far away below the Bridge or the floor of the plain beneath the Bridge. Oh, the desperate anguish of the helplessness of those poor souls—lost in that immensity of darkness and with no guide to lead them out.

But although they must have felt so, yet every one is noted and registered in the spheres of light, and, when they be ready for help, then help is sent to them, as it was even now.

Having looked about me and received information from the Captain, our guide, I bade him open all the gates about us and those leading into the cavern into which we first came. But he replied, "Sir, it is in my heart to do this; but I fear my lord, the Chief. He is terrible in his anger, sir, and even now I have a dread upon me, lest some spying hound should have sought to curry favor with him by carrying to him a report of what has already been done."

And I answered to him, "It seems to me you have been progressing speedily since we came hither to this dark city, my friend. I marked once before an advance in good feeling, but did not advertise you of it. Now, I see, I was not in error, so I give you choice. Think quickly and decisively. We are here to lead forth those who are ready to go a little way toward the light. It is for you to take your place at our side or against us. Will you come forth with us, or stay and serve your present lord? Choose quickly and presently."

For a few seconds he stood and looked at me, and then at my companions, and then at the tunnels which led further into the darkness, and then gazed upon the ground at his feet. All this he did swiftly, as I had bidden him, and then replied to me, "Sir, I thank you. I will do as you bid me and open the gates. But I will not pledge myself to come forth with you. I dare not so much—not yet."

Then, as if the resolve to obey us had given him new vitality, he swung about, and, even in that dim light, I noticed an air of decision, and his tunic seemed to fall a little more gracefully upon his naked knees, and his flesh to take on a more comely and healthful aspect. By this I knew more of the change of his estate in spirit than he himself knew. It is thus on occasion that, where strength of character has been overlaid and buried beneath a load of iniquity, it will suddenly start forth afresh and fling wide the portals of its prison and make a dash for liberty and the sunlight of God. Yes, but that he did not know, and I was not quite sure of its staying power, so I held my peace until he had gone on his way. I heard him calling, in strong voice, to the porter to open the gate. I heard him shout the same command to the second as he rushed up the tunnel towards it; and then his voice gradually became more faint as he went farther away from us towards the great cavern into which we had ourselves first come.

32

The "Spirits in Prison"

Tuesday, January 15, 1918. 5:25–7:15

THEN in concert we lifted up our voices and sent forth a loud chorus of praise. It swelled louder and louder as we sang, and it filled all that place with its melody and penetrated the tunnels and filled the galleries and the caves where the poor hopeless ones were doing service to their lord, this cruel Prince of the Darkness, who held them bond by the fierceness of his evil strength. And we were told by many later that as the strains of our singing came upon them and increased in volume, they paused to listen to that strange thing, for the music they made themselves was far different from ours, and the theme we sang was not such as they were used to hear.

What was the theme, Leader?

We made it to suit the purpose we had in hand. We sang of power and of authority, and how it was wielded in those dread cities of the darkened world. We showed its cruelty and its shame and the hopeless condition of those who found themselves within its meshes. And then we traced the effect such wickedness brought upon the land, and how darkness came

469

with darkness of spirit and blasted the trees and seared the land and clave the rocky places into caverns and many an abyss, and how the very water itself became foul and the air stank with rottenness and the decay of evil all around. And then we changed our theme, and recalled the pleasant pastures of earth and the light-tipped mountains and the waters sweet, which chased and tumbled in merriment down to the plain where verdant grass and pretty flowerets grew and turned up their sweet lips to God's own sun that he might kiss them for their beauty. We sang of the songs of birds and the song of the mother to her mite and the lover to his lass, and the songs of praise which people sang together within the sanctuaries where worship was made to Him Who sent His angels that they might bring up such prayers and adoration to the footstep of His throne, there to be presented to Him with incense of purification for His glory. We sang of all those things which make for beauty on earth, and then we lifted up our voices with full-throated ardor as we told of the homes where they were brought who had tried to do their service bravely on the earth, and who now abide in the light and glory of God His Pleasance, where the trees were very stately and the flowers of gorgeous coloring, and the whole panoply of loveliness was found for the restful joy of those who owned the sovereignty of the Savior Prince Who ruled them liege for the Father.

How many were there of you in your party, please?

Fifteen—two sevens and myself. That was our complement. And as we sang, one after another of those slaves of evil came within sight of us. A pale, gray face would half emerge from one tunnel and then from another, or from a cleft in the rock, and from holes and dens we had not noticed they looked forth upon us, until the whole of the cliffs around us were full of frightened, yet longing people, too timorous to come forth, yet gulping down the draught of refreshment like thirsty men in a desert. But others there were who looked forth in anger with red, shining eyes, which flashed their inner fires upon us, and others still who bowed their heads aground in the misery of remorse for past wrongdoing and for the memory of that mother's lullaby of which we had sung, and the way it had pointed and which they had spurned, and gone the other road—to this.

Then we grew slowly softer, and ended in a sweet, long chord of rest and peace, and one long-drawn, solemn "Amen."

Then one came forth and stood a little distance away from us and knelt and said, "Amen."

When the others saw this they drew in their breath to see what plague would strike him, for this was treason to the lord of the place. But I went forward and raised him up and took him among us, and we closed him round, so none could do him harm. Then they came forth to the number of four hundred, in twos and threes and then in dozens, and stood like children saying a lection, and murmured, as they had heard him do, "Amen." And the while, those who stood or crouched still in the shadows of the galleries and of the boulders and crags hissed curses at us and them, but none came forth to try their tilt with us. So I, seeing all were come who would, addressed the rest, "Be silent all of you who have made choice today between the light and the darkness. These who are braver than you shall go forth presently of these mines and dim places into the light and ease of which we sang to you. Be curious of your own hearts to school yourselves that, when again our fellows of God's sunlight shall come to you, you be ready to follow their leading, as these do ours today."

The chief of the City of the Mines.

And then I turned to our band of rescued souls, for they were fearful and trembling at the venture they had made, and said, "And you, my brothers, come your ways into the city, and heed none who shall threaten you with the displeasure of the Chief. For he is your lord no longer, but you shall learn the service of a brighter Lord, and wear his livery anon when you have progressed to be so worthy. But now have not any fear, except to mark our word and to obey, for the Chief of this place comes, and we must reckon first with him before your way hence shall be clear."

So we turned about toward the gate through which the Captain had gone, and through which many of the four hundred had come to swell our band. And, even as we did so, we heard a great noise far up towards the outer gate where we had entered, and the noise became louder and drew more near to us. So we awaited the coming of the Chief, who, as he passed through one cave and the next, called on his slaves to follow and do vengeance for him upon the insolent intruders into his realm who had dared his vengeance by defiance of authority. With such swelling words and many threats and oaths, he came on; and those poor craven spirits, frenzied by the dread of his presence, followed him with yells and curses, binding his blasphemous oaths upon themselves to do his bidding.

We stood before our band to receive him as he came through the gate, and at last he appeared.

What was he like, Leader—his appearance, I mean?

My friend, he was a son of God, and therefore my brother, sunk in evil as he was. For that reason I would gladly pass by the appearance of him in charity and in pity, for pity it was that most I felt for him in that hour of his great wrath and greater humiliation. But you have asked me to limn his aspect for you and I will do so, and you shall see how deep a truth may lie beneath the words, "How be the mighty fallen."

He was of stature gigantic, as tall as a man and half a man in height. His shoulders were unequal, his left lower than the right, and his head, nearly hairless, was thrust forward on a thick neck. A tunic of rusty gold and sleeveless was upon him, and a sword hung on his left side from a leather belt which passed over his right shoulder. Rusty iron greaves he wore, and shoes of untanned skin, and on his brow a chaplet of silver, tarnished and stained, and on the front of it a boss carved into the semblance of some animal which might be called a land-octopus, if such there were, symbolic of his evil power. His whole aspect was that of mock-royalty, or, more nearly, the striving after a royalty beyond his attaining. Evil passion, frenzy, lust, cruelty and hatred seemed to suffuse his dark face and to permeate his whole personality. And yet these overlaid potential nobility, and nullified what might have been great power for good, now turned to evil. He was an Archangel damned, and that is another way of saying "arch-fiend."

Do you know what he had been in earth-life?

Your questions, friend, I like to answer, and when you ask them I cannot but feel some prompting leads you so to do which must have respect of me. And, therefore, I answer them. Do not cease to ask them, no, for there may be in them reason I do not reckon with and which I could find only by inquiry. But you will not mistake my meaning. If he was a great surgeon in a large hospital for the poor in your England, that does not predicate that others are as he. Had he been a priest or a philanthropist, it had been no more strange. For the outward seeming is not ever in consonance with the real man. Well, such he was, and there you have it in a word.

Sorry, if I butted in thoughtlessly.

No, no, my son. That is not so. Do not mistake my words. Ask what you will, for what you ask would be in the minds of many, and you speak for them.

So he stood there, the King unquestioned of all that rabble, and there were thousands of them who crowded behind him and on either side. But around him was left a space—they came not too near his arm. His left hand held a heavy, cruel-looking whip with many lashes, and on this their eyes would often glance and glance away again as quickly. But he hesitated now to speak, the while we stood to silence, for he was only used for a long time past to speak with authority and in the manner of a bully, and he lacked courage to speak to us now he saw us, for we were of aspect restful and at variance with the whole fearful, trembling attitude of all those others in that place. But while we waited, facing each the others, I noticed behind him there was a man bound and held by two in the livery of the guards we had met at the Principal Gate. I looked with more care now, for he was in the shadows, and so I made him out to be our guide, the Captain. This seeing, I at once stepped forward very quickly, and, as I went by the Chief, I touched the blade of his sword in passing, and then stood before those who held the bound man and commanded them. "Loose that man of his thongs and set him forward towards our company.

At these words a yell of rage broke from the Chief and he tried to raise his sword upon me. But all the temper had left the blade, and it hung down limp as water-weed, he staring in horror at it the while, for he took it at once as a token of his authority bereft of power. I had not in mind to make of him a stock for laughter, but the others, his slaves, saw the comic element in his plight, not of humor but of malice, and from hidden places there came gusts of laughter and mockery. Then the blade withered and fell from the haft all rotten, and the haft he hurled at a point up among the rocks where some one laughed longer than his fellows. Then I turned to the guard again, and they hastily unbound the prisoner and set him before us.

Immediately the Chief threw off his air of mock-majesty, and bowed courteously to me and then to my company. Truly this man is destined in ages to come to be a great servant of our Father when his evil shall have turned to good.

"Sir," he said, "you have the freedom, it seems, of a power greater than my own. To it I bow, and would know your will with me and with these my servants who serve me so willingly and so well." For all his great command of self, he could not but discover, here and there, his inmost spirit of cynical malice. It is ever thus in those hell-regions; all is counterfeit—except slavery.

I told him of our mission, and he said, "I had not known your estate, or else had I welcomed you more fittingly. But, having been remiss, I will now be forward. Follow, and I will myself be guide to you to the Gates of this my City. Follow me, gentlemen, the while I go to lead the way."

And so we went after him, and passed through the eaves and workings, and came at last to the smaller gate which gave on to the steps which led to the trap through which we had come into the mines.

33

Out of the Mines

Friday, January 18, 1918. 5:20–7:25 P.M.

AS we had come through the mines, our company had been increased in length by those who had joined us from the caves which stretched into the darkness far away on either hand. News, so scarce among them, had been carried quickly to the farthest limits of these gloomy regions, and now our numbers were in thousands, where they had been hundreds before. As we halted before the wall, beneath the hole through which we had looked down upon the cave where now we stood, I turned about and could see little beyond the nearer part of the multitude, but I could hear those who had been in the workings farther away and deepest underground, still coming in with feverish haste and joining up behind the others, fall to silence in the presence of the Chief and his perplexing guests. Then I spoke first to him, and then to the company, and said, "In your heart there is not that to match your words of courtesy which but now you spoke to us. But we come here in pity and in blessing, be it greater or less. That you may not go empty, I will bid you now that you take heed of what shall

476

follow, both of your own thrust and of our return. Then, when we shall have gone forward on our journey with these who will shortly leave your service for that of another not so deep in the darkness of evil as yourself, ponder and wrestle with the meaning of things, and remember these words of mine for your help when you shall bite your fingers in vexation and in pride abased by your hopeless battle against us who come from those places where pride and cruelty have no place at all in the mellow light of the heavens of your King."

He stood to silence, looking upon the ground, nor would he say us yes or no, but was sullen and threatening, every muscle and every tendon taut and ready for the chance he sought, but feared to take, to our hurt. So I turned to the multitude and spoke to them, "And as for you, be not in any wise afraid of what shall come of your choice which you have made, for you have chosen the stronger part, which shall not in any wise fail you. Only be very true and do not falter in your steps, and you shall win freedom shortly and attain to the highlands, where the light is, at your journey's end."

I paused, and all were silent for a short space until the Chief lifted his head, and, looking to me, said, "Ended?" And I gave him answer, "For this time. When we be free of these galleries and in the open space without, I will gather them where they may hear me the better and give direction what they shall do." "Aye, when we be free of these dark passages, aye, that would be better," he said, and I noted the threat beneath his tongue as he said it.

Then he turned, and, having passed through the door, came soon to the window above us and told them to mount and follow him, while he led them into the City. We stood aside to let them pass, and, as they went, I sought out the Captain and told him my will with these people and with him. So he mixed himself in their midst and passed on with them out of the mines. We rallied the laggards in the rear, and at last all were passed through the door and we stood alone. Then we, too, passed through, and at length came to that bare land which was about the mouth of the mines.

There again I spoke to the people, and I told them that they should separate themselves each from the others and go through the City into those houses and dens which best they knew, and best were known, and tell the news and bring forth those who would come with them to the square of the Principal Gate where we would meet with them. So they began to leave us, and, as they went, the Chief addressed himself to us, "If it pleases you, gentlemen, who have honored us with your coming among us, I would have you consort with me to my house, while these go to gather their friends. It may chance there will blessing ensue to my household also from your presence."

"Blessing indeed shall come to you and your house of this visit of ours," I replied to him, "but that will be not at the time, nor in the manner you look for," so we went with him and he led the way. We came at last to the very middle of the City, and there in the darkness there loomed a great pile of stone. It was more castle than dwelling-house, and more prison than castle, to see it. It stood insular, with a road on every side, oblong in shape, and rising like a hill from the flat of the roadway. But it was grim; in very truth, a dark and grim abode, in tune, every line of it, with that strong and darkened soul, its builder.

We went within, and he led the way along passages and halls, and at last we came to a chamber, not very large, and there he bade us wait while he made our welcome ready. So he departed, and I smiled upon my friends and asked them, if they had fathomed the dim depths of his purpose. They were doubtful, most of them, but a few there were who felt a sense of having been deceived, so I told them we were prisoners, fast as he could make us, and when one went to the door through which we had entered he found it fast enough, bolted without. There was another on the other side of the room, which was a kind of ante-chamber to that Throne Room beyond. That also was fast bolted. You of earth would think that some at least of those fourteen would be fearful, or hurt at such a pass as this. But you must know that only those are sent on such missions as this of ours, and into regions such as these, who by long training have become strangers quite to fear, and who are strong to wield the almighty power of good, with skill so unfailing and sure, no evil can withstand it and go scatheless.

We knew what we should do without counsel or discourse, so we took hands one of another and lifted ourselves toward the light and life of our normal environment. This more gross condition we had taken upon us that we might traffic in those regions in the guise of the inhabitants who lived in them. But, as we aspired together, our condition gradually changed, and our bodies took on a nature more sublimate, so we passed hence without those walls, and stood in the square before the Principal Gate, awaiting the coming of our company.

We did not see the Chief again. He had, as we knew, planned the recapture of those whom we had freed from his servitude, and even now there were being gathered from the regions round about the city by runners sent forth, a great army, which was closing in on all sides to do vengeance on those who had made bold to flout his authority. But I have naught dramatic to tell you, my friend—no clash of arms, no cries for mercy, and no coming of an army of bright warriors to the rescue. It all fell out very tame and flat. In this wise: In that mock Throne Room he gathered his court, and, having torches lighted and, placed all round the walls, and fires kindled all along the center of the floor to light the hall, he made a great speech to his dusky retainers. Then the door of our anteroom was solemnly unbolted, and we were bidden come forth that he should do us honor. And when we were not found within, and his vengeance was thus denied to him, and his shame before his nobles manifest, and all come about by his own plans and actions, he broke down utterly, while they laughed to see him so in his abasement. Cruel jests they passed among them as they strolled away and left him alone, seated upon his stone-chair aloft on the dais, defeated.

Mark you, friend, how in these rebel states tragedy and gross buffoonery jostle one the other wherever you shall go. All is empty make-believe, for all is in opposition to the Only Reality. So these mock rulers are served by their people in mock humility, and are surrounded by mock-courtiers whose adulation is thrust through and through with stings and arrows of cynicism and ribald mockery.

* * *

Note: End of 18 January, 1918, message. Here pp. 387-393 of the original script are missing (one sitting).

The rescued people are handed over to the charge of the "Lesser Christ" who, with the Captain as his Lieutenant, establishes a Colony in a tract of open country at some distance from the City of the Mines. It is composed of those brought out of the Mines together with others of both sexes whom they had gathered out of the City. This Colony is referred to again later on January 28 and February 2, 1918.—H. W. E.

34

Toward the Light

Monday, January 21, 1918. 5:30–7:05 P.M.

OUR journey now was toward the light. And if I tell you that the Valley below the Bridge was what you would say was a dark night on earth, you will be able to see that the darkness about those further regions behind us was great indeed. In pitch darkness you cannot see aught. And yet there is a darkness more intense than that, for on earth, darkness is darkness alone, but here it has a substance in it which is a very real horror to those who are not protected from the higher spheres. Those poor people who have gravitated into that thick darkness feel the suffocation of drowning, and yet have no spar or sherd of wreck to buoy them upward, and so they suffer until frenzy and despair steal upon them, and then hell calls to hell in blasphemy, knowing not that in their own wills alone is the fulcrum on which they shall lever themselves upward till they attain to the light. Yes, there is a thickness in that darkness in the more remote regions. And yet, for those who live there, there is a dim kind of sight, by which they get no blessing, for it only brings to their consciousness things hideous and malicious and makes more poignant the pangs they have to bear. And these are people who have lived on your earth and mixed in earth society, and some have borne evil and others honored names and places. I tell you this that you may show to others what is true, for some there be who say there are no hells because the One Supreme is Love both first and last. Yes, but those who so speak of Him have attained but to the First knowledge of that Love surpassing, while we who speak to you have not by a long reach attained to the Last. But enough we have bottomed of His Wisdom—enough, but a mite, withal—to be all sure that He is Love indeed. We cannot understand, but all we have gathered of knowledge of Him has enlarged our belief, and more firmly founded it, that He is Perfect in Wisdom and Himself is Perfect Love.

Concerning the mines.

Leader, I once, in my sleep, visited some underground workings in the dark regions. Do you know of this experience of mine, and if you do will you tell me whether this was the same place to which you went to bring the people out of the mines? There was a certain resemblance, but with some differences.

I know of that experience, for before preparing you thus to write for us we made ourselves acquainted with all your life, in order that we might not err in our treatment of you. Be sure the lives of all are so studied here, for one purpose or other, and naught is passed over by those who would help them. As to that of which you question us. The place into which you were taken was one a few miles away from that city, and is governed by an under-lord of the Chief of whom we have told you. It is a place where those are taken who are rebellious of his authority, that there they may be both oppressed into subjection and also made to work at tasks under closer supervision than those in the mines and workings to which we went, who have more freedom, being themselves more suppliant and broken. To the place you name those go in most part who are newcomers into that region, and so are not conversant with the extent of the cruelty there obtaining, nor of the divers forms in which it is exercised upon them.

Animals in the hells.
What were the animals for?

They were trained to help in the overaweing and guarding of the prisoners.

But what could animals have done to merit such a hell and to be put to such a use as that?

These animals have never been in the flesh. Those go into brighter places. These are the creations of evil Powers who are able to bring them forth so far but not to project them further in advance toward incarnation on earth, so they become animals complete as ever they will be, by the complement of a body composite of the elements of the dark regions which form their environment. That is why you were somewhat perplexed to place them in their order. They have no order in the earth-economy of animal life, where only those great Creative Beings are enabled to express their faculties in the evolvement of animal tribes who have attained to high places in the Brighter spheres. Do you understand me as I am able to put an unearthly truth into language of earth?

Yes, I think so. Thank you, sir. It is a great mystery and new to me altogether. But I seem to feel it may be a key to other mysteries when one has time to think it out a little.

That is so, my son; deal with it so and you will find it helpful.

Good supreme.

Bear in mind always that although, when considered in the light of the Only Good and Beautiful, evil has a negative aspect, yet when considered obversely, that is, beginning at the opposite end and proceeding forward in opposition to the

Life Stream of the Only Good, there be great and powerful beings of darkness who are the counterpoises of the Archangels and Principalities and Thrones of Light. One great divergence, however, stands, and it is this. As through the stories of the heavens there is progress ever onward until the Sublime blends into the Ultimate Sublimity, in the darker spheres there is no such consummation, there is no Supreme. As in all other phases of activity, so in this, those dark powers stop short of completeness, and order is wanting by reason of the lack of a Godhead. Were this not so, then darkness would equal light in potency and in evolutional expansion, till light should find no place, and love and beauty might be invaded of their opposites, until no place for them should be found. Then the purpose of the Most Highest should be thrust awry, and, stumbling into byways, be wrecked in space, and among eternities be changed into confusion, and so fail to attain.

So, powerful as are those Lords of the Darkness, they are not All-powerful. This is the prerogative of One, and of Him alone. He has knowledge of His own Might so complete as to be secure in what license He permits to a progeny rebellious, and, for a few eternities, they are permitted to stray, that, in the end, they shall prove, by their capitulation, free-willed and unconditional, the supremacy of Love. Then will First and Last be clarified as to their relation each to other, and the Wisdom of God be manifest.

I am able to give you so much, my friend, of the aspect of the Kingdom which we only know ourselves in part, and who have a language for our use more serviceable than that of earth. I cannot give you more than this, I fear. But if you have any further question—

Thank you; not on that subject.

Then for the present we will let that suffice. Kathleen, I think, has it in her mind to say a few words to you, so we will leave her to her own sweet thoughts and withdraw our more grave influence from her locality, so she may be free, of her own winning self, to say her say to you. She is most kind and patient to be our writer, and we thank her very sincerely for her willing service to us. We shall meet with you again when you have opportunity for our presence. Goodnight, my friend, and God His Brightness be with you and your people who are enveloped in a radiance more than they know. It shall be revealed to them and to you some day.

35

Return to Sphere Ten

January 25, 1918. 5:25–7:43 P.M.

WHEN we came at the Bridge we crossed it from the darker side and arrived on the slopes which rise to the progressive spheres, and there awhile we rested and reviewed the work we had so far brought to a conclusion. Here there met with us a messenger from our own land, who brought tidings of what was there afoot about our mission. For never since we had left the Sphere Ten had they loosed from their being in touch with us, and as we talked with him he picked out those instances of special need when those who watched from their high place had felt necessity to send, on the instant, an access of help and guidance to us. Some of these were known to us, others were suspected, but the most of them had been times of special stress when all our faculties had been alert to deal with the matter on hand, so that we had missed the fact of outside aid impinging on our circumstances. For, down in those darker regions, having taken on the local condition greatly, we had perforce to endure some of the limitations of soul which went along with the heaviness of environment about us at the moment.

So it is with you of the earth sphere, my friend, and if you do not ever realize the help given, it is there to hand, nevertheless, and dealt out as you shall need it.

Now I will go-by the intervening journey, and tell you of our return to Sphere Ten.

The Temple of the Holy Mount

We were met on the outlying hills by a party of our good friends, who awaited our homecoming with much gladness, and with no little eagerness to hear of our adventures. These we told them as we went onward, and then at last we came to the great plain before the Temple of the Holy Mount, and ascended to the Porch thereof. We were led within, and went forward into the great Central Hall of the Sanctuary, and here we found a great concourse of people gathered. They were kneeling in adoration of the Great Unseen, and did not move as we passed quietly within and waited in their rear.

Silence in the higher spheres

You do not know what silence is on earth. There is on earth no perfect silence. You cannot go where you will leave sound behind. Here in the Tenth Sphere, and at that time in the Sanctuary was Silence, in all its majesty and awe. Away beyond the earth, if you could go through the air, you would gradually leave the sounds which are upon its surface behind you. But there would still be the atmospheric friction which would invade silence with a sense of sound. Even beyond that atmospheric belt there would be, in the ether, sound as a potential element, as planet called to planet in gravitational response. Beyond the Solar System, and between it and other systems in the void of space, you would approach to an idea of silence, while earth would be millions of light-years away, unseen, unfelt, almost unknown. But the ether would be there, and, although your ears would not hear any sound, yet ether is the realm of which atmosphere is the antechamber, and sound is its neighbor and closely akin.

But here in the Sphere Ten is an atmosphere of what ether should be if ten times refined by sublimation, and Silence is here a thing not negative so much as active in its effect upon those who bathe themselves in its ocean. Silence here is not an absence of sound, it is the Presence of the Silent One. It is a vibrating entity, but of so quick pulsation that stillness and Silence are as one. I am not able to be more plain in my description, for it is not possible for you, in your grosser element, to imagine, even by a little degree, the condition of which we partook as we entered that vast Temple Hall.

Then down the gangway in the midst there came the Seer, and, taking me by the hand, he led us toward the Altar which stood on the boundary of the Chamber where the Throne was, and from which he had dismissed us on our journey.

We came now a little weary, with our hearts full of what we had seen in those far realms of darkness. Our faces showed the effect of many a fight for the mastery—for I have but told you of our enterprise in brief, and nowise fully. We were warriors who had come through the war which is incessant between good and its opposite. But our scars and furrows would blend into harmony anon, and we should be more comely than afore we had suffered. It is so with our Royal Prince and Captain Who has shown us the way to Beauty of Spirit, as of aspect in body. And indeed He, Whose robes still read the lesson of Sacrifice its high dignity, is so beautiful as I cannot find to paint His comeliness in words of earth—or of the heavens.

A vision of the Christ Regal.

So we paused before the altar, and at some distance away, and then we too knelt down and adored the Fount of Being, the One Supreme, Who becomes manifest to us only by Presence Form, and that rarely, but mostly by His Anointed One, Who is more in tune with our present state by reason of His Humanity.

Then we at last, having received the sign, all raised our heads and looked toward the Altar. The sign we had was a sense of Presence which glowed in and around us. And as we looked we saw standing on the left of the Altar, with the Altar on His right hand, the Son of Man. He never comes twice in like fashion quite. There is ever some detail new to catch and hold the mind and speak its lesson.

In straight line above His head, hands crossed abreast, stood still, silent and suspended, seven high Angels. Their eyes were not closed, but the lids were lowered, and they seemed to be looking on the ground a little in rear of Him. They wore gossamer robes of varicolored hues. They were not really colored, these robes. They did but suggest color without displaying it. These were hues you have not on earth, but with these were also some after your style of violet, gold, faint crimson (not pink—but what I write, faint crimson), you cannot understand this, but let it rest, you will some day—and blue—only suggestions of these, but very beautiful. And for all their gossamer robes, their bodies were naked in all their surpassing loveliness. They were so very high in their holiness that the garments were of such a luster as not to clothe so much as to adorn. Their heads were encircled with a band of light about their hair, and the light was alive and moved in its radiance as their thoughts took on a disposition towards praise or love, or pity, so evenly attuned and so equal the poise of their minds, that even a very slight change of thought would affect those circlets of light, and also send a shimmer of crimson through a blue robe, or a shimmer of gold through one of violet.

The Christ Who stood by the Altar was both more emphasized in His visibility, and also the details of His countenance were to us more plain than was the case with those attendant Angels. He wore upon His head a double crown, one within the other. The larger and outer one was of purple, and the inner was of white mixed with crimson. Bars of gold joined the two into one structure, and between them were set jewels of sapphire—a very pretty piece, and the light from it was a cloud about His bead. He was clad in a robe of shimmering silver, and upon it was a mantle of crimson-purple—you have no color of it on earth. About His middle was a belt of metal, between silver and copper in color. I am doing my best to give you what His appearance was, and so I must use strange mixtures of earth-words, and even then I cannot come near to doing what I list to do. Upon His breast was a chain of rubies, which held His mantle about His shoulders. In His hand He held a stick of alabaster, varicolored, which He rested upon the Altar in repose. His left hand was upon His hip, thumb in belt, so that the mantle fell away on that side. The grace of His figure was matched by the graciousness of His face.

Was His face anything like the conventional idea we have in pictures of Him?

But little, friend, but little. But you must know that His face is not of the same features in detail in every Manifestation of Him. In essentials it is unchanging. As I saw Him now, His face was that of a King. The Sufferer was there, but Regality was the dominant note. We read Him as one who had won His Kingdom. What elements of battle remained were transmuted into that restfulness which comes with attainment. You are wondering if He had a beard, as in your pictures of Him. Not as I saw Him then. Indeed, I have never seen Him yet with a beard; I have seen Him some fifty or sixty times. But that does not settle the matter. There is no reason why He should not appear bearded, and He may do so on occasion. I have not seen Him so, that is all I can say.

When we had looked on Him, and on the Angels above Him, He spoke to us. You would not understand the import of His theme to the great congregation of people assembled. But when He came to speak to us, the Fifteen just returned, His words were such as these, but not spoken as you speak words: "And you who have been down into the outlands of gloom, know you that I am there also. Manifest to those, My strayed ones, I may not be, except in part and seldom. But when I had penetrated to the outer realms of My Father's expression of Himself, then, before returning this way onward, I went, as you have done, and spoke to many people, and they awoke to hear My voice, and a large number set their faces forward towards these realms. But some there were who turned away from Me to darker spheres, because they might not endure the sense of the Presence of Me, which at that time became intensified in the atmosphere of those regions, and should so remain. You did not reach so far as to the refuge of those who fled from Me then. But I am there with them also, and they shall be here with Me some day.

"But now, My own and earnest missioners, you have been afoot of My business, and I have noted your work from My own place. You have not come forth of your battle without scathe. They gave me wounds also. You have not in everything been given due credence for your honesty of purpose in your calling of men into the sunlight of these spheres. Of Me also they said I did not well but evil. Your hearts have sometimes been very full of pain when you beheld the pangs of our brethren in those drear lands. And at times you have stooped to wonder why the Father is so called—times when most the anguish of others bore you down with its millstone of woe, and crushed you nearly. My beloved and fellow-laborers in those far fields, remember how I, too, as in all things else, so in this, plumbed the deeps of human experience. I, too, knew darkness when His face was turned away."

He spoke in quiet, calm, and equal tones, and, as He spoke, His eyes seemed to dissolve into a mist, a vista of great distance, as if, while telling of these things and people, He was there in the midst of them, feeling and suffering with them in those dim places far away, and not here in the Sanctuary amid all the beauty of holiness and bright with the seven shining Beings glowing above Him. But there was no passion in His words, only a great majesty of pity and of power over all the ills of which He spoke. But to His words again, so far as I can translate them to you:

"But now I give you to wear, when you do worship to the Father His goodness and loving bounty, a sign and seal of your journey and service, and of your suffering."

He spoke of the new gem which was then added to our diadem of worship which we wore.

Then He raised His left hand and slowly circled it over the heads of the kneeling multitude, and said, "My legate I leave with you, to tell you further of the business next ahead of you in this place. For that work I am with you to help you, for it is a great emprise I entrust to you. Do not hurry to begin, and, when begun, be strenuous and strong to end it in good fashion, that it need no repairing of others more in advance of you in knowledge as in power. Call—and I will answer. But call not more than needs be. This is for the betterment, not only of the spheres inferior, but for your proving also. Remember that, and do what you are able with strength already yours. Yet do not let the work suffer for lack of calling on Me, for I am there to answer. And that this work at your hands be well done is greater to your minds than your own advancement, for the work is My Father's and Mine."

Then He raised His hand in blessing and worship blended, and said very slowly, "God is."

And as He said this, both He and the Seven slowly faded from our gaze as they withdrew, into their own Sphere and left us alone in the Silence. And in that Silence was the Beloved His Presence, and we, being wrapt about by the Silence, knew that it was His voice, and it spoke for us, and we paused, because it was He who was speaking, and, pausing, heard and worshipped.

36

The Diadem of Worship

Monday, January 28, 1918. 5:24–7:06 P.M.

THUS, then, our journey and our mission ended as we have narrated to you. Have you any questions you would ask of us concerning what we have told you? I think I see some questions taking form in your mind, and this is perhaps a convenient place for their answering.

Yes, I would like to put a few inquiries to you. First, what did you mean by your diadem of worship, or some such phrase you used, in your last message?

No emotion, no thought here is without its outer manifestation. All you see around you from your place upon the earth is the manifestation of thought. All thought is ultimate in the Being from Whom all life proceeds. From the outer inwardly all thought finds its focus in Him. Conversely, the Source of all thought is He from Whom it proceeds, and to Whom it returns in never-ending cycle. Between-times, this thought-stream passes through the mentality of Personalities of varying degree of authority, and also of loyalty or oneness with Him. This thought-stream, passing through these Princes, Archangels,

Angels and Spirits, becomes manifest through them externally in Heavens, Hells, Constellations of suns, Sun-systems, Races, Nations, Animals, Plants, and all those entities which you call things. All these come into existence by means of persons thinking from themselves outward, when their thoughts take on expression tangible to the senses of those who inhabit the sphere in which the thinkers dwell or with which they are in touch.

Nay, more, the thoughts of all, in all spheres, whether Earth or Hells or Heavens, are manifest to those who are, by their degree of power, competent to sense them. So it is not more than true to say that all your thoughts, my friend, are registered both here in these lower Heavens and also in those sublime regions which throb with the pulsation of the very Heart of the Holiest and Highest, the One Universal and Supreme.

As in matters majestic, so is it also in matters of detail. Thus the thoughts of a company in these heavenly regions become manifest in the temperature and tint of the atmospheric environment. (I use earth words, for in them only can I give my meaning to you.) So the quality and degree of the person here are manifest in more ways than one: in the texture, shape and color of his robes; in the form, stature and texture of his body, and in the color and luster of the jewels which he wears.

Thus, on our return from our mission in those far regions we, having assimilated into our personalities qualities before lacking, were given one gem more to wear in our diadem.

This action on the part of the Christ was not of an arbitrary nature. All here is done in strict and exact equity, but in the manner most gracious. I called this circlet our diadem of worship, because it is not visible upon our heads at all times, but only when our thoughts and emotions are focused on worship. Then it appears upon our hair, binding it about and clasping it behind the ears. All the gems which go to adorn it are not so much selected as evolved by those qualities we have accumulated in our progress from sphere to sphere. And now we were given one more in token, as the result of our achievements in those lower spheres where that our mission lay.

There is much more in respect of jewels and gems which you would not understand, even could I put my meaning into words. Some day you will know of their beauty and their symbolism and of the life which animates them, and of their powers. But not now. Shall we say that shall suffice for the time, and pass on to other questions?

The progress of the people of Barnabas.
Thank you, Leader. Can you tell me anything of the Colony to which you took those you had rescued, and left them with the one whom I will call the Lesser Christ?

You do well to call him so; he is worthy of the name.

Yes. With a few of the party who went with me on that journey, I have visited that Colony several times, as I promised him. I found he had not disappointed my hopes of him. Mark me well in this, that I am entirely satisfied with his work. But this was his proving, and, in result, it did not eventuate quite as I had expected. It has been very interesting for me to go there from time to time, and also to receive reports of others my commissioners, who go there in my name and bring me word of what is agait there.

On my first visit I found that they had arranged a City, in fashion orderly enough, but the buildings were rude and not elegant, even as the materials to hand in that region could have made them. There seemed to be a lack of completeness. I said words of approval of what had been done, and of encouragement to further endeavor, and left them to work the scheme out for themselves.

I found, as time went on, that—for comfort I will call that Lesser Christ by a name—we will speak of him as "Barnabas," that will serve very well—I found that his power was not in leadership of command; it lay rather in the more persuasive leadership of love. This was a great power among his people, as they more and more came to understand, and to be able by development to respond.

Wisdom he had in plenty, but not command. By his wisdom he came to see this, and by his humility he was able to acknowledge it readily and without shame. So, while in the deeper and more spiritual affairs he led, and leads today, he committed more and more, but gradually, the organization to his lieutenant the Captain. This is a very strong personality, and he will one day stand resplendent in these Heavens of light, a mighty Prince, to dare and do great things greatly; a man of large emprise.

By slow degrees he awakened in those poor darkened brains what skill they once had on earth in their various callings, and got them to work. Smiths, wood-workers and carvers, masons, architects, and also artists and musicians, each to his own calling. Every time I went, I found the City improving in order and in appearance, the people more happy. And one thing else I found.

When I brought them there as I came back from the deeper darkness beyond, the light was, at best, a glimmer over the land. But every time I went I noticed an access to the degree of light and visibility prevailing over the City, and, from the City, spreading its gleams over the country surrounding. This was one effect of the quiet activity of Barnabas himself. He it was who bent the spirit of each of his people towards their true destiny. By his love he enthused their spiritual aspirations, and as these became more real, so the people themselves advanced in light which, beginning inwardly, was radiated outwardly, and the result was seen in the increased and ever increasing brightness of their atmosphere.

So these two, loyally coordinating each his powers to those of the other, have done great things, and will do more anon, to my very great joy and the joy of all of those who suffered with me when we trod the dark by-paths of that underworld in search of souls who had lost their way.

Do the inhabitants of the surrounding regions ever molest them?

To your question, my son, as worded presently, the answer is No. None molest them now, nor seek to do so. But at the first, when they were weakly and least able to deal with their enemies, they were much harassed by them.

I will tell you. Now, first I will tell you what will strike strange on your mind. You remember the twelve times twelve thousand redeemed of whom Johannes writes. Yes; well, the number of our redeemed was that number. You would ask me why and how this came to pass. It came to pass in the counsels of those who conceived that enterprise; spheres far above mine they be, and their reason is not known to me; but it has relation to future ages of progress. You are wondering whether the number has anything in contact with those other of John's redeemed. No, not explicitly, at least. Implicitly there is a reason. That reason will work out in future development of that company, who will form of themselves hereafter a new and self-contained—what shall I say so you will understand me?— department in the Heavens. Not a new Heaven, no, but a new heavenly department; so.

Now to your question. At first they were much hindered and much vexed by surrounding tribes, who came, and, finding what was on hand there in their midst, snarled insults at the people and departed. But they reported to other tribes, and many an assault was made on parties of workers as opportunity was found. Then these minor attacks ceased for a long period. But the Captain was ever regaining his one-time alertness and ability, and had his watchers posted on outlying hillocks and in watch-houses all round. And from these he knew that a battle was impending, for the tribes were gathering a large army, and drilling their soldiers, with much display and talk of glory, as their manners go in those regions of false-reality so to group words.

But all the time our people grew in strength and also in brightness, and when the attack came they were able to beat off their foemen. It was a long and a very bitter battle of forces and wills. But they won, as they were bound by their destiny to win, what, strange as it may sound to you, and a paradox was a real and strenuous fight. What helped them greatly was their increased luster of person and atmosphere. This was very painful to their adversaries, who were still immersed in their darker condition, and they cried out in agonized frenzy when they came within the radius and felt the sting of the unresponsive aura of that City and Colony of progressive people.

Improvement has still proceeded, and, in ratio to their increasing brightness, the Colony has been gradually removed from its original state and has approached the spheres of light. And so I come upon a principle of interrelation between state and place obtaining here in these realms, and which you may find it hard to understand—nay, impossible. So I will not enlarge on it. I will say their enemies found it harder to come near to them, while the Colonists found that every time a trial of approach was made the radius of their City's immunity from danger had increased and still continued to increase, and their enemies perforce stopped in their tracks farther and farther away.

So small parties were settled on the ever-brightening lands around to farm and to till them, and to establish forests and mines. These were the last to be taken in hand, for the people shrank from the idea by reason of bitter memories. But metal was wanted, and some of the bolder and more determined set about to dig them, and they found that to work as slaves and to work as freemen were very diverse in effect upon them, and now they have no lack of happy volunteers to their help.

So it is that their increasing in goodness increases the light about their dwellings and their City. And that is their strength, for it is token of their advance towards higher estate, and that means greater power to them. Therefore it is that their enemies are powerless to come at them to their hurt.

My son, do you mark that well, for it is not without gladness for whose who in their earthly pilgrimage are encompassed with enemies also. And, be these enemies incarnate or spirit, they differ in nowise, mark you, from those who encompass the City of Barnabas, but ever at larger range as the City emerges more and more into the light, and they are left more and more in the darkness behind, below.

My love to you, my son, and our blessing.

37

Zabdiel's Band

Friday, February 1, 1918. 5:38–6:35 P.M.

K ATHLEEN has a word for you, my son, and then, when she has spoken, we will ourselves speak to you.

Well, Kathleen?

Yes, I wanted to tell you that we have been in touch with the Zabdiel Band, and they have sent a message to you by me. They wish me to tell you that your mind may rest at ease. Since they came into our neighborhood, when we were speaking to your wife, you have been questioning whether it was Zabdiel himself, or one of his Band, who gave you that series of messages in his name. It was the Leader Zabdiel himself who came personally, but with a few of his friends, and spoke to you. It was not one of his band, but himself. He wishes you to know this.

Some of you, who came a few evenings ago, told my wife that they had seen the name Zabdiel on—was it on their belts?

That is right, yes.

I didn't know he had a band until then, and have been wondering whether I had mistaken one of them for Zabdiel himself, as

I have heard that such spirits often give messages in the name of their Leader.

That is so. It is quite an orderly and regular custom. But in this case it was Zabdiel who came and did the work himself.

Thank you, Kathleen. Is that all you wished to say?

Yes. Now you can ask your questions of Leader. He knows you have them in your mind, and is waiting to answer them.

Concerning the future of the people of Barnabas.
Very well. First, Leader, reverting to the subject of our last meeting, I wish to ask you this: In that future Department of the Redeemed 144,000, what part will you yourself play? I have a feeling, that you will have some connection with them in some way. Is that so?

It is not without significance that that precise number should have been selected to form the new heavenly Department. Personally, I did not know of their number until my second visit to them after their settlement with Barnabas. Since then I have felt that what you suspect may have some truth in it. Nothing definite has been told me, for the time of which you speak is not yet. They still need much preparation before they emerge into the Light toward which they are steadily making their way. Also, their rate of progress is that of the slowest and most backward of them, or their number, settled with such evident care and design, would become meaningless.

For were they to be advanced individually as they came to merit advancement, they would become divided, and the arrangement would come to naught.

As I say, I have not yet been given any further charge concerning them and their future course. I watch over their present progress and am well content, and find much joy of our work. The rest awaits the decision of those who direct us from the Higher Spheres.

This, however, I may say. You mind me that I told you of our number. It was Fifteen. I told you further that the Fifteen were made up of two Sevens and myself as Leader. If you think of us as two bands, each of Six, with a Governor, and of those as subject to a Ruler over the whole Department, then you will have our complement complete in Fifteen. It will be interesting for you to watch this new Colony of the Heavenly Realms. You have taken a part in its present inception, or, at least, its early development, and will no doubt be always interested in its progress.

How have I taken a part in its development?

But yes, most surely. You are the instrument by which an account of the present condition of this people has been given forth of these spheres into that of earth. Those good and thoughtful who read of it will pray for them, and think kindly of them, and of us their helpers. Thus they and you will help on their development.

I fear I haven't thought to pray for them yet.

Because you have not had time to grasp the actual reality of what you have written at our instance. When you do you will pray for them, or I mistake you. Nay, I ask you to do so.

Certainly I will do so.

Yes, and when you come over here you will see that people with your own eyes, and will rejoice that you have helped them thus, for they will not be ready for advancement very far until a long time after you are here with us. Pray for them, therefore, and you will have many who will give you their love and gratitude, as to one who gave his kindly sympathy when they needed it so much, as now. Speak of them, think of them as the People of Barnabas.

Why not think of them, as your people, Leader?

Nay, friend, they are not yet mine. You go too fast. I think they one day will be so, and I hope to that end, for they be to me as my children, my own little children, so helpless, begotten from among the dead. You may image in your heart what that is to me. So do I ask you to pray for them and to send them your kindly thoughts of love, as also to Barnabas and the Captain. They be all your brethren, my son, and you, through us, have been put into real touch with them. Ask others to pray for them also.

Thank you for explaining what I fear I had overlooked.

Yes, and pray for those others of whom we have spoken, for they be in sore need of prayer and help to uplift them—I speak of their sometime Chief in that dark City of the Mines, and also of the others of whom we have told you. Could earth people come to realize what they might do for those in the Hells, they would lessen, by their prayers for them, the ills they themselves suffer. For by lifting those poor spirits more into the light, and softening their anguish, they would lessen both the numbers and the malice of those who rush to earth to trouble those of like nature with themselves, and, through them, the whole of mankind.

It is well for men to look upward and strive towards the light. It is of more virtue to look downward towards those who have sore need of strength so they may rise out of their unhappy spheres. For, bethink you, friend, this the Christ did long ago, and thus They do today.

God give you of that bounty bountifully, my son, which then He sent to earth. And may He attune you in your spirit and your acts to the mind of Him Who brought it. I mean the Bounty of the Father, which His Son once brought to man in this dark sphere of earth, and does today, and always.

Remember this, and you shall not then choose but to give to others as you have yourself received, to your greater peace and joy.

* * *

Note: The messages following the above were continued on the evening of February 5, 1918, and continued with one or two intermissions until April 3, 1919, and are published in Volume IV of *The Life Beyond the Veil,* entitled "The Battalions of Heaven."

Book IV

THE BATTALIONS
OF HEAVEN

Poem:
The Battalions of Heaven

Battalions of the Heavenly Siege,
    Encircling Earth above, below,
How did You leave Your Homes of bliss
    To come on service such as this,
To seek a Kingdom for Your Life?
    Is it the Christ would have it so?

The Christ Who sometime bending down,
    Breathed into man His benison,
And Jesus His Divinity?—
    We gave Him back Gethsemane,
And of Hell's brambles wove a crown
    To set His royal brow upon.

The Angel Hosts bemist all space,
    Like cloudy cosmos come to birth,
And down those Clouds far echoes ring
    It is the Slogan of the King,
"Up, royal brood of Priestly race,
    For I Will reign Upon my Earth!"

We sons of men take heart anew,
    Our faces lift and shout amain,
"We fling your slogan back again
    You shall not reign without us men!
Lead, valiant Christ; we follow you!
    Together we on Earth will reign!"

* * *

Note: Received at our weekly sittings for communion in July, 1920.—G.V.O.

1

Temple of the Holy Mount

Tuesday, February 5, 1918. 5:37–7:10 P.M.

Its origin and purpose

YOU would like us to give you some account of the origin and aspect of the Temple of the Holy Mount.

It stands between the Spheres Ten and Eleven, and when we say that, we mean that it is visible from both of those spheres, and yet is wholly encompassed by neither one nor other.

Its origin was in this wise. Ages ago there were many who passed from the one sphere into the other who were qualified by training. But Sphere Ten is, in a manner, a sphere wherein are rounded off and ordered all those attributes of power and character which have been gathered in their journey by those who have passed here through the spheres inferior. Here ends one grand stage of their journey, and the next stage is one wherein advance is made of somewhat different order of evolution and development than heretofore has obtained.

Hitherto the duties performed by those spirits in their advance have been, on the whole, of protective and strengthening

507

quality. Guardian angels you would call them, mayhap. This help truly develops and becomes of more spiritual tone as they rise higher. But essentially it is of the same order, if of different aspect, in its application to those who are watched and aided, both in the earth-sphere, and in all those spheres intervening up to the Tenth.

But those who enter the Sphere Eleven now take on another series of duties. Their service now develops into that which is Creative. They begin to learn the great mysteries of the Universe of Life, not now as to its operative power as more outwardly manifest, but as to its more inward Potency, as it is found nearer to those Holy Ones Who dwell about the Father's Home. So do they add the greater of those lesser qualities already assimilated into their personalities, and becoming attuned by degrees to the sphere ahead, prepare for their advance into that realm where Creation opens out to them in all its grand panoply of might and of majestic beauty.

This is one of the uses of that Temple, and indeed its principal use, and of the others we have no need at this time to speak. For you would that we should try to limn for you its plan and elevation. We will try to do so, but you will keep within your mind that, as in the present description of its uses, so now in our description of its aspect we speak but imperfectly, for not only stands the Temple to crown a Sphere not of matter but of spirit substance, but also of spirit atmosphere and environment intensified, by sublimation, tenfold. What that means in terms of dynamics and of potentiality of forces we do not pause to hazard, for we should fail to make any reasonable tale for you in your speech of earth.

This Temple was raised for the purpose of blending the two spheres, with their varying aspects of service, together. Here, then, those who are about to leave the one for the other are brought together and dwell here usually for a lengthy period, going forth, from time to time, into the Sphere Ten and those inferior, on their service as of old to help, or to protect, or to instruct, or to develop those whose abode is therein.

But they also begin to escort those from the spheres superior on their missions into Sphere Eleven. At first they go not far, nor for long. But as they become stronger and more attuned to the finer Pulsations of that sphere, so they go farther afield therein, and stay for longer and longer time. Returning they rest in the Temple, and, mayhap, in the interim, they go into one of the spheres inferior on duties of service there. You have already received a description of one of these missions being sent on a journey through the lower realms and into those of nether gloom. That mission of ours, friend, was a very severe test, for it encompassed, in its entirety, not one or two, but the whole gamut of the spheres between earth and this, and also invaded those farther afield. This very strenuous test of endurance, adaptability in condition and in the attuning of our minds, as well as our bodies, to deal with problems so far removed from our normal condition and temperament of life and service, was given with intent. It was a final test of me who had dwelt within the Temple and was ready for advance into Sphere Eleven, and for those my good friends who were for me an escort it was a test also for their advancement from the Sphere Nine into Sphere Ten, and of two of them from Sphere Ten to be henceforward Dwellers in the Temple.

Also, you will note a certain significance in the fact that I was charged to go and gather that company of people from the utter darkness, and bring them towards the light, as a final test of service before my calling into the series of spheres wherein the Creative faculty is quickened and trained. I did not understand it then, nor do I even now, yet my enlightening is already begun, and I seem to see a little of the glories ahead for those who once were in so grievous a plight, and now are almost at their ease, and at least are able to know what happiness is to those who go forward on their appointed way.

Have you, then, passed from the Tenth to the Eleventh Sphere?

Not yet of permanence. I am still a Temple-dweller, but more and more I become attuned with the conditions of Sphere Eleven. So many are the items which go to make up the sum of our life here, and yet which are each of much import, that while I hesitate to overpass one of them, yet you have neither time nor material on which to write a thousandth part of them. Here is one:

The period of residence in that Temple is almost always a very long period. In my case it will be longer than with most. For this reason: I have a charge (I mean the People of Barnabas) to watch, to aid, and to conserve in the path of progress onward. I must, from time to time, visit them in person and visibly; I must therefore keep in good fettle to condition myself speedily, not to a sphere once or twice removed from my present normal realm, but one far away in the dim ends of space, so to say it.

Mine is therefore a double task. I stand here on the Tableland, and I must keep one hand extended upward to grip, and the other extended downward to give. Well, well, there you have it, friend, I need not enlarge. You will see my meaning.

Zabdiel has passed into Sphere Eleven, hasn't he?

Yes, so far as his service in principal is considered. But yet he also comes to the Temple on occasion, and, attuning himself once more to his old estate, passes onward towards earth on some mission to those lower planes of life. Returning, he will pass through the Temple on the way to his proper place of service.

And now enough, for this occasion, of condition and environment. Let me tell you of the Temple itself. But cease now; you are spent of power.

Leader gives his name.

Before I go, Leader, I would like you to tell me your name. "Leader" is the only one I know you by, and it does not commend itself much to me.

Well, well, my son, maybe there is something in a name, withal, for all your good sage his dictum, I am known by another name in those spheres which are to that Temple superior. But in those below I am called by the name "Arnel." That you may call me also, if it please you better, my son.

My mother told me of one named "Arnol."

There is no earth letter-scheme to compass heavenly names, and enmesh them in earth phrase. I am he of whom your mother told you—write it with one or other letter, as you will: it shall suffice that you know me by that name hereafter. Will that please you—shall I say "commend" me to you, my son?

That's a knock for me, sir. Well, I can take it.

Aye, you can take it, for you have taken harder ere now, and not so kindly meant. So now, goodnight—as strange a sound on these lips of mine which never breathe night air as my name shall be on yours.

ARNEL+[1]

---

[1] It was at this sitting that Arnel first affixed his name and thereafter he signed each of his communications, always adding the sign of the cross.

2

Aspect and Plan
of the Temple

Friday, February 8, 1918. 5:35–6:30 P.M.

I HAVE told you of the use of the Temple of the Holy Mount. I now give you some account of the structure itself, but not in detail, for that were not possible.

A sheer edifice rises above the grassland, and on the table-land above stands the Temple. That portion of it viewed from the plain below is but one small wing, and not the main building. A multitude there assembled, and looking up, sees the porch and the flanking arches of the wing which fronts that way. From its lofty position, its size and its proportional elements of architecture, it is, as thus viewed, both stately and beautiful. Entering by this porch, and passing through it, we turn to the right, and skirt an open-air colonnade, roofed but with no side-walls to it, which runs quite round the main building, and at a distance from it, but is broken at intervals where corridors pass across, on the left leading towards the Central Temple, and to our right leading to other detached wings with their porches. All these, however, front upon districts in Sphere Eleven, and

512

only that one of which you have already knowledge looks towards Sphere Ten. Those wings are each devoted to special use, and are in number Ten. This number has not reference to the Ten Spheres inferior, but to those which are in advance.

Does this number include the Porch fronting on the Tenth Sphere?

No, that is as of itself alone, and has reference only to those spheres below. These ten have reference to the Eleventh and succeeding spheres. In each wing is a great Hall; and the wings are not identical in shape, no two are alike. In a way you would not understand, each of these Halls is tinctured with the elements of the sphere to which it has reference, and is also in communion with that sphere. It is hither that messages are received from those spheres, transcribed into the language of Sphere Eleven, and dealt with there, or are sent out to what district they concern.

Also, when companies of Temple-dwellers go forth into those spheres superior, touch is always maintained with them in these Wings, and, as they pass from one sphere to another, so the link is taken up by the wing in touch with that sphere into which their journey has taken them.

We turn to the left down one of these corridors bisecting the circular colonnade. It passes through court-yards and gardens and woods, all beautifully kept, and containing fountains, statuary, lakes, paths of varicolored marbles, arbors, temples— some in replica of temples in far spheres, but not on so grand a scale. And at length we come to the main group of buildings.

These also have ten Porches, but they do not give on to the corridors, but are each about equidistant between two corridors, as these end upon the wall of the main group. The Porches stand out into those sections of the grounds which lie each between two of the corridors, and are far-stretching. On earth you would call each of these sections a park, for the Temple is very vast in area, and the Colony of Temple-dwellers number many thousands, yet each has plenty of room, both house and gardens.

We will pause before the Porch which is set between the Wings of Spheres Twelve and Thirteen—they are not so numbered here, but I call them so for your less confusion. There is a broad terrace here, running on each side of the Porch, passing high above the beautiful grounds which stretch away towards the mountains which stand sentinel afar on the horizon and which mark the boundary proper of Sphere Eleven—for the Temple is built merely in the outlands of that Sphere. The Porch breaks into the terrace, and projects beyond it into the square, from which ascent is given by steps of dazzling amber, with a light within itself glowing and meeting the light from without in a blend, which changes according to the personality of those who be ascending the steps at the time. Here, you shall remember, all which you would call dead or inanimate is responsive to all else. Stone is affected by, and does also affect, verdure and trees; trees are affected by the presence of people, according to the nature both of people and trees. So is it with houses and all buildings.

The Porch itself is of much beauty. It is not rounded nor squared, but of a shape you cannot image. If I should say it is not so much a shape as a sentiment, you would think I spoke in allegory. Yet it is permanent with a permanency more perfect than that of any earth building. Call it mother-of-pearl, or liquid glass, in substance, and that must suffice.

Passing within we come on a large oblong space, covered with a roof of trellis-work interwoven with plants and flowers, some of which have their roots without in the, grounds, and some are planted within. But I must hasten on. We enter at last the Great Hall of the Temple.

Is it that in which you saw the Christ on the return from your journey?

The same. It has no roof, such as you would say was a roof. Yet it is not open to space. The arches tower high and majestic up into the place, where the roof would be, and are supported on pillars of multicolored crystal. But their arches end in a running line upon which rests what has the appearance of a cloud of light, but light of such a quality as to be impenetrable by those who, for the most part, assemble there. The roof-cloud is not ever of one tint, but changes according to the manner of ceremony proceeding below in the Hall.

I have already told you of the Altar, and of the Throne Room behind it. Round the sides of the Hall are other rooms such as that. One is a Robing-Room. Now that may sound very earthlike. But I will give you to know that the Robing which is there enacted is not merely the changing of a coat or cloak, but a ceremony of a most momentous kind. Let me tell you.

There are at times transactions enacted in the Great Hall which are fraught with electric power from spheres much advanced. At such times it is necessary that those from the Sphere Eleven, or any sphere inferior to that from which the influence comes, be each so conditioned that the life-stream be received upon his body so it be to his benefit and not to his hurt. So the ceremony of this Robing is diligently carried through in the Robing-Room, where they are very carefully treated by those expert in holiness and power, so that their garments change to the requisite hue and texture and shape. This is achieved only through the personality of the wearer. The inner qualities of him are denoted by the aspect of his robes. Only so may one safely enter that Hall and take part in the ceremony toward.

It may be that there is on hand the commission of a band on service into other spheres—a Dismissal ceremony. At such time the assembly meet to give of the combined influence of their strength to those thus sent forth. It is therefore required that all be done so that the harmony of blend be perfect. Those of less estate, or newcomers, have, to this end, to undergo very careful attunement in the Robing-Room, and then even they may lend of their mite of profit to the missioners.

Or a Manifestation shall perhaps be on hand. It may be a Manifestation of some aspect of the Godhead, or of some very High One, or of the Christ Himself. Then such robing is most carefully done, or harm, and not good, would ensue. But I have never heard of a mistake having been made in this matter. Albeit, in theory most certainly it is possible.

Frequently, however, the more recent comers find themselves weakening as they approach the Hall, when the Presence of some very powerful Person or some other intense influence suffuses it. Then they go back for that time. It is a test, and by it they get at what is required in their training. So they are not without blessing also.

If you go towards the mountains and view the Temple from some hillside, it will appear like a city, with its multitude of towers and archways and domes and trees and parklands. And the sight is most beautiful because of the gems which gleam out of its midst and shine afar. For each dome or pinnacle is a gemlike structure glowing and flashing with heavenly light and language—for each item of the building and every color and group of colors or of gems has a meaning which can be read by those who dwell there. Themselves are not less lovely as they move to and fro about those porticoes, or upon the balconies or roofs of the buildings, or in the parks. They mingle with the other beauties and glories of the place, and add to its peace, as to its splendor. For they and the Temple are each part of other, or, as I have said before, responsive, so that no unharmony is there, but all is in perfect poise of grouping and of color. And if I were asked to give that Temple City a name in one word, I would call it the Kingdom of Harmony. For therein is perfect unison of sound and color and shape and the temperament of those who abide there.

Arnel+

3

Twin Spirits—
A Dimissal Ceremony

Monday, February 11, 1918. 5:30–7:15 P.M.

AND now, my son, I will that you give me your mind while I try to limn for you one of those incidents of the Temple which I have called by the name Dismissal Service and Manifestation, for this was both.

Converging on the Central Hall were streams of happy people who came from all parts of the Sphere at the call of the Master of the Temple. They were happy, but of thoughtful mien, for they were aware that a very impressive ceremony was afoot, and so came in such a mind as that they might take away with them so much as possible for the furtherance of their progress. For these Manifestations be of mystical and sacramental nature, and we are much exercised in rising to meet those high influences which come from the spheres superior, that we may interpret the meaning of the ceremony, and so come at what blessing it is intended to impart.

When they were all assembled within I looked up to the roof-cloud and saw that its color was changing. When I had

517

entered it had been gold with streaks of blue. Now it was absorbing and blending such hues as the multitude brought with them, and, as more arrived, so the living moving vapor changed its color; until, when all were assembled, it was of deep tone of crimson-velvet. That is so near as I can come at it in your colors of earth. But its aspect told me that it was also touched by powers of higher grade from above and that some Presence was at hand already.

Then there descended from this roof-cloud a mist, distilled from its own essence, and settled upon us with a sense of sweet odors and of music whispers and brought into us a glow of exaltation and peace which uplifted one and all in harmonious blending so that we became, not so much a multitude of individuals as an assembly of those cellular entities which go to make up the one body of a man, so much at one in sympathy of love and purpose were we.

Then we saw that before the open way into the Throne Room a cloud was condensing upon itself and taking shape. Now, so far as is possible, I will tell of this transaction, but you will bear it in your mind that, were you to describe it again to one of my fellows of this sphere, while he would recognize that incident you had in your mind to show him, yet he would say that such a description was not a true one, by reason both of omission, and also of the quite inadequate names given to what things you would tell him were seen and heard there.

The cloud was of green tint streaked with spirals of amber within itself, and capped with a canopy of blue. This cloud was continuously in motion, and at length grew into the shape of a stately pavilion whose roof was of the deepest blue-violet and the pillars of semitransparent green and amber. There were in all seven pillars round the sides and back of the semicircular shape, and also two on each side of the main opening in front. These last two were of deep violet, with spiral bands of crimson edged with white. All were pulsing with the life of those who were willing this gem of beauty into being, and from the structure proceeded a murmur of melody most lovely to feel—for we did not so much hear it as feel it. It is often more real to feel sound here than it is with you to hear it.

Then beneath the canopy, and in the midst of the pillars, there appeared a wheeled chariot with the rear of it towards us. We could see the heads and quarters of those five beautiful horses above the front-board of it as they tossed their heads and exulted at their presence in the high drama in which they were playing their part. They were of faint gold color, and their manes and tails were of deeper gold. Very beautiful they were, and their satin coats gleamed and almost reflected the colors of the pavilion.

Then within the chariot there emerged into sight of us a beautiful young woman. She was facing us, and I noted all her loveliness, and, as I looked upon her, I saw nothing else for the exceeding beauty of her. Her body was of a tint you do not know. I will call it amber, but it was not the same tone as the amber of the pillars, but of more radiance and transparency, and yet with an aspect of reality and permanency which those wanted. She wore a robe of blue gossamer, but where it covered her body the two hues blended and became a delicate green. On her arms were bands of purple metal, and on her wrists bands of ruby-colored metal. She wore upon her hair a small cap of deep red with a thin band of white and gold, and her hair was brown with a sheen of orange upon it, as if it were touched by a ray of the sun at setting-time. And her eyes were deep purple and blue.

Now as we looked upon that picture we, one and all, felt that this Queen from the High Places of the Heavenly Realm was a Mistress of—I am now at a loss, my son, I am wishful to tell you what she meant to us, what she was in reality in her own Home, and I cannot come at it to find words of such content of meaning as to be to me of use. Pause a moment, friend, and I will continue. . . .

Now take these words and write them down: Mother-Queen, maidenhood, a spirit brooding over a race of people and bringing it forth into its own self-realization as a power for progress and good: one who, by eloquence of speech, strikes shame into a people dormant and not progressive, and, at the risk of tumult and frenzy, stirs up that people into activity, while over all she sheds a sense of far eternities realized and present, when all shall blend into, and be absorbed in, a majesty of peace; fearlessness and purity, where no shame can come of nakedness, and the lure of beauty is all towards holiness and pity and love. Roll all these into one word "Queen," and you have all I can give you of what that vision was to us in its message.

Then she turned and touched the two horses nearest her, each one lightly with her hand, and they swept round and faced the multitude. Then there came down from the gallery at the opposite end of the Hall a young man, who walked up the middle gangway and stood before the pavilion. She smiled upon him, and he went to the rear of the chariot and mounted and stood beside her, and they two took each of the other's beauty, and gave back, each to other, an added measure of comeliness, as they stood there responsive, heart calling to heart in love and holy aspiration.

Could you describe the young man, sir?

He was the woman in masculine duplicate. One was the complement and counterpart of the other. In only one thing did he seem dissimilar. His robe was of a slightly ruddier tint. I did not notice aught else of moment to mark one from other. Even sex was expressed rather in spirit than bodily. Albeit, in form she was emphatically woman, and he man. But to their purpose.

They had come to head a company of those who had been prepared in that Temple and its environs and lead them forth on emprise of a large conception, and requiring much ability and power for its furtherance. This was that they should take their way to a planet which was just at that stage of evolution where intellect was beginning to realize itself, and to raise itself into distinct order out of the brute towards the man—but it would not eventuate in man such as the earth type is, but not very dissimilar, and in essentials identical. This company was to take up the work of guidance in the progress of this race just at this stage. They would not take over their task in its entirety, nor at once. This was to be their first visit to those high Creative Princes who had brought the planet to its present crisis. They would return, from time to time, hitherward for rest and counsel. They would return in part, leaving some of their number to carry on the work, to be relieved by others of them after rest, and so gradually the affairs of that planet would be gathered up entirely into their hands, the while, in this sphere and some other spheres, other bands supplementary are being trained to join them when the time shall be that the race is expanding and evolving to what stage shall require more numerous guardians and rectors at the helm of that ship as it sails the broad spaces of the heavens on its way from mist to substance, and to living creatures, and to intelligence, and, as I will say for you of earth, from animality, through human-sort, to godhead.

This band, which were to receive our good-speeding presently, were about to take their first trial, not of creative enterprise—that would follow in some eternity ahead—but in that phase which inversely should lead them to the borders of creative service—the development of life already created into new forms of being—which in itself is creative in principle, and in reality is a department of the lesser creations, but not of creation new and radical.

Note you, my son, that in this Manifestation of those two high spirits, the woman came first into the chariot, in order of sequence, and the man came later. For Motherhood is principal in this empire of theirs, and yet they two stand together and start together, abreast and equal. That is mystery: how two may be one, one principal, the other second, and both equal in unity. It is so, but I will leave it there, and you may think on it; rather you will feel the truth of it than reason is to be so, I think.

Then forward came those chosen for that solemn dignity of conquest in the infinities of spatial realms so far and so deep into the darkness, away there where matter is instead of spirit substance and environment. Ah, you little know what that means to us, to speed away from the light of the heavens into gross and ever grosser darkness toward the distant abyss of being where worlds are material, and where bodies, enshrining sparks of life of the same source as that by which we live, are material also. Yet we were once such as these. Strange, strange exceedingly, this, and yet here be I and my own friends to speak to you, yourself enmeshed in body material. But we see only your body spiritual, and to that we address ourselves. The little lady Kathleen, by some strange witchery of her own, goes farther and touches the physical brain of you. She is our hyphen, and a charming link between us.

Well, I have now, at this time, no more to tell you. You have questions, I can see. Write them down, and, at our next meeting, we will give you answer.

Arnel+

4

Mary and Joseph

Friday, February 15, 1918. 5:85–7:05 P.M.
Their origin and development.
Have you any more to tell me about the Ceremony of which you spoke at our last sitting, Arnel? If so, my questions can wait, if that will suit you.

As you will, my son. And yet there is a question you have written down which perhaps we would do well to answer here.

Do you refer to this one: Of what race were those two leaders in their earth-life?

The same. Now you must know that these two youthful angels were really very ancient in their origin. There be few who attain to their power and authority to use them in such a service as this who have not passed a very lengthy period of training and evolvement. These two were twin spirits. They both lived in those times when earth had not taken on its present condition of life, but when man was in that state of evolution to which the foremost race on that planet to which they were commissioned had attained. That period for earth was a long one. During that period they both passed through that stage of dawning intelligence and came on into the spirit spheres. Their training was taken up here; and they, being two of the foremost and most progressive of their race, were passed on from planet to planet, each more in advance of the last, until they came back to the earth-sphere and continued their progress there. At that time earth had reached the rational stage, the phase of development when man had arrived as a human being such as he is today, but of lower capacity of intelligence.

Bronze or Stone Age, or which?

There was the Bronze Age, as you have named it, for some portions of the race, and the Iron Age for others, and the Stone Age for others. Man did not evolve with universal equality. You know this, and your question was a hasty one, my son.

It was when earth was progressing in intellect, and that is as exact as you can make it. It was long before Atlantis, or that other civilization which men call Lemuria. They came into the spheres about earth; and now, having accumulated much power, and also much knowledge, and being of high degree in holiness also, they made rapid advancement through these spheres, and passed beyond into the interplanetary spheres; and, as I believe, into those spheres which are interstellar. For I am of a mind to hazard that such as they are not entrusted with such work as this to which they had been sent except they be conversant with those high forces which unify the constellations in their orbits, responsive each to others. They did not find their affinity until they came back hither, and then they were drawn together by natural gravitation of spiritual sympathy, and have since gone on their way, ascending together the stairs of the Heavens of God.

How did they come into contact with the other planets? By reincarnation?

Reincarnation would imply a re-entry into flesh of same nature and substance as they had previously worn. If this be so, and has of you acceptation, then the term "reincarnation" would not be competent to express their becoming conditioned to the material and outer manifestation of other planets than earth. For although on some planets flesh is very like that of your earth bodies, yet no two planets produce precisely the same material for habitation upon their surface, and on some worlds it is much dissimilar.

Not only, therefore, would such an operation as you have in mind be no true reincarnation, but it would be, not perhaps directly contrary to the laws which govern interplanetary cosmogony, but certainly of so irregular a nature as to be negatived as unprofitable by those who have these matters under their authority to control the onward urge of the spheres. No; they visited those far worlds, both of this Solar group and also of other groups as they did this earth, and as I do now. I come back to earth to reinforce my powers here, and I go to other planets, now and again, in like manner, seeking after greater knowledge of God His wisdom in the creation and guiding of worlds. But I do not take upon me their material condition. That would but hinder me. I get at their inner life and the real state of them, the better from the inner—that is, the spiritual—side. From my standpoint in the spirit, I can learn more of what is agait upon that world than I could do were I to go out upon its surface incarnate, and with my senses engrossed by reason of their obligation to operate through a machine so much heavier and denser than that of the body of that ethereal substance which, in comparison, clothes the spirit lightly. Does this suffice to answer you in respect of their experience by the analogy of mine, my son?

Thanks, sir, yes. I see what you mean, I think.

Yes; you will remark that, while all Creation is one, yet diversity goes a very long way into the exalted places of heavenly progress, and in unification only comes into operation far beyond the knowledge of us who, when we look ahead, feel how short a way we have come along the road from that time when we numbered our progress by day and day towards those sublime heights, expanded into infinitude, where the pendulum of the timepiece of God swings in eternity after eternity, and the rhythm of tune blends into one bar of harmony in the great orchestra of dynamic Creation.

This is the school in which I take my place on a lower form, just one remove from the probationary stage which I left on entering this my present sphere and the Temple. Those two have progressed through this school in which I learn, and have now gone on to a higher. They return hitherward, as you have seen, as teachers and leaders now of others on the way of training they themselves once trod.

I have been wanting to ask you their names, sir.

But hesitated lest I counter you as once afore. Well, they have no names you could write down. Give them what names you will, my son, and those shall serve for their identity.

I have not thought of it.

Well, think, and tell me. It were better you named them than I who know their names but may not transcribe them for you. They could not be put down in your letters. What will you call them then, my friend.

Shall we say "Mary and Joseph"?

My son, you have done what I think you do not fully understand in its inner mystery. Nay, I do not disapprove. Nay. For those are the only two names in their significance which earth history supplies which are in any degree fitting to call them by. I will not further upon this. Let him that hath ears hear. By those names, therefore, we will call them in this account: Mary, Joseph. In that order you said them; in that order let them stand. Be you curious to observe that, my son; for it is of significance.

There seems to be a great difficulty in the transmission of names, and also of dates of earth periods. Everybody seems to find this so who receives messages from your spheres. Why is this, please?

I think you confuse the matter a little, do you not, my son; are you not now speaking of earth names once owned, and of earth periods once lived?

Yes.

Yes. Now, as to earth names. These are remembered for a time after transition by death; but new names are given here, and are used in constant, to the exclusion of earth names. This has the effect of the earth name fading, becoming dim, and at last almost, or quite, vanishing from the memory. Not so much while relatives are still on the earth, but after such time as they be all come over. Then, as generations go by, the line becomes intermixed with other blood, and the connection is thinned in ratio and at last is lost altogether. Exceptions there are; but few. Then, also, in the course of time names become changed, both in spelling and pronunciation. They become different names. But most of all they fade from memory as interest in the earth period becomes of less account by its removal from the more immediate proximity of the present estate of a progressed spirit, and among the infinite variety of experience here it is forgotten. It can always be had by research of the records, but that is rarely worth while.

The difficulty of remembering earth periods is a similar one and as needless to our present concerns as to our future course, in which chiefly our interest lies. There is also the fact that the continuous receding of our earth period and the intervention of event after event in so long a line of links, that it is difficult, on the moment, to pick out that particular link at the farther end and label it with earth time of day. It is easy for one of you to spring a query on one of us who is bent on giving you some message, and whose will is all taut and strenuous and focused on that message he wishes to give. It is not so easy for us, who have other work on hand, and who live in the present so much, to make a sudden about-ship and sail for the one little section in our wake where a particular wavelet lapped our bow, and which has long ago flattened out upon the bosom of the ocean, the while the ship still sped on her way, breasting swell after swell of the ocean. Count each swell a century, and you will get some idea of my meaning.

And now, friend, our narrative must await our next coming to resume it and to tell you some little more of Mary and Joseph, Angel Commissioners of God. So.

Arnel+

* * *

Note: The manuscript of sittings between February 15 and February 22 was unfortunately lost with other manuscripts relating to messages following the sittings of January 18, 1918.

5

Stillborn Children

Friday, February 22, 1918. 5:20–6:85 P.M.

WHAT we have to tell you tonight will, perhaps, seem a little off the track of our narrative. But it is necessary to readjust your outlook in respect of a matter of some importance to those who would try to understand the differences which obtain in the life of these spheres as compared with your normal life of earth.

We speak of childbirth into these realms of those who come forth from the earth sphere but have not been endowed with a separate individuality therein. These children come here asleep, and you will realize that their first awakening is that process here which answers to birth on earth. They have never breathed the atmosphere, nor seen the light, nor heard any of the sounds of earth. In brief, none of their bodily senses have been exercised in the way for which they were prepared by their natural formation. The organs of these senses are, therefore, nearly, but not quite, perfect in their structure. Moreover, the brain has never been called upon to interpret their messages. And so the child of earth lacks earthly qualities empirically, while having them potentially. These conditions do not apply to a child who has been actually born into earth life, even though he have but a few moments, or even less, of life before he pass on hitherward.

The problem, therefore, which they have to solve who take these children in hand is not a small one; for it is necessary both that the organs be dealt with so that a natural progress may attend the child, and also that the brain receives its lesson. In the case of an infant a few minutes old this connection between the brain and the organs of sense has been established and can be used in the maturing of those faculties dependent for their exercise on those organs. But a stillborn child brings not that connection, and it has to be made on this side. Once that is done, the progress is merely a matter of orderly development, on the same lines as that of ordinary children.

To this end several means are pressed into use. There is the relationship between the child and his parents, and especially between him and his mother. He is brought into contact with her in such a way that he experiences what is as nearly as possible equivalent to birth. By this process he is made to feel his separation from her bodily, and his individualization as a separate and complete entity.

This is achieved not by his taking a body of flesh, but by his being brought into intimate association in his spiritual body with the spiritual body of his mother. This does not affect so perfect an inception of contact between brain and organic faculties as does a natural birth, but it does establish in a definite way the relationship of earthly parenthood, and from that time the child is kept in touch with his mother in order that he may, as he grows up to maturity, be as others, so far as it is possible to compass this. Still, there is always some little difference between such children and those others who have been born on earth. They are lacking in some of the sterner virtues; and, on the other hand, they are more spiritual in their personality and outlook. But as earthborn children progress in spiritual development, and the stillborn children develop their knowledge of earth by contact with their mothers, and later with their other relatives, so the difference is minimized until they are able to associate on quasi-equal terms of loving friendship, and to help in the mutual giving of what each lacks.

So the earthborn are mellowed in sweetness, and the others are strengthened in character, and, both being included in a community, infuse an element of variety which is pleasurable as it is of profit.

You will see, my son, by what I have but now told you, how great is the responsibility of earthly parents to those their offspring in these realms, for association with them is necessary to the true development of the earthborn children also. It is not an adequate life they lead if they are not kept in touch with their kin on earth—there is a hiatus which no one else can fill. And where the parents are of evil life, it is necessary that their spirit children be held aloof from their company for many years of earth time, until they be grown up and of such strength of will and quality of wisdom that they may help the guardians of those people in their watch over them for their well-being.

And most often this development is not sufficiently advanced that it be safe to expose the child to earth influences before the time of earth probation is over and the parent is called away to these realms of spirit. In such cases the only help the child can give is that of prayer.

Such a parent comes over here either with no affection for the child she has suckled at her breast, or else with no knowledge that the child exists at all. So the link between them, weak at best, grows weaker still as the child progresses upward, and the mother goes downward to her own place of purging. And by the time she had again ascended to the sphere where the child had awaited her coming all her earth life through, he has gone onward into the upper realms and is out of reach of her.

He may be cognizant of her, and send her of his help unknown to her. But the link of warm love which should be about parent and child to bind them heart to heart is not, and never can be, in the ordinary progress of heavenly life.

I have told you this, my son, because we here have noted so much of disregard among you of the burden of motherhood in the matter of which I speak. And yet these sweet flowers, plucked before the bud be opened fully to life's sunlight, be so beautiful, and their wistfulness at the lack of own parentage so marked, it fills one with great distress to see it so. Not that they be in any wise unhappy. We would not permit that to be. But there is a lack, as I say, and it is only partly supplied by those dear mothers who lacked the achieving of motherhood on earth, and find it here. So each, you will note, makes gift to the other of what that other lacks, and receives what is wanting in return. And it is very beautiful to see.

But, Arnel, why have you inserted this essay in this place? It seems to have no connection with your narrative.

But yes, my son.

I have noted that query forming in your mind as you have written, and knew you would ask it of me in due time. And it was not without intent that I chose my theme tonight. For without such knowledge it were not possible to understand the Queen and her Consort, whom you have named Mary and Joseph. It is of their relation in the long, long past I have told you tonight. So first they came together. The fruition of their love-bond you have seen.

Arnel+

6

University
of the Five Towers

Friday, March 1, 1918. 5:45–6:45 P.M.

THERE is in the Sphere Ten a vast glade amidst a forest-land. It is surrounded by the forest, from which there emerge into the open many roads which lead away into different quarters of the sphere. From these there branch off paths in all directions, which are much affected by those who would draw aside from the company of their fellows for meditation, and communion with those in other spheres. Beautiful is the peace which here prevails. The trees and flowers and the brooklets, a lake here and there, with the birds and forest animals for only company, entice the student to wander here and drink in its atmosphere of peace.

But our present business is in the glade. It is so great in area that you would perhaps name it a plain. It is filled with gardens and fountains and temples and buildings put to the use of study and research. It is University, but of such a plan that it might stand for a City Beautiful. For in motive here beauty seems to rank equal with knowledge.

It is not circular in shape, but rather oval. At one end of the oval there projects from the forest edge a high broad porch, flanked with trees on either side, and above the trees there appears a wing of the building, with a balcony running high up the wall, and giving a far view over the glade. The remaining building is embosomed in the forest, except the Towers and Dome, which you see soaring above the porch and beyond it. Were it not for these, you would not know there was a large group of buildings there, so thick are the trees about it.

There are five towers—four of equal size, but not of pattern—and, in their midst, the Dome. The Great Tower rises farthest away, and is continued to a great height, ending in a very beautiful design. This cap is in the form of a heavenly palm tree, whose leaves are interwoven in filigree to form a crown set with jewels and surmounted with a semblance of a constellation of suns, also bejeweled richly.

All this—the four Towers, the Dome, and the Great Tower—has a mystical significance, which only those who have passed into the Temple of the Holy Mount do fully understand. These explain to the students of the University so much as they are able to assimilate on occasions of great Festival; and some of the Mysteries of that place are explained by Manifestation. Of one such occasion I am minded to tell you, but will first be a little more full as to this building itself.

Beyond the Porch there lies a lake which is approached by steps on to which the porch gives, and which stretch to some distance right and left. The main building rises from the lake, and all its gardens and the clusters of lesser buildings are joined to it by bridges, mostly with roofs. The Dome covers a hall which is used for observation. This work is not like that carried on in the wings of the Temple of the Holy Mount for sending help and maintaining communication, but for the simple study of the Spheres. This study is elaborated, by classification, into a science which is continuously progressive, because the Spheres are for ever readjusting themselves in their relation each to others. So there is no finality in the pursuit of knowledge in these heavenly realms.

The Four Towers have each a group of buildings of their own. I cannot give you their names, but you may write them down as the Tower of Sleeping Life, which you would call mineral; the Tower of Dreaming Life, which you would call vegetable; the Tower of Waking Life, which you would call animal; and the Tower of Consciousness, which you would call human.

Tower of Angelic Life

The Great Tower is the Tower of Angelic Life, which watches over all those forms of life below it in degree of progress, and also crowns them all. For towards the Angelic order is all the lower creation moving.

These Towers are served by the House of the Dome, and to it they turn for any specific item of knowledge they need in their work of research and classification. On the powers generated within the Dome House they rely to help them in that matter.

The four Towers are each of different design, and you would know at once, as you looked at them from the plain, what order of Creation they were intended to picture. They are designed to that end. The work agait within them infuses them each with its own peculiar character, and from that infusion the design emerges and becomes the pattern outwardly displayed.

The Great Tower is very lovely to see. It is of no color of earth; but call it golden alabaster set about with pearls, and you get an idea of it.

It is almost like a vast and splendid fountain of liquid gems in perpetual play. But instead of the plashing of waters, there is given off a harmony of whispered music, so that none can approach that building but he is moved, almost to enchantment of ecstasy, by the influence it sends abroad.

The waters also are beautiful, for they wind in and out of the flower-gardens; and here is a rill, and there a lake in which the Towers, or Dome, or some gem of architecture, is reflected, and lies in placid, restful beauty, like an angel-child in it—cradle, so to say it for you. I will take you within the Great Tower and note a few of its qualities.

This has no broad building at its base, but springs sheer up from its foundations. We stand within and look upward, and you are struck at once with awe. There is no floor or roof between you and the sky above. Up and up and up ascend the walls—it is four-square—like a mountain precipice, until the top seems set right into the heavens among the stars. Far away the rim of the Tower appears, almost beyond the Tower itself, so high it is.

But the walls are not blank. The Tower is built of double walls, and on all four sides there are rooms and halls and dwelling-places of the Angels. So as you gaze aloft you see here a doorway, there a balcony or a hanging window, or a bridge will shoot from one dwelling to another, in a curve outward over space, and inward again to its destination. Or a diagonal line on the wall will show where a flight of steps goes from one house or pleasance to another. Even gardens are there, planted on broad ledges thrust out from the sidewalls of the Tower. And so high and so wide is this great shaft that those items, which are of roomy proportions when you mount up to them from within, yet do not impede the view into the sky above, nor alter the contour of the opening atop.

And as you look about, you see how the light alters and blends, or grows or dies away at different parts of the ascent. So, at one home, as it gives on to the well of the Tower, there seems to be shining the noonday sun. On another the evening sun seems to be setting and lighting up the ledge-garden, with its lovely green trees and arbors, with a sunset glow. At another part of the structure there is an aspect, yea and a sense, of sunrise on a fresh spring morning, with the singing of birds and the ripple of mountain rills into the meadows below—for running water is not absent here in this wonderful place.

Music, also, from one dwelling or another, comes sometimes from several at one time, and yet the interior of the building is so vast that they do not invade each the theme of the other's melody.

Now, from what I have told you—and that is but a tithe of the whole—you might deduce that you were in some place where slumber was chief resident, and ease the motive of its founding. But cast back your mind to the name I gave these Five Towers and you will see that such is not the case.

This Great Tower supervises the work of the other four, and the Dome draws from here the power required for its work. Here reside Angels of great rank, and come and go from very high realms to give of their mighty strength and far-flung experience, to aid those who now seek to tread the way they went before ages ago. Those whose abode is in the Four Towers and the Dome House are doing, in the present eternity, what themselves did in eternities bygone, whose denizens have passed on in the cycle of progress, and left their place to be possessed by the present race.

You will note also that, much advanced as their work is, yet it is still of the fostering, and not of the creating, of things, being still in Sphere Ten. But it leads on thither, and this is one of the places highest in degree in Sphere Ten.

Did you pass through that University, Arnel?

Yes; I took my course through all four Towers; that is the usual way.

And the Dome House?

That I did not enter as student, having done such work elsewhere. I passed from the Fourth Tower into the service of one of the Princes of the Tower of the Angels. It was he who trained me to proceed to the Temple, and he also, as I have found since my return, sent of his power to help when I went about the darker places of the Hells. He did this auxiliary to that of others, whose proper work it was. God's blessing, my son.

ARNEL+

7

A Manifestation
in the Palm Crown Hall

Monday, March 4, 1918. 5:50–7:25 P.M.

The Christ Creative.

WITHIN the precincts of the University of the Five Towers there is much movement but no hurry. Along the canals boats are issuing from the lanes which lead into the central waters, and are giving up their voyagers upon the landings about the various buildings. Upon the terraces and stairways coming down to the water's edge thousands are congregating, and each group arriving adds to their gladness, for they bring with them expectancy of some great Manifestation. These have been bidden hither each one personally. For not all the inhabitants of the Sphere may come within these confines, but only those who are much progressed.

The thousands being assembled, there comes from the Tower of the Angels a strain of music, and all are at attention to see what shall follow. I will describe this Manifestation in order.

As the music grew in volume the atmosphere about the Tower took on a certain mistiness, but did not obscure so much as transform it. It became more transparent, and seemed to be flowing up and down, and from within outward, and back inward upon itself, like liquid glass of many colors.

Presently we heard voices above the Angels' orchestra. They were singing a *Te Deum* to the One Alone, and to His Christ Who was about to manifest some phase of His Being to us.

Could you give me the theme of their song?

Nay, that were not possible; I will give you a version of it as well as I may. Here it is:

"We, who have listened to Thy Voice from afar, know Thou art He from Whom is Melody, for, at Thy Word, eternities brought forth Beauty.

"We who have seen Thy Face in His eyes, Who alone has shown to us Thyself, know that Thou art formless, and yet out of Thy Mind came Form, that beauty should not go naked, but be clothed in garments whose woof is light and their web the shadow.

"We, who have felt Thy Heart its beating, know that Beauty is so formed for us because Thou art all Love and no love is but of Thee.

"And of all Thy Beauty we can only know by the Beauty of Thy Christ, Who shall manifest to us, Thine offspring, in such form as Thou hast given us to wear.

"We bow our heads to worship Thee, for of Thee we are, and ever look to Thee, Center of Life, and of what Being life is screen. Behind this outer life Thou hidest Thine effulgence that it harm us not at all.

"Yet what Thou mayest show us of Thyself give to us now who wait His coming and His Peace."

The last words were slowly sung, with lingering cadence, and then all fell silent, and, with bowed heads, waited.

Then we heard His voice saying, "Peace," and we raised our heads and saw that He was standing before the entrance of the Tower of the Angels. Before Him stretched a long stairway, very broad, down to the water's edge, and, kneeling on the steps, were a great number of Angels. They were the residents of the Tower. They were many thousands in all. He stood alone, well away from the great round archway which gave into the Tower, and behind Him stood another multitude of Angels of still higher degree, who had attended Him on His coming.

The Tower now glowed like a great leaping flame, and flashed out its fire into the atmosphere until the waters flickered, shimmering like the Tower, and seemed to be alight with its ardor.

Then He raised one foot first, and then the other, and stood suspended. And we looked up to the Tower-top and saw that the Crown was changed, for it was like a beautiful living thing now. The filigree work was all in movement, and, as we looked, we saw that the palm-leaf crown was be-gemmed with clusters of angels. They sat in rows along the leaves, they stood in curves about the circlet at the base, they reclined upon the gem-bosses. Every strand of the crown was a company of angels, and every jewel was a group of seraphim, glowing and burning like flames of fire.

Slowly the whole Tower-top detached itself and moved forward into the space above the spot where He and His company stood. And then it floated slowly down until it rested upon the terrace pavement. Within were thousands of Angels already, and we also were now bidden cross the waterway and come within.

When I arrived at the stair-head I found a stream of people, lifted up in ecstasy of joy, pouring into the newly-laid palace. And so I joined them and went within, nothing fearing, all was so calm and so full of peace and joy.

Within, the Crown was like a great hall, very high and glittering with precious stones and jewels from base to top. The open-work was now filled in with a light-suffused mist, which made the chamber self-contained. The walls went up vertical for a space, and then arched over, groined, and met in the center at its highest span in one big jewel of sapphire color. This was transparent crystal, and had a wonderful quality of reflecting the heavens without, and showing who came towards the sphere and who departed. The Crown must have been thus remodeled as it descended, for, at other times, it was quite open to the sky above it.

How many were there present?

I cannot say. But those who came with Him must have numbered at least a thousand and a half, and we guests were not less than six times that number. Then there were the residents of the Tower, who were in number some three thousand, in ordinary. It was a great company.

The object of this Manifestation was one of instruction as to the science of that University. I have told you what it was. We had pursued our work of research, and had accumulated much material, and now He came to show us how it was coordinate with the knowledge of God as progressed into the spheres ahead.

Could you be more explicit, Arnel, please? This is rather general.

Yes, it is, my son, and I regret it much; but I fear I cannot make it much more simple for you. I will try.

Not to weary you too much, at once I say, He came, at that time, as God His Word made manifest.

You know that the Word it was Who, when worlds were in the making, was constituted the Medium by Whom the energy of God's Life became modified and condensed into that star-milk out of which was churned plastic matter, and of this the worlds were modeled. The Word was the Agent of Creation. The Father thought through the Word, and His thought, in its passage through the Word, took form of matter.

This had been our study for a long time past, and it was to link us on initially to the kindred, but deeper, study of the realms above us that the Christ came now to explain to us a little more than we had learned of the Word in His relation to the work of the Father in the creation of the universe. But more than that I cannot transmit to you.

Could you give me a description of Him, as He came this time?

He stood suspended in the midst of the Palm Crown Hall, and so remained. I did not at first understand why this should be so. But as the Manifestation proceeded I saw that any other position could not be in harmony with His theme.

It was not merely a pose for the sake of teaching by the eye. It was by reason of His theme that He became levitated into space, and, as He proceeded, He arose until He stood there halfway between floor and roof. It is of the dynamics of these realms, not a matter of choice, but of scientific order.

Moreover, the Angels who had be-gemmed the Crown without now were seen all about it, both walls and dome, within, living jewels to curtain the walls in living tapestry.

You wish me to describe Him to you. His robe was a tunic to the knees, of liquid green, His arms were bare, both of clothing and jewels. One jewel alone He wore. His belt about His middle was fastened by a clasp, and the clasp was a flashing blood-red stone. Midway between His hips it rested, and in that there is a mighty significance, if you will think it out. For, although He is never severed from the One of Whom He came, yet in His work in these spheres away from the Father's presence His is truly a separation. He sallies forth, as of His own strength, to do battle with worlds, and must perforce turn away His face to do it. For His will must be projected outward from Spirit into matter. That is the mystery of the ruby's emplacement. I would not have told you this, but I saw the question in your mind.

He had no mantle. His legs were bare below the tunic, and His limbs and face were those of a young prince in full strength of youthful manhood. His hair was bare, parted in the middle, and fell upon His neck in clustering brown curls. No; I cannot tell you the color of His eyes—none you know. Your mind is full of questions of Him, my son. I am trying to keep pace with you in this.

Well, when you speak of Him I always feel I want to know more of His appearance, as it may help me and others to know Him better—Himself.

I well understand. But, believe me, my son, you will come to know but little of all He is while you are in the earth sphere, and little more when you stand where I stand now, so great is He, so far ahead of any formula your cramped theology of Christendom teaches. They have tried to catch and confine Him in words and phrases. He cannot be so contained. He is free of the Heavens of God, and the whole world is but a speck of dust upon the floor of His Palace. Yet there be some of you who would not give to Him the freedom even of that small atom. I will not pursue this farther now.

Arnel's earth life.

But, Arnel, what did you believe when you were here on earth? What you have just written, I believe. But did you, when you were here, sir?

I did not, to my shame, for men had not then freed themselves from shackles of words, even so much as now they have done so. Yet, my son, believe me, I did go beyond my Church her pale, and preached of love of wider scope than they would allow. And for that I suffered. They did not kill me, but they reviled me, and made me feel very lonely, more lonely at times than you do, my son. For there are more now to keep you company than there were to me. And although I did not reach so far as you do now, yet it was far to me in those dark days. The sun begins to warm the horizon today, my son. It was winter then.

When was that, and where?

It was in Italy, my son, in Florence the beautiful. And I do not mind me when, but it was at the time when God was making things anew, and men were beginning to think strange bold thoughts, and Church frowned from one brow, and State frowned from the other, and—well, I died in mid-life and so escaped their further enmity.

What were you? A priest?

Nay, my son, no priest was I. I taught music and painting—they were oft mixed in one teacher in those early days.

The early days of the Renaissance, do you mean?

We did not call it so among us. But that was what it was, yes. God then began to make things anew as He is doing today; and when He stretches forth His hand to do so it means that men will have to help, with much travail. But they, in the work of renewal, are not alone—mind you the ruby-stone in His girdle, my son, and take heart by reason of His company.

Friday, March 8, 1918. 5:43–7:12 P.M.

When we were all assembled, the Angels who were His attendants lifted up their voices and led an anthem of praise, and we all joined them in their adoration. I see you wish me to give you the motive of the theme. It was as I write it now:

"BEING was, and from the heart of Being came forth God.

"GOD thought, and from His Mind the Word became.

"THE WORD went far abroad, but with Him went God. For God was the Life of the Word, and through the Word God's Life passed onward into Form.

"So MAN became in essence and emerged from his first eternity a creature of the Heart and Mind of God, and the Word gave to him the heart of angels and the form of man.

"Right worthy is the CHRIST MANIFEST, for He it is Who, through the Word, comes forth of God, and so declares

God's purpose, and His life through Him is poured upon the family of angels and of men.

"This is God Manifest, through the Word, by the Christ, in angels and men. This is the Body of God.

"When the Word spoke forth the will and purpose of God, the outer space took on a semblance of matter, out of which matter was made, and it reflected back the rays of light which came from God, through the Word.

"This is the Mantle of God, and of His Word and of the Christ.

"And planets danced to the music of the Word, for they were glad when they heard His Voice, because by His Voice alone might they hear of their Creator's Love, Who speaks to them through His Word.

"These are the Jewels which be-gem the Mantle of God.

"So from Being came forth God, and from God came the Word, and of the Word was the Christ of God ordained to Kingship of the Worlds for their salvation.

"And in the eternities man shall follow Him, after the long journey in places strange, and some most desolate, homeward, Godward, in the evening of the day whose hours are eternities, and whose Noon is now.

"This shall be the Kingdom of God, and of His Christ."

And, as we sang, the whole building began first to vibrate and then to dissolve, and pass away. And the Angels, who had been about its walls and arches, now formed groups, who stood, each in order, in front of his own great company, which stretched away behind him into space. For the whole heavens were filled with innumerable companies of men of different race, and animals; and all creation was there around us.

We saw the spirits of men who were in the animal stage, and others, in all degrees of progress up to the state at present reached on the foremost of the planets. We saw all forms of animal life, both of land and air, and sea-creatures in all their degrees of development also, from simple to complex form and organism.

And we saw those angelic beings, also in all their degrees of splendor, who had charge of peoples and nations, and of animals and plants in all their variety of order. These Hierarchies were most sublime, for we saw them in massed grandeur, and those who had been stationed about the Crown were now observed to have taken their places as members of those groups to which they each belonged.

It was a spectacle to fill the soul with awe and reverence at the majesty of Creation, and of Him Who stood there aloft, right in the very center of it all, about Whom all revolved as a wheel upon its hub.

I understood then, as never before, how that the Christ Manifest, either in earth or in the heavens, was but a shadow of the Christ Himself in all His fullness, just a shadow cast by the light of His Godhead upon the walls of space, and these walls were made up of the specks of dust scattered about in the great void, each speck a sun with his planets.

And yet, even so, how beautiful and full of simple majesty was He as we saw Him thus manifest at that time. All the movement of all these creations were reflected upon His tunic, or in His eyes, or upon His body—each pore, each cell and every hair of Him seemed responsive to some order of that wonderful creation displayed around us.

Did you, among the various species, see those which had gone astray, or were vicious and savage, or loathsome—tigers, spiders, snakes, and so on? Were they there also?

My son, call not anything unclean until you have looked within. When a rosebud goes wrong, as some men say, it becomes a thorn instead, yet God permits the thorns, and presses them into service, protective to the flower, like a bodyguard watching over the safety of their beautiful queen.

Yes; they were there, not roses and thorns alone, but all manner of creatures unloved by men, as thorns are unloved by them, although God does not cast them away, but uses them.

But we saw all these creatures, which you call vicious and loathsome, not as we saw them when we lived on earth, but as we had been taught to see them here. We saw them from the inside of things, and they did not appear so in our eyes, but as offshoots of the one great tree of natural and orderly progress: not evil, but less perfect: each class an endeavor of some high spirit, and his hierarchy of workers to express an idea of some minute element in the Character of God.

Some of these experiments had been brought to higher perfection than others, but until the Grand Experiment is consummate, no angel, and surely no man, may pronounce one to be a creation of good, and another to proceed from vileness. We who saw from the inside were breathless at the beauty of that fair but far-flung mantle of the Christ Who, as He stood there in the midst, seemed to be clothed and wrapped about by the distilled essence of it all, which settled upon Him in incense of worship and fond adoration.

For the time we were no longer denizens of the Tenth Sphere, but of the whole Universe, and wandered about among its continents and down the vistas of its ages, and spoke with those who planned and those who wrought in that great workshop of God. And many things new we learned, and each new thing was a joy such as only those may know who themselves come so near to creatorship as we who were now receiving an advanced lesson in our school, in order that we, even as these Mighty Ones, should go forth to do as they had done so wonderfully, yes, even those who had made a worm or a thorn. My son, you who speak lightly of these would find much ado to make either one or other. Is not that so? Well, wisdom comes with years, and greater wisdom in eternity.

Then we, who had thus been sent to school, were bidden together again from our journeys of inquiry, and, as we came towards one center, the whole dissolved into invisibility, and we stood upon the platform before the Porch of the Temple of Angelic Life.

I looked aloft, and noted that the Crown was back in its wonted place, and all was as it had been before the Ceremony had begun. All things but one—for it seems to be the rule that every such visitation shall leave some permanent token behind it. Thus, we saw upon the waters of the great lake before the Tower a small new building, dome-shaped, and raised not much above the surface. It was of crystal, and through it shone a light from within, which fell upon the waters and floated there, not in reflection but in substance. And the waters of the lake now have one more element of power than they had before.

Can you explain, please?

Nay, my son, there I stick; for it is not to be conceived in the mind of man on earth. It was one more aid to our progress in understanding the powers which permeate the spaces about the planets and their suns, and which become what you call light by friction with the denser atmosphere enveloping them. We should have to deal with that in our further studies in the Eleventh Sphere, and it was for our aid in that matter.

ARNEL+.

7:14 P.M.

Do you wish to say something, Kathleen?

Yes; I want to tell you how much I enjoy coming and helping you to catch the thoughts of Arnel and his Band. They are so beautiful and so kind to me that it is a pleasure for me to stand here and receive their thoughts and hand them on to you.

How is it that Arnel lived in Florence and yet talks not in old Florentine but old English?

He lived there, I believe, but was not of Italian birth. I fancy he was English, or at least, a native of these islands, but emigrated, or had to flee—I don't know which—when he was a young man. He then went to Florence, and stayed there. I don't know whether he ever returned to England again. There was an English Colony in Florence in his day.

Do you know in whose reign he lived?

No; but I don't think it was so early as you had in mind when you spoke of the Renaissance. I am not sure either way, however.

Thank you, Kathleen. Is that all?

Yes; and thank you for coming to write for us.

How much longer is it going to last?

Not very long, I fancy. Why? Do you want it to end?

No, I enjoy it; and I enjoy your company, and his also. But I am wondering whether I shall be able to last out; to keep up the necessary sensitiveness, I mean. There are so many distractions at present.

Yes; but you will be helped, you will find—as you have about the interruptions. You have not been interrupted since Arnel said he would deal with the matter.

Quite right. In a rather noticeable way those interruptions suddenly ceased altogether. Well, I mean to go on until you tell me you have done. God bless you, Kathleen. Goodbye for the present.

Goodnight, my dear friend.

* * *

Note: The interruptions referred to had occasionally been made by callers at the vestry in which in the hour after evensong Mr. Vale Owen was receiving the messages.—H.W.E.

8

Some Principles
of Creative Science

Monday, March 11, 1918. 5:33–7:03 P.M.

The spiral.

WILL you tell me of your experience, and of what you learned, when you made your tour among the Creative Hierarchies, on the occasion of the Manifestation in the Crown Hall?

With a company of fellow-students, I essayed into the scenes around us, and at once I found that all had been arranged for our convenience in gathering knowledge such as would be helpful to us. All was planned out orderly. Broad avenues of great length, fading into the distance, were laid between the great orders of Creation. But, inasmuch as none of these were entirely separate one from another, these avenues were not merely divisions, nor roads for traverse, but were in themselves departments blending those on either hand.

As we walked down these we were struck with the fact that certain principles were evident, as observed by all the Creative

Princes loyally. And these principles were essentially the same whether they were applied to mineral or vegetable or animal life. This is but reason when you remember that all the glamour of the diversity, so rich in wisdom and ingenuity, as displayed in those departments most evolved, had grown out of the first simple aggregation of elements, through long ages of progress, first in a few apparently trivial departures from the simple into the complex, until at length we have the richness of flamboyant display as we see it today.

Let me take an instance to illustrate my meaning.

We saw, as we went down one avenue, how worlds were made. On the left hand, as we went, we saw how the thought of God, vibrating and pulsing outward, became, by degrees, of denser element, until it issued into what you call ether. Here we were able to notice the nature of the movement, and we saw that it was spiral, but that, as any certain wave reached the top of the spiral, it continued its course by a descent, also of spiral form, but now within the atom of ether. So that the inner spiral, having a more constricted space to work in, the descent was of greater speed than that of the outer spiral. Emerging from the lower end of the atom at a greatly increased velocity the vibrations were able, of their own momentum, to continue again their outer course upward, but at a rate of movement ever a little slower, until the top was reached, and the descent begun anew interiorly, and with ever-gathering velocity.

These atoms were not round, nor were they true oval, but, by reason of the ceaseless movement within themselves, elliptic. The motive power of their self-contained motion was a gravitational pressure exerted from without, and, if we could have chased it to its source, I think that we should have found that the dynamo from which it proceeded was the Mind of God. You will note that I use the words "top" and "bottom," "up," "down," for convenience only. There is no top nor bottom to an atom of ether.

Now I have described this to you in order that it may form a model for you when you pursue the atom of ether into other substances of denser sort. When we came to those atoms which form the gases of your earth atmosphere we found that they also had a like motion. Each circulated upon itself in precisely the same way as the atom of ether. There were minor differences: the spiral was, in some cases, elongated, in others compressed; the movement was of greater speed or less. But all these movements were spiral, both without and within the atom.

When we came to the atom of the mineral we found the same principle to hold.

And what is true in the single atom obtains also in the atom in aggregate. The movement of the atoms of a planet is spiral. But here it is much retarded by reason of the grossness of the matter which goes to form a planet.

The same is also true of the movements of satellites, and of planets about suns, and of suns about their Center.

But both the mass and also the density of a unit affect the rate of velocity. The speed of the movement of their atoms is slower in those planets which have attained to more density than in others. But even in these the rule holds good that the interior movement is quicker than that on their outer surface, which drags after it very slowly, as if reluctant to move at all. But move it does, and that movement is in the form of a spiral about its axis.

Your moon still endeavors to keep the rule in regard to her orbit. She lifts herself, and she sinks again, as if in vain endeavor to perform her onetime spiral course about the earth. So does the earth in his journey about the sun. His orbit is not a true circle, nor a circle laid upon a true plane. It is erratic and elliptic, both as to pilot and also to level.

And what is true of the atom of ether, and of earth gases, and of earth itself, is also true of the sun and of the constellations. Their movements are in the form of a gigantic spiral about an elliptic formation made up of the suns and their planets.

This we saw on the one side of that broad way. On the other side we saw the spiritual counterpart of these creations: the heavens complementary. And the street between the two took the place of the Borderland which joins the two. You cross a borderland like this when you pass from the earth life into the spirit realms, my son. And so we will leave that Department and come to another, for the street you cross is that between the man of earth and the man of the heavens.

Was there any other principle you observed other than that of the spiral?

Yes. I told you of that because it seemed simple to explain, and also it is fundamental—simple, perhaps, for that reason.

I will try to tell you of another. As the basal stage is left behind the matter becomes more complex and harder of description; but I will try.

We found that the great Lords of Creation begin their work farther back than the etheric atom, and nearer the origin of all. Still, those who deal with the etheric evolution, and onward, are very great and ancient Lords. We therefore went forward to study these vibrations of thought-power where they were more retarded by the density of the material in which they moved. And we found that one of the most difficult tasks we students had ahead of us was to think and to will in the proper way. For to deal with matter creatively the first thing to master is to think in spirals. I cannot further explain that to you. But it is a most difficult habit to achieve: to think spirally.

But you ask for other principle. Let us come to sensitive creation—that of plant life.

We went down a great avenue, on the one side of which was displayed the vegetable life of earth and of other planets, and on the other side, that of their complementary heavens. We found that each species of vegetable life had an analogue in the animal world. There is a reason why this is so, and it has to do with the soul of the plant rather than with its outer manifestation in bark, branch and leaf. But not only, for even there you may glimpse, if you examine closely, the relation between the two: the animal and the vegetable.

I am afraid I don't quite follow you, sir. Could you help me a little further?

Let us begin away from those two realms, and work back to them again; it is the better way.

Here in the heavens we have different orders of beings, differing in authority, differing in power, and in character, and also in ability for one branch of work or another. This also obtains on earth.

So you will find it also in the animal kingdom. Animals have different powers, and some have skill in one direction, some in another. They also differ in character. The horse is more apt at friendship with man than is the snake; the parrot than the vulture.

Now, this principle of analogue, of which I have spoken, may be seen, if only dimly for the most part, obtaining between the vegetable and animal world. We will take the oak tree to represent the vegetable world, and the bird for the animal. The oak tree produces its seed, and lets it fall upon the earth, in order that it may become overlaid and by the warmth of the earth burst its shell and its inner life break forth into outer manifestation. The acorn and the egg are identical in all essentials, both as to their structure and also their manner of incubation. This motion of life—from the inner to the outer—is a universal law, and is never broken. It also has its origin deep down into primordial matter, from whence the present universe came. Remember my words about the etheric atom. For the initial

motion of the atom is interior, where its velocity is acceler-
ated, where it accumulates its momentum. Exteriorly both are
retarded.

So we found the rule in respect of other departments.
There were unifying principles established to which celestial
workers were bound. Among these principles was that of protective covering, and its beauty as presented outwardly, so that
so much pleasure might be afforded to the beholder as should
be consistent with the inner utility; sex, in its two divisions,
active and receptive; circulatory system, as of sap and blood;
respiratory system by pores, and other principles also.

You cannot continue longer, my son. Cease now.

Arnel+.

9

The Spiral Course
of Progress[1]

Friday, March 15, 1918. 5:30–6:27 P.M.

NOW what principles govern material things—that is, the
manifestation of life outwardly in matter—are applicable
also to realms spiritual.

First, as to the spiral, which is itself an analogue in matter of principles which are seen in operation in these spiritual
realms. That must be so, for all movement of atoms material
is the effect of will operative. The Central Will is that of God,
Whose active outpouring passes through the spheres in orderly sequence, and finds ultimate expression in matter. What,
therefore, is seen in matter is the effect of energy passing onward from these spheres. In the case we have named that en-

[1] *Note:* Prior to this message Mr. Vale Owen commenced the sitting by asking the following question: *What is your wish tonight, sir?* Arnel: "To continue our description of the lesson we learned in the Manifestation." G.V.O.: *"I
could not quite understand that last part about the analogues. It seemed rather
pointless to me. Did I get it down correctly?"* Arnel: "Quite. What you missed
was our application. You were too spent to continue. We will give it now."

ergy is seen to issue, in the atom, in spiral activity. This could not be so unless the principle was also found to be active in these spheres through which the life-energy streams. How it is seen here manifest I purpose to show you now.

The Crown of palm leaves was a symbol of this spiral principle, for in that form they were woven, and in the Manifestation I have related, the Angels who sat about the Crown were necessarily also arranged spirally. It was a token of their work as they do it, and it was to read us a lesson by the eye that they took their stations so.

Now, as applied to animal life in creation:

The first motion of sensation is seen in the plant, and there you see clearly illustrated the spiral principle. The bean climbs spirally, as do other climbing plants, some more explicitly and others less perfectly. The veins of the trees also tend to incline from the perpendicular as they traverse the trunk in its length. The plants which climb by tendrils support themselves by a spiral hook. Seeds float afield, or fall to the ground, in a similar curve. All these are consequent on the principle, active as the vibrations proceed through the sun and reach the plant life on earth. These reproduce in miniature his motion along the heavens of space, and, in themselves, mimic the orbits of the constellations.

When we come to animal life we find the same principle at work; for birds do neither fly nor swim in a straight line, but incline out of the straight, and, given a course of sufficient extent, the same formation would be apparent. To the animals, both of ocean and land, the same rule applies, but is not always seen so plainly as in the lower orders of life, because it is here modified by the exercise of free will, which produces motions erratic from the central rule. In inverse ratio, the less freewill enters into the composition the more apparent does the law become. I need only name, by way of example, the snail's shell, and many of the shells of the sea-animals, where instinct is in the place of free will.

On the other hand, where man is concerned, the principle is seen operative most in those matters where his individuality is less apparent than is the general guiding Mind of his race. Thus: civilization proceeds from east to west, from time to time encircling the earth. It obeys the lead of earth's Central Sun. But the sun's meridian does not travel in a right line along the equator, but inclines, now to north, now to south, as earth leans one way or other. This motion of earth is a remnant of the ancient rule, and shows earth's origin from the nebular state, wherein the same spiral movement, obtains. Even so, the path of civilization, encircling earth, never crosses over the same region twice in succession. By the time the civilizing wave reaches the point of longitude which marks its former revolution earth has inclined itself at its poles, the north southward and the south northward, some degrees. As the path of the impact of the sun's radiation upon earth is thus varied, so also is the path of the onward march of civilization, which, by the way, is but another way of saying "revelation." If you think of the location of Lemuria and Atlantis, and their successors in the progress of human experience, you will see my meaning.

Further, not alone in respect of the path it takes locally, but as to achievement also, the principle holds. This is harder to explain to you. Here it is clearly seen by us, for we see the inner mental working of the race, not alone more vividly, but also over a wider range of time. Thus I am able to tell you that the progress of the human race goes ever upward, but in a gigantic spiral nevertheless. I may best be able to give you a hint of my meaning by reminding you of the saying, "There is naught new under the sun." That is not true, but it echoes a truth. You hear, from time to time, that new discoveries have been made, but are found to have been anticipated some thousands of years ago. Well, I would not put it quite in that way. I would say, rather, this new discovery has come about during that period when science is traversing the inclined path just above that section of the inclined path below it in the spiral when its antecedent discovery was made. For the spiral is ever ascending, and ever returning above its circuitous course. And these new inventions are new only in the sense of being adaptations of scientific discoveries in the previous cycle of the spiral of civilization.

Could you, please, give me some illustrations?

The utilization of the molecules of ether for the service of mankind is illustrative of this. You will note that the present advanced state of this branch of science was worked up to very gradually. We will start with the process of combustion by which gas was liberated, heat was generated, and, from the heat, steam was produced. This was followed by the application of this same gas, but discarding the intervening medium of steam. Then a finer system of etheric vibrations was pressed into service, and electricity now is fast supplanting steam. But another step forward has been taken, and what you call wireless waves are beginning to be found more potent still.

Now, all this has been done before, in varying degrees of perfection, by scientists of those long ago civilizations, which have to you become almost a mythical memory. The next step is also seen ahead. It is the substitution of mental waves for the etheric waves. This also some few of the highest and most progressed of those your forerunners compassed in their science. They were not allowed to give forth their knowledge to their fellow-men, who were not progressed enough morally to use it aright. Nor will it be given to the present race of men to perfect this as an exact science until they have further progressed in spiritual competency. Otherwise harm would accrue to the race, and not benefit.

But the present cycle of progress will, in this matter, go beyond that of the cycle last preceding, for at this point in those days they stopped and went no farther. Their decline set in, and what they had come by gradually became absorbed into the spiritual spheres, to be conserved there until the next race had been prepared and brought to such a state of perfection as should qualify them to receive it back again with added momentum inspired into it by its guardians during the ages in which it has rested quiescent in their charge. Call the spiritual spheres interior, and the earth sphere external, and you have the same principle of movement reproduced which we have already attached to the atom of ether.

There is much more than this to the matter, but it is not competent in us to put it in words you would understand. Enough to say the principle we have been scheming to show to you holds good, not alone in respect of the dynamics of science, as I may name what I have instanced presently, but also of the sciences of government, of cultivation of vegetable species and of animals, and the science of astronomy and of chymics (chemistry).

Were astrology and alchemy the two analogues which corresponded with astronomy and chemistry of the present day?

But no, my son, most surely no. We have been speaking to you tonight in eons, not in centuries. Astrology and alchemy are the immediate parents of the two modern sciences. They are in the same cycle of this gigantic spiral of which I speak, and but a few inches apart, almost at the same level of ascent on the inclined plane.

No, but chymics shall serve for a theme for one word more to you ere I say goodnight.

It is the outermost expression of the activity of those High Ones who guide the stream of vibration proceeding from the One Great Central Mind into diversity and differentiation. From unity all these chymical elements proceeded by way of differentiation of that unity into parts, and then into particles, as the life-stream proceeded outward from God, through spirit, to emerge in matter. Then, having reached its lowest point, that impulse is now turned about, and is proceeding upward inwardly. The analytic chymist is obeying this impulse as to its outward course from unity into diversity. The synthetic chymist already is making stumbling and somewhat clumsy attempts to counter this tendency. His endeavors are set from diversity towards unification of elements again. He has turned the outermost spiral of the cosmic atom, when the inward course will continue that same onward urge, to emerge once again on its outer, but ever spiral, path. Remember our words concerning this which we gave you at our last coming, and check our words of tonight by them.

ARNEL+

10

The Cycle of Progress

Friday, March 22, 1918. 5:18–6:45 P.M.
Attempts to shorten the cycle and its result.

LET us this evening pursue our theme of those principles which emerge from such a study of the economic order of the universe of creation as we were able to pursue at the Manifestation which I have described to you.

I have spoken of the spiral principle of the operation of forces, and now I will tell you of another principle of which we learned.

In every department of creative life there is an underlying impulse which those who take in hand the guiding of development have to counter and adapt. That contrary influence is of very ancient origin, and is due to the effect of the endeavors of those who schemed to perfect a manifestation of the Mind of God in matter.

There were at that time, so long ago, some who had in mind to take a shorter path to perfection and others who chose a longer one. These two groups did not clash exactly, but the variety of their endeavors overlapped somewhat, and the confusion which ensued has caused all that men today call evil.

All things are working towards perfection, but so great is the field of activity that the period must necessarily be long, if you count it in days and years. As viewed by those who stand in God His Presence it is neither short nor long, but one continuous event, as a river when considered as a unit embraces the whole from source to sea.

You will see how this diversity in the development of creation emerges even into the outer realms in which your present earth-consciousness functions. For the earth itself is strewn with, and almost made up of, those former trials of wisdom which eventuated in the present accumulation, on the one hand of faculties which are still in process of development, and on the other hand of the materials which have served their purpose in the grand scheme of progress, and have been thrown aside as refuse, as the quality of life became refined and needed more intricate and delicate instruments for its expression. But while this is true of some of these ruins of ages past, others witness to the fact that, in some cases, a direction was taken which led into an impasse where the onward urge found the vehicle inadequate to its expression, became cramped, the pulse of life grew more feeble, faded into inertia, and that line of evolutionary activity came to an end.

Those great mammalia and reptilia, of which you have the remains in fossil form, were very wonderful products of creative energy most skillfully employed. But as viewed from the more advanced standpoint of this present stage of evolution, they appear rude and of clumsy workmanship. Nevertheless, it is well to remember that some of these were the great blocks which were used in the laying of those foundations upon which a very ornate temple of living and progressing energy is today still being built; and, by the contemplation of those foundations, you may estimate how much the building has been improved in design, and also you may realize how great is the altitude of that floor upon which you now stand to view the wide landscape of the heavens afar into those regions of space wherein are still being evolved the workshops of other great Hierarchies who today are, in their own way, fashioning new worlds at the stage where earth was when those foundations of present-day life were laid.

Now, the further principle of which I speak is this: The course of development shall take a twofold line of direction. That direction shall be first outward, from unity into diversity of expression, as we have already explained. But also along with this line of movement shall go its twin, which is, that progress shall take the direction from the spiritual ever towards the material. It is like two runners running their course side by side. The one is named "From Unity into Diversity," and the other is named "From Spirit into Matter." These two must keep pace together. Neither must be allowed to outstrip the other; for they run not to win except they win the outward goal together.

There were those who schemed to shorten this course by arresting the tendency untimely, before the whole outward course had been run, and turning again the urge of creative life inward toward spirit before the outermost post had been reached and rounded. That post is the material expression of this creative activity which your scientists call the Universe. It is not a universe in itself. It is the outer expression of an inner manifestation of a still deeper cycle of development behind which there are those Lords of Creation who by their willful energizing guide the great fleet of sun-systems in their constellations on its voyage through the space of matter towards the port where they shall bend their course round and homeward once again.

But when that happens they shall not sail back upon their wake. For, having accumulated all the richness of manifold expression of life in its activity, as they have traversed the outward stormy course, now they shall sail home through sunnier seas, Master Mariners every one of them, and Princes themselves who have fared forth and won, who when they set out were but rowers and cargo-men.

Now, it was when certain of the Great Creative Lords schemed to shorten that voyage that disaster came. The fleet had voyaged some eternities, and now was to turn in mid-ocean, with full-bellied sails. Here are gales and fierce seas, and the ships were so knocked about that some of them collided and were like to founder altogether. And so it was found that they must sail with the wind, and the course was once again laid toward the original destination. Well, here the fleet has arrived, but the ships are battered in hull and with torn sails and much evidence of the storms they have weathered on the way.

To clear my meaning for you: The Ocean is the realm of Being expressed in outward expansion of the Mind of the Infinite and Ultimate One. The fleet is that Universe which was brought into existence at His command and by the Creative Lords of whom I spoke. The port to which the outward course was to be laid is the present material expression of this Universe wherein you find yourself today. The homeward course is that to which you are now tending; for the outermost point has been reached and is just being rounded. It is the rounding of that point, it is the turning of the vessels out of the harbor of material inertia towards the more active element of the open sea, which is the cause of the much unrest in all directions at the present time. Soon the sails will fill and set steadily athwart the hulls, the vessels will settle down to their homeward course, and both officers and crews, now homeward bound, will be of cheery disposition, and ever, as the fleet ploughs through the ocean of being, nearer and nearer will it come to the port from which it set out so many ages ago, and gladness and peace will gather about them as they go for the welcome which awaits them aport far away ahead into the east where the light is already breaking and the smile of God is seen.

When did the trouble begin, Arnel? I mean, at what stage of progress did those Creative Lords begin to make mistakes?

Much farther back than I am able to trace it, my son. Also, although from your point of view it seems as if they erred in their reckoning, yet it is not of necessity so. I stand beyond you in the line of progress, but a little way ahead, and yet I and those who are my companions here seem to see that what we should call mistaken will be found to be, when we arrive in port, not what we should call it now. What we see and think to be evil and imperfect is only the outermost lapping of the wavelets upon the stony beach of a miniature islet, a speck in the midst of an ocean which is infinite. These wavelets seem to break up into spray. But they go back to their big mother notwithstanding, and become again—well, ocean, no more, no less. As we may not appraise the profundity of her deeps, and the majesty of her swelling bosom by the egg-cup full of spray cast upon a speck of land in her midst, so we may not estimate the wisdom of the Great Ones by what mite we are able to sense of their Infinitude.

One ant said to another, "We, my brother, are wiser than the aphis, for she is our slave to serve our needs." "Yes," said the other. But an anteater came that way, and all their wisdom came to naught, and vanished in a trice. And the anteater, as she stretched herself to doze in the sun, murmured as she lay, "That was not all the wisdom there is, which I heard as I came hither, for lo, I myself have compassed it whole. And I believe there be those who have within them greater store of wisdom even than I."

If man be as the ant for wisdom, yet there be also those who are of stature more stalwart, and of strength to match. These are slower to come at a conclusion, and they are not less wise, my son.

Arnel+

11

The Creative Hierarchies

Monday, March 25, 1918. 5:20–6:00 P.M.

SO far, my son, we have but touched the outer fringe of the garment of God, which covers, and yet reveals His form of light and beauty. And we may penetrate a little deeper, if you will give us your mind, for there be many things to say, and we would say what we are able through you according to your capacity of transmission of our thoughts.

It were well that men should bear with us when we try to express God His purpose in the events which they see enacting around them on their daily course of life. For we be very intimate in the affairs of every one of you, and are only let by what obstacles you put between the flow of our energies and their objectives in the world. And we, of whom I speak, are but very little ones in the great scheme of life as it surges through the constellations, bathing all in the one great sea of life which fills infinity with its energy and finds no door to bar it out wherever it would go.

We have already told you some of those effects, and of their causes mediate between the Universe as expressed in matter and the Great Central Source from which comes all that is, and to which all shall gather when the great field is reaped, and the Harvest Home is due.

Now, as we stood in that great Crown Hall, we were spell-bound by the pressure about us of this same great force. For there stood the Word manifest in the Christ of God aloft, calm, majestic, and clothed in beauty. And, mark you, we were at that moment in the presence of Him and of what passed outward through His Presence and came from deeps of Being unknown to us except by what we might glimpse through Him. Thus we felt this pressure of potent energy, flung outward upon us through Him, of weight and compass beyond our capacity to assimilate. But what we did understand was that He was there to radiate abroad some of the light within and behind His personality for our instruction and uplifting and more perfect joy.

Until the great display of creative departments was fully opened out around Him, He stood in perfect stillness, as if His every faculty was being pressed to its uttermost tension to produce for us these wonders. When this was done and the grand total completed, He sighed, and then there appeared a throne behind Him, and many beings of wonderful beauty emerged into visibility and stood behind it, still and adoring. He turned and mounted the seven steps, and sat within the throne, and then before the steps there appeared a pathway, which stretched outward towards that section of the encircling Hierarchies which stood before the race of Mankind. These passed up the avenue and stood before the throne and paused with one consent, and bent their gaze aground, while from their realm behind them came the sound of singing, and the hum of music, like some great diapason from the womb of space, far, far away, as if the worlds had stretched between them strings for harping, and their murmurs came to witness to their unity with those who stood in the Presence of their Lord.

Then there came from behind the throne a radiant Prince who stood to the right hand of the Christ and spoke to those who had drawn near. His words were quite distinctly heard by us, but the anthem from the worlds afar continued the while he told them that now was the Christ of God vindicated in what Sacrifice He had made for the expression of Love in the whole Universe of God.

Arnel+

* * *

THE BREAK OF A YEAR

Note by G. V.O.: Here the power failed and I was unable to proceed. The power failed because I was overtaxed with parish work—war work, keeping in touch with the lads away (over 200) and their families at home—the double harness was too much for me, so they broke off suddenly in the midst of the above message. On Wednesday, April 10, 1918, my wife, whilst using the Planchette, asked the following question: "Why was the writing with George stopped?" Then her father replied, through the Planchette, "Let me explain. George was feeling the strain very much, and wished to stop, particularly as the summer was coming on. The rest was needful, and will be beneficial. But he must not think it is finished yet."

Note by H. W. Engholm: It will be noticed that nearly a year—from March 25, 1918 to February 19, 1919—intervened between the receipt of the message given in the last chapter and the message which now follows entitled "The Christ Creative."

Some details may be added here regarding this interruption to those given in the Note from Mr. Vale Owen.

It appears that towards the close of the summer of 1918, calls to sit again in the vestry came to Mr. Vale Owen through his wife. On October 24 he resumed the sittings and continued them until November 1.

The communications received did not continue the narrative which had been interrupted on March 25, and he doubted that they were given wholly under the influence of Arnel. He discontinued the sittings.

On January 14, 1919, in response to further requests, he again began to sit. He then received a detailed narrative of the progress of one man from death through the dark realms to the borderland of the regions of light. This was completed on February 14.

In Mr. Vale Owen's opinion these communications were given him to prepare him again for the task of receiving messages from Arnel; for on February 19 Arnel resumed his account of the great assembly at the University of the Five Towers, and, from then until April 3, described the enterprise there undertaken. It will be observed that, apart from an explanatory statement of two sentences, the account was continued as if there had been no interruption.

12

The Christ Creative

Wednesday, February 19, 1919. 5:46–7:06 P.M.

WE who are with you tonight are of that company who a year ago were describing to you the ceremony in the Crown Hall. At that time we were obliged to cease, as you remember, for you were spent of power. We now take up that theme once again and continue it here and now.

The first of those hierarchies to approach the Christ in praise and That One Who sent Him was that of the human kind. Then a herald came forward and addressed the assembled multitude in their several departments. These were of development diverse, some were more forward than others. And to each he spoke in their turn, to guide and to encourage them in their forward urge of evolutionary progress.

This much in brief. Now to the next stage of the ceremony. Round the Throne in which the Great Christ Creative sat there appeared a cloud of vapor. Very beautiful it was to see it as the colors invaded it and mingled within it like web and woof. Then from the rear of the Throne and of the cloud there shot up a circle of rays, fan-shaped and spread high and wide, while He sat in the lower middle of them.

They were of blue and green and amber, these rays, and were heavenly projections of those forces which are generated from the material departments of His realm—the realm phenomenal in substance of matter of which the earth and planets and stars are made.

Then the cloud all in movement condensed upon itself and its various hues so arranged themselves that when it contracted to form a mantle we saw them once again in their appropriate and relative places. For the Mantle when it had sat itself down upon Him and had enwrapped His Form about as He sat there rapt and still was very beautiful. The great piece of it was blue, dark and deep blue, but of brightness withal. The edging was of gold and inside this edging was a border and it lay spread out upon the pavement and settled upon the steps. This border was broad and of gold, silver, green, with crimson and amber in two broad lines on the boundary of it inward. The blue robe had upon it at large intervals the semblance of a crown inverted. And it had a collar of pearl upon the shoulders of it. The collar shone forth many hues. It was not pearl-gray, but—how shall I say it to you? It shone from within and sent forth rays about His head, not obscuring His face from us but framing it in a halo of radiance. Viewed in perspective with the rayed background it looked like the nucleus from whence those rays issued forth. But this was not so, except as it appeared to us. Upon His Head was no crown but a circlet only of white and red which bound his hair about behind the ears, somewhat after the fashion of our Diadem of Worship of which I told you.

You are careful to give me these colors in detail, Arnel. What is their significance?

I cannot give you the detail of explanation as I have given to you the detail of the colors as they appeared to us and were so beautifully and intentionally disposed in their groups. But I will tell you broadly and that is as much as you could understand.

The rayed background was the universe of matter which for those who have eyes and ears serves to display the figure of Him, the Christ, and to throw into relief the benign aspect of His appearing. The circlet coronal was the distilled essential of humanity both of earth and those who had passed on into the hither spheres.

It was of red and white. Had that a meaning?

Yes. It betokened the transition of humanity out of the spheres of forcefulness, desire, and self-assertion into those of attunement with the One Light in Whom all colors blend into restful peace as they who make up those rays attune themselves in company. This is the transition from the red into the white. And yet that white light is the most perfect of all as it is most potent also. Those who stand without to view see a snowy stretch of arctic cold and stillness. But those within that light see its component hues each in its own great beauty and in their mingling feel the warmth of their glow. To them without white light is cold. To them within it is the glow of love and of peace.

Have you been within the white light, Arnel?

Nay, my son, not wholly within, but just upon the doorstep of that shrine. And there I only came by greatly daring and much forcefulness of will exerted for that purpose, but that one time alone and by permission. It was not I who laid his hand upon the door, but one great in the Service of the Christ Creative. He came behind me lest I should fail of my hold upon my will were I to look upon his high beauty at that moment. He reached over my shoulder and cast his cloak about me and before my eyes, and then pushed open the door a little way and for a moment held it so. Thus, my eyes shaded and my form veiled by his mantle, I saw and felt the radiance within that very glorious Temple of the Presence. And it has sufficed me, my son, I know what human kind shall be one day when He has dealt with all the tale of His operative energies and all is consulate in Him. Now His face is towards us lower ones, and the human race behind us, of whom we are the heavenly skirmishers. In that day He shall turn about and lead His redeemed myriads towards the Father's Throne, Himself then truly one with them. In that day also all the red in the circlet shall have become blended into the white and the white shall glow a little more warmly for its tincture.

Now, my son, you have turned me aside so that I have spoken all this upon that circlet coronal. What further shall I say of the mantle of blue than this: as the background of material essence showed up the form and shape of Him and of His mantle and His Throne; as the diadem blended in one humanity of earth with humanity's potential exaltation onward into heavens of spirit, so the robe covered all of the Body of Him by means of Whom all Creation evolved outwardly from the Father: in that robe were blended all those great forces which move and enable and vivify matter and organism. Some of these you know: electricity, ether, which is not alone inert but has a force of its own: magnetism also, and the motive force of light-rays, and also others more sublimate. These all blended in His mantle to hide His form and yet to outline it and the Throne.

What is the signification of the inverted crown—why inverted?

In place of the crown He wore that circle of red and white. One day He shall wear the crown itself when the circle has become all white and has been absorbed into the candid white of His personality. Then the mantle shall be lifted, spread out and thus it will float heavenward and now itself inverted, shall it be displayed itself as the background of Him and of His Throne in place of the rays material which shall then be no more seen. Then also, when in that far Great Day He stands to review His myriads once again, over Him and around Him shall those many bright crowns be seen, not now inverted, but erect. They are of divers species in design. But all then in their normal position shall point toward the further glories as the Christ shall marshal His redeemed and lead them onwards in their brave array.

ARNEL+

13

The Hymn of Lamel

Thursday, February 20, 1919. 5:25–6:40 P.M.

ANON the Cloak of Blue became vaporized and melted away into the atmosphere. Then the Christ Creative sat within His Throne but changed of raiment now. Upon His shoulders there was a cape of that same deep blue, but it fell away on either side of Him and beneath it was displayed a vest of gold which reached upon His knees and fell below a little as He sat there. It was belted with a broad band of green with gold in it and it had a hem of ruby color. The circlet still was upon His head and within the circlet a band of stars scintillating many hues about Him. In His right hand He held a crown of dull white metal. It was the only thing about Him which had no radiance and was by the same token the more to be marked by us who saw it.

Now He arose and laid the crown upon the steps before His feet and stood to face us. Awhile He spoke His will to us. He said,

"You have but lately seen what is toward within my Kingdom. Yet there are who may not come to look upon its inner beauties as you have done. In those far outlands they are able only with dim thoughts to think of Me, for they are not yet come to their full awakening. Tell these friends, good Lamel, of the present estate and coming destiny of those so far removed."

Then upon the first step of the Throne stood a man who was of those who attended and had waited in silence on either side the stairs. He was clad in white with a silver belt upon his left shoulder and about his loins. He therefore spoke to us these words and as he spoke them the voice of him seemed to be made up of many chords of music, not one note, but multiple. The tones were resonant, so much that they floated forth into the air about us and passed above us until each note struck some gossamer string of music and it responded. One and another aerial thong was thus set vibrating until the whole welkin was tremulant with music as if a thousand harps were at their business harmonic.

Yet were his words not the less clearly heard, but became the more tuneful and descriptive, more at one with the nature of the things and acts they signified, more full of body and substance, as you should take a picture of black on white and turn it into colors. So there was life in his song and not music only.

So he addressed himself to his theme.

"What if the Presence of Him seem to be far removed away in yonder high Realms of Glory? He is here withal, for we are progeny of Him and in His life we live.

"What if we be to them afar down in those lands where light is dim as He to us? They be our brethren still and we to them akin.

"What if they know not where their life is hid; by which they live and live amiss? They feel and grope and grip but one small quartern. Yet they do at least in this aright and stretch their hands all blindly hitherward with palm upturned.

"But in their night they stumble and then stray into the by-ward tracks. Their onward course is hindered, while they who see a little await the return of those errant who see less still, and they come forward slowly but as in one company together.

"What if the way be long, shall we not also await their coming hitherward that they and we may move together on-ward, upward, both more greatly blest in mutual love, so giving and receiving each to other, both?

"Yet shall we wait, and only wait, while they towards us stumble on their way? Or shall we go and bring them, as the Christ sometime put off His robe of glory and, clad in lowly garb and work-a-day, sought out those sheep who strayed, as these do stray, and brought to earth what earth would salve, that time ago?

"That this should be the powers on High made marvel and they who hover over cosmoi greater than this of ours bowed low before Him as, of reverence due, they made obeisance to the Son of GOD in His humility. For they who are so great in wisdom learned now more greatly still how Love was fash-ioned for the Universe, and the whole Universe is both lovable and of Love.

"So what if He be high from Whom is all? we have His Christ.

"What if there be beyond, below, those more distant set than we? the Christ reached them too.

"What if they be weak of limb and dim of sight? He is their strength and He shall be their Lamp to lead them so they stray not over much, nor finally be lost.

"And if they do not know these brighter realms as we do know them to our joy, some day they shall rejoice with us, and we with them—some day.

"But which of us shall take the crown, with strength ap-pointed to this war? Who shall essay to place it upon his head? for it is dull and heavy in its weight today.

"Yet, let him who is strong and simple in his faith stand here and take the crown.

"What if it be now lusterless? It shall some day be radiant with the light which is now hid within it, when the task is made complete, some day."

There was a silence great when he had ceased. Only the vibrations of the music ambient about us hovered still wistful and caressing, loath to still themselves into silence until the singer had been answered.

Then when no one came forth, none daring this high venture, the Christ Himself descended and took up the crown and placed it upon His head, and it sank deep upon His brow, for it was very heavy. Yea, my son, it is heavy upon Him today, but there is now beginning to show a luster about it which it had not then.

So He stood and called to us, "And who will go forth with Me of you, my brethren?"

And when we heard His voice we knelt, one and all of us, beneath His Benediction.

Arnel+

14

Earth and Mars

Wednesday, February 26, 1919. 5:35–6:50 P.M.
And what is this high venture of which you speak, Arnel?

OF that I am about to tell you, my son, and you be able to
write it down, for it is of moment to those who shall find
within their hearts some desire to understand events of these
late centuries.

You shall mark that the enterprise had not its conception at the Tower of the Angels. No, that was born ages ago in
Realms higher than those of which I have spoken hereto. At
every age, in its beginning, the High Ones, so we are told, take
counsel. Results accruing from sometime ages are gathered
and laid before them. Those of ages very ancient are rehearsed
in tabulated form and briefly. Those of the nearer ages are giv-
en in greater detail. Those of the ages last past in full. These are
considered in their bearings upon events at that time proceeding on earth. Then the cognate planets have their hearing, and
next both earth and them together. So the Council gets agait,
and, with no hurry, comes at such conclusion as, when put into
operative form for the next age, will be harmonious with the

acts of other Hierarchies who have in charge the guidings of planets other than this of earth.

Please explain the phrase "cognate" planets.

I speak of those other worlds which have most near relation to Earth both as to degree of development and of the trend of its evolution; those planets which have followed a free-willed career most like that of Earth; and also have attained to a degree of intellect and spirit most in accord with Earth in its present age. These are not only those which are most near Earth in spatial distance, but, as I say, in intellectual and spiritual content.

Can you name them?

I could, but refrain, lest I be said to expound the obvious. I see a phrase in your mind which I appropriate to my service: "to play to the gallery." Moreover there are planets which are not visible to you, albeit they be within the solar range, which must be considered in the matter. Also there are some few which are on the border of this system but obey the pull of another star, and yet are cognate much with Earth. And two there be which are not only within the Solar range—

Solar system?

Solar System, yes—not only within it but material in substance also, but of which your science at present takes no account, but will some day. But this is prophecy with which we have naught to do herein. So these counsels being well sifted, I say, the chart is marked for the next voyage of earth, commands are issued, and away goes the ship free of rudder bands, prow abreast the open sea.

What position does the Christ occupy in these Councils?

This Council, singular, you should write; only one Council, but meeting age by age. The personnel of that Council is not static in absolute, yet it changes but little in a few eons period, they are so high, those Great Creative Lords. Of them the Christ is President.

King?

I should not write it so, no. King of the Heavens inferior to that Heaven in which this Council holds court; of that Council president. This is of my knowledge delegate only, not of that to which I have attained empirically, but of that which has come to me and my brethren of this Sphere by transition through those spheres which stretch above us. See you now? Or shall I still pursue?

Thank you, sir, I think I see what you mean as well as it is possible for me to do.

So, it is well you speak what you do. It pleases me. For not I nor those in realms ahead of me some way are able to understand except in figure what those high Councils really are. In this same guise I have handed it to you and you content yourself therewith. It is well.

Now let me go forward. You see now that He Who is President of the Council, the Son of GOD elect, is He Who sallies forth to see the venture through. That is, in the eyes of those who work with me, as it should be: that He who shoulders the responsibility of a decision make bold to put it into operation and see it to an end. This did the Christ, today He is in your midst with this present Mission just beyond halfway accomplished, having reached the earth and turned about on the upward, homeward march. Do not wonder at my words. I am about to tell you of this matter in more of detail. That was an arrow in the bull. We will leave it there. It will serve as a mark to guide us to our goal, lest we stray away into the many by-paths on our journey. These have interest, and are not without instruction and much beauty also. But they concern us not here. I want to tell you of the campaign as it has reference to Earth. We leave the effect of it on those other worlds aside and speak of Earth alone, or at least in principal. Except this one alone. You were curious of our words about other planets. Now I will mention Mars. So much thought has been directed upon that solitary planet of late years that it has become foremost of interest to those who are not of science but of ordinary citizenship. That is so, my son?

Yes, I think you are not far out.

The reason is reflex. The people of Mars began it. They have directed a vast amount of thought waves in your direction and you have responded—no, more than that. The reason of this intercommunion is found in the kinship between the people of Earth and Mars. Some of your astronomers speak of them so familiarly as to call them Martians. That would amuse them as it also gives us a pleasant little shiver of happy mirth. Well, those who know the Martians so well tell you they be much ahead of you in intellectual development. Do not they so, my son?

Yes, quite correct. They do say so.

They are in error. The people of Mars are, in some things, ahead of you of Earth. In other matters not a few, they lag behind you. I have been there. I know this. But these things you shall in time compass by your science normally, and then they shall be all your own, and you will be the more justly proud to know them. That is why we often refrain and bring restraint upon our clacking tongues. It is why I do so now.

You say you have been to Mars?

Even as they of Mars have been to us and to Earth. See you, my son, we do these things here efficiently. I am one of those who were embodied in that army of the Christ at the Tower. Other armies had been gathered, and others still were added later. Not one of all those myriads but is most carefully schooled for his one individual task in hand.

You train your own armies in like manner. Some have duties on this wise and others on that. It was of moment to the able execution of my own part that I should know of the state and progress of peoples other than my own of Earth. To that end I went to one University after another, so to say it. Very good. One of those Universities was at the Temple of the Holy Mount, one at the Tower and the Five Domes, and another at Mars.

What was your special work, may I ask, Arnel?

You speak of the past when you ask me "was." My task is of the Present. I am about it tonight here with you, my son, and thank you for your good aid to its advancement.

Arnel+

15

The Christ Sphere

Thursday, February 27, 1919. 5:30–6:10 P.M.
The events you have just related occurred in Sphere Eleven, as I understand. Is that so, Arnel?

THAT is so, my son, according to the enumeration of the Spheres as my Lord Zabdiel gave it to you. I see the point of your question: I see it half-formed in your mind. I will presently deal with the matter and clear it away and then to my narrative.

I have told you already that the conception of this enterprise had its genesis not in the Sphere Eleven but in realms much more exalted. You have read of the Christ Sphere. That is a real entity, but is understood by some in one way and by some otherwise. The spheres are so constituted both as to content and bounds, as to be not competent of any rigid tabulation in your philosophic habit of thought. If we and others speak of them we must divide and classify them, however; and this we do for your better understanding. But the method of classification is not of universal acceptance. It is no dogma with us. Yet if you search beneath the outer wording you will find a certain agreement among those who transmit their messages.

Some say there are spheres seven and the Seventh is that of the Christ. Well, so be it. Zabdiel and I have spoken of spheres up to the Eleventh. Now, as we have marked them off, that of the Christ would be two sevens and one. In this way: two of these spheres of ours make one of those who speak of seven only. But methinks these should the rather say, not that the Seventh is the sphere which contains the Christ, but the highest known of those which the Christ contains.

In our enumeration the Sphere Fourteen—or the twofold Seven—is the highest Sphere of which we of Sphere Eleven have any real cognizance. We are not yet capable of assimilating instruction of what obtains in those Spheres superior to the Fourteenth. So we say that, inasmuch as we know the Christ to be omnipresent in that Sphere, needs must that He personally be of a Sphere at least one beyond. For there is no mite of all the circumference of that Sphere where He is not found in presence. If He, then, contain that Sphere in whole within Himself, Himself must also be produced beyond. Thus the two Sevens and the One. That is so far as we here are able to reach in our reasonings on what instruction we have been given. So we say that, in this manner of reckoning, the Sphere of the Christ is the Sphere Fifteen which includes within itself all those fourteen Spheres inferior. This much we say, and yet refrain from definition of the Sphere Fifteen, either as to its bounds or conditions, for of them we know not. But wherever its bounds be set, if set they be, it is from that Sphere Fifteen that power and authority are given to those who rule in the Spheres below.

That is the limit of our imagining; beyond is to us the great Unknown. I am able, however, to tell you one more thing and not break my caution—I must ever be guarded of myself that I give you not surmise under guise of knowledge.

It is this: That Council of the High Powers of which I spoke is the same which gathers for deliberation from age to age. Their decrees are registered at times in earth records when revelation is made of them to those who are able to receive them.

Thus that Council met when the material cosmos was devised.

Arnel+

16

Angel Helpers

Friday, February 28, 1919. 5:38–6:38 P.M.

IT met again when man became and stepped out of the vast chamber of agelong sleep and slow awaking into the brightening dawn of responsive activity and, for the first time, gazed abroad on those realms of future conquest to see what he would do. These, or some Council delegate of These perchance, noted the passing of Atlantis and, in later ages, those times of stress when some new element of man's potential greatness travailed in its struggle for self-assertion in the economy of further progress of the race. The late impetus was given to your sciences of the phenomenal from the same far realm. Men thought that phase the crown of the wisdom of those ages behind them. But finality is not found in this marshalling of material array, and the royal progress still continues on its road. For not here is the City of the Crowning, but away to heights beyond. You have just made transit of the valley and gathered the pebbles from the streams therein as you passed. You bring them with you now against you meet the lapidary. That shall be some day and he will burnish those pebbles bright and beautiful for the kingly crown. But he dwells not in the valley, nor among the rises where now your way is laid, but up among the highlands where the light strikes full and warm. Here is the Porch of the Palace Royal where dwells the King His Court, but Himself is afoot on active service way down there below with His myriads where He once again walks earth unseen and in His train we march who speak to you and do what work He has given us to do.

Do I understand you aright, Arnel, that the Christ is at the present time on the earth plane and that you and many others take your orders from Him?

From whom else should we take them? Note you, my son, the remarkable forces at work, and judge all fairly. Your science, intoxicated of its own exaltation, has made one more leap and toppled over out of the material into the ethereal—this against those same precepts which urged it on. Signs and wonders are spoken of of divers sorts, and what was once a whisper now gives place to declamation. Look around you and you will see, reflected in the waters over all the earth, the smiling faces of us myriads, all at work and busy always. We are silent, but you hear us; we are unseen, but our fingers ripple every wave. Men say they feel us not, and yet our presence envelops you and we make merry to be poking those same fingers of ours into every pie you make. We do not steal your plums, nay, but the pie is the sweeter for our contributions.

A tinker left his pewter trencher upon the seat where he had eaten his evening meal, out in the porch to his cottage, and went to his bed forgetting it. The old cat, in the darkness, came and found what meat he had left and ate it up. Then for bed she stepped within the circle which she had found so savory. But it was uncommon hard and many times she turned her round and round to make her a snuggery there. But naught did she save to polish that trencher with her soft fur coat as it had never been so bright before. At dawn the tinker sallied forth and in the morning sun the pewter shone like plate of gold.

"Now," said the tinker, "here be strange doings. The meat is gone, but the trencher remains to me. That the meat be gone spells 'Thief,' yet that the trencher remains, and all brightly polished, cries 'Good friend.' But, being reasonable man of mind, methinks the solution of the matter lies this way: I ate the meat myself, and while I drank my mug of ale I, meditating on the stars and other high matters, polished it the while on my jerkin, gathering combings of the clouds, as men of mind will do. And here comes cat to verify. See you, cat, is not this pewter bright and did not I, your master, burnish it? Or, of your uncanny wisdom, tell me who?" And the cat made answer, "Me," and forbore to finish her "meow," being a cautious cat. For in the trencher she saw her own face reflected. And the tinker said, "Poor dumb beast. Well, it is well your master has both wisdom and speech to voice it."

So he took the trencher within and, with pride, he laid it upon the settle for his wife to see. But she looked out of the window and said only, "Cat settles herself for sleep. Wise cat is she, and ever was."

And I suppose in this parable of yours, Arnel, you are the cat?

But one hair of the cat, my son, but just one hair am I, no more.

Arnel+

17

Purging
of the Sphere's Interior

Monday, March 8, 1919. 5:37–6:55 P.M.

OUR first business to take in hand after that stage wherein I was called to join in the enterprise was the clarification of those spheres inferior. All these were in touch with earth nearly, and had given of their guiding in the ages preceding. The inverse is also of fact, namely, that they had received into their composition such contribution as earth made from generation to generation. This of necessity, because the spheres are recruited from earth, and those nearest to earth more immediately.

As people come over by way of death's port they are, as you know, taken in hand and helped on to clearer views of life. Old errors are gradually purged away, new light is gradually accepted and assimilated. But keep it ever in mind that no rigid law binds life, either of earth or of the heavens. Free-will is sacred and operative continuously and universally. It was in consequence of this element, this supreme factor, its presence in the spheres, that it so happened that, in the process of puri-

fying those who came over, they also received into themselves
a certain degree of default. Most of the error so brought over
had undergone a process of transmutation into elements beneficent and good; but not all. This same free will, so fugitive
of logic and of all bonds soever, had permitted of some elusive
erratic particles to mingle in the life of these spheres and to
remain suspended in their atmosphere. This element had accumulated. It had not attained to any very serious proportion,
and, in the ordinary course of things, would have been left to
the development of future ages. But just at that time this was
not good to do. For this reason:

The trend of human development had been downward
and outward, toward and into matter. That was God His purpose, namely, that He manifest Himself in detail of form phenomenally. Because this way was downward set, the elements
of error increased in greater measure than the reservoir of spirit into which they were poured from earth was able to absorb,
assimilate and to transmute. It was, therefore, necessary that
on our way to earth we clarify these spheres. And this we did
preparatory to our more intensified operations on earth itself.

Why "more intensified"?

Always earth is operated on from these realms. This was to
be an intensification of those operations, an access of dynamic
urge of such degree and impetus as should serve to send the
hoop spinning safely down the lower slope and give it a good
start on the upward turn on its way toward the peaks across
the valley. This has now been accomplished, and the ascent is
well begun.

So we acted as a film of gelatinous compound acts upon a
cask of wine. As we slowly descended, a steady cloud of workers, ever vigilant and curious and close knit together, we bore
down with us and beneath us all those elements discordant,
down, ever downward, toward earth. This has continued for

generations past. And as we, being constant in our movement and irresistible, lessened the space between our far-spread array and earth its plane, those elements between us and you became ever more concentrated upon their own content. By and by they began to flatten out over earth itself like a thick vapor all in movement, ever becoming more frantic and frenzied as the elements of which it was composed jostled each the others, wanting room.

This commotion increased and extended as we pressed more closely round the sphere of earth; and ever more and more they mingled in earth's life and policies until they at last burst through the encircling envelope ethereal altogether and became of the economy of the world of men.

Behind, above us, we, looking upward, saw the heavens cleansed of this agelong rising vapor, and brighter and more beautiful for their cleansing.

Below us, where that same vapor had been compelled—well, my son, need I enlarge? He among you who has eyes to see may see the effect of our operations ever more potent these few centuries last ago. It were a dullard indeed who should say today he did not see our work in its effects.

But when these dire forces broke into your atmospheric belt—so to borrow a phrase from your sciences—then we, still pursuing them in their steps, burst through also hard at heel. And here we be, arrived and in possession of the field at last.

But, my son, my son, it has been a long, grim battle of the forces, aye, long and grim, and fierce withal betimes, my son. We have won through it with the good comradeship of the manhood of your race, and their women, all so wonderful to us who have, time and often, marveled in our joy to find such mettle in your womankind. Well, well, you have suffered, you of earth, full sorely, and we love you more because of that. But know, my son, if we gave blows straight and heavy in the fray, we also took our wounds not few nor slight. We suffered, too, with you. And we were glad we suffered when we came close enough to see how you were suffering, too, so greatly. It helped us as we helped you, both. It helped us much to see it.

Are you speaking now of the Great War, Ariel?

Of that as climax. But ever in increasing force, as I have already said, this war has gone on for these ages past. Its martyrs have been many, and many phases has the war passed through. You would count it strange were I to table for you all of these in total. I name but a few of these phases: the phase religious and theological, artistic, political and democratic, scientific, the warlike phase which took such vogue this last millennium as to absorb well-nigh all dynamics into its wide-open maw.

But we have won through together, and now together we will foot it onward up the heavenly ways toward the sunlit peaks ahead. The valley lies behind us in the gloom. So. We take our staff and turn our faces upward, and on our war-marked limbs from yonder peaks there falls a gleam which makes our wounds into garlands upon our breasts and bracelets around our wrists and of our torn and soiled raiment lace of filigree beautifully wrought. For our wounds are honorable wounds, and our garments witness to our deeds. And our great and common Captain is the Christ Who knows what battle is, aye, and wounds withal.

My blessing, my son, I am not sad tonight, but the battle is yet scarcely silent to me today, and within me stirs the heavenly slogan still, and my hand grips tight betimes to think of it and what we did, and more of what we saw, and of the tears we shed for you of earth, my son. Aye, we were tearful, more times than one were we, and more times still. For we had vision clear of Him Who led us on, and your poor sight was heavy with the mists, so you saw Him but dimly, when at all. And we were pitiful for you all, my son, because of that same thing.

And yet through all our tears, responsive of your own, we looked upon you in wonder, and not a little awe, to see you fight so. But oh, how you fought, you sons of men, how well you fought! I say we stood still to wonder, until we minded us and one another that you too were warriors of the same King and Captain even as ourselves. Then we understood and, weeping still, rejoiced and turned our gaze towards Him where He stood commanding; and so we made our worship to Him on your behalf.

My blessing, I cannot further now, my son. My blessing to you; and to my brother men of earth my greeting in great love and benediction.

Arnel+

18

Reason
for the Expedition

Wednesday, March 5, 1919. 5:30–6:22 P.M.

WHAT I have given to you, my son, is an account of the
enterprise so far as it came within my own and personal
cognizance. I have given it in a lump, and not in detail. I shall
now speak to you of some of the incidents of which I was self-
witness during the time of our progress earthward and on our
arrival. But I will begin by telling you this:

Our operative descent was continuous and irresistible. It
never rested and its pressure never was removed. The closeness of our ranks was never destroyed. Nothing from below
could break us through. But the individual details were not
ever constant. I speak in earth words and use your earth ideas
when I say that our various companies were from time to time
relieved. Then they betook them on their ways aloft to rest in
their proper homes awhile, or make some softer and less strenuous expedition among the free realms of the heavens of God.

For the enterprise pressed earthward was local and, as to
spatial comparisons, very small. The whole field of our opera-

tions did but fill a minute speck in an outlying corner of the cosmos of matter. The significance of it was of spiritual kind. I have already said that the effect of earth policies had been felt even in those spheres somewhat removed from earth. But this effect was beginning to be of wider extent and had been felt on other planets, so that some of their dwellers were experiencing a sense of shrinking, some were bewildered and muddled as to the cause, not knowing its origin. On other worlds the origin was sensed and earth writ down a troubled and troublesome member of the planetary confraternity—these the more spiritually advanced. Had not we, who knew earth by actual sometime inhabitation, taken the matter in hand, it would have been dealt with initially from those planets. Those who have become so evolved as to have compassed the art of intercommunication already had begun to exchange counsel. Their motives are very noble and spiritually high. But their methods are of their own evolvement and are not such as earth would have understood. They would have been so severe as to have produced such an access of God-denial such as would have thrown you back a brace of centuries just when you most needed a forward push. Think of this when you are troubled by thinking of the sufferings of those who have led the world these thousand years past and those who lead today.

But it was made known to those planetary worlds that the Christ had taken the matter in hand and then they summarily offered Him their aid in supplement. This He accepted and has used them in reserve, so to say it. They have sent to us of their virtues in a stream of power to reinforce our own. So have they sustained us in greater strength, and so also has the fight been shortened.

Keep these few things in your mind, therefore, the while I tell you of our doings in more detail. Those incidents are such as will serve to help you to understand something of past history from the causative point of view. In future times men will study history more from this inner side of it, and will then be able to correlate the outer events of the world's progress in more understandable form than is presently the case.

It is so strange that men should take so small account of us and our doings. For you do dwell upon the earth widespread and with large spaces unpeopled. So you in total are still but few. We encompass earth about on every hand and our ranks spread back upward through the steppes and stories of the serried heavens. So we be many, and each one of us of power greater than the most of you. Ah well, the dawning light will send its rays aloft and search us out in our hiding-places amid the light and brightness of the spheres. Then earth will feel less lonely as it rolls along the meadows of the void. Earth will know in that day that all about those meadows fairies play and elves besport themselves in their merriment and that earth is not lonely but at one with the myriads of the redeemed of earth who have linked up humankind with those afar who dwell on planets some of which you see of a clear night and others which are not visible to you of earth. Nor will they be until you put off from your low-lying shores and sail your boat toward the open sea, toward the great expanse, toward the western region of the sun.

ARNEL+

19

The Heavenly Armies of the Christ

Thursday, March 6, 1919. 5:40–6:45 P.M.

FAR out upon the heavenly steppes were flung the armies of the Christ. One beyond one recurring they rose in their ranks and degrees. I with my own companies stood upon a terrace which at that present seemed to be suspended in mid-heaven, neither atop nor at the bottom of that great ocean of beings, each drop a warrior with his own task apportioned. For a marvel had been wrought which even to us of the Sphere Eleven was new and solitary.

The preparation of us all for our entering into the fray had gone on apace with divers effects upon us. One was that, while our magnetic capacity had been enlarged in each one of us by the inpouring of virtues both from the heavens above us and from those planetary rulers of whom I told you, our faculty of vision had also been enlarged beyond the ordinary, so that we were enabled to see afar into regions sealed to us hereto. The purpose of this was the co-ordination of forces, that is to say that we were given a wider range of vision in order that we might watch the movements of those in degree above and below us, and so suit our own to theirs. Thus we should the more perfectly work together to greater advantage. Those below would take heart also of the apparent presence of those of brighter and stronger aspect from whom, moreover, they received leadership and direction in the fray.

So it was that I gazed in awe at the sight above and below and on every side of me. I had seen beauty and many great wonders, but none so great as this.

Below there appeared layers of colors manifold, one beyond the other, as I gazed earthward. These were the distinguishing colors of the spheres between my own and earth. They were the garments of the armies marshaled ready to descend. Below them all, forming a background to them; I saw the mists of vapor swirling about the earth. Murky, thick and horrid they appeared, with streaks and shooting tongues of red and dark green cleaving the dull slate-brown clouds which whirled here and there like thick gelatinous substance, as those serpents of evil darted here and yon about their ghastly business of the hells.

We did not shrink, we did not fear as we looked upon the sight. Yet we took hand, one of another, in love and comradeship, and were very solemn awhile. For our journey must be against and through that noisome mass. Earth lay within it, and we must win through to earth, for our aid was sorely needed there on that dark planet. The thought came to me as I gazed, "How can man abide within that awful hell-soup and still breathe and live?"

As to ourselves, our task was to absorb what we might into our own economies by transmutation, as I have already said. What should prove to be insoluble must be driven into the deeper hells there to decompose of itself, so to say it. A pretty meal for us, you will say, and not much savory. And that is truth. But we were safe to be enabled for our task, safe both in our myriads, and in our Leader the Christ.

Then we turned about and looked aloft. There they stood or moved softly, terrace on terrace of those brighter ones. Each terrace was a heaven, and each heaven, as then displayed before us panoramic, was a step on the great flight of stairs which stretched up and away mountains high, in dizzy space suspended, until it entered into impenetrable radiance and the top was lost to sight. Only those some spheres beyond us up the ever-brightening rises were competent to look into that light and see what was therein. To us it was a void of light, none else.

Yet it gave us strength to see those myriads within our range. How lovely were they, those most near to us, clad in robes of lustrous material of hues unknown to those below us. Those higher up beyond were enveloped in an aura gossamer-like, their bodies radiant with their beauty of form and substance, each suggestive of a stately poem or tender song of love and aspiration, each a god in grace and equipoise, each, with his peers, perfectly displayed before us. You would say, in earth words, they were distant very far from us. In truth they were so, yet we saw them whole and in detail, both of form and raiment, if raiment be any name by which to call that radiance which enveloped them.

But these were intermediate withal. There were other myriads beyond the compass of our vision. This we knew, but saw them not at all; they were too sublimate for us of our estate to see them. And atop of all we knew there stood the Christ.

If these be all so lovely, we said one to another as we gazed, what then must He be like in His native glory! Here we stuck, we could not go farther, so left the matter there. For we knew He would come to marshal us. And when He came He would assume visibility for the sake of us, conditioning Himself to the capacity of the indwellers of the descending spheres, as He passed by on His progress earthward. For it was made known to us that He who was above them all would press through and downward until He stood within the firmament of earth to lead the van.

Aye, my son, never was such leader as He. Among the gods and principalities there cannot be His peer in leadership both of angels and of men. I say this solemnly, for those Heavenly Powers and Princes be not cut to pattern, you shall know, but, as with you of earth, so here, each expresses a personality of his own. This do we, the angels; so do those above us in degree of holiness; so do those of still higher rank and so do the greatest express each the excellences of the Father in his own free personality.

So I say it, that, in respect of Leadership, the Christ is peerless among them all, I think, and those my comrades with whom I was there at speech said even as I said. But we will speak of this again to you and you shall then say if we seem to have judged aright or no.

ARNEL+

20

The Approach
of the Christ

The Advance Guard

WE waited expectant, gazing aloft along the serried heavens as they stretched away beyond and above us. There they lay like a gigantic carpet of silk unrolled and falling, all flounced and pleated, like a cascade of waters prismatic in the heavenly sunlight. Each pleat was a heaven, each flounce a borderland conjoining two and blending their dominant colors into one. It swept down from the heights in glittering waves, their hues scintillating in the celestial radiance like jewels on a kingly mantle, each crystal atom an angel of power who, as he moved, caught and reflected some new beauty of those heavenly rays.

Then, as we watched, the farthest line within our vision slowly began to change in its coloring. The normal hue was there, but suffused by another ingredient, a new effulgence. And we knew that the Christ and His retinue had come within the compass of our vision. Very beautiful it was to see, as one after another of those silken pleatings seemed to fall over and tilt the lap beneath till it fell over too and kissed the third, which likewise bent its head and laid its cheek caressingly upon the shoulder of its kin below.

This was the aspect as we viewed the coming of the Christ afar, the while He descended, step by step, towards us, ever nearer and yet vast intervals away above there, just emerged from that impenetrable light and throwing forward over the spheres the influence of His Presence as He descended toward our own. At length the light-waves which went before Him began to ripple upon the utter boundary of a region but a few spheres away, and then we could note what was toward in some more detail. We began to see His wide-flung fore-guard as they advanced and threw their beams before them as they came. But Him we saw not yet.

Then, after long ecstasy of wonderment and great uplifting at the sight of so much power and glory, we began to feel within us a glow which suffused us with a sense of love and pity and an access of resolve to put of our best into what work lay ahead of us. So we knew that He drew near in person.

But I cannot tell you how He came, or when He passed onward below us, my son. It was all too glorious. I will give you what I am able.

That glow increased until we felt so strong and able that we stood each erect and craned our necks to see His coming. First came the retinue which went before Him to prepare us. For He came now not as I have limned to you some times already. In His great glory and native strength He came this time to enable ten thousand battalions of His chosen for this great enterprise. So it was necessary that we absorb of His strength to our utmost, and for this we must also be gradually attuned. So they came and, as they passed over us and through our ranks, one gave a word of wisdom, another his blessing, another a kiss of peacefulness, as each had need. They went among us leisurely, those strong ones, and singled us out and in a trice had scanned our lack and had supplied it and passed on. Those who went above us directed them where need was. All worked together in a harmony of business which in itself was no mean lesson to us.

What happened to yourself, Arnel?

There were women with them, as there were with us. You send women to the wars of earth, my son. We also brought with us women to the rescue in their proper spheres of service.

I stood there away from my fellows, for there had been gathered together a number by one of those who came in order that he might speak to them. And as I stood so there came to me a man and a woman. They smiled and took each of them a hand of mine. The man was of greater stature than I and the woman but little less than he. A comely and most stately pair, but very simple in their humility and love, as all those great ones be. Then he put his other hand upon my shoulder, and he said, "Arnel, you are not unknown to us, who work together for the most part, combining our native qualities for the work we have in hand from time to time. So we sought you out together on our way through this your home. The lady my companion has, I think, something to say to you before we pass onward. She has kept it within her this some time past awaiting opportunity."

Now the woman was very beautiful; her radiance, joined with that of him, abashed me, and I could do naught better than gaze aground in silence. And while I did so I saw her grip tighten on my hand as she raised it a little. Then down before my lowered eyes came the crown of her beautiful head as she stooped to kiss my hand. For a little time her lips remained there and I looked upon her silken brown-gold hair, where a gold band crossed it where it parted and fell away each side. I could not speak, for the touch of them overcame me with a joy uplifting and so exquisite in its holiness as I cannot put it into words.

And then I raised my eyes to his, questioning him in my perplexity and, as she slowly lifted her head and looked at my face, he said, "She is grand-dam, my friend Arnel, to the girl Miramne."

I looked from him to her then and she smiled and said, "I thank you, Arnel, for you did for me what I was not able to do, being too far removed. But, seeing the plight of the girl, I sent to you my longing, and you readily responded to my wish. I thank you as she also soon shall come to thank you for herself."

Then she kissed me upon my brow, gently impressing me toward her, and they went upon their way, smiling upon me as they left me, so that I felt I should always be in touch with them thereafter, and never far away. It is so here.

You are wondering who is this Miramne of whom he spoke. So did I wonder, albeit I knew her well.

As I was going about my business on a time not long before I, as you perchance have done, stood still of a sudden, feeling that some one wished my attention. Well, as I stood there passive, there came to me no voice, but an impulse which forthwith I obeyed, I made haste to descend to the earth-plane and, by some exoteric influence, was led straight to a young woman who was about to pass over into the spirit life. At first I scarce knew what my duty was. Only I knew it lay there. But I soon made it out. Waiting for her passing there stood near me a man. He had been her bane on earth and was awaiting her now to claim her and drag her away with him into his wickedness.

So, to be short, I met her when she came through, warded him off with much endeavor, and bore her to a place of safety where he could not reach her in the Sphere Three. She is now two spheres advanced, and I have warded and tended her all the way. She is one of my charges. So there you have it. And now it was a great joy to me, both to know from whence came that first request, and also to know I had served the sender of it to her approval.

Such joy you cannot understand while you still be of the earth, my son. Yet He forelimned it when He said the story of the Almoners and the greeting awaiting such as were trustworthy in their duties. "Well done, good and faithful, enter you into My joy with Me." So did I then, my son, I had not lacked in that little service, and now I entered with the greater joy upon this present and larger enterprise. For I knew that her words were such as He Himself would have spoken to me. And His greater joy is ever the joy of service.

ARNEL+

21

The Herald

Monday, March 10, 1919. 5:31–6:38 P.M.

NOW you shall know that these transactions extended over many years in your earth time. Meanwhile we went about our business. When a reforming of a community of earth is proceeding people still work their work-o'-day. And so did we. Only the one great and dominating thought which permeated all our doings, and tinctured any scheme of service we chanced to have on hand, was the coming of the Christ and the conditioning of the spheres above us as He came. This we could see as we went our ways here or there; and at times we assembled to note more carefully the changing splendor of His progress. Such times we mostly came at call when some herald would enter the state of our sphere and, standing sometimes upon a mountain peak, or in mid-heaven suspended, would proclaim the assembly. Then those of us who were so called would go to the place of meeting and await what should befall.

Such an occasion was that which I narrated to you at my last coming.

But at other times we pursued our ordinary work, or were especially trained for our future service with our Prince when

609

He should call to us, or were sent on special missions into other spheres. But in this last case a more perfect line of communication was maintained than in ordinary, so that we might be notified if a sudden call should be made on our attendance.

Yet, although many things were done at this time which would be of interest to you and helpful, I will go by these presently, and, if it should be so ordained, at some future time I will return to them. It is my purpose now to tell you of the Coming of the Christ Himself.

We came together, we who were elected to follow Him, and gathered within the parklands where stood the Tower of the Angels. As we waited we looked up to the Palm Crown atop. Gradually there emerged into visibility, one after other, many angels. They were kneeling, sitting, standing, reclining among that lace-work. They did not move into their positions from within the Crown. They became vested with visibility before our eyes.

They were first there unseen, and then took on their outward shape where they were. Having done this they did not remain still, but moved about from one place to another conversing. These were of high degree and very beautiful. I have already related a similar incident to you. I do not think many of these were the same who came then. Some of them were.

When they were all set, another form was seen to be taking shape, in this wise:

There appeared a new item in the Crown—a cross rising from the center of it and above it. The last angel to come stood on one arm of the cross and rested his left hand against the upper portion. He was more resplendent than any of them. When he had fully taken on the condition of our Sphere, he raised his right hand, looking down on us the while, and gave us his benediction. Then he spoke to us in a clear bell-like voice, not loud in tone, but still reaching us way down below and all who stood within those precincts. They were scattered far and wide about the meadows and hills, and some upon the roofs or in the boats upon the waters. So he made his proclamation and he said,

"We have called you, my comrades, that you should hear the message of Him Who draws near this State in order that at His advent and His passing you understand what those should be to you and lose no blessing.

"Know you, therefore, who have seen Him times again that now He comes in other guise. As you have seen Him hitherto He came for some one purpose or another, in special phase of person, as special need required. Now He comes, not in His fullness truly, yet in much greater fullness of majesty than sometime He came. For then He descended to you upon His business peculiar. Now He comes with the mandate of His Father to the work.

"It is an emprise of great moment, for earth is in sore need of you to help. When therefore He passes by you, do you, each and every one of you, bespeak of Him what qualities you most do lack. So shall you become attuned to the task in hand and strengthened to its accomplishment.

"Be not unready, nor overawed too much, of His glory. He brings it for you. Himself has no such need. It is for you He comes all-glorious, and the beams of His radiance are for you. Bathe you in them, therefore, and appropriate to your use what of strength and ennoblement they carry in their magnetic forces.

"Now make for yourselves small companies for friendly conversation. Speak one to another of what I have said to you. My words to you have been few. Make you them into many. And where you stick these my companions will help you to re-solve your difficulty. So shall you be at ease the more when He shortly comes and, while He passes, you, seeing and hearing and feeling, shall also understand."

Then we did as he had bidden us. And those who had in-habited the Palm Crown while he spoke did not fade away into invisibility from which they had emerged. No; they descended amongst us, going where their aid was needed, and great was the peace they brought to us. So that when the Christ passed by we were not found unready. We were able to absorb into ourselves of the wonderful river of the waters of the Life which bathed us to our baptism of His inner counsel and purpose.

This was the last of those assemblies before He came. When it was over we knew we were one with Him, and so in quietness and content we awaited His good pleasure.

ARNEL+

22

The Passing of the Christ

Tuesday, March 11, 1919. 5:30–7:09 P.M.

W E were gathered together among the highlands of the Sphere Ten. A solitary place it was and with very few habitations. What buildings were there were occupied for the most part with the coordinating work of the great central Tower where outlook was kept over wide regions continually.

This, of course, was before you became a dweller in the Temple of which you have told me?

Yes, my son. It was late in His progress that we met with Him as He descended. At that time I had been advanced to the Sphere Ten, of which I had now been inhabitant for a considerable period. Here was I when He reached the boundary of that region.

We watched the mountain range in the far distance. The light upon it was crystal-bright, and in hue green-golden. Then it began to change, and green in it gave place to rosy pink, like a red rose seen through amber. This deepened in its luster until the whole range flamed red-gold, with waves of light rolling over it as the retinue moved hither and yon in their progress forward. Then we began to see their forms as they came toward us. They were outlined against the cloud of light in which the Christ Himself moved onward. They were very glorious and of mighty stature, as of strength to match.

Men and women they were, and one here and there was a dual angel—two-in-one—I leave it there; you would not understand that mystery, nor could I put it into words for you. They were neither bi-sexed nor sexless. Let it rest there. They were very lovely to see, but of softer mien than the men and more queenly than the women their companions. So.

This company passed forward, therefore, into the condition of our State and filled the whole firmament with their light and glory. They did not descend among us, these. They hovered above, dropping upon us of the dew of their sweetness and peace, so light as kisses wafted to us on a summer breeze, but full of power, and charged with understanding of mysteries very deep and holy. As these tokens of their love fell upon us we became enlightened in matters hitherto beyond our range, and so were made more competent for our work.

Some took up their stations on the highest of the peaks where few of our sphere were wont to ascend, the atmosphere at those elevations being too rarefied for endurance, and none were there at that time. The newcomers took their stand in groups, one here, another far away upon another peak, and so on, till a circle was made of the whole vast region, with groups in between where some mountains had place within their circumference.

So they called in music one to another, both instrumental and vocal, till the welkin vibrated with their harmony. Nor was that music without its effect upon us, for to what had been given to us by their peers these added a sweetness all their own, as a mother coos her babe, already resting, into rest still more profound.

Anon the horizon deepened to crimson-gold, and yet the gold was primary and the crimson interspersed, And we knew the Christ was at our gates.

He came. How shall I tell you how He came or of the glory of His Presence! As I essay to do so, my son, I pause in fear. For to bid the Court Fool display the progress to the Crowning of his liege Prince, to show with his cap the crown how it sat upon the royal head, with his staff how the scepter was held in rest, and to shake his bells for the music of the choir—well, my son, that were to do irreverence to the King. And that is how I feel to be agait of my business now.

And yet, if that poor Fool should love his royal master very well, he would do what in him lay to show both how the King had deported himself before his people, and also he would be curious to certify them of the unworthiness of his parody, lacking skill of play-acting, and of material for the play. So do I now, and He Who keeps the eagle for high heaven and the sparrow for the hedgerow will accept my little flight and twitter, so they be offered in humility and with good intent.

His circumambient radiance increased in its brightness and expansion until we were all enveloped within it. I could see my companions even to the farthest bounds quite clearly. But all the air was tinted rosy gold. Our bodies also were bathed in its liquid flood. So He enveloped us whole and several. It was within His Presence and Personality we stood, and we felt not it but Him in and around us. We were in, and parts of, the Christ. And yet, although He thus became universal to us, He did not eschew to appear in outer form.

I saw Him as He moved about, above and among us. It is very hard to tell you. He seemed to be everywhere at one time in His bodily, localized form, and yet there was but one of Him. I cannot say it better, and it is not very well said, forsooth. So He appeared to us. I doubt me much He was not seen in detail of character by each one of us identically. To me He appeared as I will tell you.

He was very large of stature, some two men high, but He did not seem so. To say "giant" would be to say a wrong idea in total. He was just man, but man ennobled in aspect as in build.

Very well. Then upon His head He wore a crown, just a broad band of continuous blending with ruby-stone and metal of gold alternate. Their rays were not intermingled, but the ruby rays were red and the gold rays were golden. These went upward, ever expanding, into the heavens and were caught upon the robes of those who hovered there which became much beautified by them.

His body shone naked, and yet not unclothed—which is paradox. I mean to say that the glory which His body emitted went into every part of the region and bathed all in its glow. And yet some seemed to be reflected back when it beat upon the screen of our reverence so that it, returning, enveloped Him in our own responsive love, like golden armor upon His form. Now that was very sweet, both to us and to Him. To us He did not scruple to surrender the sanctuary of His native beauty. And we took up the only robe worthy of the service and laid it in reverence upon Him, eyes aground; and loved Him to heartbreaking for His sweet confidence with all the exquisite tenor of our fond and worshipful love.

But we had seen His glory and we knew His power suppressed within and ready. So, although He wore no armor, He went clad in golden mail, our offering to Him. Of His own, as all is His, we returned to Him our presentation.

His feet went bare, for what we gave Him fell short by that which we had absorbed into ourselves. So the robe lacked by that much in length and stayed upon His ankles.

His face was very solemn and pitiful, as He went first to one company and then to another, and yet never seemed to leave that central place where first we beheld Him in visible form. We could read His countenance like an unrolled script. The solemnity in it came from realms ineffable where sin is not unknown but known only as a fact and not as an experience. The pity came from Calvary. And the two meeting midway between were caught in the hand of the Son of Man Divine Who, raising His hand to shade His eyes that He might look into those far high realms to see what they would do with man for his sinfulness, let fall upon His brow those drops of sin from earth to shadow His face into greater beauty. So were sublime solemnity and sorrow blended one, and pity emerged the off-spring born, henceforth to be an attribute of Divinity.

Then there was love, not that which delights to give or take; but love which into its bosom gathers all, and becomes one with all, identical. So did He envelop us and gather us into Himself at that time.

Majesty also sat upon His head, a majesty which makes a constellation into a bracelet for arm-wear, and sets in His signet a sun with planets attendant encircling.

So He came, and so He appeared at His coming. That coming passed, but He remained in presence still. We do not see Him today as we saw Him then, and yet we can re-visualize that scene and substantiate it whenever we will. This also is a mystery. Let me put it thus: He passed on earthward, but the train of His mantle lengthened as He went and covered with its light all those spheres through which He passed. He went on still descending, descending, down towards that awful hell of noxious vapor about your earth, and we who had seen that shade of pity upon the majesty of His face found in our hearts to pity Him too, and yet to admire and worship Him.

For awful as it was to Him in His spotless purity of holiness to look upon that horror there below, yet He paused not nor shrank from what He had taken in hand. Calm and invincible He approached the conflict for the purification of a world, and we knew that in Him we should prevail. No such Leader ever was so great as he, my son. He is Captain thoroughly, and not the less because there is very much of motherhood in His heart.

ARNEL+

23

Heavenly Powers and Earth Science

Wednesday, March 12, 1919. 5:28-6:46 P.M.

How the Heavenly Powers dealt with Earth Science.

NOW when the Christ passed onward we also, now of His company, pressed after Him. We were all arrayed in our several orders, but by no outward word of command. Our commission proceeded from our own hearts wherein it was given us, by means of our own preparation, to understand exactly where lay our field of service and what was required of us there. So we at ease fell into our individual places, inspired thereto by communion of His Presence, and fell to our task.

I will explain to you in brief the order of our advance earthward. As we encircled earth on every side, and all those spheres intervening, we pressed downward and inward as toward a center. This is to give it to you in terms of space—a space of three dimensions. Only so will you be able to come at some slight knowledge of the economy of this great campaign. So.

The Christ Himself, as I have said, was ubiquitous; He was omnipresent throughout the whole myriads of His far-flung armies in all their degrees of rank, from those His Lords paramount, who held authority exceeding great, to the humblest of us His rank and file. But although we were inspired from within as to our several duties, yet all was in perfect order of battle array externally.

Those who were highest and nearest to Him transmitted His commands, through those next in rank to the officers below themselves, who transmitted them to others of lesser degree in due sequence. We received our guidance from those who, being nearest above us in estate, were also visible to our sight continually. We were able as we proceeded on our way to visualize those of some three degrees superior, but received our orders, except on occasion, from those of one degree above.

We of the Sphere Ten, therefore, followed where He led and, arriving in the Sphere Nine, began our operations. We exerted our pressure upon the whole circumference on every side and gradually moved inward upon it. And, as we did so, there happened within that sphere some like experience as had come already to us when He and His retinue pressed into our own. So we gave of our higher condition to that realm and, as we passed through it, strained out some of its weakness, and other some we transmuted into soundness of strength. Thus did we and passed onward to the Sphere Eight.

But, this gained, we in turn became to those of the Sphere Nine who followed us as those of the Sphere Eleven had become to us. They looked to us now for our guidance and followed us into the Sphere Eight, which traversed, they also accepting from us our transmitted orders, handed them on to those who followed them, in due order of array into the Sphere Seven next in order below.

So did this process continue until we had come within three spheres of earth. We had gathered up our armies of the heavens, one by one, and numbered them with our myriads. But here we paused. These Three Spheres nearest earth were treated more or less as one region, for here the vapor of earth's hell-soup was thick about us, and here it is the great Armageddon must needs be fought. It was these Three Spheres which formed our battleground, and here we accepted onset from the enemy.

You of earth went on your ways and only very few were able to penetrate through the gloom surrounding you in those regions of spirit which enclosed you round. But gradually we progressed until you began to hear rumors that our coming had been sensed by some and by others certain of our advance-guard had been sighted. Many laughed at those reports. So many of you laughed that we were able to note the effect of your unholy mirth upon the atmospheric conditions about us, and we knew that you first must sorely suffer ere your minds in whole should learn reverence for Him Who came to your aid and respect for us His servants. But I go forward with too much haste.

Yet how shall I tell you of our maneuvers? I am wishful to make you understand what has come to pass of late upon you. I speak of things heavenly and hellish, and of powers of spirit, both bright and of somber gray, all locked in strenuous conflict, unseen, unheeded, unbelieved—but not unfelt. I do my best with your words and your knowledge of things and make an allegory of what took place. I can do no more than that, but so much I will essay to do here and now.

Arrived at the Three States encompassing earth we found our first task was one not of annihilation but of transmutation. We curiously surveyed the vaporous conditions and descried the element first to be dealt with. Others had arrived before us and had been at work for centuries preparing. I speak only of that period when first we of the Sphere Ten arrived.

There was an ingredient of heavy substance which weighed very heavily upon the atmosphere. It was born of the science of earth and had the effect of raising itself upward, and then settling down again toward earth and matter, and weighing down with it those who inhabited that region. But it was born of knowledge true if rudimentary, and much sincerity was mixed with it.

It was this which lifted it upward for the space of these Three Spheres. But, inasmuch as it was true only of material phenomena, to matter it needs must gravitate once again, having so little of spirit to buoy it upward. This condition we dealt with by expansion. We plunged into it, so to say it, flung far and wide our influence in aid, helped this knowledge to dilate itself to the utmost, and so fulfill itself.

Under our pressure thus applied it expanded until the boundary of the material was reached. But the impetus we had given to this material science could not there be stayed. It gradually pressed outward on its own bounds and began to emerge here and there beyond. So that the sharp line, so arbitrarily drawn between material and spiritual, began to sag and to bulge, and here and there a small breach was made—small at first, enlarging later. But small or large, mark me, no such breach was ever repaired. The dyke once gapped, the steady irresistible pressure, all-encircling without, found inlet and, from that time, a steady stream of spiritual content flowed increasingly into your science of earth, and is today continued.

So we did not destroy your science by cataclysm, as has happened in the past ages of earth not once nor twice. No. For, cramped and limited as it was, it ministered to progress as a whole, and so we held it to that degree in reverence. So we transmuted it by expansion, and are so continuing today.

This work in which the little lady Kathleen is helping me and my friends may seem but of scant relation to that which I have but now described to you. Yet it is one item in the same operation, and, if you will re-read what messages you have received from us, and those who wrote with your hand before us, you will see that what you were able to receive of scientific kind has been given you. Not over much, I grant you, but what you lack is not of will but of ability. I will tell you this however.

There are those now being prepared who are more able than yourself for this especial phase of revelation, men, aye and a few women also, of the scientific mind who will be more facile instruments for the work. I shall not be their proctor, no, for that is not so much my quality. Each of us goes to those whose make-up is found in sympathy with his own. And so I come to you, my son. I may not speak of science as others of my own degree are able to speak, being so equipped by their training. But what I am I reveal to you, and what I have I give. You, with your sweet graciousness, receive my offering; and so I am both content and pleasured.

God His greater grace be to you, my son. We will speak together again of this matter. You be some little spent of strength now.

Arnel+

24

Heavenly Powers
and Religion

Monday, March 17, 1919. 5:41–7:10 P.M.

How the Heavenly Powers dealt with Religion.

ANOTHER element to be dealt with was that of religion. This was the more difficult inasmuch as, while its praetors claimed it as a science, and a progressive science, they hampered it with a tether-rope to its founders. To speak plainly, you were permitted, as I was, to career never so fast so your ways took you not outside the circle. When that not over distant circumference was reached the rope shortly reminded you—and sometimes violently if you went too headlong—that you were tethered to the center and must by no means stray too far away. That center was, I say, the Founder of the form of religion professed. It was much the same with Islam as with Buddha his system, and not much else with Christendom.

We had much ado therefore because the fair words of religionists made a very good show, and yet had the same effect in operation as those of the old rabbis at the period of Jesus our own Lord. In all cases we, looking into these matters somewhat narrowly and in detail, found that the error proceeded from one grand cause. I leave out the minor factors of greed of gold and of power, of that strange side-shoot of earnestness called fanaticism, of hypocrisy which generates so much blindness in those who think they are sincere. You may read of them all in our own Scriptures of the goodmen of Israel and of early mother Church, as those who fell victim to those same errors did also read them all down the ages. I say I leave all those aside and speak of the one cause fundamental.

We were all one grand army, we of the campaign to earth, and all we acted and interacted together. But we also had our departments of service whereon to concentrate our energy in principal. As I had lived in Christendom, to that system of religion I was allotted, and so of that I shall speak now.

The grand cause of error of which I speak is this:

Men spoke of the Christ as the Founder of their system. So. But the Christ of Whom they spoke was enthroned way back at the beginning of the Christian era, and from thence watched the progress of His Church. Whenever men asked what should they do in this case or in that, in order that they should not fail to co-ordinate their own acts with His will, the answer was, "Look backward to Him and learn of Him." And if any man inquired further where he would be able to find the will of the Christ expressed, the answer was that such expression would be found in a book, the book of the records of His acts and words. Naught but what was therein found was to be believed as His will, and on His will as therein expressed, the doings of Christendom were shaped.

And so it came to pass that Christendom became tied with a tether to a book. The Church truly was alive with the life of Him; His Spirit filled it up like the living coursing blood in a human body. But that life was being strangled and the body began to halt, and at last to go round more slowly in that circumscribed orbit.

Truly His words and acts recorded were a most precious heritage. They were meant to be a Shekinah to guide the Church through the wilderness of the ages. But, note you well, the Shekinah went before the Children of Jacob and led them. The Book of the New Covenant did not go before, but was enthroned behind. The light cast was true light, as from a beacon atop of a hill. But it lighted men from behind and threw their shadows before them. If they would look to the light they must turn their glance over their shoulders backward. Then they stumbled. It is not of orderly advance to be turning backward in order to see how to go forward.

That was the error men made. "He is our Captain," said they, "and He goes before us and we follow Him through death and Resurrection into His Heaven beyond." But for a sight of this Captain going before them they turned round and looked to their rear, which is not, I say, conducive to orderly advance, nor agreeable with reason.

So we began to take hold of the bolder sort and help them on. Jesus had pointed onward to the doing of greater works than He had done, and to His Presence which should lead men into the truth, not drive them from behind. So some men there were who, heeding this and understanding, made bold to move forward confident in this leading. They suffered of their fellowmen, but in the next generation, or next after that, the seed they had sown sprang up and bore its harvest.

So you will understand, my son, that the mistake men made was to hamper a living, moving Life with a Book. They regarded that Book not as what it was and is, wonderful, beautiful and mostly true, but as both infallible and also complete. But the Life of Christ has been continued in the world and is continued today. The few words and acts of Him in the Book of the four evangelists are not even as the source from which the river of Christendom flows. They are merely a few ripples on its broader tide to show what way it rides to the sea.

Men are beginning to see this now and to understand that if He spoke by His angels to good men of old, so does He speak to them today. These men go forward, glad of the beacon-light behind, but with greater gladness toward the more radiant light ahead. For there He is today, as He was when He went up to Salem that time. He goes before you. Follow Him without fear. He promised He would lead you. Follow Him. He may not tarry on your hesitancy. Read what has been written of Him in the evangel. But read it while you march ahead. Do not turn back time and again to the shrine of Authority inquiring, as of the Delphian pythoness, "Shall I do this or that?" No. Bring the roll of those brief records along with you as you go forward on your journey. Unroll it on your pommel as you ride, for it is a good map for the present stage. If in some details obsolete, yet the grand contour of the country is well and boldly set out. There are other maps of later issue. Consult them also and add to the old one what details it lacks. But go forward all the time. And if some seek again to tether you, brace your tendons and set your knees firm against your horse's flanks, and, urging forward, snap the rope with which they would bind you from behind. There be plenty, alas too plenty, who, not daring forward, have fallen behind, choked with the dust raised by those who have gone onward—erringly choked and fallen by the wayside they be, and sunk into the slumber of death. You may do nothing for them, for still the Captain goes onward ahead and calls with brave and clarion voice for volunteers to lead the van. He shall not call in vain.

As to those others, well, there be all enough to company along with them. The dead shall bury the dead, and the dead past shall entomb them in its womb of night. But ahead the dawn is breaking. There be clouds upon its horizon truly, but the glad sun shall melt them into his rays—when he is at last quite fully risen. And in that day shall all men see how that, willing to bless His children every one, the Father has set but one only Sun in the midst of the firmament of His brightness. Men view that Sun at different angles according as the place of their habitation be to north or south of His heavenly path, and to some He is brighter and to others less bright. Yet He is the same Sun, and sole of His kind for earth's fair benediction.

Nor does He of Himself favor one people with more of His blessings and another people with less. He sheds His rays on all sides equally. It is the free will of the peoples which determines the ratio of their portion, each for each, in the election of the locality of their dwelling.

Read this parable aright, my son, and you shall see that if the Christ be Sun to one creed He must of necessity be Sun to all. For a Sun cannot be hid over all the surface of a world— except that world turn its face away from the Sun. Then He becomes hid truly, and yet, even so, but for a season.

ARNEL+

25

Heavenly Powers and Christendom

Tuesday, March 18, 1919. 5:58–6:57 P.M.

WE have spoken to you, my son, of the Christ, and indicated a larger view of Him than Christendom has been wont to approve. Let us now pursue this theme some little further.

As we neared earth—we of the companies whose business was with the Church of Christendom—we paused awhile and were called together in order that we might the better understand the various aspects of our task. Then the Christ Himself intensified His Presence and became in personal form before us. He stood there in mid-heaven in full view. We were now nearer in state to the earth than we were when He came to us sometime, as I have related to you. So that His appearance was now of more material aspect, and also in more detail. Thus we saw His robe plainly. It covered His body to the knees, but not His arms, which were free. It was upon this robe of Him that we were set to gaze, because it was made to reflect the sentiments of earth towards Him in the various creeds of the Churches.

I cannot tell you how this knowledge was shown to us except by saying that the light flung aloft by the worship and teaching of the religions of the world, was caught upon that robe. It acted like a spectroscope and divided the rays into their true constituent elements. These we analyzed and, so doing, we found that there was not one true white ray among them all. Every one was both sullied and also incomplete.

We studied this matter for a long time, and then it was given us to understand what remedy should be applied to the case. It was radical. Men had not only taken away from Him somewhat of His glory; they had also added other glories not His own. And yet these added glories were of so counterfeit a sort as to be unworthy of Him in total. They were glories of wordy titles and attributes. Swelling and sonorous in sound, unworthy in reality.

Could you, please, give me a few details, Arnel?

Men called Him God, and said He was Divine. They said too much and meant too little. On the one part, the Christ is not the only Supreme, the One Being of Beings consummate. The Father Himself is not so, but is the highest expression of Being man wots [knows] of. And the Father is Greater than the Christ, Who is of the Father, God's Son.

On the other part, the Lord Christ is of powers and glories greater far than any of those with which men invest the Father God. The highest of all the Beings which Christendom acknowledges is the Father Almighty. These words of attribute sound big with power. But the idea which men infuse into them is poor and small in comparison with the real majesty even of the Christ, as we who speak to you have come to know it. And we are but ten spheres removed from earth. What therefore must the real majesty of Him be!

Men say with one breath He is co-equal with the Father— that never said He. With the next breath men say the Father is Lord of All Power. What power have men held in reserve therefore with which to endow the Christ?

Men say the Christ came to earth in all the plenitude of His Being. Yet they also say that all the heaven of heavens cannot contain Him.

I will no further, my son. For I love Him so, and worship so humbly at the footstool of His Princely Throne that such jumble of broken lights focused upon Him is distressful to me, very sorely distressful to me, my son. His robe because of this was bespotted with patches of colors which blended not at all in harmony together. Were it possible to sully holiness from without, they would have sullied Him. But the robe of His Holiness protected His Body and threw back that motley array into the space about earth. They did not pass beyond Him upward into the heavens superior to that wherein we stood. They were refracted downward. Thus we read them and took note.

The remedy which was revealed to us was no less than this: the demolition of earth's Christ. That is exact truth but has a fearsome sound. It has also a fearsome reality. Let me explain.

Some buildings there be badly reared by not very skilful workmen but capable of reconstruction and repair as they stand. Some be so bad they must be broke up and scattered and new material be brought together that the house may be built anew. The only part left is that of the foundations below ground. This latter house is earth's Christ. I say not the Christ, but the Christ of earth's creeds, the dogmatic Christ of Christendom. Such Christ as appears in the accepted Creed of Christendom today is unworthy of Him as He is. That must be pulled down, its materials scattered—all but the deep-down foundations. Then new materials will be brought together, and a shrine resplendent and beautiful will rise, a shrine worthy for Him to set His Throne within, worthy to cover His head as He sits within His Throne.

This, my son, this that I call to you from where I stand a little way off is no threat. This thing of which I speak to you has already been proceeding for some century and half-century past and gone. The demolition is still not quite complete in the countries of Europe. But it is going forward. When He is stripped of the robe of His Divinity woven in the looms of earth, then we have another, a Royal Robe of Divinity woven in the looms of the Heavens, shot with rays of eternal light, made soft with the silken threads of love divine, and be-gemmed with pearls of angels' tears, caught up as they fell towards earth when they bowed their heads to look upon the doings of men, caught up and spread upon the pavement before the stairs of the Father His Pavilion. There they lay till they became beautiful with the luster of His love-rays and fit to adorn the garment of His Son. For, themselves were tears of a great love.

Arnel+

26

Heavenly Powers
and the Earth's Christ

Wednesday, March 19, 1919. 5:37–7:00 P.M.

How the Heavenly Powers dealt with the Earth's Christ.

SO this divestiture of the Christ proceeded and has a certain relation to that materialistic progress of science of which we have already told you. Albeit the treatment of that and of this matter varied in process somewhat. But the end, and our aim, are identical. The relation of which I speak is seen in the general trend towards the exaltation of the natural and the elimination of the purely spiritual.

Science in this matter worked from within outward, and burst her bounds, emerging into the realm of things spiritual. In the case of the Christ men have been working from without, not filling up, but paring away the rind, and then the pulp, until only the seed was left. But in that seed is the life, and that will break forth anon, and much beautiful fruit will become of it.

But the human mind is not to be measured with a single gauge the world over in any period. For always there is freedom of will to be reckoned in with the count. So it comes to pass that the total stripping of the Christ as to His Divinity is not of universal necessity. We have found it to be that in some communities the people are of such mind that were they to become assured that the Christ was mere man they would lose all faith in Him who guides the universe. So their faith is left to them, but not untouched. Even they have heard whisperings of people who say the Christ was mere man. They are disturbed and, wanting courage to face this matter and search to find the real truth of it, they lay it aside and cling to Authority, as to a sherd of wreckage, to buoy them up.

Others have boldness too much and say they have solved the riddle of the Christ. The answer is, say these, "Man and man merely." My son, we who speak to you on this grave matter have also searched it out. Our praetors also are very high, and of wisdom very great. Yet we have not resolved the problem hereto, and they our teachers tell us they know more of this high mystery than we do, but not all. You will mark, my son, that while some of your masters theologic lay down the nature and attributes even of Supreme Being precisely and with decision, there are those above us who venture not so far when they speak but of the Christ. Well, well, the old ram goes not so sprightly as the kid in his frolicking. But he has of wisdom, as of dignity, more than the kid.

Now although there be communities of people to whom is left their creed, yet the rehabilitation of the Christ will come not from them. It will come from among those of the bolder sort, who have gone the length, to their surprise. A little will come from the others, but the mass will come from among them who at least have read with open mind the teachings of those who have taught the mere-man doctrine. There are exceptions on both sides, I speak but on general lines.

I have tarried about this question because to Christendom it has seemed to be of primary importance. Much pain is caused to many when they hear their Savior spoken of in terms of seeming irreverence. This is because of their love for Him. I hesitate to say it, my son, yet I will say it, for I am constrained to do so: It were well for them if their knowledge of Him were great as is their love. For much of their devotion is paid to Him through clouds of mist and vapor which are not part of Him but are the result of their own imaginings. However sincere these be they are imaginings still and their effect on the devotions of those who create them is to dilute those devotions until their bulk is much reduced. This worship does reach Him, yes, but there is a fear blended with it which weakens it. It were, therefore, well if these devout ones could cast aside that fear out of their love and could love Him so truly as to be assured that He would not be displeasured by them if they would think about Him bravely, albeit with humility, even if they should, in some small details, chance to err. This do we ourselves, yet we do not fear Him, for we know we are not yet competent to understand Him whole, and that, so it be with humility and with good intent, we may search out the truth as it is in Him without disaster or reprimand.

My son, do you this also. And be assured that, as He is of larger majesty than Christendom has ever dreamed of, so is He also far beyond all your dreamings in the perfection of His love.

Some say the Christ became incarnate several times, as, for instance, in Krishna and the Buddha. Is that so?

No, my son, not in so many words. Before so teaching a man should first understand the whole nature and content of that entity which is spoken of as the Christ. Yet I have said that this is, even to us and to those above us, a mystery still.

That is the reason why, maybe, in trying to explain so much as I know I shall fall to paradox. So.

It is not true to say that the Christ Who manifested Himself, and the Father through Himself, in Jesus of Galilee is the same Christ Who manifested through the Buddha. Yet it is also not true to say there be more Christs than the one Christ. As the Christ of Jesus is one aspect of the Father Christ-manifested, so the Christ of the Buddha is another aspect of the Father Christ-manifested. Further, Jesus and the Buddha are each a different aspect of manifestation of the One Christ.

Every man is a distinct manifestation of his Creator. Yet all men are akin. So also the manifestations of the Jesus Christ and the Buddha Christ are both distinct and yet akin. But the Jesus Christ was a fuller manifestation of the One Christ than the Buddha Christ was. Yet both were true Christ manifest. I have spoken but of these two, namely, of Jesus and Buddha. Other manifestations have been and to them all the same words are applicable in principle.

It is well, my son, to fling your thoughts afar into the heavens, probing to find the Heart of God. But when you grow aweary with perplexities, such as this of the Christ, then take the simple record of the life of Jesus and read of Him as of a brother and a friend, and you in so doing shall find that, even in His sweet manhood sole, there is Divinity enough to serve both for aim and worship. When you have equaled that perfection in your life, then you shall find, over here, that He is still ahead of you. So while you look out into the heavens and aspire, do not forget you have wonders all about you very great, and much sweetness is to be found upon earth for your comfort.

Two little girl-children played before their cottage door one evening in summertime, whiles their Granny sat just within the door and mended their hosen by the light of the candle set beside her chair. Said one child to the other, "That is my planet, up there. It is bigger than all the others and brighter. Which is yours, Mary?"

And Mary answered, "My planet is the red one. It is also very big, and I like the color of it, for it is not so chill as the white ones." So they fell to argument as to which of all the planets was most worthy their admiration. And they could not come at an agreement between them. So they called to Granny to come without and show them her favorite planet, for they thought she would prove which was the best planet of them all by her own choosing. But she continued her mending, nor raised her eyes forsooth, but answered to them, "No time, my children, Granny is busy mending your hosen.

And no need: I am sitting upon it. And a very serviceable planet has it been to me.

ARNEL+

27

Why the Christ
Incarnated as a Man

Friday, March 21, 1919. 5:35–7:02 P.M.

Why the Christ Became Incarnate as a Man and not as a Woman

I WILL go by many matters which would be of interest to you, for I do not wish to make my message too long. I will mention one grand cause which has led up to the present crisis of conflict between brother men. This was the tendency to exalt the outer manifestation in matter above the inner and more dynamical activities of spirit. This element entered into every phase of life in the West, and had begun to tincture also Eastern thought and motive. It had become blended, in measure greater or less, with the conduct of business, and had its phases social, political and ecclesiastical, and even art had not escaped its influence. From what I have already told you of the outward and downward course of the evolution of the cosmos into matter and form this will not seem strange to you.

I have also spoken of the Christ in manifestation. I said that on whatever planet He became incarnate—or whatsoever state answers to that of incarnation on earth—He went to His work in form appropriate to that people with whom that work lay. As in reference to place, so also in reference to the period of His manifestation.

I speak now of that last incarnation of the Christ in Jesus of Galilee. Men have missed the great significance of the fact that, while in the Godhead there is no divided sex—so far as we know—neither male nor female, yet when He came to earth that time, as all times before that time, He came as a Man. It is this mystery I wish to explain to you.

Hitherto the evolution of the whole cosmos has been toward self-assertion, which expresses itself in form. Spirit, essential and absolute, has not form in any sense in which you of earth understand that quality. In this long period of evolution, now ending, man has taken the leadership, not woman. That of necessity. Self-expression is masculine, not feminine. A man asserts his own individuality and incorporates his chosen woman within that his individuality. He protects her, nourishes her, claims her for his own against all others. His will is her will, to his will she submits her own. As a man be the more refined of nature, or the less refined, so is this assertion of his will over that of his wife tempered with sweetness and love the more or the less. But such refinement is not towards the masculine ideal, but towards the feminine ideal. Note you this: it is not without its significance.

So, to speak of earth, and not of other worlds for this time, the ages have developed this expression of the dominance of strength bodily and intellectual. This dual expression of strength has been the dynamical element in all branches of progress, political, scientific, social and other. It has been the guiding principle in the life of the world to this time. "Man the leader," has been emblazoned upon the Banner of Mankind. That is why the Christ came to earth not as woman, but as Man.

The climax has now but lately been passed. Nay, it is still but passing. The outer expression of that climax was the late War.

We have had so much of the War of late, Arnel. You are not going to speak of that, are you?

Not at length, my son. But were I to keep silence on the matter of that catastrophic event I should be missing out the culmination of many important and converging lines of evolution. These found natural and inevitable expression in the War. If you view this without passion you will see that, while the better side of the principle of self-assertion is that a man should in his own life show forth what likeness is his Creator, on the grosser side it leads to monopoly and absorption. While the one man of refined character will give honor to the woman, the man brutal will dominate her. Even so a refined nation will seek to be of service to other nations and, if those others be weak, will help them with its greater strength. But a gross people will not do this, but will seek to enslave the weaker nations; to absorb them.

But whether the higher or the lower, still the act is masculine, and depends on the pleasure of the man. The good man will give, and the bad man will take. But both giving and taking wait on the pleasure of the man, not of the woman. In the man giving is counted for merit and gratuitous; in the woman it is normal. In the man it is an added grace: it is included in the unity of womanhood.

The Christ showed forth in Himself this principle of self-assertion which was the guiding motive of the race to whom He came. He claimed all, and took all, as a man does; as a woman does not.

Having asserted this principle He renounced all, and gave all, as a man should do. Yet if He do this he is acting not according to his masculine ideal but according to the feminine ideal.

And yet, this doing, he is the more perfect man than lacking to do this. You shall see my justification of this paradox shortly. I now remind you of a few of the sayings of the Jesus Christ, Who in His nature showed Himself, while Man in outer bodily form, yet a very perfect expression of that Divinity in Whom both elements, male and female, insist conjointly.

"Greater love has none than this that he lay down his own life for his friends." So. And yet there is a greater love than this of man. It is that he lay down his life for his enemies. And when I behold the clinging love of some women for those men who use them ill I could image this greater act of love as peculiarly her own. Jesus did give His life for His ill-users, and that was, it seems to me, at the prompting of the feminine element within His nature, rather than of the masculine.

So also His words how "it is the more blessed to give than to take." It is hard for a man to realize these words in thought or act, but it is easy and natural to a woman. Man will assent to this truth, and continue his taking. Woman acts and seeks her blessing in what she gives. If she return not manifold measure for what she accepts she rests unsatisfied. You may read this with reverence into that mystery by which the race is continued.

The feeding of the people with the bread was an acted lection on this same theme.

But I will not pursue this farther now.

What I have tried to show you is this: The world has served for a stage on which the heroic element in humankind should be shown forth in all its aspects. The phrase "Manly strength" attunes itself naturally with our minds and has no such strange vibrations as if we should say, "womanly strength."

But man is the expression of one aspect of Divinity, and of one alone. That aspect has been amply displayed during the long line of ages past. There remains the other aspect now to be displayed before mankind shall be complete in experience.

Hitherto he has led the van, and we have seen the outcome of his leading. The future ages hold in store another and more pleasurable endowment for humanity.

ARNEL+

28

The Future of Womanhood

Monday, March 24, 1919. 5:23–7:10 P.M.

WRITE what we give you and do not stay to question it. When the whole is written then read it whole and judge our message whole and not in part. I say this to you, my son, because we have that to give you which will not conform to the mind of the many. Write it down notwithstanding, for we have to say what we say: and there you have it in brief.

Until the time of the coming of the Christ in Jesus of Galilee evolution had proceeded on the lines of dominance of intellect and force of a man's right arm. That was the masculine element in the progress of the race of mankind. Where other notions prevailed these were exceptional to the general trend of evolution, like small runnels tributary to the main stream. We speak now of the general and not of the particular.

Jesus came and into the maelstrom of human activity He threw His flask of oil. He explained to those who would listen to Him that ultimate victory was not to the strong, either of arm or of intellect, but that the meek shall inherit the earth—inherit, not take it. You note that He spoke of the future.

Men took up His teaching and acknowledged it to be both beautiful and true, if practicable. For two millennia nigh they have been striving to blend the two together; to graft the meekness on to the dominance, to mix the two together in affairs national, international, social and other. The two have failed to blend together; so much so that some have said that Christianity is not possible in public affairs. They are wrong in their conclusion. The teaching of the Christ is the only durable and perpetual element in the life of earth.

So men, therefore, have confessed that violence and force have been proven fallacious. Their remedy hereto has been to retain the fallacious element and to try to soften it with the softer element of meekness. They have endeavored to retain to the man his dominance, while trying to soften that dominance with the feminine element of meekness. The resultant is failure. Do you see the inference, my son? The one course left is the abjuration of the fallacious element and the gradual emergence into the premier place in the world's life of the element of meekness, which is feminine.

The past of the world has been man's past; the future of the world will be woman's future. The woman has felt this stirring within her as a new thing to be brought forth for the salvation of her sex. That is an unworthy thought, because partial, and therefore inadequate. When a woman brought forth a Savior aforetime He came as Savior not of a sex but of the whole human race. Such will be the outcome of woman's present throes.

Feeling this new thing stirring within she has set herself about preparing for her offspring. She has been making his clothes. I say "his" clothes, for the garments she has been making are for a man-child. For them she has gone to the same mart where men buy and sell their wares and has challenged them in barter. "We can do your work," says she. But she does not yet understand that she is putting new wine into old wineskins thus. Well, they both shall perish together. Meantime woman must learn her lesson as man has had to do. Man has learned where failure lies, yet does not know where to turn for success. With one hand he holds fast to the past; the other he holds out to the future. But that hand is empty yet, and no one has taken hold, nor will do so until he let go of the past with the other.

The woman now is doing as he did; she is seeking to join with him in his dominance of affairs. Her future lies not that way. Woman shall not rule the race, neither solely nor with man conjointly. She shall guide the race hereafter, not rule it.

As I have before said to you, the evolution of earth has been downward toward the material. Here man led the way, and the suit of armor necessary to such rough conflict with matter fitted him well. Now the lowest curve of the descent has been rounded, and is just being left behind, and the race has begun on the upward path of spiritual development. In spirit we know no such dominance of rule as men have fashioned. We know the leading of love. And here woman will lead by guidance when she has learned her lesson of failure to rule by dominance.

My son, it is very difficult, as I find it, to make in any way clear to you what this future leading of the woman shall be. For all such leading hereto among you has a dual content in the human mind, namely, the governing and the governed, the dominant and the subservient. This duality has no place in the future leading. Even this word "leading" has a sense of one company going on before and the other company following after, and that of compulsion. That is not the leading we have been shown as that which awaits the human race.

Let me put it in this wise. It is manifest in the Christ of Jesus. In Him you see all the excellencies of the man without their accompaniment of traits unlovable and unlovely. And in Him also blended you see all the sweetness of the woman without the weaknesses. So in the future shall the two, the man and the woman, become, not two sexes, however perfectly assimilated the one to the other, but two aspects merely of one sex sole.

Where force rules the word is "I lead: you follow." Where love rules there is no word needed, but heart beats out to heart the message, "We go on together, beloved."

See you aught in this of what I strive to tell you, my son?

I think so, Arnel. But to one who has been used to the present order of things it is a little difficult to grasp the fact that progress can be made unless one leads and the other follows.

So, my son. You very well illustrate the difficulty you feel even in your wording of your ideas. For you use such phrases as appertain to what the world understands as organization and orderly regulations, as an army or a great business is organized from top to bottom of it.

Now orderly arrangement is found also here in the heavenly spheres: but that is based not so much on more power or less power but on that which is behind all power—and that is Love.

Try to image, even never so faintly, what that means in its operation. In a very real sense it means that there are no higher and lower, no greater or lesser in the world's sense of these words. For as concerning the relation between an archangel and a newly-arrived spirit there is always present the potential factor. That young spirit is potentially not an archangel alone, but a Prince and a Virtue and a Power beyond the archangelic degree.

And as concerning the relation between, say, an angel and the Father—well, in earth sense truly the angel is the lesser; but in the atmosphere of the heavens that relation is absorbed into the one grand reality: the Unity of God, for that angel knows that he is one with God. Greater and lesser have here no essential place. It is of the outer robes, as a jewel or hem, and enters not into the heart's inner sanctuary.

This is what is brought home to us in every Manifestation of the Christ. We always feel that, while He is King and we His subjects, yet that He is one with His Kingdom, and that all His subjects share His Throne. He commands and He leads us, and we obey and follow, not so much in that He commands, but rather because we love Him and He us. See you, my son? Well, now cast some of this heavenly light upon the future of the human race and you shall perchance come at some glimpse of the way ahead as it has been shown to us who speak to you.

And this remember also, that reason is of the qualities masculine, and thus an imperfect instrument by which to descry the future of which I speak. Intuition is of the feminine, and will make a better lens for your spying-glass. Albeit, methinks what women shall read this will assimilate my meaning more easily than the men, who are not content unless they understand. Woman seeks not understanding very eagerly, for she values logic scarce at all. She has little need of it. She has her intuition and it serves her very well, and shall serve both her and man the better still anon.

Arnel, don't you think there is a call for one of your little parables here?

The parable of the goldsmith and the diamond.

A goldsmith took up into his hand two stones, a ruby and an emerald, to choose which he should set into a bracelet for the wife of his King. He was perplexed thereabout, however, for the ruby was favorite with the King, and the emerald with the King his lady. So when he could not come at a decision with himself he called his wife and asked her what she would do in such a case and she said she would set the bracelet with a diamond. "For why," said the goldsmith, "since that is not of either color?" "Make a trial," said his wife. And so he did. But when he took it to the Palace he went in some fear of the displeasure of the King, or of the Queen, or of both. But when the King saw it he said, "You have done very well, goldsmith. That diamond is of an excellent water, for it sends forth rich rays of red. Take it to my lady that she may see it also." So the goldsmith went and showed it to the Queen. And the Queen was also much pleasured, and she said, "Goldsmith, you have a good taste in gems. This diamond is very fine for the rays of emerald it has. You shall complete the jewel and bring it back to me." Now the goldsmith went home sore perplexed, and asked his wife why she had told him to set the diamond in the bracelet. "How went the matter at the Palace?" she asked, and he replied, "They were both much pleasured; for the King saw it crystal and red, and the Queen saw it crystal and emerald." "And yet," answered the good wife, "they both were right, for both red and emerald rays come forth of white when split up, and therein are other colors also. For Love has within its bosom all the virtues blended, and each virtue separate is just one of the rays of Love. The King and his Queen both saw in the brightness of the crystal the color-ray of their choice. Yet was there no disquietude of difference between them. No, their own favorite rays blended together in the crystal where their identity merged into its native brightness. Because they greatly love."

Arnel+

29

Womanhood
of the Future

Tuesday, March 25, 1919. 5:48–6:50 P.M.

AND now, having shot our arrow into the future, we must return to the taw and modulate somewhat our message that we have already given to you. I have spoken on general lines, taking those features most outstanding in the progress of the human race. But the economy into which mankind has entered is not simple but complex. As sphere interpenetrates with sphere, even so do several streams of progress mingle together in the one broad river of human evolution.

Thus, when I tell you that the dominance of the man shall give place to the meekness of the woman, I do not say that such dominance shall be annihilated. No. The evolution of mankind into matter and form had a purpose from his Creator, and no such purpose is attained merely to be cast aside. For this period of evolution just ending was essentially for man's spiritual benefit. And so the masterfulness he has learned shall be blended into the new composite now forming for his future exaltation.

The ruby rays shall not be eliminated from the diamond or its brilliance would lack some of its beauty. But those rays shall become more subdued in their manifestation as the gem receives upon its facets the light of the future at a new angle. Thus for a period the rays most evidential in its scintillation shall not be ruby, as heretofore, but emerald.

And as there are other rays which have had their turn of notice in time past, before the ruby rays, so there are, within the heart of the crystal, still other rays which shall find their normal environment in outer manifestation in the eternities ahead, after the emerald rays have had their turn.

Moreover, the new age of the woman shall not come catastrophic, but very slow, as you men of earth count progress. That age is not yet come to the birth, I say. But it shall be born in due time. And when that time is at hand, well—the Savior was born by night, and few took heed of it. And yet He was the fount and source of His own new age. Then the world went onward in its normal course of life, and no break was apparent to those who reckoned their years A.U.C. Yet today, because of that obscure Babe's birth in the night, the whole of Christendom reckons A.D. and A.U.C. has ceased from your calends. Read this a parable, as you are so gentle as to like my parables, my son, and you shall see a significance therein.

Further, you will remember how I told you of our experience of the Manifestation of the Christ Creative at the Tower of the Angels. Now, that was a part of our training for this present mission of ours to earth. And you will see from my account of it how thorough that training was. It based itself upon the creation of the cosmoi, and showed us the constitution of the atom out of which these are made. We were shown the evolution of the mineral and the vegetable and the animal and man in a long and majestic sweep of .life progression. Other instruction followed by which we were enabled to appraise the various elements which enter into the composite life of earth in particular, and so to deal with them severally and effectually. Then we were glimpsed of the future. And that brings me up to this present term of my message to you.

Now, I cannot tell you all of the Manifestation by which we were shown this future of humankind. There are rays within the diamond's heart which emerge not visibly from the angles of the spectroscope. But such as you can appreciate of that very grand spectacle, so full of sweet beauty, and so full of confidence and of cheer for us, I will show to you.

There came a time when the vapors about earth had, by means of our heavenly chymistry, been separated into their native elements. These were segregated and dealt with separately, each by those specially trained for that particular service. They were transmuted and, when the process of re-blending them into a more healthful mass was nearing completion, we were called apart for rest, others taking up our task the while.

So it came to pass that we in our myriads assembled, tier on tier, up into the storied heavens. A sight of much splendor it was, heartening us all by the unity of our purpose so displayed. For every one of that vast array had borne a part in the redemption of our brethren of earth, and that purpose was personified in Him Who led the campaign.

Far away they reached like a thousand rainbows seen from within their arc of colors manifold, all ranked and ordered. And every angel and archangel there was a veteran come from the field—not as he went returning, but tinctured to richer hue of robe and body, and enriched also by much spoil of tribute given in homage to Love, and not taken by right of mastery gained.

Then into the void in our midst, a hollow sphere in size a universe, came that entity of silence, of which I have already told you, wherein is the Presence of our Prince. And when the silence came upon us we bowed our heads in worship, as we ever do at such a time. And we waited well content in the sweetness of our awe of reverence, and in the unity of our Love which found its focus in Him, our invisible Guest.

Arnel+

30

The Manifestation
Description Resumed

Friday, March 28, 1919. 5:28–7:00 P.M.

AT this time we had re-assumed our normal condition according to our heavens of abode. Therefore, although we were set as a hollow sphere all looking inward toward earth, yet earth was not visible to us. I speak of my own estate and not of those whose proper home was nearer earth, for to them I think there would be at least a semblance of the planet to view. But that of which I now tell you is told according to my own seeing.

I looked inward into that great void and all was vacancy except that, while the circumference was made bright by our encircling presence, yet as the depths of the interior of that sphere were neared, darkness gathered. And in the very center of it all it was very dark indeed. So we waited, and then from the empty blackness in the midst there arose a sound of wailing, and it spread outward on every side in its swelling as it came toward us who formed the spatial sphere. But as it came it grew more loud, and then we heard another element mingle in its tone, and yet another, until a chord of manifold notes was made. At first this was in disharmony, but it also, as it neared us, gradually cleared itself until at length the whole sphere vibrated with one deep tone, not now of wailing but of virile diapason.

This some more while persisted and then slowly there began to blend with it a lighter tone until from bass it grew to tenor. Still it changed until the whole space within our circles was filled with the clear ringing of a sustained choir of women's voices.

As this harmony developed so the vibrations of light answered to its progress, and when the consummation of sound was reached then also the whole space interior to us was illumined with a radiance of very beautiful tints. And in the midst, far away from any and all of us, we saw that the Manifestation had begun to assume visibility.

Earth came to view like a ball of crystal, and there stood upon it a little boy. Then there appeared by his side a girl-child, and they took hands one of another. Their sweet young faces were turned aloft and, as they gazed, they became gradually transfigured into a youth and maid, while the globe on which they stood expanded until it was of a goodly size. There now appeared a canopied throne upon its highest curve, and the maid led the youth to the steps of the throne and, while she knelt there, he ascended and sat within it.

A host of servitors came and stood round the throne and presented him with crown and sword, and upon his shoulders cast a richly embroidered mantle of deep red. Then minstrels tuned up their pieces of music and sang to him this benison:

"Out of spirit you came, Master of all life of earth.

"Into the outer universe, where form is, you stepped, and took your look around you. And you being set firm upon your feet, felt it was a good world mixed with somewhat of discomfort. Daring the one, you proclaimed yourself master of the other. And, after conquest made and ended, found that both were yours.

"Then you looked about you once again for the appraisement of your possessions. And you, in your highest mood, whispered your love to the fairest thing you found there. So woman became your dearest treasure among all the jewels which the Father of all brought forth for you out of the sanctuary of His treasure-house.

"Are these things so as we have sung to you, Master of earth in right of conquest won?"

And the young man laid down his sword athwart his thighs as he made answer to those who had sung his benison.

"It is as you have sung it, you who have watched my long warfare of many battles from your own place over earth. You see true, and you speak true, for you are liege men and women of our common Lord.

"And now I have justified and established what I set out to claim, and there is no equal of mine in prowess upon earth. This is my inheritance. I have claimed it, and I have established my claim.

"And yet I am not fully at my ease, for now that this rough quest is ended, where shall I find further quarry for my aim? Earth, unrestful for so long ages past, is now composed, and yet unrested. And earth wearies of disquiet, for she longs for her rest that she may leave behind the today of conflict for the tomorrow of peace.

"So you who have guided me in my humanity, hereto, my angel friends, show me what way I should take in my future journey, for I have not ever pleased you in your counsels when I have been more set upon the fray than wisdom whispered I should be. This has been to my own hurt, yet I have more of that wisdom now, bought at a great price, but my own now for the buying.

"I have a better bearing for your words of counsel today, for I have ended my fight and am a little weary by reason of the roughness of the ascent by which I climbed hither to this Throne."

And then all those ministers stood divided on each side the steps of the Throne, and a lane was made between them, while in the midst of the lane the maid appeared in her white robe of silver hemmed with blue. So she waited, hands clasped before her simply, and with sweet meekness. But she looked straight before her into the face of the young king who sat above her and gazed upon her intently.

At long last he slowly took the sword from off his thighs, and the crown from off his head, and came down the steps and stood before her. Within her arms he laid the sword, and upon her head he placed the crown. Then he bowed and kissed her upon the brow and said to her:

"I have been hereto your guard and strength against the dangers of our way in the long journey which I and you have made together. Against the winds I cast my cloak about you. Through many a swift river I set my strength against its on-set for you. But now the dangers of the road are behind us, and wind and flood have faded into the music of the summer-breeze. And I have you, beloved, safe this day, and all my own.

"But now I give to you my sword and my crown. With the one I kept the other safe against all question. And I find they are not sweet to me unless I give them both to you and you are kind and accept my gift. They are no mean trophy of my achievement, my beloved, and they are my own, and I give them, with all they betoken, into your sweet keeping. Be still your own gentle self to me and, as in love I offer them, so do you in love receive them. They are all I have to give you, my beloved—a world and these."

Then she set the sword against her left shoulder, and she put forth her right hand and took his hand and led him up the steps toward the throne till they stood on the level before it. Here a pause was made, and in a while, having meditated on what he should do, he stepped aside and bowed to her and she, not shrinking, sat within the Throne, while he stood to the side and looked toward her, well content that it should be so.

But when I looked upon them now I saw that the sword against her left breast was a sword no longer, but a palm-branch set with jewels of rainbow tints. The crown also was changed and, where before its heavy gold and iron circle had rested, there was now a daisy-chain about her pretty brown hair gleaming with star-like jewels of blue and green and white and a deep yellow color, but you have no yellow on earth like it for its glow.

The young king also was changed. His face was more placid and his form more restful, and the only robe he wore was one which was not for the journey nor for the battle but full and flowing, and in hue a faint gold, with rose-color lurking in its folds.

So he turned to her and said, "I thank you for your acceptance of what I had to give you. Show me now our future way wherein it shall be no longer I and you, but you and I, who go."

And she said, "Nay, for as I am to you so are you to me, beloved. It is we who will tread our future way together. Yet I will set the compass of our course, and I will set it true. But it is yourself who must read it, my beloved."

Arnel+

31

Future Evolution of the Earth

Tuesday, April 1, 1919. 5:29–6:20 P.M.

A WHILE the whole space within our ranks was filled once more with silence. And they two sat together within the Throne, for she had bidden him sit beside her.

Then we heard the voice of one of the great ones who had led those who came to the Sphere Ten and prepared us therein for our advance earthward. He stood behind the Throne and above it, and he cried:

"I speak to those who are of my own company, and to those who were called to array themselves with us descending earthward. For to you this Manifestation is given in order that you may with understanding get you to the further work. We who came to you to lead you had even then been given to know these things. But to you they now shall be shown new. Therefore take very good heed of them that you may step without hesitancy on the road which lies ahead of you. God our Father sends to you of His strength for the work by the commission of His Beloved, Who leads us, and through Him that Stream is poured upon us and shall enable us to the work. To Him our Author be all worship always."

And now there came a radiant mist upon the Throne, and encompassed the earth about till it was not to be seen of us any more. This slowly expanded and filled some quartern part of the sphere of space and then stayed in its enlarging. It began to revolve and seemed to take upon itself somewhat of solidity, but was not solid as matter is solid. If you will image an earth material still but yet etherealized halfway into transparency, there you have the look of it.

As it went round upon its axis there appeared shapes of lands and waters upon its outer circumference. These were not coterminous in outline with those of earth as they are today. We were now being shown our future sphere of work, and these were changing as they are now changing on earth's surface, but more quickly. The ages ahead of you were foreshortened for us and we read them as a moving model.

There appeared also the cities and their peoples and animals also, and the engines which the people made for their several uses. And as the globe turned its surface to us, continually revolving, we were able to see the progress of it all.

I mean this: take, in token of other lands, your own islands. I noted them first as they will be a few years hence. Then they sailed round out of view. When they came before us again they had become changed a little in configuration of coastlines, and as to their cities and people. So, as the globe revolved, these lands, and the whole human race and their works of building and engines of locomotion and all their handiwork progressed in their ages, but condensed from millennia into hours. I must suit my words to your way of thinking, my son. Years have not the same significance to us as they have to you.

Now it would not be permitted to me to fish for you in the deeps of future ages. You of earth must net your own supper.

That is as it should be. Nevertheless, it is permitted to me to tell you where the fishing-grounds are like to be. Then those who will think of me as a good admiral will set their sail to my chart, and out upon their quest. So.

Now, the earth became more beautiful as it sailed round upon its voyage of the ages. The light increased upon its surface, and its mass became more radiant from within. The peoples also hurried not so greatly here and there, for nature had become more at one with them and yielded more genially to their abundance. So their lives were less fevered and more given to meditation. Thus they became ever more in harmony one with others, and all of them more nearly attuned to us who were able, in our turn, to spend upon them a larger degree of our power and of our sweeter peace.

As this attunement advanced it enthused us with a largess of happiness to know we had gained for ourselves, after much stress of warfare, these younger companions of our ancient race. It was very sweet to us, my son.

And gradually earth itself was changed. Let me tell you.

Psychometry

You have a new word among you which I have seen in the mind of you and of others: psychometry. I understand it signifies that faculty by which from solid things some incident of the past is read by reason of a sort of vibrant record left in those solids by events in which they have had a part.

Now, there is a truth here which will not be fully known to you until the substance which you call ether has yielded up to your scientists the secrets of its composition and the forces inherent in its atoms. The time will come—we saw this plainly as we watched the globe revolving—when you will be able to deal, both analytically and synthetically, with this cosmic ballast which you call ether. You will deal with it as now you deal with liquids and with gases. But that is not yet, for your bodies are still much too gross that you should be permitted this great power with safety. Meanwhile your men of scientific mind will be preparing the way.

    Arnel+

32

Cosmic Psychometry

Wednesday, April 2, 1919. 5:85–7:10 P.M.

THESE psychometric vibrations, therefore, are—so we have concluded after study of the matter—writ, or indented upon the ether, which suffuses matter. But not that alone. The ether acts upon the substance of matter, and according to the inherent properties which energize through this ether, so does matter become transmuted into a more sublimated substance. These properties come upon ether from the outside of it, invade it, and, using it as a medium between themselves and matter, act upon matter through the ether. For the particles material are held in solution in the ether, as your men of chymics have told. But they have not yet ventured farther than the vestibule. There lies ahead of them the Temple, and within the Temple the Sanctuary. When they have ventured beyond the vestibule of the material into the temple of the ethereal then, and not until that time, will they begin to understand that this Sanctuary is the dynamo from which the ether, and through it matter also, is energized. The Sanctuary is the abode of Spirit.

And so you get the scheme of this affair in its due order, namely, Spirit impinges upon ether dynamically from the outside, that is, from that realm which is superior, both in powers as in degree of sublimity as to its basic substance. It energizes ether, which, in its turn, acts on and refines those particles which, with itself, make up the substance matter.

But this action is not automatic; it is willful. Where will is there also is implied personality. It is individuals expressing their personality who give character to the ether, and the consequence is faithfully carried on into matter. It therefore issues in this: that according to the degree in holiness of those spiritual entities who operate on matter through ether, so is that matter the more gross or less gross in substance of its mass.

The quality of the matter of which earth and all things thereon are made is, therefore, responsive to the character of those spiritual individuals who act upon it willfully. These are spirits both incarnate and discarnate.

And so it came to pass that as the people of earth progressed spiritually higher, so earth itself gradually but faithfully answered to their influence which was registered upon the substance of which earth is built up. Matter became less gross and more ethereal. That is why it became brighter with radiance from within as we saw it revolving. It was no more nor no less than cosmic psychometry in mass, but essentially identical with that you at present know manifested in detail.

As earth and its peoples became more and more etherealized, so the hosts spiritual were able with greater ease to consort with those peoples, and their conversation was both more frequent and more free than it is today. And, to shorten my story, we came to that period when progress had been made to such a degree that the communion of spirits with people of earth was normal and continual. Then it became possible that one great Manifestation be made of which I will tell you anon.

But this first: I leave out constellations and speak now of our own sun and his planetary system, so—

Those planets which your scientists have charted are, say they, material.

They have noted further that the matter of which these planets are made is not identical in the proportions of those ingredients which go to make up their material mass. But they have not yet proceeded to register one other factor which enters into the causes of difference of density. This is the spiritual factor of which I have told you, and which has entered into the evolution of some of these planets so as to produce them forward on their evolutionary pilgrimage ahead of earth.

Etheric planets

There are others which are not visible to you of earth for they are those which have progressed in their etherealization beyond the material, and have become ethereal. They may be seen by those who live on planets of like substance. They are not spiritual, but between the material and the spiritual estate. Their inhabitants are cognizant of the other planets of which earth is one. And they act upon these planets very powerfully, being at the same time more progressed than earth people, and yet nearer in estate than the spiritual people are.

These of which I speak are true planets of themselves. But there are other ethereal planets, so to say it. One of these encompasses earth. For it is of the engrossened ether of which this ethereal planet is composed that earth is suffused. This is not merely a belt of ether solely for service of earth. It has its own continents and oceans and peoples. Most of these have lived on earth in bygone ages, and some have never been earth-dwellers, never having reached material manifestation in body of flesh and blood.

Is that what some call the Astral Plane?

That name is not understood equally by those who use it. But, as yourself have read of it and understand it, this ethereal planet of which I speak is not it. It is what I have said of it. Those of human-kind who have come to be there are old denizens as we have been told, and their residence there is uncertain as to its future duration. They are a kind of by-product of humanity of earth in long ages past.

Do you pass through this ethereal planet on your way to earth from the higher spheres?

Locally we must do so. But we are not responsive to its environment in normal as we pass through it. We are not sensibly conscious of its presence. It has not relation to the spheres one, two, three, as I have spoken of them in their degree by numbers. It is another order of creation, and a very strange one. It lies away off the highway of our goings, so that I know little of detail concerning it. What I have told you, and a little more, was explained to us in order to help us to account for some erratic events which perplexed us much until this new factor was brought to our knowledge. And then we understood.

Arnel+

33

The Christ Manifestation Consummate

Thursday, April 3, 1919. 5:20–6:50 P.M.

NOW that we have cleared the ground, my son, we will tell you of the Manifestation which was given us. Its purport was to show us to what end the present evolution was tending, in order that we might with the greater assurance set our course ahead.

Earth, as we beheld it before us, had come to that stage when the ethereal and the material had almost equal place in content. The bodies of men were still of matter, but purified and more readily co-responsive with the heavens of spirit life than in former times—these same times in which you live today.

Earth had responded to the upliftment, and the vegetation which it produced lay upon its bosom almost as sentient as a babe upon his mother's breast.

No kingdoms were upon earth, but one confederacy of peoples whose colors were not so diverse, each from other, as they are today.

Science also was not the science of Europe as it is now, but the powers of ethereal dynamics being understood, the whole life of men was transformed. I will not farther in detail. That is no affair of mine. I lay the stage in its setting only so you may the more clearly discern what came upon us for our instruction.

The light grew ever brighter from within earth, still spinning upon its axis slowly, until it shone upon the encircling hosts of us, and we were brighter also for its radiance. Then out of this terrestrial light there came forth in their myriads all those half-rational forces which have their place among the elements of earth. These were very strange in their shapes, and also in their movements. I had not seen these until now, and I was very greatly intent upon their manners. These I speak of were those impersonal forces which insure cohesion in minerals, and those by which the vegetation is enthused with its life, and those who were guardians of animals in their kinds. The mineral entities were not much sentient in themselves until magnetized by those great Lords of Creation whose province it was to sustain this realm in its orders. But the vegetable entities had in themselves a formed and subjective faculty of sensation with which to respond to the forces poured upon them by their own Rulers. That is why change in substance is of quicker operation in the vegetable than in the mineral as it issues visibly in growth.

And for this same cause the obverse is consequent when the personality of man is introduced in interference with their normal state of development. When two opposing, or two affinitative minerals are brought into contact in solution, as in chymistry, their action toward or against one another respectively is immediately and violently displayed, because they have so little sentience to oppose to this exoteric influence. But when the vegetable world is invaded by the cultivator the response of the plant is more tardy and deliberate, because it. opposes its inherent sentience to such disturbance of its normal method of growth.

The animal entities, however, had fully sensation in themselves, and also a modicum of personality. And their Lords were very splendid in their array.

These all came forth of earth and, leaving its surface, took up their stations in middle space between us and earth. Then from the void between us and them emerged into visibility their Rulers. I cannot limn their aspect to you because you have nothing for comparison on earth, albeit they are very busy in your midst, nevertheless. I will be content with saying that as we looked upon each we knew, from the aspect of him, that department of nature of which he was Ruler. Whether it were atmosphere or gold or oak or tiger, his dominion was writ upon him plainly, in all its beauty. Form, and the substance of his body, and countenance, and raiment all expressed his kingdom. Some had raiment, some had none. But the grandeur of these great Lords is very majestic in strength and comeliness. All had their retinue who were ordered in their degrees. These had charge of the subdivisions of their kingdoms and linked up their Lords with the animals or forces which those Lords controlled.

Now, how shall I tell you of their contact when they mingled together with their creatures who emerged out of the earth-light? I will say it thus: As their retinues approached the earth-creatures a movement was made among them by which they encompassed their Lord. They did not hide him, and yet they clothed him. Then the earth-forces also, as they met with these higher formations, became blended with them, and the result was a panoply over earth which armored earth while it enshrined it.

In effect earth, radiant now more than it was before, became in the midst of a canopy of living entities which draped above and on all sides of it like the curtains of a pavilion enshrining a throne. Earth now shone like one great and very beautiful pearl, but with veins of green and gold and crimson and amber and blue upon it. And within it shone its native light aglow with fire of worship about its heart, which throbbed with life and happiness as the impulses of the Creative Lords and their myriads invaded it and wooed from it this responsive and shimmering loveliness.

Then beneath that living canopy the form of the Christ appeared. It was as the Christ Consummate that He now appeared. I have been hard put to tell you how He looked when I had seen Him aforetime. How shall I tell you of His appearing now?

His body was of translucent substance and in perfect equipoise of harmony it blended within itself all those distinctive colors, both of earth and of the myriads surrounding. He stood upon the great radiant pearl. It still revolved beneath His feet, yet He stood steadfast. Its movement had no effect upon His station there.

He had no raiment, but the glory of all the various departments of life suspended around Him surged through their own great Lords and was directed upon Him in streams of worship. This became instead of robe about Him, and filled the shrine within which He stood with a radiance of beauty.

His face was calm and reposeful, but His brow wore an aspect of great majesty of power. Divinity seemed to clothe Him like a cloak upon His shoulders and fell behind Him in rich folds of violet-tinted light.

Now we were all around and above and below Him encompassing earth. Yet there was no front or rear, and no above and below to Him. All of us and each of us saw Him whole—front, rear and through and through. You will not understand this. I say it and leave it. It was so, as we saw Him then.

Then there came voices of all those myriad orders, each great company in its own proper order grouped, and each sounding its own appropriate anthem of worship, and yet all blended together as one chord of creative harmony which filled our heavens and all the spaces about the planets in their orbits, and had response of those who in the outlands of space held vigil over their special planetary charges.

Such a hymn as this, it is plain, I cannot put into words of a single people of our planet earth. But, using your English words, I will tell you, so far as I am able, of what we enchanted, blending our worship with that of those other orders of the universe in one grand stream of concerted praise:

"What lies beyond you in the deeps of space we know not yet, and earth is but a mote in the rays of your Heavenly Sun. But this we know, since we have seen this Province of your Kingdom, Christ of the Father, that what is there beyond is wholly good.

"What comes to meet us out of the eternities ahead of us, on the road we go, what peoples there abide, what sort of Princes rule—these, too, we know not now. Yet we go forward fearless, for we follow you, 0 Christ. Upon your shoulders sit twin power and love embracing each other in your crown of majesty.

"Who the Father is we know, for we have seen you His Beloved, and we have loved you also. So our love meets with the Father's love in you as trysting place. We know Him in you, and we are content.

"You are very wonderful and beautiful, Beloved, yet all your beauty cannot be shown to us so great.

"But in that future emprise we adventure forth all strong of heart and buoyant and unafraid. And you still lead us we will follow you, Christ Consummate of wisdom, of strength and of creative love.

"We pay you our due worship, ordered and arrayed in our degrees. Content us with the benediction of your Peace."

ARNEL+